Louis XIV
and the parlements

MANCHESTER
UNIVERSITY PRESS

Louis XIV
and the parlements

The assertion
of royal authority

John J. Hurt

Manchester University Press

Manchester and New York

distributed exclusively in the USA by Palgrave

Copyright © John J. Hurt 2002

The right of John J. Hurt to be identified as the author of this work has been asserted
by him in accordance with the Copyright, Designs and Patents Act 1988.

Published by Manchester University Press
Oxford Road, Manchester M13 9NR, UK
and Room 400, 175 Fifth Avenue, New York, NY 10010, USA
www.manchesteruniversitypress.co.uk

Distributed exclusively in the USA by
Palgrave, 175 Fifth Avenue, New York,
NY 10010, USA

Distributed exclusively in Canada by
UBC Press, University of British Columbia, 2029 West Mall,
Vancouver, BC, Canada V6T 1Z2

British Library Cataloguing-in-Publication Data
A catalogue record for this book is available from the British Library

Library of Congress Cataloging-in-Publication Data applied for

ISBN 0 7190 6235 7 *hardback*

First published 2002

10 09 08 07 06 05 04 03 02   10 9 8 7 6 5 4 3 2 1

Typeset in Monotype Photina 10/12 pt
by Servis Filmsetting Ltd, Manchester
Printed in Great Britain
by Bookcraft (Bath) Ltd, Midsomer Norton

For Joyce

Contents

List of tables

Preface and acknowledgements

Few historians today believe that there was anything very 'absolute' about what was once reflexively called the absolute monarchy of seventeenth- and eighteenth-century France. A revisionist view that treats the Bourbon monarchy as limited in its authority and conciliatory in its methods has swept the field and entrenched itself in original scholarship and works of synthesis, textbooks and manuals. Revisionism also serves as a context for articles and book reviews. One can but admire the magnitude of this triumph, all the more impressive for having been won without any particular resistance, a victory without a battle. Indeed, I myself do not write in an effort to overthrow the main tenets of this revisionist history; I admire the quality of the core scholarship that has almost made revisionism into a new orthodoxy. I do think that we have pushed the revisionist thesis beyond its appropriate limits, possibly because we have given up looking for evidence that contradicts it.

I have examined two aspects of the history of the parlements under Louis XIV, the king's suppression of their political independence and his extortion of money from the magistrates who served in them. As the subtitle to this book suggests, I believe that an understanding of these subjects shows that Louis XIV acted as an absolute monarch when he needed to and that, therefore, the revisionist thesis needs qualification. Any statement characterizing the Bourbon system as inherently limited and conciliatory ought to contain a modifying clause, dependent or main, to make clear that there was something 'absolute' about the monarchy after all.

Although this study belongs more to the realm of scholarship than to polemic, one ought to state a little more clearly, if only briefly, where revisionism came from and what it amounts to. The ablest representatives of the school, indeed in a sense its founders, are Albert N. Hamscher and William Beik. In 1976, Hamscher published *The Parlement of Paris after the Fronde, 1653–1673*, a superb monograph which argued that the government of Louis XIV consulted, cooperated with, and sometimes deferred to that tribunal on important judicial, political and financial issues. As Hamscher saw it, Louis XIV skilfully 'managed' the judges of the Parlement, respecting their economic interests, compromising with them and compensating them when, on occasion, he did reduce their institutional power. Although different in concept and execution, socio-economic rather than political and institutional, William Beik's *Absolutism and Society in Seventeenth-Century France. State Power and Provincial Aristocracy in Languedoc*, appearing in 1985, ran parallel to Hamscher. Beik had comparatively little to say about the Parlement of Toulouse, but he used the ideas of compromise and cooperation as much if not more than Hamscher did. Indeed, Beik argued that the government of Louis XIV owed its effectiveness in Languedoc to a bargain it instinctively struck with the provincial 'ruling class', including but by no means limited to the judges of the Parlement. Under this bargain, the king co-opted an entire provincial elite into his system of government and promoted its social and economic interests. Although the rulers of Languedoc obeyed the king more readily than their forebears had done, they were also obeying themselves, in the sense that they enjoyed a collaborative 'partnership' with the monarchy. The two studies, the one focused on Paris and the other on a major province, nicely complemented each other.[1]

Hamscher and Beik had their predecessors, of course, notably the great Ernest Lavisse, whose synthesis of the reign of Louis XIV, published in 1905, stood for decades as a point of reference. In addition to his Third Republic esteem for the economic policies and administrative skills of Colbert, Lavisse clearly stated that absolute government had inherent limits and that the king formed a 'coalition of interests' with the French elite and respected their social status and institutional powers, thus anticipating both Hamscher and Beik. After Lavisse published, various scholars, with a range of interests, discovered one example after another of local authorities successfully resisting the government, an indication of their residual power and thus the limits of the monarchy. Patron-client studies, initiated by Orest Ranum and taken to a high point by Sharon Kettering, emphasized the personal nature of seventeenth-century politics, lending themselves naturally to the new concepts. Russell Major had powerfully argued that what he called the 'Renaissance monarchy' was innately consultative in nature. The new studies, especially those of Hamscher and Beik, supplied the intellectual and empirical authority to broaden Major's ideas about consultation and to extend them through, and indeed beyond, the reign of Louis XIV. All the recent surveys and syntheses show how deeply the Hamscher/Beik theses of cooperation, collaboration and compromise have worked themselves into the history of seventeenth-century France. Most contemporary students of Louis XIV's reign would probably associate the word absolutism with 'limits' if not indeed 'myth'. Lavisse pointed the way, but we are all revisionists now; or so it would seem.[2]

In calling for a time-out, so to speak, before this consensus hardens any further, I am suggesting that we have pushed ahead of what the empirical research has shown and that we have not yet gathered all the information that we need in order to form a general view. In particular, we ought to know a good deal more about what happened to the parlements and their magistrates under Louis XIV. In an important companion study on the jurisdictional relationship between the parlements and the royal council, Hamscher himself called eloquently for even more investigation of the tribunals on other topics and extending through the entire reign. Besides, his first book, which is more closely related to this study, ended in 1673, and Beik's in about 1683 so the opportunity to do a bit more chronologically certainly exists. A study of the parlements, moreover, would seem potentially to be of more general importance than one focused upon provincial estates, where royal policies often depended upon individual circumstances.[3]

Since even with the parlements no one can tackle everything at once, I have focused upon the two topics specified earlier – the successful effort of Louis XIV's government to deprive the parlements of their political powers and the equally successful effort to take large sums of money out of the pockets of the judges. These topics not only had their inherent importance, as the Introduction to this book will argue, but intertwined, the one linking to the other. The kings understood the connection and periodically tried to subdue the parlements politically by altering the financial terms upon which the magistrates held office. First President Matthieu Molé of the Parlement of Paris and Madame de Motteville, well-informed participants in the mid-century Fronde, saw that struggle as involving both the political authority of the tribunal and the financial status of the judges, parts of a whole. Scholars, indeed, have long treated the relationship as fundamental, seeing power and wealth as reinforcing each other.[4]

Most readers of this study will already understand the nature of the parlements of the Old Regime, but a brief description of them should help those unfamiliar with these institutions. Parlements were royal appellate law courts that judged civil and criminal cases on appeal, definitively, handing down decrees or *arrêts*, a word that in French indicates finality. Parlements also judged certain types of lawsuits in the first instance. In addition, an aggrieved party with good legal grounds might induce the royal council to overturn a parlement's supposedly definitive ruling or transfer the lawsuit to another parlement, although this was not easy to do. The tribunals also exercised broad administrative powers and, within their jurisdictions, kept an eye on the activities and behaviour of subordinate office-holders.

The Parlement of Paris was the oldest of these tribunals. It emerged gradually from the judicial section of the council of medieval kings, acquired a distinct institutional status in the 1200s, and settled into a royal palace on the Île de la Cité, the site of the present Palais de Justice. In due course, the kings also created parlements in the larger provinces and some of the smaller ones: Toulouse (1443) for Languedoc and surrounding territories, Grenoble (1453) for Dauphiné, Bordeaux (1462) for Guyenne and western Gascony, Dijon

(1476) for Burgundy, Rouen (1499) for Normandy, Aix (1501) for Provence, Rennes (1554) for Brittany, Pau (1620) for Béarn and Navarre, and Metz (1633) for the bishoprics of Metz, Toul and Verdun. Although Toulouse claimed precedence among the provincials, as the oldest among them and because of the size of Languedoc, none of these could really compare with the senior tribunal in the capital. The Parlement of Paris, exercising by far the largest jurisdiction, ruled in a judicial sense over a wide swath running from Flanders in the north-east through the centre of France and out to the Atlantic Ocean, more than half the realm. It also boasted the largest number of judges, more than two hundred, while most of the provincial parlements had between about fifty and a hundred magistrates.

Almost all the judges in these parlements served in either the Grand-Chambre or a Chambre des Enquêtes, starting their careers in the latter and advancing by seniority into the former. The Grand-Chambre, the senior chamber, heard the most important cases both in the first instance and on appeal, essentially those in which the evidence consisted of oral testimony and pleadings. The Enquêtes, of which there could be more than one (the Parlement of Paris had five), dealt with cases requiring scrutiny of the sworn testimony of witnesses as recorded in documents. Magistrates from all these chambers took turns serving in a criminal chamber, the Tournelle. In most parlements, a smaller Chambre des Requêtes adjudicated disputes involving dignitaries who, by virtue of a royal privilege called *committimus*, could bring their affairs, as plaintiffs or defenders, directly to a parlement, without proceeding through subordinate tribunals. (The Parlement of Paris had two Requêtes chambers.) Requêtes judges, although incorporated into a parlement, did not enjoy quite the same status as Grand-Chambre and Enquêtes magistrates. In Paris, a *chambre des vacations* met intermittently during the magistrates' summer break, from mid-August until the onset of the judicial year on 12 November; and some provincial tribunals had similar arrangements. Until 1679, Huguenots had access to a special chamber attached to the Parlements of Paris, Bordeaux, Toulouse and Grenoble, the *mi-partie*, consisting of both Catholic and Calvinist magistrates.[5]

A first president, or *premier président*, stood at the head of each tribunal and presided at sessions of the Grand-Chambre and at plenary sessions, when all the magistrates met together. *Présidents à mortier* sat beside him in the Grand-Chambre, and the senior among them presided in his absence. *Présidents des enquêtes* or *requêtes* took charge at those chambers. The king appointed the first president directly and controlled the appointments of the *gens du roi*, the *procureur général* and the *avocats généraux*, usually two to a tribunal. The *gens du roi* functioned collectively as state's attorneys, responsible for enforcing the king's laws and looking after his affairs, with the *procureur général* as their unofficial chief. He drafted and signed documents sent to a parlement, while an *avocat général* presented them to the tribunal and spoke to it in person, the difference between *plume* and *parole*. The great majority of the magistrates held the title of *conseiller du roi en son parlement de . . .*, or simply councillor. In Paris and most provincial tribunals, beneficed clergy, and laymen by dispensation, served as *conseillers clercs* (who did not sit in the Tournelle); most councillors, however, classified as lay councillors. In the Parlement of Rennes, where this distinction did not exist, the councillors were about equally divided between *originaires*, those native to the province, and *non-originaires*, or non-Bretons, a royal contrivance intended to counter provincial solidarity. Both the Parlement of Rennes and the Parlement of Metz were divided into 'semesters', each semester consisting of half the judges and convening for six months of the year.

For routine business, the magistrates wore black robes with large open sleeves over black cassocks that descended to their heels; they donned splendid red robes for special ceremonies. The councillors also wore hats with wide round rims, while the presidents boasted *mortiers* – round velvet headgear trimmed in gold and resembling a mortar and pestle, with ends pulled up around the sides and a peak rising at the crown.[6]

The University of Delaware and the American Philosophical Society provided indispensable research funding for the study. At Delaware, moreover, I benefited from the advice and counsel of my colleagues David Allmendinger, Reed Geiger and Jotham Parsons, and from the work of a skilled research assistant, Oanh Hoang. Outside my institution, I am grateful for the various favours extended over the years by William Beik, Joseph Bergin, Richard Bonney, François Bluche, James Collins, Pierre Goubert, Jean Meyer, Johann P. Sommerville and Donald Sutherland. I have drawn heavily upon the critical expertise of Robin Briggs, William Doyle, Mack P. Holt, Sharon Kettering, T.J.A. Le Goff, David Parker, Orest Ranum and J.H.M. Salmon, all of whom read substantial portions of the manuscript in one or more of its incarnations. I owe a profound debt to the talented Albert N. Hamscher for his generous assistance in every possible way over many years. My professors in graduate school – John M. Headley, Werner P. Friederich, James E. King and my valued mentor George V. Taylor – set standards worthy of anyone's emulation. Even at this late date, I profited from the precepts and examples of my undergraduate history teachers – Willis B. Glover, Spencer B. King, Malcolm Lester and Henry Warnock. The professional staff of numerous archives and libraries throughout France helped me enormously, as did Alison Whittle and the editorial staff of Manchester University Press. Naturally, I assume full responsibility for the errors and deficiencies remaining in this study.

Notes

1   Albert N. Hamscher, *The Parlement of Paris after the Fronde, 1653–1673* (Pittsburgh, 1976); William Beik, *Absolutism and Society in Seventeenth-Century France. State Power and Provincial Aristocracy in Languedoc* (Cambridge, 1985).

2 Ernest Lavisse, *Louis XIV. La Fronde. Le Roi. Colbert (1643–1685)*, vol. 7, pt I, of *Histoire de France depuis les origines jusqu'à la Révolution* (Paris, 1905), pp. 366–367, 403. Charles W. Cole, *Colbert and a Century of French Mercantilism* (2 vols; New York, 1939); Herbert Lüthy, *La banque protestante en France, de la révocation de l'Édit de Nantes à la Révolution* (2 vols; Paris, 1959–1961); and Eugene L. Asher, *The Resistance to the Maritime Classes: The Survival of Feudalism in the France of Colbert* (Berkeley, 1960) all noted the survival of elite and institutional resistance to the government well into the reign of Louis XIV. A. Lloyd Moote anticipated revisionism in the epilogue to his *The Revolt of the Judges. The Parlement of Paris and the Fronde 1643–1652* (Princeton, NJ, 1971). On clientage Orest Ranum's pioneering study is *Richelieu and the Councillors of Louis XIII: A Study of the Secretaries of State and Superintendents of Finance in the Ministry of Richelieu* (Oxford, 1963), while Sharon Kettering's *Patrons, Brokers, and Clients in Seventeenth-Century France* (New York and Oxford, 1987) took this mode of analysis to a high point. The interpretations of J. Russell Major are conveniently summarized in his latest book, *From Renaissance Monarchy to Absolute Monarchy. French Kings, Nobles, & Estates* (Baltimore and London, 1994). For the growing strength of the revisionist interpretation in syntheses of the period, see and compare David Parker, *The Making of French Absolutism* (New York, 1983) and idem, *Class and State in Ancien Régime France. The Road to Modernity?* (London and New York, 1996), ch. 6 (more nuanced); Roger Mettam, *Power and Faction in Louis XIV's France* (Oxford, 1988); James B. Collins, *The State in Early Modern France* (Cambridge, 1995); David J. Sturdy, *Louis XIV* (New York, 1998); and Bernard Barbiche, *Les institutions de la monarchie française à l'époque moderne, XVIe-XVIIIe siècle* (Paris, 1999). Note the titles in Richard Bonney, *The Limits of Absolutism in Ancien Régime France* (Aldershot, Hampshire, and Brookfield, Vt, 1995), and Nicholas Henshall, *The Myth of Absolutism: Change and Continuity in Early Modern European Monarchy* (London, 1992). Among recent monographs, James Collins aggressively advanced the revisionist thesis in his *Fiscal Limits to Absolutism. Direct Taxation in Early Seventeenth-Century France* (Berkeley, 1988), while Daniel Hickey, in partial contrast, detected increasing absolutism in Dauphiné but attributed it not to a grand design of the government but to conflict and disunion among provincial authorities: *The Coming of French Absolutism: The Struggle for Tax Reform in the Province of Dauphiné, 1540–1640* (Toronto, 1986).

3 Albert N. Hamscher, *The Conseil Privé and the Parlements in the Age of Louis XIV: A Study in French Absolutism* (Philadelphia, 1987), pp. 32, 147 and n. 1, and the endorsement of this appeal by J.H. Shennan in his book review in *French History*, II (no. 3, 1988), 356; like Beik, James Collins concentrated upon a provincial estates in his *Classes, Estates, and Order in Early Modern Brittany* (Cambridge, 1994).

4 For the views of Molé and Madame de Motteville, see n. 28, Introduction. Orest Ranum recently drew attention to the interaction of wealth and power in the relations of the Parlement of Paris with the government in his *The Fronde. A French Revolution, 1648–1652* (New York and London, 1993), pp. 18, 76–77. Charles Loyseau, the great authority on office-holding, conceived of offices as combining political power and economic opportunity: *Ordre des cinq livres des offices*, in *Les oeuvres de maistre Charles Loyseau*, new edn (Paris, 1678), Bk I, ch. vi, par. i.

5 In general, I prefer not to italicize such French words as parlement or Chambre, on the theory that they are close enough to English to appear as plain text. I have,

however, italicized such expressions as *committimus*, etc., when they seemed distinctively French or, in this case, Latin.

6 For the origins, structure and personnel of the Parlement of Paris, see John H. Shennan, *The Parlement of Paris* (Ithaca, NY, 1968), pp. 9–49, and Bailey Stone, *The Parlement of Paris, 1774–1789* (Chapel Hill, NC, 1981), pp. 14–33. For the provincial parlements as well as the Parlement of Paris, see Adolphe Chéruel, *Dictionnaire historique des institutions, moeurs, et coutumes de la France*, 2nd edn (2 vols; Paris, 1865), II, 951–953; Roland E. Mousnier, *The Organs of State and Society*, vol. II of *The Institutions of France under the Absolute Monarchy, 1598–1789*, trans. Arthur Goldhammer (Chicago and London, 1984), pp. 253–261, 302; Lucien Bély, ed., *Dictionnaire de l'Ancien Régime. Royaume de France, XVIe–XVIIIe siècle* (Paris, 1996), pp. 603–604, 960–965; and, on its particular subject, the still indispensable Gustave Saulnier de La Pinelais, *Les gens du roi au Parlement de Bretagne* (Rennes and Paris, 1902). The Parlements of Dijon, Grenoble and Rennes were also Cour des Aides, superior courts with jurisdiction over taxes and related issues. The Parlement of Metz and, in the late reign of Louis XIV, the Parlement of Pau were not only Cours des Aides but also Chambres des Comptes, superior courts responsible for auditing royal accounts and adjudicating disputes over royal funds. On the organization of the parlements, see also BN, *Fonds fr.*, MS 16,871, ff. 45r–46v (Parlement of Toulouse, 1654) and ff. 249r–256r (Parlement of Bordeaux, 1675); MS 16,873, ff. 353r–363r (Parlement of Rennes, 1673).

List of abbreviations

AAE	Archives des Affaires Étrangères, Paris
Actes R.	Actes Royaux, Bibliothèque Nationale, Paris
AD	Archives Départementales
AM	Archives Municipales
AN	Archives Nationales, Paris
B-R	Bouches-du-Rhône
BM	Bibliothèque Municipale
BN	Bibliothèque Nationale, Paris
C-O	Côte-d-Or
Fonds fr.	Fonds français, Bibliothèque Nationale, Paris
H-G	Haute-Garonne
I-V	Ille-et-Vilaine
Mél. Colbert	Mélanges Colbert, Bibliothèque Nationale, Paris
N.a.f.	Nouvelles acquisitions françaises, Bibliothèque Nationale, Paris
P-A	Pyrénées-Atlantiques
S-M	Seine-Maritime

Introduction: sovereignty and registration of the laws

Recent scholarship on the parlements has minimized their differences with royal administrations. According to the current view, any disputes involving the parlements were less than fundamental, involving no vital interest, and artificial, a ritual ballet in which both sides accepted unwritten rules and kept inside invisible boundaries. Thus the basic issue of royal sovereignty could never come into play, by mutual consent.[1] This view is only partially correct. It is true that the parlements did not openly challenge sovereignty or the nature of the monarchy. They looked for no Bastille to storm. But it is not true that they posed no fundamental obstacle to royal government, merely that their behaviour was insidious, marked by stealth. They cloaked their intentions in procedural ambiguity and acted under the cover of a trademark rhetorical dissimulation, seeking not to overturn royal power but to infiltrate and weaken it. Sometimes, however, the disputes involved irreconcilable issues that artifice could not elide. This was eventually the case with the way the parlements treated the king's new laws.

Jean Bodin, the most incisive political thinker of sixteenth-century France, identified the giving of laws to all subjects without their consent as the hallmark of sovereignty, by which he meant supreme, permanent power in the state. In France, sovereignty belonged to the king, so that legislative sovereignty coincided with royal sovereignty, or *puissance absolue*. Bodin also said that sovereignty could not be divided, shared or delegated. On the surface, magistrates of the Parlement of Paris accepted all of this and periodically, sometimes frequently, affirmed their steadfast belief in the king's full legislative sovereignty. But as framers of the American constitution would one day discover, things grew more complicated when political theory gave way to the actual making of laws.[2]

The kings issued laws and sent them to their parlements to be registered, in order to bring the new legislation to public attention and to make it enforceable within the parlements' jurisdictions. Reduced to its essentials, registration meant that the parlements 'published' the laws by reading them aloud in open court, copied them into folio registers and sent them in printed form to subordinate law courts. But the parlements claimed that registration involved more than this minimalist procedure. They argued that in registering the laws, they also validated them, bestowing a seal of approval and conferring public standing.[3]

A school of sixteenth-century legal scholars, known as 'constitutionalists', associated themselves with this premise. Like 'absolutist' theorists, with whom they shared many ideas and values, constitutionalists accepted that the kings held absolute power and exercised it subject to divine and natural law, thus keeping the monarchy from degenerating into tyranny. Unlike most absolutists, constitutionalists also thought that the kings had chosen to govern under the additional restraints of French laws and customs, gaining moral stature by voluntarily renouncing the full exercise of their power. This paradox, in which constitutionalists saw royal power as both absolute and limited, caused them to focus upon registration procedure.

In the second volume of his formidable *Les Recherches de la France*, published in 1565, the learned constitutional scholar Étienne Pasquier assimilated registration procedure to the idea of bridling royal power, proposed by Claude de Seyssel in 1519. Pasquier deeply influenced constitutional thinkers of his day and for the next half century. In 1617, Bernard de La Roche-Flavin, a *président aux requêtes* at the Parlement of Toulouse, incorporated the arguments of Pasquier and his successors into his *Treize livres des Parlements de France*, an opus which demonstrated the essential concord of the constitutionalists by copying verbatim from most of them, without attribution.[4]

According to these scholars, royal legislation did not become enforceable or take effect until the parlements had *verified* it. Constitutionalists believed that verification entailed a close scrutiny of the laws to see that they did not conflict with the abstract principles of justice, reason and virtue, and with the concrete provisions of royal ordinances and legal precedent. To conduct this scrutiny, magistrates of the parlements attended a plenary session called assembled chambers, heard the laws read aloud and in full, analysed them in detail, discussed them at length and then expressed their approval or disapproval by means of an free vote, *liberté des suffrages*. The principles of *vérification* and *liberté des suffrages* became recurring features of constitutional thought and the rhetoric of the parlements.[5]

If a new law failed verification scrutiny, constitutionalists argued that a parlement could reform it by deleting articles that it disliked. As if it had passed through a pharmacist's alembic, to use Pasquier's metaphor, a law purged of its impurities naturally improved in quality. The parlements might also improve laws by inserting articles drafted on the spot to settle any issues remaining in dispute. Both these procedures made up what constitutionalists and parlements called 'modification'. Constitutionalist thinkers took it for granted that the parlements could alter new laws in either way, especially the latter, without necessarily troubling the king by informing him of what they had done.[6]

The parlements also undermined laws that they disliked by stretching the registration process over a long, indefinite period, the tactic of delay. If a tribunal escaped detection as it thus marked time, the new law would eventually die of neglect. Then, too, a truly long delay might soften the king's commitment to the law, persuading him to change it in order to get it registered. Submitting remonstrances also held up the progress of new legislation. A remonstrance was an oral or written argument against the law in question. Simply by voting to issue a remonstrance, a parlement tabled the law and froze the registration process. Time passed slowly while the magistrates, often at a leisurely pace, drafted, revised, approved and at last sent the remonstrance to the king. He responded much more quickly, ordinarily by rejecting the remonstrance straight away. But the constitutionalists recommended that the parlement submit a fresh remonstrance, in case of a turndown, and then another, putting the king off again and again until he agreed to alter or withdraw the disputed law.[7] The tactic of delay fitted well with that of modification; and the two lent considerable strength to *vérification* and *liberté des suffrages*.

Absolutist theorists from Bodin to Cardin Le Bret developed a different reading of the proper legislative role of the parlements. Absolutists held that registration proclaimed rather than certified the laws and served primarily to bring laws to the attention of the king's subjects. Parlements could remonstrate against legislation if they did so in a timely fashion. But they could not modify legislation or delay registration for very long, especially after the king had answered their remonstrances. Otherwise, the Bodinian principle of undivided sovereignty would suffer injury. Le Bret had the parlements in mind when he issued his unforgettable dictum that sovereignty was no more divisible than a geometric point.[8]

A succession of royal administrators, starting in 1561 with the reformist Chancellor Michel de L'Hôpital, opposed the parlements' registration claims in similar ways. L'Hôpital, who appears to have influenced Bodin, denied that the parlements could amend legislation on their own authority; scolded them for delaying registration of the laws after the king had answered remonstrances; and, returning to a theme of Francis I (1515–1547), insisted that parlements were merely judicial institutions that should not get involved in finance and government. Michel de Marillac, keeper of the seals for Louis XIII, inveighed against constitutionalist tenets in much the same way, even denying that the king needed to submit his laws for parlementary verification. The regency government of Anne of Austria adopted all these counter-arguments and bequeathed them intact to Louis XIV.

However, the constitutionalists had influenced learned opinion to such a degree that most absolutists did not altogether contradict them on the registration of laws. Although absolutists stressed the authority of the king over the tribunals, most of them, including Bodin, agreed that the parlements properly deliberated upon new laws, a concession that brought them close to constitutionalist principles. Marillac acknowledged that on occasion parlements ought to 'make difficulties' in registering contested legislation; this was, he said, 'often very useful' in slowing or halting 'many . . . things'. Even Le Bret agreed that parlements should use 'all sorts of methods' to impede a bad law, while looking to the king to reform it. Constitutionalist ideas, unrefuted in any thorough way, thus enjoyed a degree of acceptance throughout the French political elite. In the Estates General of 1576, for example, both the clergy and the third estate firmly endorsed the principles of parlementary verification of the laws.[9]

Meanwhile, the royal administration tried to get its way in the parlements by intervening directly in registration procedure, using as its first weapon a peremptory order called the *lettre de jussion*. A *jussion*, the king's command in writing, should by itself have secured immediate registration of the laws, but the parlements tended to ignore it. The king could issue a second or third *jussion*; but repetition dulled the sharp edges of the weapon, reducing it to a gambit in the process. If and when the peremptory order failed, the king could resort to face to face compulsion by confronting a parlement in person.[10]

Monarchs could attend sessions in the Parlement of Paris and occasionally did so, just to observe the proceedings. In the 1400s, they also visited the tribunal in an effort to compel it to register legislation. Charles VIII (1483–1498), Louis XII (1498–1515) and Francis I (1515–1547) all had recourse to the royal visit for just this purpose. In hopes of coercing the Parlement into registering edicts of religious toleration, Charles IX (1560–1574) elevated the visit into a ceremony called a *lit de justice*, which his successors adopted and developed to a high point. Henry III (1574–1589) often tried to force fiscal laws through the Parlement in a *lit de justice*; and Louis XIII (1610–1643) did so with even greater frequency. The regency government of the young Louis XIV made selective but provocative use of the *lit de justice*, again from fiscal motives.[11] To justify their resort to coercion, Henry III and his successors invoked the medieval principle of necessity, *necessitas legem non habet*, arguing that military emergency had placed the kingdom at risk and justified extraordinary measures.[12]

When he held his *lit de justice* in the Parlement of Paris, the king entered the Grand-Chambre to the sound of drums and trumpets, accompanied by his chancellor, princes of the blood, dukes and peers, marshals of France and other dignitaries.The magistrates, having climbed into their ceremonial red robes with scarlet hoods, watched respectfully as the monarch took his seat on a cushioned throne in the corner of the Grand-Chambre, the *lit de justice* itself. The chancellor made an opening statement, and a clerk read aloud from the law or laws in question. After pretending to consult dignitaries and senior judges, the chancellor invoked the authority of the king and ordered the Parlement to register and publish the laws. Since the monarch was the source of the law, registration was to follow from his personal act.

The king might also hold a *lit de justice* in the provincial parlements in an effort get new laws registered, but ordinarily he depended upon his governors and intendants to get this job done. Bearing the written orders of the king, these officials would enter parlements, present the law or laws at issue, command the magistrates to register them at once, and stand around until they complied. This procedure, the functional equivalent of a *lit de justice*, had no particular name; it was simply a forced or involuntary registration, a generic term that included the *lit de justice*.[13]

In principle, the king should have prevailed once he invoked his personal authority, but the magistrates resented coercion because it violated constitutionalist maxims. Already in the *lits de justice* of Henry III, Achille I de Harlay, first president of the Parlement of Paris, vigorously denounced registration by compulsion, using constitutionalist rhetoric that magistrates would deploy all through the seventeenth and eighteenth centuries. At the pre-Fronde *lit de justice* of 15 January 1648, the *avocat général*, Omer Talon, whose post compelled him to endorse the new fiscal edicts, nevertheless castigated the proceedings as a moral illusion, a political contradiction and a violation of *liberté des suffrages*. First President Molé also denounced the *lit de justice* on constitutionalist grounds. To mark their disapproval of coerced registrations, the parlements often inserted the judgemental phrase *du très exprès commandement du roi* into their registration decrees. These words served to cry foul and to flag an abuse. They gave the registration a taint of illegality and jeopardized public acceptance of the law.[14]

Even after a *lit de justice*, the magistrates had to instruct their clerks to copy the new law into the folio register; and this in itself gave rise to deliberations, scrutiny and remonstrances – something very much like verification procedure itself. When Louis XIII held a *lit de justice* in the Parlement of Paris in December 1635, the magistrates deliberated in the weeks that followed upon the very legislation that the king thought he had forced through. To the consternation of the government, parlements might even try to revise *lit de justice* edicts, as the Parlement of Paris did on the eve of the Fronde. As late as 1667, First President Lamoignon of the Parlement of Paris paid homage to these precedents. Moreover, the *lit de justice* could well increase opposition to new laws, inflaming the magistrates rather than subduing them. Recent scholars have depicted the *lit de justice* as 'a high risk tactic . . . likely to misfire' (Robin Briggs) and 'fraught with dangers' (Roger Mettam).[15]

Since they could not depend upon involuntary registrations, the kings also attempted to control what the parlements could and could not do as they handled the laws. The ordinance of Moulins of 1566 (the work of Chancellor L'Hôpital), the ordinance of 1629 called the 'Code Michaud' (after its author, Keeper of the Seals Michel de Marillac), and an edict of 1641 issued by Louis XIII all established guidelines for remonstrances and stipulated that the parlements should register new legislation without delay. The kings did not object to remonstrances as such, then or later; so long as remonstrances resembled supplications, they did not offend. They troubled the government primarily because the parlements continued to issue them after the king had spoken. The Moulins ordinance therefore proscribed the use of repeated remonstrances; and although a subsequent declaration rescinded that ban, both the Code Michaud and the 1641 edict restored it in one way or another. The Code Michaud required the parlements to issue remonstrances within two months of the date of the legislation. The 1641 edict permitted only one remonstrance after a *lit de justice* registration and only two for all other laws, provided in the latter case that the king gave permission in advance. It also forbade the parlements to modify fiscal legislation in any way; they could only remonstrate against it.[16]

But the restraints that these laws imposed never really took hold, falling victim to various kinds of parlementary subterfuge. The Parlement of Paris negotiated changes in the Moulins ordinance and then ignored it. It delayed registering the Code Michaud even after receiving it in a *lit de justice* and forgot all about it after Marillac fell from power and landed in prison. The death of Louis XIII in 1643 appears to have ended enforcement of the 1641 edict. Indeed, parlements argued that the coerced registration of the Moulins ordinance and the Code Michaud cast doubt upon their legitimacy and took away any responsibility to obey them. The kings therefore met with disappointment in their efforts to control registration procedure, just as they had done with compulsory registrations. In addition, precedent had conferred upon the parlements a number of registration victories, which they could usefully cite when confronted with new rules.[17]

For example, the Parlement of Paris took a long time to register the great ordinances of judicial reform issued from Orléans (1561), Moulins (1566) and Blois (1579), and the government finally had to accept substantive changes in all of them. Virtually all the parlements opposed the sixteenth-century edicts of religious toleration, modified these edicts significantly and delayed registering them for many months. The Parlement of Rouen, the last one to hold out, did not register the Edict of Nantes, issued in 1598, until 1609. The parlements also delayed registering fiscal edicts and modified them in order to reduce their rates, scope and yield. Henry IV (1598–1610) frequently suffered from the parlementary tactics of modification and delay, even in the face of the military emergencies in the last years of the Wars of Religion.[18]

The reign of Louis XIII brought these tensions to new heights, as in 1635 France became a belligerent in the Thirty Years War. To finance the war, the government increased existing taxes, invented new ones and put new public offices up for sale. It grew dependent upon *traitants* (revenue farmers), financiers who advanced the king money on the basis of the potential yield of new fiscal edicts and made profits by collecting the taxes or selling the offices that the edicts established. But the revenue farmers could not collect anything until the parlements registered the edicts; and the parlements, declining to cooperate, obliged the king to resort to coercion. Louis XIII held so many *lits de justice* in the Parlement of Paris that he all but made the Grand-Chambre into a throne room. He ordered forced registrations in the provinces with equal frequency. Despite this pressure, the parlements resisted registering fiscal edicts or modified them so significantly that, even when registered, the crown failed to harvest the revenue that it originally anticipated.[19]

The edicts that provoked the strongest resistance and involved the highest stakes affected the most important private interest of the magistrates, their financial investment in venal offices. In the Old Regime, offices were saleable or vendible, the word venality designating property in office. A magistrate typically inherited his office or purchased it from a sitting judge; and it accounted for a large part of his personal fortune. Seekers of office might also hope to purchase new posts created by the king. In the sixteenth century, the monarchy created offices on a heroic scale; and newly minted judges swelled the rolls of the parlements. The Parlement of Bordeaux doubled under Francis I, and the Parlement of Paris doubled under Henry II. The Parlement of Toulouse tripled over the two reigns; and the Parlement of Rennes, created under Henry II, doubled and then tripled under Henry III. The Parlement of Aix grew apace. In 1524, Francis I created the *parties casuelles*, an office in the treasury that received this occasional (hence 'casual') income from venal office; it yielded steadily rising sums.[20]

But the parlements always resisted this increase in the number of their magistrates, fearing that the new posts would depress the prices of existing offices, hitherto rising. In fact, prices held more or less steady during the new sales, before resuming their upward march, but this became clear only in retrospect. As new magistrates poured into the tribunals, moreover, the sitting judges had to share with them the common income from judicial fees (*épices*), entailing smaller portions all around. In 1521–1522, Francis created twenty new offices in the Parlement of Paris, the first king to sell in bulk; but the sale proceeded very slowly. The judges did not register the edict in question for a long time and, once they had done so, took still more time to admit the newcomers, a warning to prospective buyers. This resistance became standard practice in all the tribunals, and eventually the kings had to scale back their plans to create offices. Fearing opposition, Henry IV refused even to consider a potentially lucrative proposal to establish a new parlement at Lyons. The growing recalcitrance of the parlements led Louis XIII to accept compromises on this vital issue.[21]

When in 1635 the Parlement of Paris balked at the creation of twenty-four councillors, the king had to lower their number to seventeen. The Parlement of Rouen fought its way to a similar arrangement in 1637, getting a planned sale of twelve councillor offices reduced to four. Opposition by the Parlements of Bordeaux and Toulouse in 1636–1639 also induced the government to lower the number of new judges that it had wanted to create. In 1641, the Parlement of Aix had to accept the creation of a Chambre des Requêtes, but it delayed admitting the new judges and then harassed those who took their seats. These tactics forced a compromise in 1649. In 1641, the crown attempted to double the magistrates of the Parlement of Rouen by adding a 'semester' of more than fifty new judges, one semester sharing the judicial year with the other; but this led to such an uproar that, in 1643, the king revoked the semester, at least for the time being.[22] Because of this opposition, Louis XIII could not sell as many new offices in the tribunals as he wished nor, arguably, as many as the market would absorb. It would seem indeed that the parlements were gaining strength on this issue, enjoying more success in opposing the office sales of the Bourbon than of the Valois monarchs.[23]

The royal administration also attempted to extract loans from the magistrates, using as leverage their interest in bequeathing their offices to their heirs or to selling them to third parties. The kings had long set the terms for the transfer of office and repossessed the office if an unfortunate owner failed to meet the terms. Francis I ruled that a resigning magistrate had to live at least forty days after the chancellery had given his designated successor the necessary papers, a process which could easily take three months. This made deathbed sales impossible, creating anxiety throughout the world of venality; but only a few could afford the costly dispensations that the king occasionally made available.[24] A declaration of 1604 lifted the forty-day requirement from all office-holders who paid the king an annual sum equal to one-sixtieth of the value of the office, as appraised by the royal council. Office-holders, including judges in the parlements, regarded these payments as more an insurance premium than an exaction, cheap at the price. They gladly paid what was called both by its official name, the *droit annuel* (annual payment), and the *paulette*, its colloquial designation.[25]

The popularity of the *paulette* led to a controversy that lasted into the reign of Louis XIV, since holders of office wanted to preserve the terms of 1604, while the government sought to alter those terms to bring in more money. Louis XIII ordinarily granted the *paulette* for nine years and renewed it just before it expired, in 1620, 1630 and 1638. But each of the renewal declarations required office-holders, including the parlementaires, to loan the king sums equal to 5 percent (1620), 25 percent (1630), or 12.5 percent (1638) of the appraised value of their offices before they would be 'admitted' to the new *paulette*. No one expected the government to repay this money, which amounted to several thousand livres from each of the judges in the parlements. The Parlement of Paris stubbornly resisted the loans, issuing remonstrances and seeking audiences with the king to heighten its protest; and opposition in the provincial parlements added to the fracas. In the end, the parlements triumphed: the king excused them from the loans and gave them free access to the *paulette*.[26]

Another dispute sprang up over a loan called an *augmentations de gages*, a 'salary increase' only in a misleading sense. To obtain such an increase, a magistrate had to pay the government a large sum of new money, making an *augmentations de gages* the interest payment on a loan. The parlements opposed *augmentations de gages* with their customary stubbornness. Either they did not register *augmentations de gages* edicts, or by virtue of a modifying clause they made the payments voluntary. Down to the reign of Louis XIV, only those judges who wanted to buy *augmentations de gages* did so, another victory for the tribunals.[27]

In the first phase of the Fronde (1648–1653), the Parlement of Paris and its sister tribunals drew up twenty-seven reform articles to cure what they saw as abuses of government. They devoted particular attention to their grievances about registration procedure and venal office, both of which had grown more acute in the regency government of Anne of Austria. Six articles asserted the need for proper verification of the laws, of which three defended *liberté des suffrages*. Verification procedures themselves provided a solid defence against assaults upon venality; but just to make sure, one of the articles called for a four-year moratorium on new offices.

As these articles showed, the Fronde had persuaded the magistrates that the government was damaging their constitutional role by jeopardizing their venal offices, a provocative fusing of issues. Although the government emerged victorious from the Fronde, the parlements could take satisfaction from having defended these entwined issues with reasonable success. After the Fronde, the tribunals obstructed, modified and delayed royal legislation much as before, obliging the Mazarin administration to compromise with them on contested points. Sensitive to their interests in venal office, Mazarin renewed the *paulette* unconditionally, did not seek loans from the judges and sold new offices in only three provincial parlements, and not until the late 1650s at that.[28] In the century or more since registration procedure had become so troublesome, over venal as well as other issues, the parlements had won at least as much as they had lost, although they sometimes ran the risk of appearing to disobey the king.

As royal institutions, the parlements depended upon the king for their jurisdiction, authority and their very existence: they had no standing, legal or otherwise, to defy him outright. Needing to reconcile their behaviour with the principles of monarchy, the magistrates found in rhetoric a convenient disguise. When Charles IX complained in 1572 about the slow progress of nine fiscal edicts in the Parlement of Paris, the magistrates replied that their duty to him required them to take their time ('This delay is not disobedience'). When the magistrates denounced a law issued by Henry III as 'useless, pernicious, and damaging to the public', they insisted that such harsh language only served the king's interests. When it modified laws in the later 1500s, the Parlement asserted ritualistically that it acted on the 'will of the king' and with his 'good pleasure'. Rhetorical versatility not only reflected constitutional theory; it shielded the judges against charges of disobedience. Henry IV and Louis XIII both accused the Parlement of Paris of disobedience, but it was hard to make the accusation stick, once the parlements had mastered a rhetoric of subservient resistance. The Parlement of Paris used the 'good pleasure' phrase repeatedly in the run-up to the Fronde.[29]

All these matters – constitutional theory, the parlements' treatment of the laws, the ineffective royal attempts to regulate or coerce them, studied ambiguity – raised the question whether the tribunals had trespassed into the fortress of sovereignty through a back door. Had they somehow impaired Bodin's concept of the king as a giver of law to each and to all, without their consent? The parlements denied it, and many scholars, although noting the question, have hesitated to find them guilty. It can indeed be argued that the institutional ambiguities of the Old Regime made government flexible enough to accommodate their behaviour. But the ambiguities in registration procedure became theoretically worrisome, when pushed beyond a certain point, at some critical moment.[30]

Such a moment arrived when the Parlement of Paris began to modify one of the seven fiscal edicts presented in the *lit de justice* of January 1648, declaring in the usual way that it was acting under the 'good pleasure' of the king. The regency inquired pointedly if the Parlement claimed the power to alter an edict registered by royal authority in a *lit de justice*. The duc d'Orléans, uncle of the king, Prime Minister Mazarin and Chancellor Séguier all asked the judges this precise question: did they mean to substitute their authority for that of the king when, by modifying an edict, they executed it only in part? The regency probably hoped to lure the Parlement into a constitutional debate about legislative sovereignty and the proper limits of verification procedure, a debate that no tribunal ever wanted to have. In the event, the magistrates hummed and hawed, chopped and changed, and finally declined to answer on the grounds that any response would carry them on to a 'dangerous shoal'. Omar Talon, the *avocat général*, said that the judges deliberately elected not to address 'the most important and most difficult question of polity'.[31]

This deliberate silence went hand in hand with constitutionalist theory and legal precedent, neither of which recognized a point where unqualified registration of the laws had to take place. Theorists acknowledged that parlements must eventually do what the king commanded, but they did not say just when that obedience must occur. They never intended fully to explore or chart the maze of registration procedure; they might stumble into some intersection where the parlements must finally register the laws. It was best to leave these coordinates undiscovered, as the Parlement of Paris well understood.

Despite and because of such silences, the monarchy harboured a deep suspicion that the claims of registration procedure threatened serious harm to the principle of legislative sovereignty. Cardinal Richelieu had nurtured these anxieties, and the regency government shared his concerns, in 1648. Louis XIV's memoirs alluded to ancient worries about usurped authority in the Fronde, as though the issue had never disturbed his personal rule; but there he was less than candid. At a session of his Council of Justice in 1665, the councillor of state François Verthamont denounced the parlements for continuing to remonstrate after the king had answered a remonstrance. Repeated remonstrances, he contended, undermined the king's legislative sovereignty, because no one could know whether his will or that of the parlements would ultimately prevail. Verthamont would surely have extended this condemnation to verification procedure as a whole.

In 1718, a keeper of the seals, d'Argenson, also presented his struggle with the Parlement of Paris as deciding whether or not the king truly enjoyed legislative sovereignty, as did Chancellor Maupeou a half century later. When so confronted, the parlements, especially the Parlement of Paris, obfuscated as in the past and touted their devotion to the unqualified sovereignty of the king; but an eighteenth-century president in the Parlement of Aix confessed privately that modification alone 'totally' undermined royal sovereignty and placed the king 'beneath the magistrate'.[32]

Thomas Hobbes would have agreed. Living in France from 1640 to 1651, the great English thinker both witnessed much of the Fronde and wrote his treatise *Leviathan* (1651) during his stay. In that book, which owed something to Bodin, he took up 'verification' and dismissed it. Hobbes could see no proper role for verification except the innocent one of establishing that the authentic sovereign had actually issued the law in question – an identity check, to prove that the law was not counterfeit. Once the law had met this simple test, it immediately took effect, having been validated by the will of the sovereign when he issued it. Hobbes would have heard all about the parlements' version of verification before and during the Fronde; in all probability, he believed, like the royal administration, that *vérification* and *liberté des suffrages* conflicted with sovereignty, all protests to the contrary notwithstanding.[33]

It would have helped us to resolve this question had the parlements flatly opposed the principle of royal legislative sovereignty, dropping the mask. Jean-Sylvain Bailly, the first president of the revolutionary Constitutent Assembly of 1789, did just this when, in his memoirs, he expressed contempt for the idea that 'legislative power was concentrated uniquely in the hands of the monarch'. His views probably coincided with those of many magistrates in the seventeenth and eighteenth centuries. Although the actual judges never indulged in this much clarity, the royal administrations had good reason to believe that the parlements did not completely accept the legislative sovereignty of the king.[34]

The France of 1661, in which the principles of obedience and authority still lacked clarity and definition, was not altogether an absolutist state. Despite their protests, the parlements did not believe that the principles of monarchy meant that they must accept undue subordination in the registration of the king's laws. Henry IV deplored the sluggishness of the Parlement in registering his edicts as well as its tendency to change them. Other monarchs would certainly have agreed, but First President Molé and the *avocat-général* Talon, in effect speaking for the magistracy as a whole, staunchly defended the importance of modification and delay and constitutionalist thought in general.[35] Louis XIV's magistrates inherited these constitutionalist ideas, the precedents with which they had been upheld, and a generally successful defence of their interests in venal office.

The controversy over registration procedure, seemingly inherent in the system, might easily have gone on repetitiously decade after decade, until the end of the Old Regime, with the institution of venality enjoying its continuous protection. Consequently, it was no foregone conclusion, and neither predicted nor predictable, that Louis XIV would throw off the twin burdens of constitutional theory and parlementary precedent and impose his will upon the tribunals in the registration of the laws and on issues of venal office. Although it took him some time to do so, that is indeed what he accomplished; and it was no small thing. He triumphed on the issue of legislative sovereignty and harvested the fruits of victory in a way that his predecessors would have envied.

Chapters 1 and 2 of this study will tell how the king gained control of registration procedure. They re-create the sequence of events, context and interplay of interests by which, in the end, the tribunals lost their power to delay, alter or oppose royal legislation, thus forfeiting their old constitutional role. Chapters 3 and 4 will show how Louis XIV overcame the parlements' defence of venality, forcing them to pay for repeated *augmentations de gages* and to accept the creation of as many offices as the king could sell, at the cost to the magistrates of falling office prices and heavy personal debt, the social and economic consequences of political defeat. Chapters 5–7 explain how the parlements tried, and failed, to recover from these interrelated losses in the post-1715 regency of Philippe d'Orléans. Louis XIV's gains would largely endure; he had indeed inserted the keystone into the arch of absolute government.

Little or nothing in the pages to come supports the optimistic view of revisionists, notably that of William Beik, who portrayed the ruling class of Languedoc as allied with Louis XIV, nurtured, protected and 'basking in the sun' of his benign reign. The experience of the parlements teaches that absolute government came at the expense of once influential institutions and subjects and weakened them for a long time, perhaps permanently. There is something to be said after all for the claim of Ernest Lavisse, that the government of Louis XIV rested upon columns that the king himself had hollowed out.[36]

Notes

1 Jonathan Dewald, 'The "Perfect Magistrate": Parlementaires and Crime in Sixteenth-Century Rouen', *Archiv für Reformationsgeschichte* 67 (1976), 291–292; John Rogister, 'Parlementaires, Sovereignty, and Legal Opposition in France under

Louis XV: An Introduction', *Parliaments, Estates & Representation* 6 (June 1986), 25–32; Michel de Waele, 'De Paris à Tours: la crise d'identité des magistrats parisiens de 1589 à 1594', *Revue Historique* 299/3 (1998), 573; William Doyle, 'The Parlements', in *The French Revolution and the Creation of Modern Political Culture*, vol. 1 of *The Political Culture of the Old Regime*, ed. K.M. Baker (Oxford, 1987), 162.

2 Jean Bodin, *Les six livres de la République* (Paris, 1583), Bk I, chs viii and x; Richard Bonney, *L'absolutisme* (Paris, 1989), pp. 23–30; Roger Doucet, *Les institutions de la France au seizième siècle* (2 vols; Paris, 1948), I, 72–81, 89–95; Jules Flammermont, ed., *Remontrances du Parlement de Paris au XVIIIe siècle* (3 vols; Paris, 1888–1898), I, 42–46, 70–73, 77–84, 88–98 (affirmations of royal legislative sovereignty).

3 Édouard Maugis, *Histoire du Parlement de Paris* (3 vols; 1913–1916; reprint, Geneva, 1977), I, 522–543, 629–630; Shennan, *Parlement of Paris*, pp. 4, 165–166, 186–187, 220; Hélène Michaud, *La grande chancellerie et les écritures royales au seizième siècle (1515–1589)* (Paris, 1967), pp. 373–383; Michel Antoine, 'La chancellerie de France au XVIe siècle', in idem, *Le dur métier de roi* (Paris, 1986), 27.

4 André Lemaire, *Les lois fondamentales de la monarchie française* (1907; reprint, Geneva, 1975), pp. 71–75, 84–91, 164–165; William F. Church, *Constitutional Thought in Sixteenth-Century France* (Cambridge, Mass., 1941), pp. 3–21, 74–77, 129–155; Donald R. Kelley, *Foundations of Modern Historical Scholarship* (New York and London, 1970), pp. 271–300; Julian H. Franklin, *Jean Bodin and the Rise of Absolutist Theory* (Cambridge, 1973), pp. 1–21; J.H.M. Salmon, 'The Legacy of Jean Bodin: Absolutism, Populism or Constitutionalism?', *History of Political Thought* 17 (Winter 1996), 500–522; Étienne Pasquier, *Les Recherches de la France* (Paris, 1665); Bernard de La Roche-Flavin, *Treize livres des Parlemens de France* (Geneva, 1621); Claude de Seyssel, *The Monarchy of France*, trans. J.H. Hexter and Michael Sherman (New Haven, Conn., and London, 1981), pp. 49–51, 54–56, 89–93.

5 BN, *N.a.f.* 9,771 ('Remontrances présentées au Roy Henry IV . . .', 1597), f. 27r.

6 Louis [Charondas] Le Caron, *Pandectes ou Digestes du droit françois* (Lyon, 1596), Bk I, ch. v, p. 46; ch. iii, p. 15; ch. xxiii, p. 334; René Choppin, 'Éloge', in *Oeuvres de René Choppin* (5 vols; Paris, 1662), III, 409; François Grimaudet, 'De la Loy', in *Oeuvres* (Paris, 1613), p. 635; Charles de Figon, *Discours des estats et offices* (Paris, 1579), p. 16; La Roche-Flavin, *Treize livres*, Bk XIII, ch. xvii, art. iii (this article is largely transposed from Le Caron); Antoine Furetière, *Dictionnaire universel* (4 vols; 1727; reprint, Geneva, 1972), III, n.p. For modification in the sixteenth-century Parlement of Paris, see Michaud, *Grande chancellerie*, p. 380.

7 Le Caron, *Pandectes*, Bk I, ch. iii, p. 15; ch. xix, pp. 224–226; ch. xxiii, pp. 333–334; Grimaudet, 'De la Loy', pp. 635–636; La Roche-Flavin, *Treize livres*, Bk XIII, ch. viii, art. ii, and ch. xvii, art. xiv.

8 Henri Sée, *Les idées politiques en France au XVIIe siècle* (1923; reprint, Geneva, 1978), pp. 16–32; Church, *Constitutional Thought*, pp. 326–327; Bodin, *Les six livres de la République*, Bk I, ch. viii; Bk III, ch. ii; Cardin Le Bret, *De la souveraineté du roi*, in *Les oeuvres* (Paris, 1689), Bk I, ch. ix.

9 Seong-Hak Kim, *Michel de L'Hôpital. The Vision of a Reformist Chancellor during the French Religious Wars* (Kirksville, Mo., 1997), pp. 118–134, and 'The Chancellor's Crusade: Michel de L'Hôpital and the *Parlement* of Paris', *French History* 7 (March 1993), 18–20, 24; Michel de L'Hôpital, *Discours pour la majorité de Charles IX et trois autres discours*, ed. Robert Descimon (Paris, 1993), pp. 107–108; Michel de Marillac,

'Mémoire . . . contre l'authorité du Parlement', BN, *Fonds fr.*, 7,549, ff. 90v–91r; Le Bret, *Souveraineté*, Bk II, ch. ix; Georges Picot, *Histoire des États Généraux* (4 vols; Paris, 1872), II, 561–562.

10 François Olivier-Martin, *L'organisation corporative de la France d'ancien régime* (Paris, 1938), p.439; Georges d'Avenel, vicomte, *Richelieu et la monarchie absolue*, 2nd ed. (4 vols; Paris, 1895), I, 99–100; Marcel Marion, *Dictionnaire des institutions de la France aux XVIIe et XVIIIe siècles* (Paris, 1923), p.314.

11 Elizabeth A.R. Brown and Richard C. Famiglietti, *The Lit de Justice. Semantics, Ceremonial, and the Parlement of Paris, 1300–1600* (Sigmaringen, 1994) is a strong argument for the late medieval origins of the *lit de justice*, in partial refutation of Sarah Hanley, *The Lit de Justice of the Kings of France* (Princeton, NJ, 1982), who contended that the first *lits de justice* were those of Francis I in 1527 and 1537. Mack P. Holt, 'The King in Parlement: the Problem of the *Lit de Justice* in Sixteenth-Century France', *The Historical Journal* 21 (1988), 507–523, argued persuasively that Henry III used the *lit de justice* to compel the Parlement to register fiscal laws, whereas Hanley believed that this practice dated from 1597. See also R.J. Knecht, 'Francis I and the "Lit de Justice"': A "Legend" Defended', *French History* 7 (March 1993), 53–83.

12 Hanley, *Lit de Justice*, pp. 215, 226, 292–293; Richard Bonney, *Political Change in France under Richelieu and Mazarin* (Oxford, 1978), pp. 115–116.

13 Joseph-Nicolas Guyot, *Répertoire universel et raisonné de jurisprudence civile et criminelle, canonique et bénéficiale*, new ed. (17 vols; Paris, 1784–1785), X, 882–883; Chéruel, *Dictionnaire historique*, II, 670–671. For *lits de justice* under Louis XIV, see Olivier Lefèvre d'Ormesson, *Journal*, ed. Pierre-Adolphe Chéruel (2 vols; Paris, 1860–1861), II, 129–131, 428–431.

14 René Filhol, *Le premier président Christofle de Thou et la réformation des coutumes* (Paris, 1937), p. 27, n. 3; Guillaume Du Vair, 'Monsieur le Premier President', in *Les oeuvres du sieur du Vair* (Paris, 1618), pp. 140–143 (the Harlay discourse); Hubert Mailfait, *Un magistrat de l'ancien régime. Omer Talon, sa vie et ses oeuvres, 1595–1652* (1902; reprint, Geneva, 1971), pp. 228–230; Omer Talon, *Mémoires* (Paris, 1836–1839), pp. 209–212. Molé's statement is in AN, U (Le Nain) 28: 21 January 1648, f. 134rv.

15 Hanley, *Lit de Justice*, pp. 283–284, 291–293; Achille de Harlay, BN, *Fonds fr.*, 7,548 ('Établissement du Parlement de Paris'), ff. 20v–21v; BN, *Fonds fr.*, 7,217 (Procès verbal de l'ordonnance du mois d'avril 1667), f. 200 (Lamoignon); Robin Briggs, 'Richelieu and Reform. Rhetoric and Political Reality', in *Richelieu and His Age*, eds Joseph Bergin and Laurence Brockliss (Oxford, 1992), p. 93; Roger Mettam, *Power and Faction in Louis XIV's France* (Oxford, 1988), p. 129. Moote, *Revolt of the Judges*, pp. 34, 104, also stressed the limited effectiveness of the *lit de justice*.

16 François-André Isambert, *et al.*, eds, *Recueil général des anciennes lois françaises* (29 vols; Paris, 1822–1833), XIV, 190–191; XVI, 239; XVI, 529–535.

17 Maugis, *Parlement*, I, 615–618; Ernest-Désiré Glasson, *Le Parlement de Paris* (2 vols; 1901; reprint, Geneva, 1974), I, 136, 167–171; J. Russell Major, *Representative Government in Early Modern France* (New Haven, Conn., 1980), pp. 512–518; Léon Desjonquères, *Le garde des sceaux Michel de Marillac* (Paris, 1908), pp. 202–213.

18 Richard Bonney, *The King's Debts: Finance and Politics in France, 1598–1661* (New York, 1981), pp. 47, 51; Glasson, *Parlement*, I, 33–36, 38–40, 97–109; Shennan,

Parlement, pp. 216, 233–237; Hanley, *Lit de Justice*, pp. 224–225; Holt, 'King in Parlement', pp. 510–521; Jean-Louis Bourgeon, 'La Fronde parlementaire à la veille de la Saint-Barthélemy', *Bibliothèque de l'École des Chartes* 148 (1991), pp. 27–52; J. Russell Major, *Bellièvre, Sully, and the Assembly of Notables of 1596*, Transactions of the American Philosophical Society, n.s., 64, pt 2 (Philadelphia, 1974), 7, 19, 24; Jean-Pierre Babelon, *Henri IV* (Paris, 1982), pp. 620–621, 687, 728–729.

19 Françoise Bayard, *Le monde des financiers au XVIIe siècle* (Paris, 1988), pp. 189–190; Bonney, *Political Change*, pp. 172, 246, 250, 302–303; *idem, King's Debts*, pp. 180–181, 199; Sharon Kettering, *Judicial Politics and Urban Revolt in Seventeenth-Century France. The Parlement of Aix, 1629–1659* (Princeton, NJ, 1978), pp. 62, 188, 193, 201–206; Glasson, *Parlement*, I, 149–166, 215–221; Moote, *Revolt of the Judges*, pp. 97–120; Hamscher, *Parlement*, pp. 88–96; Hanley, *Lit de Justice*, pp. 282–292.

20 Roland Mousnier, *La vénalité des offices sous Henri IV et Louis XIII*, 2nd ed (Paris, 1971), pp. 8–10, 40–47, 68, 86–89, 132, 95–116, 195; Maugis, *Parlement*, I, 136–268; Henri Carré, *Le Parlement de Bretagne après la Ligue* (Paris, 1888), pp. 10–13; Martin Wolfe, *The Fiscal System of Renaissance France* (New Haven, Conn., 1972), p. 80; Bonney, *King's Debts*, pp. 98–99, 175–177, 198–199.

21 Christopher W. Stocker, 'The Politics of the Parlement of Paris in 1525', *French Historical Studies* 8 (Autumn, 1973), 192–198; Maugis, *Parlement*, I, 136–268; Mousnier, *Vénalité*, pp. 83, 197–199; Jonathan Dewald, *The Formation of a Provincial Nobility: The Magistrates of the Parlement of Rouen, 1499–1610* (Princeton, NJ, 1980), pp. 137–140.

22 Glasson, *Parlement*, I, 150–159; Mousnier, *Vénalité*, pp. 130–131, 149, 199–204, 207, 213–218; Bonney, *King's Debts*, pp. 175–177, 197–198; Madeleine Foisil, *La révolte des nu-pieds et les révoltes normandes de 1639* (Paris, 1970), pp. 325–337; Beik, *Absolutism and Society*, p. 84; Kettering, *Judicial Politics*, pp. 185–186, 190–195, 202–203, 271; Prosper Cabasse, *Essais historiques sur le Parlement de Provence* (3 vols; Paris, 1826), II, 214–223, 280–281.

23 Bayard, *Monde des financiers*, pp. 177–189; Mousnier, *Vénalité*, pp. 129, 158–162, 196.

24 Mousnier, *Vénalité*, pp. 22–29, 44–50; Christopher Stocker, 'Public and Private Enterprise in the Administration of a Renaissance Monarchy: The First Sales of Office in the Parlement of Paris (1512–1524)', *The Sixteenth Century Journal* 9 (July 1978), 15.

25 Mousnier, *Vénalité*, pp. 223–243. Charles Paulet, who gave his name to the *droit annuel*, was the chief operating officer of the first group of revenue farmers to purchase the right to collect it.

26 *Ibid.*, pp. 283–296, 300–303.

27 *Ibid.*, pp. 308, 400–415; Moote, *Revolt of the Judges*, pp. 60–62; D'Estampes de Valançay, intendant, Rennes, to Chancellor Séguier, 12 September 1636, in Roland Mousnier, ed., *Lettres et mémoires adressés au Chancelier Séguier (1633–1649)* (2 vols; Paris, 1964), I, 347–348.

28 Paul Rice Doolin, *The Fronde* (Cambridge, Mass., 1935), pp. 15, 20; Ernst Heinrich Kossmann, *La Fronde* (Leiden, 1954), pp. 52, 139–143; Moote, *Revolt of the Judges*, pp. 78–84, 159–160, 213; Hamscher, *Parlement*, pp. 9–10, 82–98; for the link between constitutional and venality issues, see Talon, *Mémoires*, pp. 208–209, 222;

Mathieu Molé, *Mémoires* (4 vols; Paris, 1855–1857), III, 215; and Françoise-Bertault de Motteville, *Mémoires* (Paris, 1836), p. 157; edicts for the creation of parlementary offices in BN, *Actes R.*, F.23,612 (440) (Dijon) and AN, G7, 250 (Grenoble); M. de La Cuisine, *Le Parlement de Bourgogne* (3 vols; Dijon and Paris, 1864), III, 79–98; Daniel de Cosnac, *Mémoires*, ed. J. de Cosnac (2 vols; Paris, 1852), I, 275–278 (for Grenoble).

29 AN, U 159 (1572–1576) and U 160 (1576–1583) show how the sixteenth-century Parlement of Paris used this language to good effect; Moote, *Revolt of the Judges*, pp. 114–117, should not read as though the 'good pleasure' phrase was new.

30 Denis Richet, *La France moderne: l'esprit des institutions* (Paris, 1973), pp. 32–33; Parker, *French Absolutism*, pp. 1–2, 106; Shennan, *Parlement*, pp. 160–165, 214, 261–262, all noted the difficulty parlementary registration created for sovereignty but did not pursue the point. Michel Antoine, *Le Conseil du roi sous le règne de Louis XV* (Geneva, 1970), pp. 32–33, saw such contradictions as preventing the Old Regime from being a despotism.

31 AN, U 28: (1 February–6 March 1648), ff. 139v–149v; Jean Le Boindre, *Débats du Parlement de Paris pendant la Minorité de Louis XIV*, eds Robert Descimon *et al.* (Paris, 1997), pp. 51–61. For a scholarly treatment of these sessions, see Ranum, *Fronde*, pp. 92–97 *et passim*. Moote, *Revolt of the Judges*, pp. 112–114, underestimated the importance of the question.

32 Louis André, ed., *Testament politique du Cardinal de Richelieu* (Paris, 1947), p. 165; Paul Sonnino, ed. and trans., *Louis XIV. Mémoires for the Instruction of the Dauphin* (New York, 1974), pp. 23, 42–44; Jean-Baptiste Colbert, *Lettres, instructions, et mémoires*, ed. Pierre Clément (8 vols; Paris, 1861–1882), VI, p. 378 (Verthamont in the Council of Justice); Durand Echeverria, *The Maupeou Revolution* (Baton Rouge and London, 1985), pp. 129–130; President d'Eguilles of Aix is quoted in Jean Egret, *Louis XV et l'opposition parlementaire* (Paris, 1970), p. 10.

33 Thomas Hobbes, *Leviathan*, ed. Edwin Curley (Indianapolis, 1994), ch. xxvi, par. 16, 'Difference between Verifying and Authorising'; Quentin Skinner, 'Thomas Hobbes and His Disciples in France and England', *Comparative Studies in Society and History* 8 (January 1966), 153–167; Professor Johann P. Sommerville has kindly advised me that Hobbes could not plausibly have used the word verification to refer to anything in English political experience: he must have had France in mind.

34 Jean-Sylvain Bailly, *Mémoires de Bailly* (3 vols; Paris, 1821–1822), I, 221.

35 Yves-Marie Bercé, *La naissance dramatique de l'absolutisme, 1598–1661* (Paris, 1992), pp. 174, 189; Lavisse, *Le Roi. Colbert*, pp. 167–168, 267; BN, *Fonds fr.*, 7,548 ('Établissement du Parlement'), ff. 11v–12r (quoting Henry IV); Molé, *Mémoires*, III, 211; Talon, *Mémoires*, p. 214.

36 Lavisse, *Le Roi. Colbert*, p. 404.

1

Compulsory registration
and its limits, 1665–1671

Every student of French history knows that Louis XIV deprived the parlements of their most important power and function – that of opposing new legislation, especially fiscal legislation, when it first appeared before them. Given the tendency of the parlements to obstruct new legislation, frequently under Henry IV and Louis XII and periodically under Louis XV and Louis XVI, the reign of Louis XIV stands in sharp contrast in this regard. Curiously, however, even the most recent studies offer little in the way of narrative, analysis or background to explain how, why and under what circumstances the parlements lost their powers to obstruct new laws for the first time in their history. In treating this subject, most historians point to the ordinance of civil procedure of 1667, which curtailed the use of remonstrances by the parlements, and the declaration of February 1673, which regulated the procedure by which the tribunals registered the laws. But other kings had restricted remonstrances in ways that resembled the provisions of the ordinance; and few historians have appreciated the original features of the declaration, let alone explained why the government needed to enact it, once it had issued the ordinance. In any event, the mere citation of the laws of 1667 and 1673 cannot tell us how and why, or much about when, the government of Louis XIV, in contrast with both its predecessors and its successors, imposed its will upon the parlements in the registration of laws.[1] The issue merits a fresh examination.

Like his predecessors, Louis XIV had to deal with two essential questions, those involving extraordinary and ordinary registration: 1) whether the king could resolve legislation disputes by the extraordinary method of compulsory registration, as in a *lit de justice* or its provincial counterpart; and 2) whether the king could make the parlements stop modifying and delaying laws that they received in the ordinary way, by mail or by courier. In 1667, Louis XIV tried to deal with both these issues in title I of his new ordinance on civil procedure. He succeeded only with the first, although that success amounted to a big step forward. Unlike any of his predecessors, this king made the *lit de justice* and the provincial forced registration into effective ways to get his laws registered, once and for all. He made compulsion work. This chapter explains the circumstances and the process by which Louis XIV achieved that result. Even so, the ordinance did not enable the king to gain full control over the registration powers of the tribunals, especially those of modification and delay, the second part of the question. For that, he would have to exert himself all over again, as the next chapter explains.

When Cardinal Mazarin, his only prime minister, died on 9 March 1661, Louis XIV came into his own as ruler of France. In the beginning, the king governed with the ministers he inherited from Mazarin, but he did make an important new appointment. Jean-Baptiste Colbert (1619–1683), a descendant of a family of judicial and financial officials who rose in the service of Mazarin, gained Louis's confidence soon after the cardinal's death. Realizing that the monarch disliked and feared Nicolas Fouquet, the superintendent of finances, Colbert helped bring about Fouquet's arrest on 5 September 1661, dislodging the rival who had blocked his personal ascent. The king made Colbert a royal minister (*ministre d'état*), or member of the High Council, the cabinet in whose sessions the monarch adopted, administered and enforced his policies. Colbert also served on the Council of Dispatches and the new Royal Council of Finances, the other bodies that together with the High Council enjoyed the status of governing councils. By virtue of these positions Colbert exerted considerable influence over policies affecting the parlements. In addition, he presided at sessions of an important administrative council, the *Conseil d'État et des Finances*, which also issued decrees concerning the tribunals. Even before he became controller general of finances in 1665, Colbert had taken over all political and financial relations with the law courts, having driven the aging Chancellor Séguier out of most areas of domestic administration, a sharp break with traditional practice.[2]

For the most part, Colbert approached the Parlement of Paris and the provincial tribunals with firmness but with no a priori intention of reducing their role in French public life, let alone in the registration of laws. He did not at first envision a future in which the parlements would passively accept involuntary registrations or register new legislation automatically, without modification or delay. Surprisingly, Colbert did not even take a particularly strong stand when the government first addressed registration issues. In his memorandum of 1665 for the new Council of Justice, appointed to draw up an ordinance on civil procedure, he was resolutely moderate, urging restraint in dealing with the parlements and opposing any resort to 'a single blow' in the form of some harsh new law contrived to curb their excesses. Only weak kings, such as Charles IX or Louis XIII, resorted to shock therapy, he maintained; and once they died, the parlements quickly recovered any ground that the monarchy had gained. Instead of some bold stroke, Colbert wanted to apply moderate pressure over a long term, hoping to improve the behaviour of the parlements step by gradual step and for all time. Although Colbert would eventually change his mind, he was, as the Council began its work, a dove among hawks. His moderation is even a bit surprising since his father, the financier Nicolas Colbert, once went bankrupt with a *traité* owing to difficulties created by the Parlement of Rouen.[3]

In addition to Colbert, members of the Council of Justice included Chancellor Séguier and veteran councillors of state, masters of requests and prominent Parisian barristers. Henri Pussort, Colbert's choleric uncle, who had newly risen to prominence, also secured an appointment. Pussort advocated a much firmer line on the parlements than Colbert and advanced his views when the Council deliberated on appropriate procedure for the registration of laws, the first item on its agenda. On 25 October 1665, the Council finished title I, the king himself having participated in its sessions. Three articles of this title treated registration procedure.[4]

Of these, the most important was certainly article iv, which dealt with compulsory registration, even though this article has not received much historical attention. The article applied to *lits de justice*, in which the king himself brought legislation to a tribunal, ordinarily the Parlement of Paris. The words 'persons whom we have commissioned for this task' extended its scope to include forced registrations conducted in the other high courts of Paris by members of the royal family and in provincial parlements by governors and intendants. Article iv provided that all laws registered in the presence of the king or at the hands of his representatives should be 'kept and observed' from that very day forward. This operative phrase required the parlements to implement at once, and without any further deliberations or decrees, any laws registered under duress, a change that previous monarchs had tried unsuccessfully to introduce on several occasions.[5] In other words, article iv intended to make compulsory registration that final word in the registration process which constitutional theory and parlementary precedent had so carefully avoided for so long. It proclaimed that the king could register laws on his own authority and that once he had done so, the parlements lacked any further recourse.

The members of the Council of Justice drafted the article for this very purpose, as the *procès-verbal*, the summary of their discussions, revealed. Pussort, who spoke often and at length, explained that the words 'published in our presence' were intended to override the magistrates' contentions that laws took effect as a result of their deliberations and their *liberté de suffrages*. To the contrary, Pussort argued, the king made the laws valid when he issued them, as the 'only sovereign' and 'only legislator'. The way in which the parlements registered laws did not affect those laws at all. One could not distinguish between laws certified by the parlements as a result of a free vote and laws registered by the will of the king alone, as though the former were morally and legally superior to the latter. Pussort thus led a verbal assault upon the fortress of constitutionalist thought, but he did not attack the bastions alone; other members of the Council endorsed his views.[6]

François Verthamont, a councillor of state, agreed that the Parlement must implement any laws registered in a *lit de justice* without delay, any further deliberations on its part being out of order once a compulsory registration had occurred. Vincent Hotman, an *intendant des finances*, denounced the notion that the king somehow compromised the laws by asserting his authority in a *lit de justice*. Nicolas de La Reynie, the future *lieutenant général de police* of Paris, summed it up when he said that once the king had expressed his will, it became irrelevant whether or not the parlements verified laws. The king's command, so far from being a constitutional excess, made legislation more binding than the consent of the parlements could ever do.[7]

The Council sessions of 1665 showed a clear break with the tradition under which even royal administrators occasionally deferred to constitutionalist ideas and revealed that absolutist thought had now won an ideological victory over constitutionalism. As if to exploit this triumph, members of the Council of Justice also proscribed constitutionalist vocabulary, dumping ideologically offensive words into a lexicographical trash can. Thus the Council purposefully extirpated the word 'remonstrance', judged contaminated from its usage in the Fronde, and replaced it with a clumsy circumlocution, 'represent to us what they (the parlements and other courts) judge appropriate'. In addition, the Council replaced 'sovereign courts' with 'superior courts' as the generic name for the parlements and their sister tribunals, thinking that subjects had no right to the word 'sovereign'. These roundabout expressions took their place in title I of the ordinance and lasted, in official usage, for the balance of the Old Regime. Such anti-constitutionalist bias no doubt reflected the experience of the generation of the Fronde, which once in power laboured to reinforce the absolute state.[8]

The fate of title I depended at the beginning on the king's relationship with the Parlement of Paris, where Colbert was gaining influence with the first president and other high officials. Though much depended upon their particular skills and instincts, the first presidents ordinarily set the agenda of their parlements and influenced the political attitudes and behaviour of the judges. Unlike most magistrates, they served by virtue of a royal commission and not as owners of venal office; they answered only to the king or to Colbert as the king's representative. At the same time, the first presidents needed the support of their subordinates and could not truckle too obviously to the government or visibly waver in their defence of the magistrates' interests.[9]

Louis XIV delegated to Colbert the power to appoint the first presidents; and Colbert incorporated them into a clientage system that he reshaped in the service of the king. Under the set of personal ties called clientage, ambitious men placed themselves at the disposal of a superior, promising him fidelity and service in exchange for appointments, favours and protection. Louis XIII and Richelieu created the first network of royal clients for the kingdom as a whole, but the network fell apart after the deaths of both the king and the prime minister, to be restored by Mazarin during and after the Fronde. Colbert inherited Mazarin's network and built upon it.[10]

In 1658, Guillaume de Lamoignon became first president of the Parlement of Paris as a client of both Mazarin and Fouquet, who was also *procureur général* in the tribunal. After the fall of Fouquet, Lamoignon shifted his loyalties to the king and Colbert. But the first president also had independent traits, and Colbert found an even more loyal client in Achille II de Harlay, a grandson of the first president of the sixteenth century. Harlay became *procureur général* when Fouquet, prior to his arrest, was induced to resign that office, and set a new standard for political reliability. His son, Achille III, succeeded him as *procureur général* and became first president in 1689, in recognition of his even more dedicated service. The royal clients Lamoignon and Achille II de Harlay built a sympathetic group of loyalist judges, a political asset in reducing the friction that developed over the principle of the judicial supremacy of the royal council, asserted in 1661, and the king's decision to try Fouquet by a special tribunal instead of in the Parlement. It remained to be seen if these gains would carry over into the sphere of registration procedure.[11]

In December 1665, only weeks after the Council had finished title I, the king held a *lit de justice* to register a declaration for the reform of venal office. Since the declaration rolled back the prices of offices and seemed certain to cost the judges tens of thousands of livres, some of them began to pressure Lamoignon to convene an assembly of chambers to deliberate on the new law. Evidently they hoped to prevent it from taking effect, *lit de justice* or no *lit de justice*, much as the Parlement had tried to do with fiscal laws in the sessions before the Fronde. At first, the king banned any additional deliberations, wishing to preserve the integrity of his *lit de justice*. But in January 1666, a growing number of magistrates clamoured for a plenary session and a full scrutiny of the new law.

At this point Louis XIV took a firm stand, no doubt reinforced by his support in the Council of Justice and aware that the magistrates were in effect putting article iv at risk. Although kings and ministers before him usually worked to prevent plenary sessions from taking place, dreading the influence of opposition firebrands and their feverish discourses, Louis XIV ordered Lamoignon to convene the chambers at once. But he also told the first president that, once the magistrates had gathered, he should command them to abstain from all deliberations on the new law. The chambers could meet, but the judges must keep quiet. As Louis said in his memoirs, he intended 'to make a conspicuous example, either of the entire subjection of this court or of my just severity in punishing its assaults'. Lamoignon duly assembled the judges and repeated the king's order verbatim, whereupon they sat stunned and silent. Several tense moments passed. After a while, the session broke up without anyone saying a word, only yielding silently to the king and accepting the results of the *lit de justice*. Ormesson, a master of requests and an attentive observer, underlined the unprecedented nature of this session, without parallel in the history of the Parlement. As the king said, with evident satisfaction, the Parlement had accepted its 'subjection' and chosen 'the best course for itself'.[12]

In a larger sense, Louis XIV saw the question as involving his royal authority, stood his ground, triumphed and preserved the spirit of article iv. This act of authority was the first tangible result of the Council discussions on title I, as yet unpublished, and had more significance than the magistrates then realized. Perhaps the event marked a turning point as the king, having this time invoked his authority with success, would resort to forced registrations twice more in this decade, always with good results.

After some discussion, the government chose to register the ordinance of civil procedure, completed in early 1667, in another *lit de justice* in the Parlement, held with great fanfare on 20 April. The ceremony took on the aspect of celebration as it focused attention on the landmark reforms of the ordinance, which provided the first comprehensive description of the procedural steps in preparing, initiating, and pursuing a lawsuit. But the *lit de justice*, for all its trappings, could not disguise the degree of compulsion that the government was prepared to exert on behalf of the ordinance.[13] The king prepared for the *lit de justice* by naming a commission of judges and members of the Council of Justice to examine the newly drafted ordinance title by title, and this commission had met fifteen times at the home of Chancellor Séguier, concluding on 17 March 1667. But these sessions were consultative in appearance only. First President Lamoignon argued for several amendments; but Pussort, as spokesman for the Council, overrode him on every important point. Significantly, the king had excluded title I from the agenda, even before the commission began to meet.[14]

The *lit de justice* for the ordinance of civil procedure took place on 20 April 1667, and the king forbade the Parlement to deliberate upon it, insisting upon the corporate silence that he had imposed after the *lit de justice* of 1665. When four magistrates called for deliberations anyway, the king exiled them all to distant places and later relieved three of their offices. He thus re-emphasized the essential point of article iv, that the magistrates could not deliberate on legislation registered by authority, nor modify it or delay its enforcement. Louis XIV even forbade Lamoignon and the Parlement from seeking the return of the exiles. Twenty years later, when he himself was first president, Achille III de Harlay wrote that this session had introduced a new age of royal power.[15]

In the provinces the king registered the ordinance not only by compulsion but also by surprise, the latter aspect contrasting with the treatment of the Parlement of Paris. It is not known why the government behaved differently towards the provincial parlements, but Colbert may have thought that they needed a lesson in respect for new laws. Besides, the king was about to depart for Flanders and the War of Devolution, and the government may have wished to take a strong stand at a critical moment. But all we know for sure is that the king decided in early July to employ coercion in the provincial parlements and to begin with the Parlement of Dijon.[16]

On 8 August 1667, the comte d'Amanzé, the king's lieutenant general in Burgundy, entered the Parlement with the intendant Claude Bouchu at his side. When the magistrates had assembled in a hastily convened plenary session, d'Amanzé read aloud from a *lettre de cachet* (orders issued under the royal seal) instructing the Parlement to register the ordinance purely and simply, i.e. immediately and without restrictions or modifications, commands that Bouchu repeated. After a mild response from First President Brûlart, who on short notice had worked into the night to prepare some emollient remarks, a clerk read aloud from the preamble to the ordinance and from its first few articles. Although that left the main body of the ordinance unread, the *procureur général* recommended its registration, the first president called upon dependable magistrates for concurring opinions, and the Parlement voted the 'pure and simple' registration decree required of it. The whole business took only a few minutes, despite the importance and scope of the new law.[17]

The experience of the Parlement of Dijon prefigured what would happen in every provincial tribunal. On 26 August the duc de Montausier, the governor of Normandy, and Barrin de La Galissonière, the intendant, entered the Parlement of Rouen, carrying the ordinance and similar orders for its immediate, unqualified registration. President Bigot, the presiding judge, recommended obeying the monarch's explicit orders; and the Parlement registered the ordinance at that very session, without having heard a word of it.[18] The Parlement of Bordeaux received identical treatment on 7 September and also voted forthwith to register and publish the ordinance.[19]

The other tribunals fell rapidly into line. The ordinance was registered in the same way at Toulouse (12 September), Aix (3 October), Metz (27 October), Rennes (16 November) and Grenoble (21 November). Governors or lieutenant governors, always accompanied by intendants, entered the tribunals, read aloud from the king's orders and perhaps a few lines from the ordinance, and then commanded the magistrates to register it at once and without any changes. These parlements also complied without resistance.[20]

The provincial parlements nevertheless resented the way in which the government had abused constitutionalist maxims and denied them the right to study the ordinance and to take a free vote on whether to register it. Even the first presidents, royal clients all, had to bow to pressure from their colleagues and complain to Colbert, at least for the record. On behalf of the Parlement of Bordeaux, First President Pontac objected that the government had disregarded all the precedents by which the magistrates had previously enjoyed ample time to study major legislation. He strongly protested the order to register such an important ordinance, 'without reading it'. First President Brûlart at Dijon also complained, albeit tardily, that the forced registration of an ordinance violated all precedents and the important principle of *liberté des suffrages*.[21] Pontac and

Brûlart no doubt spoke for almost all the judges in all the other parlements, wedded as they were to constitutionalist thought, practice and precedent, all of which the Council of Justice had chosen to disregard.

In what was likely the first coordinated round of forced registrations in Paris and throughout the provinces, Louis XIV succeeded everywhere. He made these involuntary registrations stick, protests notwithstanding, and effectively exercised the authority he had assumed in article iv, not for the last time either. Moreover, the government enforced the ordinance rigorously, wherever it detected any failure of the parlements to apply it correctly.[22]

Registration issues subsided until May 1669, when the Parlement of Paris abruptly issued an oral remonstrance against an edict that, among other things, restricted the privilege by which parlementary office conferred heredi-tary nobility. No record of this remonstrance survives, but we do know that First President Lamoignon spoke so forcefully in presenting it that he irritated the king as much as he pleased his colleagues.[23]

In the annals of parlementary resistance to new laws, this episode seems scarcely worthy of mention; but it revealed a restlessness in the Parlement which may have prompted the king to order a second round of involuntary reg-istrations in all the tribunals. Perhaps other causes assumed equal, if not greater importance. Certainly the provincial parlements were still dragging their feet in registering the king's laws, title I or no title I; and the government may have wanted to signal its overall displeasure in an unmistakable way. To stick with the facts, however, all we know for sure is that in the summer of 1669 Louis XIV ordered a new round of compulsory registrations in the parlements, starting with a previously unnoticed *lit de justice* in Paris and continuing in the provinces through the autumn and into the winter.

As dawn broke on 13 August 1669, the judges of the Parlement of Paris donned their red robes and assembled in the Grand-Chambre for a *lit de justice*, announced to them by the Grand Master of Ceremonies the day before. Outside the Palace of Justice, units of the French and Swiss Guards lined the streets leading to the Saint-Honoré gate. Chancellor Séguier, now eighty-one, appeared at the Palace at 8 a.m.; a deputation of senior judges helped him to his place. Louis XIV reached the gate at 9 a.m. and proceeded to the Palace in the company of his soldiers. After hearing Mass in the adjacent Sainte-Chapelle, he entered the Grand-Chambre escorted by the usual deputation of magistrates but also by a company of Swiss Guards and amid the sound of drums, trumpets and fifes, an unusual military panoply.

At the king's command, Séguier rose and spoke haltingly, given his failing memory. He seems to have blandly celebrated the virtues of the legislation about to be unveiled, without giving any particular reason why the king had resorted to a *lit de justice* to register it. Responding to the chancellor, Lamoignon disclosed that he knew nothing about the new laws, an implicit condemnation of the *lit de justice*, earning him the approval of his fellow magistrates. Then

Louis Berryer, a secretary of the royal council and one of Colbert's henchmen, handed the chief clerk the new legislation for him to read aloud in the ceremony. As he stood before the tribunal, the clerk might almost have sagged beneath the weight of the thick folder that Berryer thrust upon him.

The king registered some twenty-five legislative acts at this *lit de justice* – an extraordinary number and perhaps more than in any *lit de justice* ever held. Given this quantity of legislation, itself an affront to the traditions of the Parlement, the clerk could read these laws only in part, a few lines from the beginning and the end of each item, making it impossible to assess their contents. When the clerk had finished, Séguier went through the motions of consultation, after which he proclaimed these laws registered in the name of the king. When the ceremony ended, Louis XIV left the Grand-Chambre abruptly and without speaking, barely nodding to those magistrates along the aisle down which he marched with his soldiers. Where the *lit de justice* of 1667 had shown respect for the dignity of the Parlement, this one seemed designed to humiliate it.[24]

The least welcome of these laws addressed judicial issues but were also fiscal in nature. Edicts creating a *contrôle des exploits* and a *consignation des amendes* amplified certain titles of the civil procedure ordinance and imposed taxes upon litigants at various points in procedure. A related edict required litigants to pay a tax when clerks recorded expenses for *voyages et séjours*, inspections and assessments of contested property. All these edicts increased the expenses of litigation and thus threatened to reduce the quantity of lawsuits, making it likely that the judicial fees collected by judges would diminish. The provincial parlements would interfere with such laws in the 1670s, hoping to diminish their effect; the Parlement of Paris would likely have balked at registering them in 1669, had it been free to do so. One can understand why the king chose to register them by constraint.[25]

But Berryer also handed the clerk almost twenty additional laws, and it is not at all clear why the *lit de justice* included them, as they seem unlikely to have provoked much controversy. For example, one of these edicts permitted nobles to invest in overseas commerce, provided that they did not practise retail trade – part of Colbert's plan to increase the investment capital available to merchant entrepreneurs. Another forbade the king's subjects to leave the kingdom without permission, perhaps part of an effort to block Protestant emigration. Various edicts interpreted technical aspects of the ordinance. The new water and forest ordinance, another of Colbert's reforms, was perhaps among the *lit de justice* legislation.

But there seems to be no reason why any of these laws would have caused enough opposition to make it worthwhile to register them under duress; and some would not have provoked any controversy at all. The water and forest ordinance, which might have set off a jurisdictional conflict with the royal council, never aroused any such criticism. Another act, a sharply worded council decree, denounced the Parlement for having tried to assert jurisdiction over a commercial court at Lyons, an 'inexcusable' violation of a regulation of 23 December 1668; but this issue does not seem quite weighty enough for a *lit de justice* either. Unlike his predecessors and without any apparent precedents, Louis XIV coerced the parlements into registering laws that were more ordinary than extraordinary – routine legislation some of which the parlements would surely have registered on their own. Why did the king and Colbert do this?[26]

It seems most likely that they chose to make a pre-emptive strike and to elim-inate with this warning any future tendencies of the Parlement to resist legis-lation in any way. The government probably put all those laws into this *lit de justice* as a forceful means of reminding everyone that it could invoke royal authority any time it wanted. On this reading of things, the king wanted to tell the Parlement of Paris and, almost immediately, the provincial parlements to register all his legislation more quickly in the future. Since the forced registra-tions in the provincial parlements included only about nine of the twenty-five *lit de justice* laws, it is also likely that the king, without taking it easy on the pro-vincials, had given the Parlement of Paris something of an extra warning, if not an outright rebuke.

A replay of the *lit de justice* took place in the provinces almost immediately. Once again, as in 1667, the king sent provincial governors or lieutenant governors, accompanied by intendants, to stage compulsory registrations of the core edicts of the *lit de justice* in all the provincial parlements. These regis-trations occurred in Rouen on 29 November 1669, in Dijon on 9 December, in Rennes on 17 December, in Metz on 23 December and in Aix and Toulouse on 8 January and 5 February 1670, and no doubt also in Bordeaux, Grenoble and Pau, where, however, records fail us. In every tribunal, the actors read from much the same script, extolling the glory of the king and the wisdom of the new laws. But they also ordered the parlements to register all the legislation without delay, modification or discussion lest they incur the charge of damaging the authority of the king. After the discourses, the *procureurs généraux* read a few lines from the beginning and the end of each legislative item, as the clerk had done in Paris; and the tribunals had to register and publish the whole corpus in those very sessions.[27]

The odd exception aside, all the provincial tribunals registered the same laws. In addition to the water and forest ordinance, the legislation sent to the provinces included the *contrôle des exploits* and the *consignation des amendes*, the prohibition against foreign travel without permission, revisions to the ordi-nance of civil procedure, and so on – all of it familiar from the ceremony in Paris, a mixture of fiscal and non-fiscal legislation. As they had done when pre-sented with the ordinance of civil procedure, the parlements bowed to this assertion of royal authority and registered the new laws then and there.

As a result of the *lit de justice* of 1665 and the compulsory registrations of 1667 and 1669, it became clear that the king and his ministers, in accordance with article iv of title I of the ordinance, had made registration under duress effective in all the tribunals. Anne of Austria, and to a lesser degree Louis XIII, risked provoking the resentment of the parlements and a dispute if not a crisis when they held *lits de justice* and forced registrations; also they failed to achieve their goals.[28] Louis XIV overcame these problems in the first decade of his reign, applying force without hesitation and to good effect. He made compulsory registrations work.

But the king and his council could not stage involuntary registrations every time they wanted to introduce some law of which the magistrates might disapprove. The king also needed to control ordinary registration procedure and to deal with the parlementary tactics of modification and delay. The Council of Justice had addressed this second issue, in articles v and vi of title I. Paradoxically, however, article v, the title's most familiar article, made only a weak attempt to counter the obstructionist tactics which the parlements had used so effectively and for so long. Article vi was no better.

Article v required the Parlement of Paris to issue any remonstrance within one week after it received a law and gave the provincial parlements six weeks in which to submit their remonstrances. Once these intervals had expired, the legislation, wherever it stood procedurally in the parlements, was to be regarded as registered and published. The parlements were to send such a law to subordinate courts in their jurisdictions, as though they had registered it freely. Article vi complemented article v by ordering the parlements to register the laws as soon as they received them, suspending all judicial business at that point.

Unlike article iv on involuntary registrations, articles v and vi did not represent anything particularly new. They reworked provisions in the ordinance of Moulins (1566), the Code Michaud (1629) and Louis XIII's edict of 1641 on registration procedure, all of which insisted upon timely remonstrances and prompt registration of the laws once the kings had answered remonstrances. While the government had not previously declared that it would deem laws registered once the deadlines for remonstrances had passed, no one knew if this would, in the absence of actual registration, make the laws enforceable. In any event, Louis XIV never invoked that clause of the article. As another weakness, article v virtually ignored, when it should have explicitly banned, the modification of laws by the parlements, an omission that possibly resulted from simple oversight. At one point in the Council of Justice sessions, Chancellor Séguier had emphatically maintained that no parlement had any right to modify the laws, and everyone agreed with him; but the ordinance had little to say on the subject. On balance, articles v and vi merely reaffirmed existing maxims that the parlements had long ignored, making it unlikely that they would change their ways now.[29] To measure the full effect of these weaknesses and omissions, we must next concentrate upon the provincial parlements.

Already in 1661, the king had awarded Colbert the power to select the first presidents of the provincial parlements; and the minister responded by organizing all the first presidents, those currently in office and those whom he would name to vacancies, into a royal client group. After his first new appointment, that of François d'Argouges, a protégé of Anne of Austria, for the Parlement of Rennes, Colbert preferred naming magistrates who belonged in some way to his extended family. For example, he arranged for the intendant Claude Pellot to marry his cousin, Madeleine Colbert, and in 1670 selected him as the first president at Rouen.[30] Other newly appointed provincial first presidents also enjoyed some family connection with Colbert. But clientage and family ties notwithstanding, Colbert and the first presidents had a hard time gaining control of the provincial parlements because of resistance from well-organized, uncooperative judges.

In 1663–1665, Colbert ordered reports on the loyalties of the most important magistrates in each parlement and learned more about the dimensions of the problem. The intendants and other officials who gathered this political intelligence identified some troublemakers by name, although there were many others.[31] For example, Alexandre Bigot de Monville, a *président à mortier* in the Parlement of Rouen, headed a large opposition group that still existed when Pellot arrived. *Président à mortier* La Chaine took the role of resistance chief at Aix and made problems for First President Oppède. At Rennes, Claude de Marbeuf, a wealthy *président à mortier*, worked relentlessly against d'Argouges, as did Christophe Fouquet de Chalain, a relative of the deposed superintendent. In 1664, Colbert had to issue a written rebuke to a refractory faction in the Parlement of Grenoble. At a heated session of the Parlement of Toulouse in 1670, the *président à mortier* Potier de La Terasse and First President Fieubet exchanged personal insults and rude gestures and almost came to blows. For this mischief, Potier was sent into exile, along with two colleagues who supported him; but in 1671 all three returned unsubdued to Toulouse and declared openly that they remained the enemies of Fieubet. Oppède spoke for many first presidents when he complained that in Aix those judges who took the strongest stand against the king's interests earned the most respect from their peers.[32]

With the exception of First President Brûlart at Dijon, no first president in the 1660s exercised much substantive control over his parlement. Even so, the first presidents rendered Colbert a valuable service by providing him with a constant flow of personal and political information about their tribunals. Although it took more than a decade for him to learn all that he needed to know, Colbert eventually understood more about the provincial judges and their motives than anyone else in the government, and probably more than any minister before him.

All during the 1660s, the provincial parlements exercised their powers of registration as if they still lived in a pre-Louis XIV past. Just as in the sixteenth and early seventeenth centuries, they felt free to modify any new law that they thought conflicted with local interests and precedents. Any law, moreover, controversial or not, could easily take more than a year to be registered, and delays of two to three years were also common. As always, the excuse of a remonstrance, prepared with suspicious sloth, automatically halted the registration process. The parlements also drew political benefits from defacto alliances with provincial estates in Languedoc, Brittany, Burgundy and Provence (where an Assembly of Communities took the place of an estate). Depending on the province, provincial estates met at intervals of one to three years and negotiated with a royal commission over proposed taxes in the province and the size of a 'free gift' of money to the king. The parlements frequently sent disputed laws to their estates, which placed them on the bargaining agenda, even if the next estates session would not occur for a year or more. When pressed by Colbert, first presidents, like Fieubet at Toulouse in 1669, often admitted that they had no power to get their colleagues to register laws promptly and without change.[33] This remained true even after the involuntary registration of the civil procedure ordinance.

In the autumn of 1667, the Parlement of Aix dealt almost cavalierly with an October edict for the creation of *auditeurs des comptes* and *experts jurés*, sworn auditors and appraisers in financial disputes and property settlements. Virtually the same as an edict of 1639 that had aroused resentment in the whole province, this edict would have converted local officials currently appointed by town consuls and the Parlement into holders of venal office, requiring them to purchase the new offices at prices set by the government and a group of revenue farmers.[34] The Parlement took no notice of the edict, the secret registers do not record its existence, and the magistrates never even deliberated on it. In June 1668, the royal council sent the Parlement a *lettre de jussion* to register the new law; but the tribunal claimed that it could not muster a quorum of magistrates in the summer. When a sufficient number of judges at last assembled on 26 November, they tabled the edict on the grounds that deputies to the Assembly of Communities were then trying to get it revoked.[35]

This was no coincidence. A few months earlier, the Parlement had itself sent the edict to the *procureurs* (representatives) of the Assembly for scrutiny; and, unsurprisingly, the *procureurs* asked the Parlement not to register it until the Assembly could examine it. When it convened in the autumn of 1668, the Assembly asked the government to withdraw the edict, confident that the Parlement would take no further action. First President Oppède, a royal commissioner to the Assembly, advised Colbert that he expected little progress with the *auditeurs* and *procureurs* issue now that the two institutions had united against it.[36]

This open disregard for the recent ordinance at last provoked the royal council into the strongest reaction seen against a parlement since 1661. In a session attended by both the king and Colbert, the council decided to punish three magistrates of the Parlement and to threaten the entire tribunal with sanctions if all the judges did not mend their ways. In a robust decree of 13

February 1669, the council suspended the *rapporteur* (briefing judge) of the edict from office and exiled him and two senior magistrates, denouncing them for violating article v of title I and the *lettres de jussion* of 1668. Then the decree condemned the entire Parlement for its 'bad intentions' and its 'open disobedience' of the king. Although the decree said that all the judges deserved a punishment, the king 'this time' would deal with these three judges only. Oppède, in invoking what he called the king's 'justified resentment', no doubt drew attention to this implied threat. A suddenly cowed tribunal finally registered the *auditeurs* and *experts* edict; and the disgraced magistrates departed Aix just as the decree ordered. So in the end the government got its way with the Parlement; but it had taken a year and a half to do so, and the tribunal had demonstrated that it did not take title I seriously.[37]

The Parlement of Toulouse also ignored the title, as became clear in a similar controversy. In December 1667, only weeks after the coerced registration of the ordinance of civil procedure, the Parlement received a *lettre de jussion* rejecting its recent remonstrance against an edict of September 1666 that would have made venal office-holders of *procureurs* (solicitors) who practised in the Parlement. The edict would have cost the *procureurs* 500 livres apiece and reduced their numbers by 33, from 153 to 120. Although the *jussion* ordered the Parlement to register the edict immediately, the magistrates decided to table it upon the request of Boyer, the *syndic général* (executive administrator) of the Estates of Languedoc. This would give the Estates time to seek concessions from the government, at its next session. When it learned what the Parlement had done, the council on 13 March 1668, condemned its arrangement with the Estates as an 'extraordinary procedure' intended only to cause delay. A decree of that date quashed the deliberations of the Parlement and the intervention of Boyer and ordered the immediate, 'pure and simple' registration of the edict and the *lettre de jussion*.

Not so easily subdued, the Parlement took another year to register the edict, which it finally did in July 1669, almost three years after the king had issued it; but its delaying tactics yielded strategic gains. The Estates remonstrated against the edict when it voted its 'free gift', and the government reduced the 'tax' on the *procureurs* from five hundred to three hundred livres. This concession rewarded the tribunal's stalling tactics and its disregard of title I. The government had made so little impression upon the magistrates that the *président à mortier* Potier de La Terasse and the councillor Frezals, obstructionists of long standing, mounted an effort to persuade the *procureurs* to refuse to buy offices even at reduced prices, attempting to subvert the edict. It took more than a year for First President Fieubet to enforce the *procureurs* law in a parlement that, as of 1670, had not accepted that it should register new laws with which it disagreed.[38]

When, in August 1670, the king issued his new ordinance of criminal procedure, Colbert sent it to the parlements to be registered in the ordinary way, by means of uncoerced voting. This turned out to be a mistake. In the Parlement of Paris, First President Lamoignon tried to get his judges to register the ordinance purely and simply but succeeded only in part. On 23 August, the Parlement voted to register the new law but not to publish it, an attempt to deprive it of any real effect. In a strong letter written the next day, the king demanded that the ordinance be read aloud in open court in the customary manner; and the judges finally complied. Even so, this episode showed that the Parlement of Paris, although less assertive than the provincials, had not completely accepted the discipline of registering the laws quickly and without change. In 1671, it amended a declaration for a *ustensile* tax, imposed on the faubourg Saint-Germain for a musketeers barracks there, and got a sharp rebuke from the council on the grounds that it was undermining the authority of the king.[39]

The provincial tribunals treated the new criminal procedure ordinance with even less regard than the Parlement of Paris. The Parlement of Rouen scrutinized it in four lengthy sessions and issued twenty-nine decrees of modification to twelve of its twenty-eight titles. In its registration decree, the Parlement noted that it made these changes pending a remonstrance to the king. But it transmitted the amended ordinance to subordinate courts and did not even begin work on the remonstrance. When the government learned of this lapse, probably informed by Pellot, the new first president, it naturally found the tribunal in violation of the ordinance of 1667. The Parlement was commanded to register the new ordinance in its original form and to send it out again to all those lower courts. The magistrates obeyed their orders on this occasion, but they had already made clear that despite the requirements of title I they expected to treat royal legislation with the freedom that they had exercised in the past.

After receiving the criminal procedure ordinance in January 1671, the Parlement of Aix confided it to a select commission, which did not report until 3 June, a delay of almost five months. Their recommendations, which do not survive, must have found fault, for the Parlement decided to withhold registration and to write its own regulation for criminal prosecutions. The government must have discovered this evasion at some point, but we can only guess when this occurred. The Parlement of Rennes, which suspended the ordinance pending a remonstrance (never written), escaped detection until November 1675. It is probable that the other provincial parlements evaded the new ordinance in similar ways.[40]

As the first decade of his personal rule ended, Louis XIV had shown that he could make the parlements register his laws when he invoked his personal authority, a significant gain for absolute government and one that had eluded all his predecessors. To be sure, he enjoyed a position to which those predecessors could only aspire, as a monarch ruling a united kingdom in peacetime,

master of his council and his nobility. But these favourable circumstances should not obscure the fact that the young king made the important political decision to assert his authority over the tribunals on a critical issue of legislative sovereignty, and succeeded.

At the same time, the parlements still clung to their traditional tactics of modification, delay and general obstruction when they registered laws in the absence of duress, despite title I of the civil procedure ordinance of 1667. One can only speculate as to why, at the close of the decade, the king and his council left their job in the parlements half done, but some speculation does seem to be in order. Since Colbert's initial financial reforms led him to reduce taxes overall, this meant that the most contentious fiscal issues of the recent past had largely disappeared, making it possible to tolerate, if just barely, lingering resistance. In addition, the king's ministers probably thought that in getting their way on the issue of compulsory registration they had dealt the tribunals a decisive blow at a strategic point and that total victory on all the issues of registration procedure would inevitably follow, without any additional effort on their part. Any such belief underrated the stamina and resourcefulness of the magistrates, who had long experience in dealing craftily with royal efforts to control registration procedure.

Another guess is that for political reasons Colbert deliberately held back from applying heavy pressure against the parlements. He was never the parlements' worst enemy and had recommended a policy of moderation towards them when the Council of Justice began to meet, in 1665. He would have had some reason to revive this policy after the publication of the ordinance. With his clientele of first presidents, Colbert might have hoped to get the magistrates as a group on his side, adding to his strength in the royal council and enhancing his chances for advancement, up to and including the position of chancellor, for which he would one day candidate, if in vain. But all this is largely guesswork. All that we can say for sure is that as late as 1671, and despite his breakthrough on the issue of forced registrations, Louis XIV would have to revisit registration issues before he could be sure that the parlements would always register his laws, on time, without change.

Notes

1 Hamscher, *Parlement*, pp. 140–146, has superseded Glasson, *Parlement de Paris*, II, 412–414, previously the standard source for this topic. Hassen El Annabi, *Le Parlement de Paris sous le règne personnel de Louis XIV. L'Institution, le Pouvoir et la Société* (Tunis, 1989), does not address this issue directly. The nineteenth-century studies of provincial parlements by local scholars occasionally provide good information about the disappearance of legislative resistance under Louis XIV. See, for example, Pierre-Amable Floquet, *Histoire du Parlement de Normandie* (7 vols; Rouen, 1840–1842), V, 559–595.

2 For the composition of the royal council, see Hamscher, *Conseil Privé*, pp. 5–11, esp.

nn. 1, 6–7, 10–11, with a valuable bibliographical guide, along with Michel Antoine, *Le fonds du Conseil d'état du Roi aux Archives Nationales* (Paris, 1955); *idem.*, 'Colbert et la révolution de 1661', in *Un nouveau Colbert*, dir. Roland Mousnier (Paris, 1985), pp. 99–109; Georges Pagès, *La monarchie d'ancien régime en France (de Henri IV à Louis XIV)* (Paris, 1932; reprint, Paris, 1952), pp. 140–148.

3 Colbert, *Lettres*, VI, 15–17; Jean-Louis Bourgeon, *Les Colbert avant Colbert. Destin d'une famille marchande* (Paris, 1973), pp. 203–212.

4 BN, *Clairambault*, 613, ff. 3–16, 315–351, 395–456 (for representative memoranda); Hamscher, *Parlement*, pp. 157–164; René Pillorget, 'Henri Pussort, Oncle de Colbert (1615–1697)', in *Le Conseil du Roi de Louis XII à la Révolution*, ed. Roland Mousnier (Paris, 1970), 255–274.

5 Philippe Bornier, *Conférences des nouvelles ordonnances de Louis XIV* (2 vols; Paris, 1694), I, 5, who could cite no precedent for article iv.

6 Procès-verbal des conférences tenues devant Louis XIV pour la Réformation de la Justice', in Colbert, *Lettres*, VI, 380.

7 *Ibid.*, pp. 379–382, and ff.

8 Bornier, *Conférences*, I, 5–8; 'Procès-verbal', pp. 385, 388; Francis Monnier, *Guillaume de Lamoignon et Colbert. Essai sur la législation française au XVIIe siècle* (Paris, 1862), pp. 56–60; Nannerl O. Keohane, *Philosophy and the State in France. The Renaissance to the Enlightenment* (Princeton, NJ, 1980), p. 313; Bercé, *Naissance dramatique de l'absolutisme*, p. 189.

9 Marcel Rousselet, *Histoire de la magistrature française des origines à nos jours* (Paris, 1957), I, 55–57; Filhol, *Le premier président Christofle de Thou*. Brûlart, first president, Dijon, to Jobelot, first president, Besançon, April 1679, in Nicolas Brûlart de La Borde, *Choix de lettres inédites*, ed. Lacuisine (2 vols; Dijon, 1859), II, 207–209, described the functions, powers, and honorific rights of the office; Ormesson, *Journal*, II, 561, 565, 570, 601, illustrates the critical scrutiny to which parlements subjected these magistrates.

10 Kettering, *Patrons, Brokers, and Clients*, pp. 3–5, 13–20, 142, 147, 157–161, 161–166, 212, and idem, 'Patronage in Early Modern France', *French Historical Studies* 17 (Autumn, 1992), 839–862; Roland Mousnier, *Society and the State*, trans. Brian Pearce, vol. 1 of *The Institutions of France under the Absolute Monarchy, 1598–1789* (Chicago and London, 1979), pp. 99–107; vol. 2, *The Organs of State and Society*, trans. Arthur Goldhammer, pp. 148–151.

11 BN, *Dossiers bleus*, 379 (Lamoignon); Hamscher, *Parlement*, pp. 105, 127–128, 133–134; François Dornic, *Une ascension sociale au XVIIe siècle. Louis Berryer, agent de Mazarin et de Colbert* (Caen, 1968), p. 127 (Lamoignon used Berryer as an intermediary with the king); E. Pilastre, *Achille III de Harlay. Premier Président du Parlement de Paris sous le règne de Louis XIV* (Paris, n.d.); Jules Lair, *Nicolas Fouquet, procureur général, surintendant des finances, ministre d'état de Louis XIV* (2 vols; Paris, 1890), II, 163–165.

12 Glasson, *Parlement*, I, 410–412; Ormesson, *Journal*, II, 431–437; Louis XIV, *Mémoires*, p. 137. The edict is in BN, *Actes R.*, F. 23,612 (842): edict of December 1665. On the issue of venal office reform, see below, ch. 3.

13 Ernest-Désiré Glasson, *Histoire du droit et des institutions de la France* (8 vols; Paris, 1887–1903), VIII, 176–188; Arthur Engelmann *et al.*, *A History of Continental Civil Procedure*, trans. Robert W. Millar (Boston, 1927), pp. 714–739.

14 *Procez-verbal des conférences tenues par ordre du roi, entre Messieurs les Commissaires du Conseil, et Messieurs les Députés du Parlement de Paris pour l'examen des Articles de l'ordonnance civile du mois d'Avril, 1667 et de l'ordonnance criminelle du mois d'Aout, 1670,* 2d edn (Louvain, 1700), p. 509; Pillorget, 'Pussort', p. 263; Monnier, *Lamoignon et Colbert,* pp. 68–96; Hamscher, *Parlement,* pp. 143–144, 175–178. At the last session of the joint commission, Lamoignon was able to address some articles in title I, but not those that dealt with the registration of the laws.

15 AN, X1A (Conseil Secret), 8395: 20 April 1667, ff. 89r–93v; AN, AD+ 391 (for the other edicts registered in the ceremony); and Hamscher, *Parlement,* p. 144. See Harlay's remark in his 'Établissement du Parlement', f. 24v.

16 The *lettres de cachet* which ordered the forced registrations in the provinces were written between 10 and 20 July 1667. The prince de Condé notified Brûlart, first president, Dijon, by letter of 30 July 1667: BM, Dijon, MS 541, f. 276r. See also Vincent Hotman, *intendant des finances,* to Brûlart, 14 August 1667, *ibid.,* ff. 251v–252r. Paul Sonnino, *Louis XIV and the Origins of the Dutch War* (Cambridge, 1988), pp. 9–27, describes the cautious state of mind in the government during the War of Devolution.

17 BM, Dijon, MS 768 (Registres du Parlement), 8–9 August 1667, ff. 76–81; Brûlart, first president, to Hotman, 9 August 1667, and Brûlart to Colbert, 9 August 1667, MS 541, ff. 278r–279v. See also Brûlart, *Choix de lettres inédites,* II, 69–72; and Alexandre-Gérard Thomas, *Une province sous Louis XIV. Situation politique et administrative de la Bourgogne de 1661 à 1715* (Paris, 1844), pp. 382–383.

18 BM, Rouen, MS Y 2l4/24 (Registres secrets), 26 August 1667, ff. 273–275; Floquet, *Parlement de Normandie,* V, 562–563.

19 AM, Bordeaux, MS 795 (Registre secret), 7 September 1667, ff. 601–607; C.B.F. Boscheron des Portes, *Histoire du Parlement de Bordeaux* (2 vols; Bordeaux, 1877), II, 196–198. Two magistrates who denounced the forced registration were exiled to La Rochelle.

20 AD, H-G, B (Enregistrement des Actes, Parlement of Toulouse) 1919: 12 September 1667, ff. 1rv–58rv, which includes the ordinance itself and orders, dated 20 July 1667, to hold the forced registration, issued to the lieutenant general and the intendant; BM, Aix, MS 975 (Délibérations du Parlement), 3 October 1667, ff. 394r–395r; Oppède, first president, Aix, to Tubeuf, unidentified, 20 September 1667, BN, *Mél. Colbert,* MS 145, f. 356v (Oppède also referred to the forced registration at Toulouse); AD, Moselle, B (Registres secrets, Metz) 264: 27 October 1667, ff. 28rv–30rv; AD, I-V (Rennes), IBb 229 (Registres secrets), 16 November 1667, f. 36r–v (staged with the assistance of an unidentified councillor of state, since Brittany had as yet no permanent intendant). There are no secret registers for the Parlement of Grenoble, but the forced registration is documented in AD, Isère, B 2355** (Enregistrement, 1665–1667), 21 November 1667, ff. 343r–409v. Unfortunately, the secret registers for the Parlement of Pau do not exist for 1667: AD, P-A, B 4538 (1637–1683), but we can assume that Pau was no exception to the forced registrations of 1667.

21 AM, Bordeaux, MS 795 (Registre secret), 7 September 1667, ff. 601–607; Brûlart, Dijon, to Colbert, and to Hotman, 9 August 1667, BM, Dijon, MS 541, ff. 278r–279v.

22 Hamscher, *Parlement,* pp. 180–185; Glasson, *Histoire du droit,* VIII, 190; AN, E

1742–1744 and 1753 contain numerous decrees of council, 1668–1670, enforcing the ordinance in almost all the provincial parlements.

23 Ormesson, *Journal*, II, 565–566; BN, *Actes R.*, F. 23,613 (no. 21; edict, April 1669). It rescinded the privilege granted in 1644, by which parlementary office bestowed hereditary or personal nobility if a judge occupied his office for twenty years or died in service. On parlementary nobility, see Franklin L. Ford, *Robe and Sword. The Regrouping of the French Aristocracy after Louis XIV*, 2nd edn (Cambridge, Mass., 1962), pp. 63–65.

24 Ormesson, *Journal*, II, 569–570 (an eye-witness account); 'Lit de Justice tenu au Parlement par Louis XIV', BN, *N.a.f.*, 9,750, ff. 173rv–174rv; and AN, X1B (Parlement de Paris. Civil. Minutes) 8868. The Parlement's secret register does not record this *lit de justice*, which explains why Glasson, *Parlement*, I, 398–399, and Hamscher, *Parlement*, p. 242, overlooked it. Hanley, *Lit de Justice*, pp. 325–326 and n. 43, speculated that the *lit de justice* had 'probably' been held. The *lit de justice* legislation is in AN, X1A (Parlement. Lettres Patentes, Ordonnances.) 8667: ff. 204r–362r; AN, AD+ 406; and Isambert, *Recueil général*, XVIII, 217–366.

25 AN, AD+ 406; AN, X1A 8667, ff. 240r–243r, 250r–253v; Isambert, *Recueil général*, XVIII, 333–339.

26 AN, X1A, 8667: ff. 253v–292v, 298v–301r.

27 BM, Rouen, MS Y 214/25 (Registres secrets), 29 November 1669, ff. 172–175, and AD, S-M, F. Parlement, 'Table chronologique des édits, ordonnances', etc., lists the laws of the forced registration of 29 November 1669; BM, Dijon, MS 768 (Registres du Parlement), 9 December 1669, ff. 156–160, and Brûlart to Châteauneuf, secretary of state, 11 December 1669, MS 541, ff. 353v–354v; AD, C-O (Dijon), B 12,108 (Enregistrement, 1663–1679), ff. iv–xxxvi; AD, I-V (Rennes), IBb 233 (Registres secrets), ff. 67v–69v (with the participation of Chamillart, intendant, Caen); AD, Moselle, B 268 (Registres secrets, Metz): 23 December 1669, ff. 51r–54rv; BM, Aix, MS 976 (Délibérations du Parlement), ff. 1rv–2v, and AD, Aix, B 3363 (Lettres royaux), ff. 507–539, 651rv–728rv; AD, H-G (Toulouse), B 1919 (Enregistrement des actes, 1667–1672): 5 February 1670, ff. 156rv–170rv; AM, Bordeaux, MS 795 (Registre secret), f. 884, indicates that a forced registration is impending. The secret register of Pau contains no entries for this portion of 1669, and there are no secret registers for the Parlement of Grenoble. However, it seems safe to assume that the government carried out forced registrations in these tribunals also.

28 For the risk the government incurred in holding a *lit de justice*, see above, Introduction, n. 15.

29 Bornier, *Conférences des nouvelles ordonnances*, I, 5–6; 'Procès-verbal', pp. 384–385.

30 BN, *Dossiers Bleus*, 150 (Le Camus) and 203 (Colbert); Henri de Frondeville, *Les présidents au Parlement de Normandie (1499–1790). Recueil généalogique* (Rouen and Paris, 1953), pp. 82–83.

31 Georges Depping, ed., *Correspondance administrative sous le règne de Louis XIV* (4 vols; Paris, 1850–1855), II, 33–133.

32 Robert Mandrou, *Magistrats et sorciers en France au XVIIe siècle, une analyse de psychologie historique* (Paris, 1968), pp. 452–458 (Bigot de Monville's rivalry with Pellot); Alexandre Bigot de Monville, *Mémoires du président Bigot de Monville. Le Parlement de Rouen, 1640–1643*, ed. Madeleine Foisil (Paris, 1976), p. 33; Oppède,

first president, to Colbert, 15 October 1661, 26 June 1666, BN, *Mél. Colbert*, 103, f. 641r; 138bis, f. 763rv (for Oppède's animosity towards the La Chaine family, see Kettering, *Patrons, Brokers, and Clients*, p. 56); d'Argouges, first president, Rennes, to Colbert, 10 February, 22 June, 23 July and 6 August 1664, and 29 May 1666, in *Mél. Colbert*, 119; 121bis, ff. 817r, 242r; 122, f. 757r; 123, f. 149r; and 137bis, ff. 931v–932r; Parlement of Dauphiné to Colbert, 15 October 1664, *ibid.*, 125, ff. 302rv–303r; Marbeuf, *président à mortier*, Rennes, to Colbert, 5 August 1665, *ibid.*, 131, ff. 169r–170r; Foucault, intendant, Caen, to Colbert, 21 May 1666, *ibid.*, 137, f. 859r.

For the Toulouse episode, see AAE, *Petits Fonds*, 1639 (Languedoc, 1658–1699): extracts of *registres* of Parlement of Toulouse, ff. 243rv–244rv; Fieubet, first president, to Colbert, 4 July 1670; 8 April, 6 May and 17 June 1671; Bezons, intendant, to Colbert, 12 May 1671, and 'Rélation de ce qui s'est passé dans Toulouse, au retour de Messieurs de Ciron, de la Terrasse & de Frezals', BN, *Clairambault*, 759.

33 Fieubet, first president, Toulouse, to Colbert, 12 June 1669, BN, *Mél. Colbert*, 153, f. 369v. Provincial estates and parlements are supposed to have feuded more than they cooperated; but numerous examples of such cooperation will appear in this study.

34 For hostile reactions to the earlier edict, see Kossmann, *Fronde*, pp. 119–120; Kettering, *Parlement of Aix*, pp. 62, 88, 203.

35 Aix, BM, MS 946: François Thomassin *et al.*, 'Histoire du Parlement de Provence...', II, 240–241. The Assembly of Communities, composed of deputies from thirty-six towns, substituted for the Estates of Provence, which had not met since 1639.

36 AD, B-R, C 43 (États de Provence, 1666–1668), ff. 285v, 286r, 309v–310r, 359v, and ff.; Oppède to Colbert, 4 September, 13 October and 10 November 1668 in BN, *Mél. Colbert*, 148bis, f. 521v; 149, ff. 54r, 372v; Thomassin, 'Histoire du Parlement de Provence', II, 240–241.

37 AN, E 1753: decree of 13 February 1669, no. 73; Oppède, first president, to Colbert, 12 March and 28 March 1669, in BN, *Mél. Colbert*, 150bis, ff. 816rv and 949rv. In 1670, the government accepted 70,000 livres from the Assembly and withdrew the edict: BM, Aix, MS 976 (Délibérations du Parlement): 24 April 1670, f. 7v.

38 AN, E 1743: decree of 13 March 1668, no. 51, and E 1749: decree of 10 August 1669, no. 307; Fieubet, first president, to Colbert, 12 June 1669, BN, *Mél. Colbert*, 153, f. 369v; AD, H-G, C 2316 (Estates of Languedoc, 1667–1668), 3 January 1668, ff. 26v–27r. For the continuing resistance to the *procureurs* edict, see the letters of 1670 from Fieubet to Colbert in BN, *Clairambault*, 759, and AN, E 448A: decree of 8 February 1672, no. 27; Beik's thesis that in the 1660s the Parlement largely cooperated with the government should be adjusted to reflect this focal point of resistance: *Absolutism and Society*, pp. 308–309.

39 Glasson, *Histoire du Droit*, VIII, 193–195; AN, X1A 8396 (Conseil Secret, Paris), 23 August 1670; 'Lettre du Roy au Parlement', 24 August 1670, BN, *Fonds fr.*, 6652, ff. 308v–309r; Ormesson, *Journal*, II, 601; AN, E 1765: decree of 28 September 1671 (no. 106).

40 BN, *Fonds fr.*, 22,455 (Parlement de Rouen), pp. 298–312; BM, Rouen, MS Y 214/25 (Registres secrets): 18 November 1670, pp. 275–276, and 7 January 1671, pp. 282–284; AD, S-M, 1B 199 (Registres secrets): 9, 12, 13 and 16 December

1670, ff. 11r–18v, and 7 January 1671, f. 29rv; BM, Aix, MS 976 (Délibérations du Parlement): January to 3 June 1671, ff. 15r–20r; AD, I-V (Rennes), IBb 245 (Registres secrets): 29 November 1675, ff. 48v–52r; BM, Rennes, MS 586, f. 442r (*lettre de cachet*, 14 November 1675, commanding Parlement to register the criminal procedure ordinance).

2

Victory over the parlements,
1671–1675

In 1663, Colbert instructed the intendants to gather political and financial information about the leading institutions and personalities of provincial France. In what he saw as an all-inclusive survey, he identified the political behaviour of the parlements as 'the most important affair' to consider. Colbert particularly wanted to know whether the parlements, having behaved badly in the Fronde, would make trouble in the future. The intendants were to scrutinize individual judges and determine their political loyalties, down to the last detail. Obviously Colbert respected the parlements and worried about how to cope with them.[1]

Within little more than a decade, however, he lost this anxiety and even his interest in the internal politics of the tribunals. When, in 1679, the intendant Herbigny reported on opposition judges in the Parlement of Grenoble, Colbert replied that Herbigny was wasting his time, as no one cared about the magistrates any more. The royal administration could not even remember why the parlements had been important in the past, 'and it is to their advantage that it is this way now'.[2] If Colbert had lost so much interest in the parlements, this could only mean that the king had finally rendered them politically harmless, completing the work begun in the ordinance of civil procedure. This chapter will explain when and how this important change occurred and what it meant in terms of issues, events and circumstances. For the most part our interest in this chapter lies with the provincial parlements, inasmuch as the Parlement of Paris, having been chastised in the *lit de justice* of 1669, remained reasonably calm.

The resistance of the provincial parlements, 1671–1673

Soon after he joined the High Council, Colbert took control of the royal domain and began an effort to increase its revenue stream. The domain consisted of real property in all its forms and revenue-generating rights that the king enjoyed as sovereign, the difference between its corporeal and incorporeal elements.

Colbert believed that both parts of the domain could generate more income: old rights could be collected more effectively and new ones invented.[3] These goals led him to strike alliances with revenue farmers (*traitants* or *fermiers*), financiers who made money by advancing funds to the crown against the yield of taxes and other fiscal devices. Colbert chose to make some revenue farmers into royal clients and to support their interests, provided that they supplied the money he needed. He thus put into place a close fiscal/administrative partnership that would outlive himself and Louis XIV and ultimately make the government dependent upon monied interests, as has recently been argued. At the onset, however, the financiers needed the strong support in the council that only Colbert could give.[4]

Colbert rewarded a hand-picked cadre of revenue farmers with administration of the tax farm, or lease, of the royal domain. On 26 October 1669, thirteen new farmers, acting under the collective, fictitious name of Claude Vialet, signed a six-year lease to collect domain taxes and duties, beginning on 1 January 1670.[5] Colbert gave the Vialet group control over income produced by *greffes*, the processing of legal documents, and *amendes*, fines levied upon defeated or convicted litigants. These sums helped fund the judicial system, but the parlements liked to use anything left over to pay for maintenance of their palaces of justice, along with refreshments and other amenities. They resented both the loss of money and of their financial autonomy. Colbert's new financial allies, the Vialet, were their natural enemies, since the money generated by the judicial system counted as part of the incorporeal domain.[6]

The tribunals also disliked the Vialet partners because they collected the proceeds from such edicts as the *contrôle des exploits* and the *consignation des amendes*, both registered under duress in 1669. An *exploit* was a writ or a summons that commanded someone to do something ordered by a law court or a judge, such as paying a sum to a victorious litigant. The new edict required litigants to register the *exploit* in a tribunal, at a cost of five sous, payable to the Vialet. The parlements believed that even this modest sum would cool the ardour of litigants and reduce the lawsuits from which they drew income.[7] The *amendes* edict tried to reduce the shocking number of appeals that worked their way up the French judicial ladder until they reached the parlements, which benefited from, and naturally encouraged, this proliferation. This edict ordered all parlements to levy a fine of twelve livres upon litigants who lost their cases, a penalty intended to discourage appeals in a general way and previously applied only in the jurisdiction of the Parlement of Paris. As a new feature, the edict required appellants to deposit (*consigner*) the fine of twelve livres with a parlement's receiver of fines before the lawsuit could proceed. The litigant recovered the twelve livres if the case was won, but a defeat meant that the Vialet group kept the money. Of course, the *consignation* displeased the parlements just as much as the *contrôle*.[8]

In March 1671, the king issued two new edicts for the *contrôle des exploits* and the *consignation des amendes*. These edicts led to months of resistance from the provincial parlements, which reflexively adopted their proven tactics of modification and delay. At another time, the government might have compromised with the judges; but the new relationship with the Vialet group meant that Colbert had to get the parlements to register fiscal laws unmodified and quickly. Moreover, the current royal budget showed a deficit for the first time in ten years, and Colbert needed the revenue from the two edicts to help close the gap between income and expenditure.[9]

The edict of 1671 for the *contrôle des exploits* updated the 1669 original by specifying all the types of writs, summonses and subpoenas which came under the *contrôle*, an effort to eliminate recent parlementary evasions. For example, the Parlement of Aix had exempted certain *exploits* from the *contrôle*, placing them beyond the reach of the Vialet group. The council nullified those particular exemptions, and the new edict made them illegal throughout the kingdom. In addition, designated Vialet clerks, working in newly established offices, were to administer and collect the *contrôle*, replacing the regular court clerks who had previously attended to these duties. The new clerks could be trusted to enforce the edict rigorously, with the proceeds going straight to the domain farmers.[10] In like manner, the 1671 edict for the *consignation des amendes* eliminated various judicial devices invented by the parlements to elude it.[11]

The most contentious point concerned the *requête civile* or 'civil request', a petition which a dissatisfied litigant could submit to a parlement, asking it to reconsider a judicial decision, which in principle it had judged definitively, and allow the lawsuit to begin all over again. The civil request had long helped ancient litigation recycle endlessly and expensively through the parlements and their subordinate tribunals, at some cost to the kingdom's economy.[12] In an effort to curtail such abuses, the ordinance of civil procedure required litigants who filed a *requête civile* to deposit 450 livres (the *consignation*) in advance; they would forfeit this substantial sum if the tribunal rejected their petition. In 1670, the Vialet group began to administer the *consignation*, on the promise of receiving 300 livres out of every forfeited deposit. The Parlements of Toulouse and Bordeaux interfered with the *consignation* at once, forcing the Vialet group to appeal to the council that, under Colbert's watchful eye, ruled in its favour. But the other parlements behaved much the same way and escaped detection, putting the *consignaton* at risk. The edict of 1671 closed all loopholes in the *consignation* requirement and specified the authority of the domain farmers in its regard, awarding them new powers.[13]

Although the parlements had good reason to resist the new versions of both the *contrôle* and the *consignation*, the government did not take the precaution of registering them under duress, a mistake. To be sure, the Parlement of Paris registered the edicts on 29 April with what Colbert later described as *liberté de suffrages*, which probably meant that his parlementary clients had overcome any lingering opposition.[14] But the provincial tribunals, where dissident groups were stronger, sought instead to impede registration in all the ways that they had perfected, continuing their sublime disregard for title I of the ordinance of 1667.

Colbert began by arranging for the first presidents of the parlements and the Vialet farmers to work together in support of these edicts, a benefit he derived from the client networks that included both groups. The meetings went quite well. Brûlart of Dijon strongly supported the interests of the domain farm with his magistrates. The Vialet partners commended First President d'Argouges for his 'singular zeal' in protecting their Breton interests. First President Pellot held long conversations with them in Paris and promised to do his best to get the edicts registered in Rouen. Whatever problems remained with getting fiscal laws registered in the provincial parlements, they did not begin at the top. By the early 1670s, the first presidents, nurtured and appointed by Colbert, served his interests and tried to execute his orders.[15]

Despite the best efforts of the first presidents, the Parlements of Dijon, Toulouse, Rennes and Aix all voted to communicate the edicts to their respective estates, without even deliberating on them. Obviously they hoped to use the estates' fiscal and negotiating powers against the edicts, and they succeeded everywhere except in Burgundy. On 19 June 1671, the Parlement of Dijon voted to transmit the edicts to the *procureur syndic*, who took them to the *élus*, the executive committee of the Estates. Disappointingly, however, the *élus* chose not to ask the Parlement to delay registering the edicts, definitively ending the political relationship between the two institutions. We do not really know why; but it is likely that the intendant Bouchu, who had clients in the Estates, heavily influenced its decision on this point. In any event, the Parlement registered the edicts on 1 July, the first provincial parlement to do so and, for a long time, the only cooperative tribunal in the provinces.[16]

On 17 June in Toulouse, Presidents Ciron and Potier and the veteran Councilor Frezals, the old opposition leaders, persuaded the Parlement to submit the edicts to the *syndic* of the Estates of Languedoc. As First President Fieubet noted, they hoped that the *syndic*, the administrator and representative of the Estates between sessions, would oppose registration, helping the tribunal to prolong the affair. On 30 June, the *syndic* gratifyingly urged the Parlement to stop work on the edicts; and the enemies of Fieubet leaped to their feet in triumph. They denounced the edicts in one fiery speech after another, to general acclaim. With only a few judges supporting Fieubet, the Parlement refused to register either the *contrôle* or the *consignation* and voted remonstrances against them both. The edicts went unregistered and unenforced in Languedoc, depriving the Vialet group of anticipated revenue.[17]

On 19 June, the Parlement of Rennes also voted both to issue a remonstrance and to deliver the edicts to the *procureur syndic* of the Estates of Brittany, whose next session would take place in August. The Parlement took it for granted that the Estates would accept custody of the edicts and did not, therefore, register either one. It did not even begin its remonstrance until September, during the Estates session, a clear violation of the ordinance. In another year, the Estates might have withheld its 'free gift' until it obtained satisfaction on the edicts; but in 1671, the new governor, the influential duc de Chaulnes, made clear that the king would no longer tolerate such tactics and brought his personal prestige to bear. The Estates voted an unconditional 'free gift' of 2.5 million livres, without any promises about the *consignation* and *contrôle*. The royal commissioners read the remonstrances of the Parlement and the Estates at the same time, there being no essential difference between the two documents, and rejected them both.[18] But this did not really settle *consignation* and *contrôle* issues in Brittany; the Estates and the Parlement had just changed their tactics. The *procureur syndic* urged the Parlement to continue opposing the edicts; and the magistrates gladly left them unregistered, just as in Languedoc.

In like manner, the Parlement of Aix had recourse to its local estates, the Assembly of Communities of Provence. The Assembly's *procureur* and *syndic* of the nobility told the Parlement that they did not want the edicts registered; and the Parlement dropped them altogether, not even troubling to issue a remonstrance. First President Oppède died on 13 November; and the government appointed Grimaldi de Régusse, a senior *président à mortier*, as his temporary replacement. This turnover presumably made it easier for the Parlement to ignore the new laws.[19]

At first the Parlements of Rouen and Bordeaux, located in provinces where estates no longer met, did not seem uncooperative. The two edicts arrived in Rouen on 2 June 1671, and the Parlement began to consider them right away. When its *commissaires*, a committee appointed to examine the laws, recommended against the edicts, the Parlement voted to remonstrate, the normal sign of intent to delay. However, the judges finished their remonstrance in July and sent it off promptly to the government. The Parlement of Bordeaux, reacting in much the same way, considered the edicts on 21 June, voted to remonstrate, and sent its remonstrance to Paris on 11 August. Neither parlement had precisely observed the six-week time limit of the ordinance, but neither had indulged in unusual delay or obstruction.[20]

By the late summer of 1671, however, only one provincial parlement, that of Dijon, had registered the *consignation* and *contrôle* edicts, issued almost six months earlier. All the other parlements for which we have information had tabled the edicts, pending the outcome of remonstrances or the action of provincial estates. The council could have taken offence at these violations of title I of the ordinance and ordered another round of forced registrations, as in 1667 and in 1669. Instead, it issued perfunctory decrees of 26 August against Rouen, 11 September against Toulouse and 9 October against Bordeaux, rejecting the remonstrances of those tribunals and ordering registration of the edicts. These decrees contented themselves with laconic orders to the parlements to register the edicts, without citing violations of the ordinance or claiming that royal authority had been compromised. Colbert and his colleagues must have thought that this round of resistance would quickly subside.[21]

Their temperate approach worked with the Parlement of Toulouse. Once the council spoke, the tribunal registered the edicts, joining the Parlement of Dijon in full compliance.[22] But as the months passed, the other delinquents just became more stubborn. On 20 November 1671, Colbert wrote a friendly letter to his favourite first president, Pellot at Rouen, reminding him that the Parlement had not obeyed the 26 August decree to register the edicts. The first president dutifully assembled chambers on 26 November and tried to persuade his judges to obey both the recent ordinance and that of Moulins, which required parlements to register laws once the government had answered their remonstrances. But his colleagues ignored both ordinances and tabled the two edicts anyway,[23] prompting Colbert to warn him in an unusually stern letter that nothing offended the king more than failing to register his laws. At this, the Rouen magistrates relented to the point of registering the *contrôle*, on 15 January 1672, although they added the disapproving phrase, *du très exprès commandement du Roy*. But they would not register the *consignation* edict.[24]

On 28 January 1672, at the urging of its first president, the Parlement of Bordeaux finally agreed to reconsider the edicts. Deferring in a way to the council decree of 9 October, the Parlement voted to register both edicts but then suspended execution of its own registration decree, leaving things the way they were before. At about the same time, the Parlement of Grenoble joined the list of recalcitrant tribunals, declining to register the *contrôle*.[25]

On 12 and 19 March 1672, the council issued several decrees to deal with this recalcitrance. The new decrees rebuked the Parlements of Aix and Rennes for failing to register the edicts, the Parlement of Rouen for rejecting the *consignation*, and the Parlement of Grenoble for ignoring the *contrôle*. The decrees charged that these tribunals had prevented the Vialet group from collecting its revenues, another sign of the close relationship between the Vialet partners and Colbert. Finally, the council commanded these tribunals to register the *consignation* and the *contrôle* without any further delay.[26]

The Parlements of Rouen and Grenoble ignored the decrees, while Aix and Rennes became even more aggressive in their opposition to the edicts. On 20 May, Acting First President Régusse of Aix urged his judges to obey the decree and register the edicts, now that almost a year had elapsed since they had been issued. Commissioners appointed to study the edicts also recommended a 'pure and simple' registration. But the Parlement discharged those commissioners, appointed new ones to replace them, and set no date for a fresh report. The session then concluded, leaving the first president baffled and the edicts in judicial oblivion.[27] On 23 May, with the encouragement of the *procureur syndic* of the Estates, the Parlement of Rennes finally registered the edicts, but modified both quite significantly. The judges fixed edict tariffs at the 1669 rates, setting aside a council decree for higher rates to be collected by the Vialet. When Colbert queried the Parlement about the edicts, the tribunal decided to write a fresh remonstrance. But, as usual, the magistrates took a long time to draft it, adding the tactic of delay to that of modification.[28]

Because the Dutch War had begun in April 1672, with all its fiscal demands, Colbert could no longer tolerate this state of affairs; he needed a free hand with fiscal policy and someone to help him get it. Henri Pussort, who had taken a firm line in the Council of Justice, joined the Royal Council of Finances on 25 April 1672, no doubt at the instigation of his nephew Colbert. Pussort became *rapporteur* for the cases involving the Parlements of Aix, Rennes and Bordeaux. Decrees against these parlements soon crackled with outrage and threats, reflecting the stern views of Pussort that parlements jeopardized legislative sovereignty when they obstructed new laws.

On 7 June 1672, the royal council firmly rejected the remonstrance of the Parlement of Bordeaux all over again, ordered a 'pure and simple' registration of the edicts, and pointedly instructed the *procureur général* to tell the king within one month if the Parlement had complied. At this firm command, together with its implied threat, the Parlement accepted defeat and registered the edicts then and there, a distinct gain for the council and Pussort.[29]

On 17 September, they used equal firmness against the Parlement of Rennes, condemning it for violating title I of the ordinance and for what they described, raising the rhetorical stakes, as an 'attack upon royal authority'. The council voided the Parlement's modification decree as well as other decrees it had issued to interfere with the edicts and summoned some judges to Paris to explain their conduct to the king. Unexpectedly, the council also told the Parlement that it should never again, for any reason at all, communicate legislation to the *procureur syndic* or to the Estates, severing at a stroke one of the most effective methods by which the Parlement had prevented new laws from taking effect. Finally, the council instructed the tribunal's chief clerk to record the discourses of any magistrates who spoke against the edicts and to send his notes to the king. Faced with this vigorous decree, the Parlement registered the *contrôle* and *consignation* on 22 October 1672, a full surrender after a resistance of almost a year and a half.[30]

On 8 October 1672, another bruising council decree voided the decrees of the Parlement of Aix which had transmitted the edicts to the Assembly of Communities and, as at Rennes, forbade the magistrates from sending any future legislation to the Assembly on any grounds, upon pain of suspension from office. The Parlement was instructed to register the decrees, purely and simply, within three days and without fail. As at Rennes, a clerk was to record all discourses on the edicts, to be used by the king to punish dissidents.[31]

When President Régusse assembled the Parlement, he drew attention to this decree's 'extraordinary clauses' and bluntly warned his colleagues that they were now in (unspecified) danger, having grievously offended the king. At this, the Parlement finally registered the edict, and Régusse informed Colbert of its 'blind submission' to the monarch. The council had won a fresh triumph over a recalcitrant tribunal, but it had taken another year and a half, just as at Bordeaux and Rennes.[32]

Only the Parlement of Rouen could not be moved. On 13 and 20 August 1672, the Norman tribunal defied the council and declared that it would not register the *consignation* unless the Vialet changed it in several ways, an unacceptable demand. Months passed, with Colbert protecting the Parlement because of his relation with Pellot, until his patience finally ended; and he jolted the first president with an angry, threatening letter, of 6 January 1673.[33] Pellot convened the Parlement on 12 January and gravely told his judges that they had displeased the king at a deep personal level and angered all the members of his council. With all the rhetorical skill he could muster, he urged the Parlement to register the edict and reminded the judges that all the other parlements had already done so.

His address persuaded the veteran judges in the Grand-Chambre, but not the ardent younger magistrates in Enquêtes. Believing that the Parlement must defend *liberté des suffrages*, they repeated their impossible demand that the government rewrite the edict. Pellot had failed again. On 20 January 1673, the controller general told him that the king planned to take 'a strong resolution' in Rouen and wanted the names of the 'cabal' of Enquêtes judges, whom he intended to punish. Indeed an *Enquêtes* president was promptly sent into exile. But almost two years had passed since the king had issued his edict for the *consignation des amendes*, and nothing, it seemed, could make this Parlement register it.[34]

Although Rouen was a special case, most of the other parlements had stymied the collection efforts of the Vialet partners for many months; and they almost all made new trouble with the additional fiscal legislation being churned out to fund the Dutch war, added as always to the steadily growing Vialet farm. A declaration of 23 March 1672, 'confirmed' the heredity of office conferred upon notaries in 1664 and restored it to *procureurs* (solicitors) in the parlements and subordinate courts. This meant that in order to retain their offices the notaries and *procureurs* had to pay such sums as the council would assess, a requirement they were certain to resist. In addition, an edict of March 1672 required non-noble holders of real property classified as noble to redeem *franc-fief* duties, which they paid annually, by disbursing in advance a sum equal to three years of the property's income. The parlements had fiercely resisted this exaction when the government attempted to impose it on the eve of the Fronde and in 1656.[35]

Only the Parlement of Dijon, the first tribunal to register the *consignation* and *contrôle*, accepted the new edicts right away. It registered the heredity and *franc-fief* laws on 13 August 1672, in what the first president proudly reported as a 'grand submission'. Brûlart had reason to boast. He had induced his magistrates to register the edicts even before the government distributed them in printed form, only their titles being available when he convened the tribunal. Moreover, the first president had received those titles from the local revenue farmers, who had purchased the rights from the Vialet group and were in a hurry to get started. Brûlart made the Parlement of Dijon a model of acquiescence to the Vialet.[36]

But the more obstinate tribunals remained obstinate. The new legislation probably arrived in Aix in late August, but the Parlement postponed discussion of it until October or November. The judges then declined to register the declaration for the heredity of judicial officials and restricted the *franc-fief* levy to only one year of income. The council had not yet issued its harsh decree of 8 October on the *consignation* and the *contrôle*, so the tribunal felt free to adopt much the same attitude towards the new edicts as it had towards the earlier ones.[37] Bordeaux and Toulouse appear to have registered the heredity declaration, but they both balked at the *franc-fief* edict, which Toulouse tabled while it drew up a remonstrance.[38]

The Parlement of Rennes ignored the heredity and *franc-fief* laws into the late autumn of 1672, at which point the government resorted to a highly visible form of duress. Letters patent of 8 December 1672, commissioned Guy Chamillart,[39] intendant at Caen, and the marquis de Coëtlogon, governor of Rennes, to convene the Parlement for the registration of the *franc-fief* and heredity edicts and four new fiscal edicts into the bargain, all of them likely to provoke a hostile reaction. Chamillart and Coëtlogon appeared in the tribunal on 19 December, prepared to force the edicts into its register in an assembly of chambers. But the session did not go the way they expected. From the senior councillor, the *doyen*, to the newest judge in Enquêtes, the magistrates rose to denounce both the new laws and the use of coercion, delivering discourses that Chamillart found politically extreme. No one took the side of the government, and d'Argouges's clients ran for cover, earning the contempt of Chamillart: 'most unworthy (he wrote of them) . . . none took the position he should have . . . [they would not do] their duty'. The Parlement refused to register anything, flouting the orders of Chamillart, who retired to Caen in confusion.[40] On 5 January 1673, the tribunal sent a deputation of senior judges to Paris, bearing oral and written remonstrances, intending to plead their case with the king in person.[41]

Meanwhile, the council, reacting to this fresh round of parlementary mischief, was already issuing admonitory decrees to the offending tribunals. Under the compulsion of a council decree, Bordeaux finally surrendered and registered the *franc-fief* edict on 28 September 1672. Another forceful decree, issued on 16 November, overturned the decree of the Parlement of Aix modifying the *franc-fief* edict and suspended the decree's *rapporteur* from office along with the judge who had presided at that session. It rebuked the whole Parlement for violating the ordinance of 1667. Only ten days had elapsed since the Parlement had bowed to that strongly worded decree of 8 October, threatening the entire tribunal with interdiction. So the Parlement, at least somewhat impressed, registered the *franc-fief* edict on 7 December; but it did not register the heredity of office declaration until January 1673, after hearing the complaints of the officials affected by it. The Parlement of Toulouse probably registered the *franc-fief* edict in January 1673, after a council decree rejected its remonstrance. In the end, Colbert and the council overcame the opposition of the parlements of Aix, Bordeaux and Toulouse; but it had taken time and effort for them to do so, and the Parlement of Rennes posed a special problem.[42]

The Breton tribunal had openly defied royal agents in an act that could not go unpunished. Evidently those magistrates summoned to Paris for the *consignation* and the *contrôle* had already received a particularly strong reprimand. In a letter of 28 December, they warned the Parlement that it would suffer 'total ruin' and 'misfortunes beyond imagination' if it did not register the new edicts and apologize to the king. By the time this warning arrived, the Parlement's deputation was on its way to Paris with the new remonstrance. But on 7 January 1673, an impatient council issued another powerful decree against the Parlement of Brittany.[43]

This decree rebuked the Breton judges for disobeying the king on 19 December and condemned them for violating article ii of title I (the article which proscribed delay in registering laws). It nullified the Parlement's 23 December decree ordering remonstrances, since it affronted the authority of the king, and commanded the Parlement to register the new edicts at once. To ensure that the tribunal complied, the council ordered Chamillart to return to Rennes to stage another forced registration. This time he was to tear the Parlement's offensive 23 December decree from the register and insert the council's decree of 7 January in its place, a permanent reminder of the reach of royal authority. A supplementary decree sent five magistrates of the Parlement into exile.[44]

When Coëtlogon learned that he and Chamillart had more work to do, his courage faltered. All the magistrates, he wrote to Colbert, had united in opposition to the edicts and awaited the return of Chamillart with grim determination. Their resistance had spread to 'people of all conditions and trades', creating the danger of violence in the streets. He himself had become the object of general hatred and feared being literally 'cut to pieces'.[45] Filled with similar misgivings, Chamillart slipped into Rennes on 17 January and, with the anxious Coëtlogon beside him, shuffled off to the Palais de Justice and its angry magistrates.

Despite tense moments in a speedily convened plenary session, the Parlement endured its punishment in stony silence. Chamillart read the council's decree of 7 January and walked out with the Parlement's secret register, which he took from the chief clerk, causing the session to be terminated in an irregular fashion. When he and Coëtlogon returned the next day, they ordered a *huissier* (bailiff) equipped with scissors to excise the entry for the entire session of 23 December. That entry extended to eight pages, the scissors were dull and the bailiff took a long time to get the job done. But at last the council decree of 7 January took its place in the mangled portion of the register. Chamillart instructed a clerk to read a few lines from the November edicts, and Coëtlogon offered the magistrates the chance to speak.

But the *doyen*, Charles Le Febvre, said nothing, and the others followed his example, leading to an uncomfortably long period of silence. At last the presiding judge, the *président à mortier* Claude Cornulier, declared, 'Monsieur, all we owe on this occasion is our presence at the execution of the king's orders', that passive disavowal of compulsory registrations long demanded by constitutionalism. Chamillart, taking little notice, declared the edicts registered and published and concluded the session. Contrary to his apprehensions, everything had gone smoothly, not altogether by accident. Royal officials had already escorted three of the exiled magistrates (the others were in Paris, with the deputation) out of Rennes, making all the judges more docile.[46] After a long delay, the *franc-fief* and heredity edicts, along with the four others, were at last registered in the Parlement of Rennes.

In the Parlement of Rouen, which still had not registered the *consignation*, Pellot worried about how his colleagues would treat the new edicts. As it turned out, the tribunal merely registered them with requests that the king honour exemptions granted to the province in the past. While these were not quite the 'pure and simple' registrations that a relieved Pellot reported to Colbert, they did not amount to obstruction. But the Parlement dug in its heels on yet another edict of March 1672, which dealt with a tax on Norman woodlands called the *tiers et danger*.[47]

The *tiers*, corresponding to the seigneurial duty of the *triage*, awarded the king one-third of the value of harvested timber; and the *danger* tacked on another 10 percent. For decades the Parlement had excused private landowners from paying the *tiers et danger*, most recently in a decree of 11 August 1667. However, the forest ordinance of 1669 cancelled these exemptions, and the edict of 1672 ordered Norman proprietors to pay arrears of as much as thirty years. A royal commission had already begun to assess both *tiers et danger* and *franc-fief* taxes, while also trying to collect from all the officials subject to the heredity of office edicts. Inevitably, the Vialet partners administered all the edicts.[48]

The commission operated under the authority of the forest ordinance and despite the refusal of the Parlement to register the *tiers et danger* edict, so the Parlement's resistance to the *consignation des amendes* coincided with its opposition to the *tiers et danger*. Indeed, the magistrates probably hated the latter more than the former, since they themselves had to pay substantial *tiers et danger* fines. They met often in plenary sessions and submitted remonstrances, over the objections of Pellot. This attitude encouraged resistance from landowners in

Normandy, obliging the council to issue repeated decrees to speed things up, none of which succeeded.[49] In Normandy, the *tiers et danger*, like the *consignation*, was at an impasse.

Redefining registration procedure

This widespread resistance, on the part of so many parlements, to so much new legislation created a dilemma for the government. To be sure, one could picture the problem as merely local, involving only this or that tribunal. Colbert himself wrote to Pellot on 6 January 1673, that 'your Company is much slower in obeying the king than the others'.[50] But this was misleading, for on 20 January 1673, Colbert also wrote to Chamillart that the Parlement of Rennes was 'the only Company in the kingdom which resists the king's wishes . . .'[51] On 27 January moreover, Colbert told the new intendant of Provence that he expected the Parlement of Aix to interfere with all new legislation, despite its capitulation on the laws just issued.[52] The behaviour of Bordeaux, Toulouse and Metz could not have pleased him either. Bordeaux had resisted the *franc-fief* edict; and Toulouse had only registered it in obedience to a council decree of 17 January 1673. The Parlement of Metz blocked it for the entire year.[53] Although Rouen and Rennes offered the most opposition, the council's quarrel with provincial parlements involved more than one or two tribunals.

By 1673, to be sure, decrees of council had at last taken hold as a generally effective method with which to subdue this resistance. Explicitly worded, using vigorous language that wounded pride, both threatening punishments and administering them, the decrees of 1672–1673 had begun to command a respect and obedience that had not existed even in the recent past, establishing at least for the moment that principle of the supremacy of council decrees, asserted in 1661. Aix, Bordeaux, Rennes, Rouen and Toulouse had all succumbed to these robust decrees. But the council could not issue its decrees fast enough to compel the parlements to register the laws as rapidly as Colbert and the revenue farmers wanted. Even in private judicial matters the council was cautious about nullifying parlementary decrees and careful to observe the requirements of law and procedure when it did so.[54] When it dealt with political opposition, the council acted with equal circumspection. It took the time it needed to identify blameworthy judges or to gather the evidence to condemn an entire tribunal. The distance between Paris and provincial capitals added to the delay. As we have seen, it could take months, even more than a year, for a council decree to be issued and enforced.

In addition, two parlements were interpreting title I differently from what its framers intended. Article v, which commanded the provincial parlements to present their remonstrances within six weeks, had seemed clear enough when it was written. But the Parlement of Rouen learned to read the article in a new way. Article v also provided that legislation would be 'deemed' registered within six weeks of its arrival in a parlement, whether or not a tribunal had acted upon it. In adding that clause, the Council of Justice intended to dispel any tendency to ignore legislation in hopes that the government would lose interest in it. But in 1671, the magistrates of Rouen contended that the article excused them from registering the edicts for the *consignation* and the *contrôle* once the six weeks had elapsed. Calling the bluff, so to speak, they invited the government to deem the edicts registered if it wanted. In his address of 26 November, Pellot argued against that eccentric interpretation; but the judges simply ignored him.[55]

After its humiliation of 17–18 January 1673, the Parlement of Rennes concocted an even more peculiar exegesis. In a lengthy argument carried to Paris by still another deputation of senior judges, the Parlement maintained that article v justified its remonstrances of December 1672, condemned by the royal council as illegal. The article, argued Rennes, implied that even forced registrations could not take effect until remonstrances had been issued and answered. The Parlement was entitled to submit its remonstrances to the king and to have its deputies read the remonstrances aloud to him, delivering any statements (*discours*) that they wanted. Of course, article v did not really apply to legislation registered by compulsion; and the council decree of 7 January rightly found that the Parlement had also violated article ii, which forbade parlements to suspend the execution of laws under the 'pretext' of remonstrances. Even so, the Parlement of Rennes had discovered an unorthodox way to interpret these articles.[56]

Several parlements had also found creative judicial ways to frustrate the Vialet revenue farmers as they tried to collect the new taxes. Throughout 1671 and 1672, the Parlements of Bordeaux, Rouen and Toulouse declined, on various specious grounds, to enforce the *requête civile* deposit of 450 livres. The Parlements of Aix, Rennes and Rouen issued decrees restricting the scope of the *contrôle des exploits*. Rennes refused to award the Vialet the proceeds from fines and on its own dubious authority reduced rates on the royal postal service. The first presidents usually informed the revenue farmers when their tribunals went astray in this manner; and the Vialet group could rely upon the royal council to strike down these violations. But these harassing tactics reduced the short-term yield of the new fiscal legislation and impeded financial planning.[57]

These two years of obstruction in all its various forms at last forced the government to consider once again the question of how the parlements should treat the king's laws. On 24 February 1673, Louis XIV issued a new declaration on registration procedures. This one took its place in the long line of such regulations, from the ordinance of Moulins of 1566 to the civil procedure ordinance of 1667. Like its predecessors, the declaration proscribed the tactics of delay, commanded parlements to register laws without modifying them, and set time limits on the use of remonstrances. These similarities have led scholars to dismiss the declaration of 1673 as redundant, limited in importance, and in no way new. It has even been claimed, wrongly, that the declaration applied only narrowly to laws issued as letters patent and not to the more consequential ordinances, edicts and declarations.[58] But we ought to remember that this declaration defined Louis XIV's attitude towards registration for the duration of his reign. Not only was it his last word on the subject, it was the monarchy's final answer to its century-long dispute with the parlements over registration procedure. It necessarily broke new ground.

In about one thousand words, the main body of the declaration created new rules to close all the loopholes through which parlements had dodged registration requirements in the past. Under the new system, the *procureur général* in a parlement was to notify the first president as soon as he received new legislation. The first president was to convene a plenary session within three days, whereupon the *procureur général* would announce the arrival of the new law. A *rapporteur*, to be appointed in that very session, would have three days in which to appear before another plenary session with a summary of the law. When the briefing judge reported, the parlement had to vote on the new law in that very session, i.e. within seven days of receiving it, a requirement made so detailed and precise as to preclude any delaying tactics whatsoever.

When a tribunal considered the new law, the magistrates could not speak against it. Clerks were to take notes on all their discourses. If any judge broke this rule, the clerks were to send their notes to the government, ensuring swift punishment for any violation. The declaration thus suppressed freedom of speech in the parlements, and not for the judges only. Representatives of provincial estates were barred from intervening against laws, as were any groups, communities or individuals, unless the law involved only some narrow, local issue. This, of course, generalized the ban, previously applied only to Aix and Rennes, against communicating legislation to provincial estates.

Along with the right to speak against the laws, the judges also lost their right to vote against them. At their final session on a law, the magistrates could only vote in its favour, a provision that ended *liberté des suffrages* for the rest of the reign. In addition, it could not modify the laws in any way, even under that old formula of the king's *bon plaisir*; nor could its registration decree refer to pending remonstrances, as though registration and remonstrances were wrapped up together. In brief, a parlement could take no steps other than to register the law then and there, purely and simply.

With regard to remonstrances, the declaration repeated the restrictions in the ordinance of 1667: the Parlement of Paris must submit its remonstrances within one week after it had received new laws and the provincial parlements must do so within six weeks. After this, the declaration imposed a brand new requirement when it ordered the parlements to register the law first, even before they remonstrated against it. A copy of the 'pure and simple' registration decree had to accompany any remonstrance that the parlements chose to make. This single requirement, without precedent and unanticipated even in absolutist thought, stripped remonstrances of most of their influence. For the first time in French history, a parlement had to enforce the laws even while it was remonstrating against them, ending the classic tactic of delay and speeding the work of revenue farmers.

The obligation to register a law before remonstrating so changed traditional practice that it came to stand for the declaration as whole, pejoratively. From the beginning, the magistrates singled out this requirement as a grave abuse of their functions and powers and automatically suspect because it was so new. As chancellor under the post-1715 regency, the respected Henri d'Aguesseau, who had served as *procureur général* of the Parlement of Paris in the late reign of Louis XIV, noted disapprovingly that only that king had ever reduced remonstrances to this state. No contemporary would have agreed with current revisionism that Louis XIV did not 'challenge' the principle of remonstrance; they thought he had trounced it. But the other clauses in the declaration also broke sharply with the past. No monarch had ever forbidden the magistrates to criticize laws during registration, barred them from hearing the complaints of other parties and deprived them of the right to vote no. In proscribing freedom of expression and all but suppressing the right to vote, the declaration subverted the principle of verification altogether, as the judges did not forget. When the king died in 1715, magistrates in the Parlement of Paris condemned the declaration for having plunged the monarchy into 'despotism'.[59]

While kings had repeatedly directed the parlements to register laws soon after receiving them, the new declaration made it impossible to do otherwise. The declaration thus answered the question of what degree of obedience the parlements owed the king in registering his laws. They now had to obey him completely and promptly or incur the risk of punishment for open disobedience. On 6 January 1673, Colbert had instructed Pellot to set the agenda of the Parlement of Rouen so that it must either register the *consignation des amendes* or refuse it in an act of open defiance that the king could justifiably punish.[60] The 1673 declaration compelled all the parlements to make this choice every time they voted on a new law. On the subject of obedience, the government of Louis XIV had peeled away the evasions and dispelled the mists of ambiguity created by more than a century of constitutionalist thought and precedent.

Significantly, the crackdown on the parlements occurred at about the same time that the government established its control over the vote of 'free gifts' voted by the provincial estates. Rather than negotiating the size of the 'free gift' as in the past, bargaining and haggling until both sides arrived at some middle ground, the government decided to stipulate the amount of the 'free gift' the day a provincial estates opened and to insist on the full sum, without further discussion, a goal that Francis I had tried without success to achieve. In 1672, the Assembly of Communities of Provence, in deference to this new policy, agreed without delay to the 500,000 livres fixed in advance by the government, a sharp contrast with its quarrelsome behaviour at the session of 1671. In 1673, the Estates of Brittany granted in a single session the 2.6 million livres the king demanded and honoured that precedent to the end of the reign. In Languedoc, the Estates of 1673–1674 voted the 'free gift' of 2 million livres at the very session in which royal commissioners asked for it. The Estates of Burgundy also fell into line. So, too, did the Assembly of the Clergy which, meeting in 1670 and 1675 in its regular quinquennial sessions, voted its 'free gift' unconditionally. In getting its way with all these institutions, the government promised favourable treatment and occasionally paid bribes to friendly deputies. But as a sovereign, Louis XIV had objected in principle to negotiating with, or bribing, his subjects; he also applied pressure to estates deputies, as he did to magistrates of parlements.[61]

The surrender of the parlements

The king registered the February declaration in a *lit de justice* at the Parlement of Paris on 23 March 1673, the last *lit de justice* of the reign. He included fifteen new fiscal edicts along with it. Although less numerous than the twenty-five acts registered at the *lit de justice* of 13 August 1669, this batch was more important. It represented Colbert's first efforts to finance the Dutch War, which was turning into a long, costly struggle.[62]

The most important measure created *formules*, forms stamped at the top with a *fleur-de-lis* and providing space in which solicitors were to note that litigants had fulfilled the appropriate procedural steps. The Vialet farmers were to sell the *formules* in offices that they would establish in every important town and city, another extension of their fiscal empire. The other edicts created such new officials as clerks for the registration of leases, mortgages and royal *rentes* (bonds), and legal agents to serve as intermediaries between French subjects and the papacy. An edict for *arts et métiers* required independent craftsmen in towns and cities to form guilds and to pay to have their guilds registered with the king. Another edict established procedures for assessing the fees paid to judges by litigants. The *lit de justice* probably included the commercial ordinance of March 1673, one of the last of Colbert's reform ordinances. Previous governments, notably those of Richelieu or Mazarin, had introduced most of these laws only to withdraw or scale them back when they met the inevitable opposition. By virtue of his new authority over registering laws, Louis XIV fulfilled an old fiscal agenda.[63]

The government also used compulsion to register the declaration of February 1673 in the provinces, along with the accompanying financial edicts. In all the parlementary cities, governors or lieutenant governors and intendants staged forced registrations in one tribunal after another, starting with Dijon on 8 May and proceeding through Grenoble (12 May), Metz (15 May), Aix (16 May), Rouen (17 May), Bordeaux (2 June) and Rennes (7 June), before finishing at Toulouse on 20 June. Re-enacting the scenarios of 1667 and 1669, governors and intendants entered the parlements and commanded the judges to register the new laws at once. The Vialet revenue farmers began immediately to exploit them, to the satisfaction of Colbert.[64]

After the reign ended, d'Aguesseau maintained that the Parlement of Paris had denounced the February declaration in a strong remonstrance that he described as the 'last cry' of dying liberty. Unfortunately, this remonstrance has not survived and may never have existed, since d'Aguesseau, born in 1668, is not an unimpeachable source. But the remonstrance could only have reaffirmed the precepts of constitutionalist thought, as at least two provincial parlements chose to do, substituting so to speak for the Parlement of Paris and indeed all the tribunals.[65]

First Presidents Brûlart at Dijon and Pellot at Rouen both staunchly protested the implications of the new declaration. Of course, their colleagues pressured them to do so; and as royal clients, they knew that they could not go too far. But they did express, for the record anyway, the constitutionalist principles to which the parlements still adhered. Thus Brûlart denounced the declaration as a sharp break with principles and precedents long sanctioned by the monarchy, an innovation that would prevent the parlements from serving the king as intermediaries with the people, their traditional role. He questioned the wisdom of replacing deliberations and persuasion with the king's 'eternal' command.[66] In like manner, Pellot lamented the loss of *liberté des suffrages* and freedom of speech. The government should not confuse the new procedures and their 'coerced silence' with a proper verification of the laws, which the parlements could no longer give. Brûlart and Pellot stopped just short of stating the obvious: from the constitutionalist view, the new declaration was illegal. It had relegated the old maxims, *liberté des suffrages* and the others, to the rubbish heap. It turned all registrations into registrations under duress, making even the *lit de justice* redundant. If the Parlement of Paris indeed remonstrated, it would inevitably have said about the same thing.[67]

Of course, these protests no longer made any difference with the government, given the decline of constitutionalist authority. With the forced registrations of 1673, the government first subjected the tribunals to that full legislative discipline which marked the reign down to its end, the onset of a new era. Henceforth the parlements registered all the legislation issued to fund the Dutch War promptly and without qualifications, in marked contrast to the way in which they had treated fiscal legislation before the new declaration on registration procedure.

In July 1673, for example, the government extended the use of formatted paper, the *formule*: all the parlements registered the new edict on schedule, without trying to modify it. 'Everything took place in accordance with the recent laws', Pellot reported from Rouen, sounding a new note. The tribunals did not try to interfere with the Vialet administration of the edict, either. The intendant of Provence, Rouillé, and the acting first president, Régusse, reported that the new edict would be executed in full. Colbert had only to issue his orders to *procureur général* Harlay for the Vialet to get all the *formule* help they needed in the vast jurisdiction of the Parlement of Paris. In 1674, Colbert abolished formatted paper in favour of *papier timbré* – blank sheets bearing a *fleur-de-lis* stamp. The Vialet farmers sold the stamped paper to litigants at costs specified in an edict of August 1674, also registered and enforced by the parlements with only one exception, to be treated below.[68]

A declaration of February 1674 imposed a tax upon pewter ware, appreciated for its domestic usefulness and because, as a semi-precious metal, it retained value, like a savings instrument. The pewter declaration, along with other unspecified fiscal edicts, caused some concern among senior magistrates of the Parlement of Paris when they convened privately one evening at the home of Lamoignon. No doubt they resented this fresh example of the implications of the new declaration on registration procedure. Presidents and veteran councillors objected to each Act and asked themselves whether they should try to resist them. A long, uncomfortable silence ensued, broken at last when Nicolas Potier de Novion, a *président à mortier*, said that the Parlement should register the edicts without troubling the king further. Such was his influence at that point that the other magistrates adopted his views; and the full Parlement fell into line, accepting once and for all the registration discipline in the declaration of February 1673. (In 1678, Potier succeeded Lamoignon as first president.) In the provinces, too, the parlements registered the pewter declaration and the other fiscal edicts in accordance with the new rules.[69]

The government resolutely stamped out any lingering traces of resistance. In 1674, the Parlement of Toulouse picked a fight with the farmers of the government monopoly and tax upon salt, the *gabelle*. As a privilege of their office, the magistrates enjoyed a free annual supply of salt, and the salt tax paid their salaries. In 1673, however, the government reduced their free salt by half, increasing the revenues of the *gabelle* farmers at the expense of the judges. When the farmers temporarily failed to pay the judges' salaries in late 1673, probably due to the requirements of the Dutch War, indignation in the Parlement rose to a crescendo. The *président à mortier* Donneville, leading an angry group of judges, threatened to imprison the salt tax farmers and even to hang them unless they restored all the free salt and paid salaries on time. On 30 December 1673, the council issued a strong decree condemning this behaviour. Any magistrate who obstructed or harassed *gabelle* officials, warned the decree, would face prosecution by the intendant d'Aguesseau in a lower court, with no right to appeal, a violation of the *committimus* privilege which allowed the magistrates to be judged in their own parlement. Before the decree arrived in Toulouse, the Parlement commissioned a young judge named Tournier to proceed to the nearest salt depot, at Narbonne, and to bring a wagonload back to Toulouse, so the magistrates could draw their usual portions. As Tournier prepared to depart, this defiance excited the people of Toulouse, arousing the concerns of the first president and the intendant.

When they got this news, the king and Colbert acted decisively. A *lettre de cachet* exiling Donneville to the town of Aumale arrived on 17 January; and he left the next day, announcing, as he glared at Fieubet, that he had no wish to serve under 'a certain person'. Tournier was arrested on the spot and taken under guard to the fortress at Montpellier, one of the few magistrates known to have been imprisoned by Louis XIV. In a harsh letter to the Parlement, read aloud by the first president on 31 January 1674, Colbert warned that 'outbursts of this sort' would always meet with punishment. Indeed, Tournier languished in the Montpellier fortress for weeks before the king finally released him. Donneville suffered an exile of six years, an unusually long period. But this harsh treatment helped bring about some welcome changes. When Donneville returned to Toulouse in 1679, he openly promised his old enemy Fieubet to cooperate fully in the future and pledged his devotion to the service of the king. In 1671, dissident magistrates had also returned from exile, but unrepentant and unchanged in their behaviour. This time the lead actor had undergone a genuine conversion, caused by the new policy of repressing resistance in the parlements.[70]

Meanwhile, the Parlement of Rennes, alone among the tribunals, fought a rearguard action against the recent fiscal edicts, registering the laws but declining to enforce them. Even before 1673, it had refused to assess appeal fines in cases where the law now required them, obstructed the efforts of tax farmers to enforce fiscal legislation, and tried to reclaim the revenues from *greffes* and fines. Local revenue farmers detected these transgressions and had them quashed in the royal council, which grew steadily more efficient in dealing with this conduct. But the Parlement of Rennes did not mend its ways. The Bretons occasionally modified royal legislation even after the declaration of February 1673 had taken effect. When the Parlement registered the stamped paper edict of August 1674, it attempted to postpone its enforcement until 1 February 1675, when its current semester ended. Colbert had the council nullify this modification in a sharp reprimand to the Parlement for breaking the new rules.[71]

Soon, however, the government faced more dangerous opposition, a popular revolt in western France. The stamped paper, tobacco and pewter taxes provoked an uprising in Bordeaux in March 1675 and sympathetic rioting in Rennes in April. Peasants in western Brittany staged an insurrection in July and August, more disruptive and more violent than the upheavals in the cities. These disturbances obliged the king to take army regiments from the Rhine theatre, to which the Dutch War had spread, and send them to Guyenne and Brittany, where they finally suppressed the revolts with grim efficiency. As it restored order in the streets and in the country, the government decided also to punish the Parlements of Rennes and Bordeaux, on the grounds that the magistrates had aided the insurrections.

The king transferred the Parlement of Rennes – its magistrates and clerks, its legal registers and sacks of litigation materials – to the Breton port of Vannes, in order to render its future remonstrances 'more agreeable' to the king, as Pomponne, the secretary of state for Brittany, caustically put it. As directed, the judges took up a cramped residence in this 'small disagreeable town' (as it was described in 1663) on 29 October 1675. Similarly, the king banished the Parlement of Bordeaux to the modest country town of Condom. The government denied that it was punishing these parlements and said instead that it had relocated them only to ensure their safety. But this thin veil could not conceal the fact that both parlements had fallen into disgrace, deemed guilty of encouraging the insurgents.

The Parlement of Rennes had indeed shirked its responsibility to maintain order once the revolt broke out in that city. The magistrates chose not to issue decrees against the rioters and instead invited them to the Parlement to protest the new taxes. When the crowd vandalized the Vialet offices for the *contrôle des exploits*, stamped paper and pewter, the Parlement declined to restore those offices until the duc de Chaulnes, governor of Brittany, ordered it to do so. Indeed, solicitors from the Parlement, angered by the recent edicts for the conversion of their offices, took part in the rebellion, probably encouraged by the judges. As Chaulnes said, 'The deep silence of the parlement gave free reign to the mutineers.' The Parlement of Bordeaux, although it punished the rebels once order had been restored, had previously suspended the stamped paper and other taxes; and this act, public knowledge in Rennes, fed the disorders in the Breton capital. All during 1674, Colbert had warned the parlements that they were responsible for enforcing new taxes even in the face of public unrest. It is easy to see why he held these tribunals accountable, particularly the Parlement of Rennes, which had tried hard to keep the edicts from being enforced. The fact that in Bordeaux the magistrates were in physical danger, to the point that one councillor was shot and killed and three others taken hostage, did not, for reasons that are less clear, qualify as an extenuating circumstance. The exiles of the Parlements of Bordeaux and Rennes lasted until 1690, almost fifteen years, the longest exiles ever suffered by any parlement or parlements during the Old Regime, a visible reminder all during that period of the penalty for disregarding the laws of Louis XIV.[72]

Obeying the declaration of 1673

The secret registers of the parlements, which recorded their actions, and the great folio law registers, into which clerks transcribed the new laws, show us that the king enforced the declaration of February 1673 down to the end of the reign. These sources also indicate that the parlements almost always followed the new registration procedures, usually to the letter. In most cases registration became reflexive, and even discussion of the laws all but disappeared.[73] Indeed, the occasional lapses that did occur, so far from affording any sign of resistance, seem merely legalistic in nature, exceptions that confirm the rule.

In addition to getting its laws registered, the government improved its ability to enforce them. From the conclusion of the Dutch War to the end of his administration, Colbert instructed the intendants to look for any lapses by parlements or other law courts concerning such disputed taxes as the stamped paper or the *consignation des amendes*. His successors continued the surveillance, so that the parlements were never again free of some watchful eye.[74] Local revenue farmers, junior partners of the Vialet, lent a hand, reliably reporting such violations as did occur, in the certain knowledge that the royal council would intervene promptly. In 1678, the council overturned seventy-four decrees of the Parlement of Aix, which had failed to enforce the *consignation* of twelve livres, violating the edict of August 1669 and the declaration of March 1671. The Parlement of Bordeaux came under scrutiny in 1691 and 1702 for similar infractions, and had to mend its ways. In 1682, the government sharply questioned the Parlement of Dijon about unauthorized rulings on stamped paper. When the Parlement of Rennes neglected to enforce the tobacco duty, Colbert threatened to install a permanent intendant in Brittany, a fate that the province had escaped up to that point; the tribunal immediately became more obedient on the subject of tobacco.[75] For the most part, however, the Vialet enforced their edicts without real problems.

Colbert and his revenue farmers could thus impose and collect their taxes confident that as long as they kept an eye on the parlements they had nothing to fear from them. In the late 1670s, the remonstrances of the Estates of Burgundy and of Brittany lamented the existence of the very taxes the parlements had failed to obstruct; but the estates could only protest, without impeding, the new operations of the fiscal machine.[76] Colbert also succeeded, finally, in coercing the solicitors of the parlements into becoming holders of venal office. Starting in 1674, the solicitors, along with notaries, clerks and others, surrendered everywhere. Indeed, the registers of the Chambre des Comptes of Paris contain for the middle and late 1670s a surfeit of receipts for capital payments from the solicitors, evidence of their forced march into compliance. In 1679, the comments of Colbert to the intendants of Burgundy and Languedoc showed that the whole business was now routine, no longer a source of conflict.[77]

Most historians have believed that the parlements of Louis XIV ceased to issue remonstrances after 1673, falling silent for the duration of the reign. This view originated with Chancellor d'Aguesseau, who in the succeeding regency government, contended that the 1673 declaration effectively abolished remonstrances until after Louis XIV died: 'There are no more examples of remonstrances until the death of the late king'. In his *Le siècle de Louis XIV*, Voltaire said much the same thing, and virtually all historians have accepted these views.[78] This position has misled us about what the 1673 declaration said about remonstrances. True, the declaration required the parlements to register legislation before they remonstrated against it, but it did not abolish remonstrances at all; indeed, it promised that once a parlement had registered a law, the government would judge a remonstrance on its merits, as Colbert reaffirmed to the Bordeaux intendant in 1679.[79] A recent study has proved that remonstrances from the superior courts continued all though the reign, correcting this scholarly mistake;[80] and the parlements actually remonstrated even more than this study acknowledged. But they always followed the new order to register the law first.

The Parlement of Paris submitted a written remonstrance as early as 1675, on a technical legal point; but it had already registered the law in question and included the registration decree along with its remonstrance, as was now required. The royal council accepted its argument and amended the law slightly, fulfilling Colbert's promise to take obedient remonstrances into due consideration. Although no other parlement met with similar success, they all observed the new rules.

In 1673, the government converted the *tiers et danger* tax upon timber in Normandy into a lump sum payable by virtually all owners of forest land. A supplementary declaration of November 1674 fixed advantageous financial terms for the Vialet administrators. The Parlement of Rouen registered the declaration and then filed a remonstrance, all within the six weeks provided by law. The Norman tribunal also obeyed the new rules in 1677 and 1678 when it remonstrated against the creation of judicial and administrative officials. In 1674, the Parlement of Dijon remonstrated against the pewter and tobacco taxes and the stamped paper; but, again, its remonstrance adhered to the new regulations. The government rejected all these provincial remonstrances, and none deterred the revenue farmers from collecting the taxes on schedule. In Normandy, the magistrates even started paying the Vialet group the *tiers et danger* tax that they owed personally, all the while remonstrating against it.[81] So remonstrances did not altogether disappear from the scene, but the government had stripped them of their political significance, just as it had done with registration procedure in all its component parts.

In this chapter, we have seen how the king, in 1671–1675, finally suppressed the ability of the parlements to impede or prevent the registration of new laws, prying them loose from the practices and precedents that had sustained them over the decades and overriding the principles upon which they claimed to act. In retrospect, it is only surprising that it took this administration as long as it did to achieve this result. Once Louis XIV, guided by Colbert, chose to pitch his fiscal machine at a higher level, he had finally had no choice but to overcome the constitutionalism of the parlements and establish the political discipline that became a hallmark of his reign and a signal victory for absolute government.

Notes

1 Mémoire pour messieurs les maîtres des requêtes commissaires départis dans les provinces', in Louis Trénard, ed., *Les mémoires des intendants pour l'instruction du duc de Bourgogne (1698)* (Paris, 1975), pp. 72–73.

2 Colbert to Herbigny, intendant, Grenoble, 23 November 1679, BN, *Clairambault*, 462, f. 470.

3 Antoine, *Le Conseil du roi*, pp. 460–463; Jean Meyer, *Colbert* (Paris, 1981), pp. 128–134, 182–216; Jean Jacquart, 'Colbert et la réformation du domaine', in *Un nouveau Colbert*, ed. Roland Mousnier (Paris, 1985), pp. 151–165; Mousnier, *Organs of State and Society*, pp. 435–439; Jean-Jules Clamageran, *Histoire de l'impôt en France depuis l'époque romaine jusqu' à 1774* (3 vols; 1867–1876), II, 658.

4 Daniel Dessert, *Argent, pouvoir et société au Grand Siècle* (Paris, 1984), pp. 311–340, 411–430; Daniel Dessert and Jean-Louis Journet, 'Le lobby Colbert. Un royaume, ou une affaire de famille?', *Annales. E.S.C.* 30 (November–December 1975), 1303–1336; Mousnier, *Organs of State and Society*, pp. 441–442.

5 Dessert, *Argent, pouvoir, et société*, pp. 163, 448–449.

6 BN, *Fonds fr.*, 7753, 'Recueil de pièces sur les finances', f. 88rv ('Traité des Greffes') and AN, E 448b: 22 February 1672, no. 11, f. 178rv (*greffes*, Parlement of Rennes); *Mél. Colbert*, 248, ff. 407rv–443rv, 447rv–519rv (*amendes*, Parlement of Paris and provincial parlements).

7 Claude-Joseph de Ferrière, *Dictionnaire de droit et de pratique*, 2nd edn (2 vols; Paris, 1740), I, 569–570, 839; II, 698, 918; Gabrielle Vilar-Berrogain, *Guide des recherches dans les fonds d'enregistrement sous l'ancien régime* (Paris, 1958), pp. 47–48.

8 Engelmann, *Continental Civil Procedure*, pp. 729–738; Ferrière, *Dictionnaire de droit*, I, 506–508.

9 Clamageran, *Impôt*, II, 671.

10 BN, *Actes R.*, F. 23,618 (200): the edict. Decrees of council had repeatedly quashed efforts of the Parlement of Aix to interfere with the *contrôle des exploits*: AN, E 1759: 10 February 1670, f. 21rv; E 433/A: 30 October 1670, no. 50; and E 434/B: 22 December 1670, no. 6.

11 BN, *Actes R.*, F. 23,613 (201); Isambert, *Recueil*, XVIII, 427–431.

12 La Roche-Flavin, *Treize livres des Parlements*, Bk XIII, ch. lxxxii, art. ii; Ferrière, *Dictionnaire de droit*, II, 729–739; Hamscher, *Conseil privé*, pp. 98–100.

13 Isambert, *Recueil*, XVIII, 174–180 ('Des Requêtes Civiles'); AN, AD+ 418: *consignation des amendes*, 21 March 1671; AN, E 440b: 18 June 1671, no. 66, f. 36rv (Toulouse), and E 1768: 21 February 1672, no. 47 (Bordeaux).

14 Colbert to Pellot, first president, Rouen, 6 January 1673, Clément, *Lettres*, II, i, 260.

15 Pellot, first president, Rouen, to Colbert, 8 May 1672, BN, *Mél. Colbert*, 159, f. 183r; Brûlart, first president, Dijon, to Colbert, 13 August 1672, and an undated letter, in BM, Dijon, MS 54l, ff. 496r, 472r; AN, E 452: decree of 7 June 1672, no. 44, ff. 111rv–112r (d'Argouges's commendation); duc de Chaulnes, governor of Brittany, to Colbert, 16 June 1675, BN, *Mél. Colbert*, 171bis, f. 568r; Colbert to Ris, intendant, Bordeaux, 15 June 1682, BN, *Clairambault*, 466, f. 21v.

16 BM, Dijon, MS 768 (Registres du Parlement), 19 June and 1 July 1671, ff. 202–203;

AD, C-O, C 3116 (Décrets des États et Délibérations des élus, 1671), ff. 247v, 254v–255r; C 3329 (Cahiers des remontrances), ff. 1–16 (remontrances of 1671).

17 See the Fieubet letters of 17 June and 30 June 1671, to Colbert and a letter of 30 June from the Bishop of Saint Papoul, also to Colbert, in BN, *Clairambault*, 759, ff. 75rv–95rv. For ongoing cooperation between the Estates and Parlement of Burgundy, see: AD, H-G, C 2318 (1671–1672), f. 54r (*cahier*, 19 January 1672).

18 AD, I-V, IBb (Registres secrets) 236: 19 and 25 June 1671, ff. 93v, 98v–105v; C (États de Bretagne) 2658: session of 1671, ff. 10v–57v; madame de Sévigné, Les Rochers and Vitré, to madame de Grignan, 19 August 1671, *Lettres*, ed. Gerard-Gailly (3 vols; Paris, 1953–1963) I, 363; Boucherat, commissaire du roi, Vitré, to Colbert, 16 August 1671, BN, *Mél. Colbert*, 157, f. 258rv; Armand Rebillon, *Les États de Bretagne de 1661 à 1789: Leur organisation – L'évolution de leurs pouvoirs. – Leur administration financière* (Paris and Rennes, 1932), pp. 235–236, n. 10.

19 Grimaldi de Régusse, acting first president, Aix, to Colbert, 26 November 1672, BN, *Clairambault*, 759, ff. 349r–350r; AN, E 1762: decree of 15 January 1672, ff. 233rv–234r.

20 BN, *Fonds fr.*, 22,455 (Parlement de Rouen), pp. 315–316; BM, Rouen, MS Y 214/25 (Registres secrets), 2 June and 9 July 1671, ff. 317, 328; AD, Gironde, B (Parlement Bordeaux. Arrêts.): 21 June 1671.

21 AN, E 1764: decrees of 26 August, 16 September and 9 October 1671.

22 As reported by First President Pellot to the Parlement of Rouen, BM, Rouen, MS Y 214/25 (Registres secrets): 15 January 1672, pp. 370–371.

23 Colbert to Pellot, 20 November 1671, Clément, *Lettres*, IV, 64; BM, Rouen, MS Y 214/25 (Registres secrets), ff. 349–351 (26 November 1671).

24 Colbert to Pellot, first president, Rouen, 8 January 1672, in Clément, *Lettres*, II, pt i, 79; BM, Rouen, MS Y 214/25 (Registres secrets), ff. 370–371 (15 January 1672).

25 AD, Gironde, B (Parlement Bordeaux. Arrêts.): 28 January 1672; AN, E 449: decree of 12 March 1672, no. 22, f. 177rv (Parlement of Grenoble and the *contrôle*).

26 AN, E 449: 12 March 1672: nos. 21, 22, and 24, ff. 175rv–181rv; 19 March 1672: nos. 22, 23, and 24: ff. 313r–317r. The Vialet *fermiers* petitioned for these decrees.

27 BM, Aix, MS 976 (Délibérations du Parlement): 17 and 20 May 1672, ff. 36v–37r.

28 AD, I-V, IBb (Registres secrets) 238: 23 May 1672, ff. 56rv–58rv; 239: 29 August and 17 September 1672, ff. 15rv, 24v–25r.

29 AN, E 1668: decree of 7 June 1672.

30 AN, E 1762: decree of 17 September 1672, ff. 335rv–339rv; and BM, Rennes, MS 586, ff. 487rv–489rv (a copy); AD, I-V, IBb (Registres secrets) 239: 22 October 1672, ff. 44r–51v (Parlement's registration decree).

31 AN, E 1762: decree of 8 October 1672, ff. 385rv–388r.

32 BM, Aix, MS 976 (Délibérations du Parlement), f. 54r; Régusse, acting first president, Aix, to Colbert, 26 November 1672, BN, *Clairambault*, 759, ff. 349r–350.

33 BM, Rouen, MS Y 214/25 (Registres secrets): 13 and 30 August 1672, ff. 441, 443; Pellot, first president, Rouen, to Colbert, 8 December 1672, BN, *Mél. Colbert*, 162, f. 467r; Colbert to Pellot, 6 January 1673, Clément, *Lettres*, II, pt i, 260–261.

34 BM, Rouen, MS Y 214/26 (Registres secrets): 12 and 13 January 1673, ff. 16–19; BN, *Fonds fr.*, 22,455 (Parlement de Rouen), pp. 341–343; Pellot, *Mémoires*, II, 153–155; Colbert to Pellot, first president, Rouen, 20 January 1673, Clément, *Lettres*, II, pt. i, p. 265.

35 For the heredity edict, see Isambert, *Recueil*, XIX, 5–8, and a supplementary declaration of 16 April 1674 in BN, *Actes R.*, F. 23,613 (580); AN, AD+ 425 (the *franc-fief* edict); for the Vialet group, see AN, E 463: decree of 13 May 1673.

36 BM, Dijon, MS 768 (Registres du Parlement): 13 August 1672, f. 237; Brûlart to Colbert, 13 August 1672, and an undated letter from Brûlart to Colbert, BM, Dijon, MS 54l, ff. 496r, 472r. The Estates of Burgundy subsequently redeemed the *franc-fief* edict for 180,000 livres, plus 10 per cent: AN, E 463: decree of 13 May 1673.

37 Régusse, acting first president, Aix, to Colbert, 9 November 1672, BN, *Clairambault*, 759, ff. 341r–343r. The Parlement kept the heredity edict out of its secret registers and made only a laconic entry, on 21 October 1672, on the *franc-fief*: BM, Aix, MS 976 (Délibérations du Parlement): f. 50r.

38 Pontac, first president, Bordeaux, to Colbert, 1 August 1672, BN, *Mél. Colbert*, 161, f. 21r; Colbert to Pontac, 2 September 1672, Clément, *Lettres*, VI, 38; AN, E 1772: decree of 17 January 1673, f. 11r (Parlement of Toulouse).

39 Guy Chamillart, a client of Colbert, was the father of Michel Chamillart, the future controller general of finances (1699–1708) and minister of war (1701–1709).

40 AD, I-V, IBb (Registres secrets) 239: 19 December 1672, ff. 89r-92rv; Chamillart, intendant, to Colbert, 7 January 1673, BN, *Clairambault*, 759, f. 685rv, and 'Extraict des Registres de Parlement', BN, *Fonds fr.*, 16,873, ff. 29rv–41r; John J. Hurt, 'La politique du Parlement de Bretagne (1661–1675)', *Annales de Bretagne et des Pays de l'Ouest* 81 (1974), 118–124.

41 AD, I-V, IBb (Registres secrets) 239: 23–24 December 1672, ff. 99rv–108r; 5 January 1673, f. 108v; BN, *Fonds fr.* 16,873, ff. 29rv–41r (23 December 1672).

42 AD, Gironde, B (Parlement Bordeaux. Arrêts.): 28 September 1672; Aix: AN, E 1762: decree of 16 November 1672, f. 404rv; BM, Aix, MS 976 (Délibérations du Parlement): 5 and 7 December 1672, f. 54rv; Régusse, acting first president, to Colbert, 8 December 1672, BN, *Clairambault*, 759, ff. 352r–353r; Colbert to Régusse, 9 December 1672, Clément, *Lettres*, VI, 41; Colbert to Rouillé de Meslay, intendant, Aix, 27 January 1673, *ibid.*, II, pt. i, 267; for Toulouse, see AN, E 1772: decree of 17 January 1673, f. 11r.

43 Boisgelin, Descartes, and Lopriac to Parlement of Rennes, 28 December 1672, BM, Rennes, MS 586, ff. 551v–552r; Coëtlogon, governor of Rennes, to Colbert, 8 January 1673, BN, *Clairambault*, 759, f. 687v.

44 AN, E 1773: decree of 7 January 1673, ff. 5rv–6r; BM, Rennes, MS 586, ff. 498rv–499rv.

45 Coëtlogon to Colbert, 8, 15 and 17 January 1673, BN, *Clairambault*, 759, ff. 675r–687rv.

46 AD, I-V, IBb (Registres secrets), 239: 17 and 18 January 1673, ff. 116v–119r; IBb (Registres secrets), 569; AN, E 1773: decree of 21 February 1673, ff. 21r–25r, rejecting the remonstrance; Coëtlogon to Colbert, 15 January 1673, and Huchet de La Bédoyère, *procureur général*, 15 January 1673, to Colbert, BN, *Clairambault*, 759, ff. 677r, 693r.

47 BN, *Fonds fr.*, 22,455 (Parlement de Rouen), pp. 334–335; BM, Rouen, MS Y 214/25 (Registres secrets): 30–31 May 1672, f. 401; Pellot, first president, Rouen, to Colbert, 8, 12 and 31 May 1672, BN, *Mél. Colbert*, 159, ff. 193r, 221r, and 354r.

48 Floquet, *Parlement de Normandie*, V, 565, n., 567–572; Marion, *Dictionnaire*, p. 535; BN, *Fonds fr.*, 22,455 (Parlement de Rouen), pp. 252–253; BM, Rouen, Y 214/24

(Registres secrets), p. 269: decree of 11 August 1667 restricting the incidence of the *tiers et danger*.

49 Pellot, first president, Rouen, to Colbert, 21 and 31 August 1672, BN, *Mél. Colbert*, 161, ff. 210r, 288r; 19 and 21 December 1672, *ibid.*, 162, ff. 582r, 609r; BM, Rouen, MS Y 214/25 (Registres secrets), 30 August and 10 October 1672, ff. 442–444, 451–452; BN, *Fonds fr.*, 22,455 (Parlement de Rouen), p. 345; Colbert to Pellot, 26 August 1672, Clément, *Lettres*, II, pt. i, 261; council decrees in AN, E 448b: 22 February 1672, no. 5, f. 174r; 454a: 9 August 1672, f. 26rv; 455a: 6 September 1672, f. 208rv, and 20 September 1672, ff. 482rv–483r; and 465b: 22 July 1673, ff. 217rv–218r.

50 Colbert to Pellot, 6 January 1673, Clément, *Lettres*, II, pt. i, 260–261.

51 Colbert to Chamillart, 20 January 1673, Clément, *Lettres*, II, pt. i, 264.

52 Colbert to Rouillé de Meslay, intendant at Aix, 27 January 1673, *ibid.*, II, pt. i, 267.

53 AD, Gironde, (Parlement Bordeaux. Arrêts.): 28 September 1672; AN, E 1772: decree of 17 January 1673 rejecting the *franc-fief* remonstrance of Parlement of Toulouse. In 1673, the government allowed the Estates of Languedoc to redeem this and other edicts for 450,000 livres: Beik, *Absolutism and Society*, pp. 136–137, more than it would have received if Parlement had not registered these edicts already; AN, E 1773: decree of 30 October 1673, f. 93r: rejecting the *franc-fief* remonstrance of Parlement of Metz.

54 Hamscher, *Conseil privé*, pp. 37–42, 48–63, 144, 148.

55 BM, Rouen, MS Y 214/25 (Registres secrets), ff. 349/2–351 (26 November 1671).

56 Parlement of Rennes to d'Argouges, first president, at Paris, undated, BM, Rennes, MS 586, ff. 557v–558r; Parlement's remonstrance statement of 25 January 1673, BN, *Clairambault*, 759: ff. 697rv–699r.

57 On the *contrôle des exploits*, see the disciplinary decrees of the royal council in AN, E 1759: 10 February 1670, f. 21rv (Parlement of Aix); E 452: 13 June 1672, no. 59, ff. 298rv–299r (Parlement of Rouen); and E 454b: 30 August 1672, no. 63, ff. 364rv–365r (Parlement of Rennes). On the *consignation des amendes*, see E 454a: 9 August 1672, no. 40, ff. 96rv–97r (Parlement of Toulouse); E 456b: 26 October 1672, no. 60, f. 455rv (Parlement of Rouen); and E 1768: 21 February 1672, no. 47 (Parlement of Bordeaux). On income from parlementary *amendes* and *greffes*: see the decree of 15 January 1672 against the Parlement of Aix, E 1762, ff. 233rv–234r, and the decree of 3 February 1672 against the parlements in general, AN, E 448a, no. 25, f. 56rv. Almost all these decrees were issued upon the complaint of Claude Vialet or one of the group's *sous-fermiers*, such as Jacques des Forges in Brittany, Maurice Millot in Guyenne and Louis Boucherar in Languedoc.

58 For the declaration, see Isambert, *Recueil*, XIX, 70–73. The revisionist view originated with Fritz Hartung and Roland Mousnier, 'Quelques problèmes concernant la monarchie absolue', *Relazoni del X congresso internazionale di science storiche* 4 (Florence, 1955), 10, which most scholars have taken as definitive. The declaration of February 1673 used the expression letters patent in a generic sense to designate all the forms in which legislation appeared. For this generic usage, see: François Olivier-Martin, *Les lois du roi* (reprint; Paris, 1988), pp. 154–155, and Antoine, *Conseil du roi*, p. 339. Mettam, *Power and Faction*, pp. 266–267, got this wrong.

59 Henri-François d'Aguesseau, 'Fragmens sur l'origine et l'usage des remontrances', *Oeuvres complètes* (16 vols; Paris, 1819–1829), X, 9; 'Maximes tirés des

Ordonnances', in *ibid.*, XIII, 272. François de Boutaric, *Explication de l'ordonnance de Louis XIV . . . sur les matières civiles* (n.p., 1743), p. 7, explained that the declaration changed the nature of remonstrances by abolishing their power to suspend the execution of the laws. Boutaric was a professor of French law at the University of Toulouse. The revisionist remark is that of Roger Mettam, 'France', in *Absolutism in Seventeenth-Century Europe*, ed. John Miller (London, 1990), p. 54. For the hostility of the Paris judges towards the declaration, see chapter 5.

60 Colbert to Pellot, first president, Rouen, 6 January 1673, Clément, *Lettres*, II, pt. i, 260.

61 Major, *Representative Government*, pp. 631–636, 644–652, 663–664; *idem*, *Renaissance Monarchy to Absolute Monarchy*, pp. 343–352; Beik, *Absolutism and Society*, pp. 136–137; Bernard Hildesheimer, *Les assemblées générales des communautés de Provence* (Paris, 1935), pp. 77–81, 148; Rebillon, *États de Bretagne*, p. 263; Colbert to duc de Chaulnes, governor, Brittany, 23 December 1673, Clément, *Lettres*, II, i, 317; Chaulnes to Colbert, 12 September 1677, BN, *Mél. Colbert*, 175, f. 120r; Anette Smedley-Weill, *Les intendants de Louis XIV* (Paris, 1995), pp. 183–186; Kettering, *Patrons, Brokers and Clients*, pp. 167–172; Pierre Blet, *Les assemblées du clergé et Louis XIV de 1670 à 1693* (Rome, 1972), pp. 15, 18, 85; Philippe Hamon, *L'argent du roi: les finances sous François Ier* (Paris, 1994), pp. 484–485 (for the Francis I precedent).

62 Isambert, *Recueil général*, XIX, 73–109, and AN, AD+ 432 (the *lit de justice* edicts). The entry in the Parlement's secret register, AN, X1A 8397 (23 March 1673) is very brief, leading to skimpy coverage in scholarly treatments.

63 J.H.M. Salmon, *Society in Crisis: France in the Sixteenth Century* (New York, 1976), pp. 228, 312; Clamageran, *Impôt*, II, 657–658; Olivier-Martin, *Organisation corporative*, pp. 102–104; Cole, *Colbert*, II, 443–444; Blet, *Assemblées du clergé*, pp. 69–76, 104–109; and Vilar-Berrogain, *Guide des recherches*, p. 48.

64 BM, Dijon, MS 768 (Registres secrets): 8 May 1673, pp. 251–255; AD, Isère (Grenoble), B 2357 (Enregistrement, 1670–1673): 12 May 1673; AD, Moselle (Metz), B 275 (Registres secrets): 15 May 1673, ff. 20rv–21rv; BM, Aix, MS 976 (Délibérations du Parlement): 16 May 1673; BM, Rouen, Y 214/26 (Registres secrets): 17 May 1673, pp. 43–54; César d'Albret, lieutenant governor of Guyenne, to Colbert, 2 June 1673, BN, *Mél. Colbert*, 164, f. 309rv; AD, I-V (Rennes), IBb (Registres secrets) 240: 7 June 1673, f. 46; AD, H-G (Toulouse), B (Enregistrement des Actes, 1672–1674) 1920: 20 June 1673, ff. 54r–93r; Colbert to d'Aguesseau, intendant, Toulouse, 24 November 1673, AN, H1, 1692.

65 D'Aguesseau, 'Fragmens', p. 15; Michel Antoine, 'Les remontrances des cours supérieures sous le règne de Louis XIV (1673–1715)', *Bibliothèque de l'École des Chartes* 151 (January–June 1993), 89–90.

66 Quoted in Thomas, *Une province*, p. 389.

67 BM, Rouen, MS Y214/26 (Registres secrets): 17 May 1673, pp. 43–54; BN, *Fonds fr.*, 22,455 (Parlement de Rouen), pp. 347–350.

68 On registering the *formules* and *papier timbré*, see: AN, X1A 8397 (Conseil secret): 10 July 1673; AD, C-O, B 12, 109 (Enregistrement, Parlement of Dijon, 1671–1676): 9 August 1673, ff. 141r–145v; AD, I-V (Rennes), 1Bb 241 and 243 (Registres secrets): 4 August 1673, ff. 3v–4v, and 10 October 1674, f. 28rv; AD, Isère, B 2358 (Enregistrement), ff. 108rv–110rv. For its enforcement, see: Pellot,

first president, Rouen, to Colbert, 21 July 1673, BN, *Mél. Colbert*, 165, f. 194r, and 19 December 1673, *ibid.*, 166bis, f. 661r; Régusse, *président à mortier*, Aix, to Colbert, 21 July 1673, BN, *Clairambault*, 759, ff. 563r–565r; Fieubet, first president, Toulouse, to Colbert, *ibid.*, f. 121v; and Colbert to Harlay, *procureur général*, Paris, 8 April 1674, BN, *Fonds fr.*, 17,413 (Harlay), f. 259r.

69 Harlay, *procureur général*, Parlement of Paris, to Colbert, 'Lundy', 9 p.m., February 1674, BN, *Mél. Colbert*, 167, f. 341r. Examples of registration of the pewter and tobacco legislation in the provincial parlements are: BM, Dijon, MS 768 (Registres du Parlement): 1 December 1674, p. 323, and AD, I-V (Rennes), 1Bb 243 (Registres secrets): 14 November 1674, ff. 47v–49v. In the provinces, the secret registers became less informative after the declaration of February 1673.

70 BN, *Clairambault*, 759, ff. 131–194 (letters and memoranda); AN, E 468: 14 October 1673, no. 14; E 470B, 30 December 1673, no. 30. On the *gabelle* in Languedoc, see Françoise Moreil, ed., *L'intendance de Languedoc à la fin du XVIIe siècle. Édition critique des mémoires 'pour l'instruction du duc de Bourgogne'* (Paris, 1985), pp. 212–215.

71 AN, E 469B-470A: 2 December 1673, no. 20; 477A: 4 August 1674, no. 1; 470B: 16 December 1673, no. 8; 480B: 8 and 15 December 1674, nos. 12 and 28; 1773: 28 October 1674, f. 211r (condemning the Parlement for modifying the stamped paper edict).

72 William Beik, *Urban Protest in Seventeenth-Century France. The Culture of Retribution* (Cambridge, 1997), pp. 145–172; John J. Hurt, 'The Parlement of Brittany and the Crown, 1665–1675', *French Historical Studies* 4 (1966), 428–433; duc de Chaulnes, governor, to Colbert, 21 June 1675, BN, *Mél. Colbert*, 171bis, f. 645r (for the quotation); Arnauld de Pomponne, secretary of state, to Parlement of Brittany, 26 October 1675, BM, Rennes, MS 586, f. 441v.

73 AN, X 1A (Parlement of Paris. Lettres patentes, ordonnances etc.) 8670 (1672–1674), 8671 (1674–1675), and succeeding volumes; AD, S-M (Rouen), 'F. Parlement', and other records show rapid registration of laws after 1675, as do AD, I-V (Rennes), IBa (Enregistrement) 23 (1672–1674) and succeeding volumes; AD, Gironde, 1B (Registres d'enregistrement, Parlement de Bordeaux) 31–34 (1688–1702); AD, C-O (Dijon) B 12071/4 (Table générale chronologique et alphabétique), article 'Édits', ff. 209rv–215rv.

74 For his surveillance of the parlements, see Colbert to Ris, intendant, Bordeaux, 6 January 1679, and Colbert to d'Aguesseau, intendant, Toulouse, 11 May 1679, BN, *Clairambault*, 461, ff. 19–20, f. 488.

75 AN, E 1795: decree of 5 November 1678, ff. 189–192 (Parlement of Aix); E 596–597/A: decree of 1 May 1691 (Parlement of Bordeaux); Armenonville, *directeur des finances*, to La Tresne, first president, Bordeaux, 9 May 1702, AM, Bordeaux, MS 722; Colbert to Bouchu, intendant, Dijon, 12 March 1682, BN, *Clairambault*, 466; Colbert to Pontchartrain, first president, Rennes, 11 June 1681, *ibid.*

76 AD, C-O, C 3329 (Remonstrances of Estates of Burgundy, 1677), f. 29r; remonstrances of Estates of Brittany, 1675–1679: AAE, *Petits fonds. Brittany*, 1511; AD, I-V, C 2658 (Estates of 1677), ff. 311r–317r. For statistics on the growth of the royal fisc in this period, see J. Mallet, *Comptes rendus de l'administration des finances du Royaume de France* (Paris, 1789), pp. 18–20, 253–257 and 319–321; Beik, *Absolutism and Society*, pp. 142–143, figure 5. A memorandum submitted to the

Regency Council in 1717 celebrated the revenue-generating capacity of the *consignation des amendes* since 1669: AN, E 3651: 13 March 1717, ff. 147v–151r.

77 Colbert to Rouillé, intendant, Aix, 22 September 1673, Clément, *Lettres*, II, pt. i, 293; Brûlart, first president, Dijon, to Colbert, 20 April, 7 May and 6 July 1673, Lacuisine, *Lettres*, II, 161–162, 174; Harlay, *procureur général*, Paris, to Colbert, 9 April 1674, BN, *Mél. Colbert*, 168, f. 21r; Huchet de La Bédoyère, *procureur général*, Rennes, to Colbert, 18 January 1673, and an unsigned correspondent to Colbert, 29 March 1673, in BN, *Clairambault*, 759. For payments from the *procureurs*, notaries, *et al.*, see: AN, P (Chambre des Comptes) 3290, 3291, 3295, 3299, 3797–3799.

78 D'Aguesseau, 'Fragmens', p. 15; Voltaire, *Le siècle de Louis XIV*, ch. xxx; Glasson, *Parlement*, I, 436, and Shennan, *Parlement of Paris*, p. 278, among many others, accepted this mistake.

79 Colbert to Ris, intendant, Bordeaux, 21 September 1679, BN, *Clairambault*, 462, f. 263r.

80 Antoine, 'Les remontrances des cours supérieures', 88–121.

81 AN, E 1779: decree of 30 January 1675, ff. 73–74: answering a remonstrance of the Parlement of Paris about a declaration of 1674 for *mesureurs de grain*. It is not true, as even Antoine believed, that the Parlement of Paris issued no remonstrances after 1673. For Rouen, see BM, Rouen, MS Y214/26 (Registres secrets): 26 November 1674, pp. 253, 260–269 (the text of the remonstrances) and 290–291. For the remonstrances of Rouen of 1677 and 1678, see Pellot, first president, to Colbert, 1 and 19 August 1677, BN, *Mél. Colbert*, 174bis, ff. 494r, 633r, and Colbert to Le Blanc, intendant, Rouen, 27 August 1677 and 1 July 1678, BN, *Fonds fr.*, 8751, ff. 201r, 323r; AD, S-M, 1B 5276–5279 (domain farmer registers); BN, *Fonds fr.*, 7753 ('Recueil de pièces sur les finances'), ff. 48r–70v, for examples of *tiers et danger* payments by parlementaires. The redemption of the *tiers et danger* was worth up to 4,000,000 livres. BM, Dijon, MS 768 (Registres du Parlement), 1 December 1674, p. 323.

3

Venal office and
the royal breakthrough

The magistrates of the parlements, like office-holders throughout the royal administration, held their offices as property in almost the same sense that one owned real estate or moveables – almost, but not quite. More precisely, an office-holder owned the *finance* or financial assets in the office; he exercised its title, function and authority as a temporary delegation from the king, a usufruct. The king could reclaim the office by refunding the *finance* to the office-holder; but only rarely did he have the money or the inclination to do so. Most office-holders held on to their posts for life.[1]

In edicts dealing with parlementary venality, kings often stipulated that office was the most important element in the wealth of the judges and accepted some responsibility for preserving its value. The magistrates happily accepted these assurances and looked to the king when financially pressed. They maintained that wealth imparted status, evoked respect and went hand in hand with the administration of justice, while poverty would render them incapable of serving. Even Richelieu, who considered abolishing venality, consoled himself with this rationalization.[2]

Modern scholars have adopted a corollary of this thesis, suggesting that the office-holders became so numerous and so heavily invested in venality that they constituted a check upon royal power. Lavisse and Mousnier, although representing different scholarly traditions, shared this opinion, and contemporary revisionists have founded their interpretation upon it. Moote believed that the Fronde taught the monarchy such a political lesson that it resolved never again to risk its authority by endangering interests in venal office. Parker and Mettam, expanding upon Moote and inspired by Beik, thought that the kings reached a social compromise with office-holders, intentionally making them into partners of absolute government by respecting their venal interests and bolstering their economic and social position. Revisionism firmly insists that Louis XIV treated the venal interests of the parlementary judges with particular delicacy. It argues, in the manner of Lavisse and Mousnier, that on the issue of venality the upper magistracy still limited the authority of the king. On this reading,

Louis XIV's victory on the registration of the laws would be incomplete, if not suspect.[3]

In fact, the Sun King exploited the venal property of the magistrates without regard for their wealth and social position and without any inclination to treat them as political partners. On the question of venality, politics and the parlements, revisionism is wrong. To see what really happened, we must examine the two issues that had always threatened the venal interests of the judges: forced loans and the sale of new offices.

Forced loans

In 1664, Louis XIV created the East and West India Companies in an effort to challenge the Dutch and English for worldwide commercial supremacy. To capitalize the companies, the king obtained funds from the great nobles at court; and Colbert looked to the leading financial and judicial officials, such as the parlementaires. At Colbert's orders, the first presidents persuaded their colleagues to make India commitments ranging from several hundred livres from councillors to a thousand livres from *présidents à mortier*. The first presidents themselves pledged up to ten thousand livres apiece. The magistrates were to pay their pledges within five years, in three instalments; but as of 1669 most had missed one and some had missed all of their payments.[4]

To deal with this situation, the king declared, upon renewing the *paulette* in 1669, that all office-holders had to meet their India pledges before they could pay their annual *paulette* premiums. Significantly, some tribunals had to borrow money to meet this demand and bring their India payments up to date. The Parlement of Rennes, which had promised 90,000 livres, cleared its accounts by paying the king from the *gages* of its delinquents. But that was almost the least of the dilemma. The Parlement of Aix noted discerningly that an important principle, previously defended with success, was beginning to crumble, the principle that admission to the *paulette* should not depend upon the judges paying anything extra in advance.[5] That warning soon came true.

When the *paulette* expired in 1674, the burgeoning Dutch War drove the government to exploit the India example more strongly than the Aix judges could have imagined. A declaration of October 1674 renewed the *paulette* for the customary nine years – 1 January 1675, to 31 December 1683. But to obtain the *paulette*, a judge had first to pay for a substantial *augmentations de gages*; if he did not buy this *augmentations de gages*, the king would not accept his *droit annuel*, i.e. the annual *paulette* payment. Without the *droit annuel*, a magistrate could not count on preserving his office for his heirs. The king's demand for *augmentations de gages* raised the old question, recently articulated by the Parlement of Aix: whether the government could make the parlements pay extra money to get the *paulette* renewed.[6]

As the magistrates had virtually ceased to resist legislation, it seemed unlikely that they would refuse to pay this *augmentations de gages*. Even so, Colbert worried that unruly judges might make trouble of some kind, and he ordered the intendants to keep an eye on the parlements when they received the new declaration. In addition, he flatly denied a request from the Parlement of Rennes that he reduce the amount of money it was required to pay. All the parlements, he said, had to comply with the terms of the declaration, without negotiation or compromise.[7]

Colbert need not have worried, for the newly disciplined parlements quietly succumbed, registering intact an accompanying declaration that created the *augmentations de gages* and quietly paying the money demanded of them.[8] At Montpellier, an amazed foreign visitor, John Locke, watched as magistrates of the local Chambre des Comptes, also covered by the *paulette*, submissively purchased their *augmentations de gages*: 'Otherwise they . . . [would have] . . . lost their places'.[9] He would have seen the same thing in any parlementary seat.

Under the new policy, a magistrate had to buy an *augmentations de gages* equal in value to his annual *paulette*, set at one-sixtieth of the appraised value of the office. Since office values differed significantly from one parlement to the next, the *droit annuel* and *augmentations de gages* varied in proportion. But all the judges determined how much money they needed for an *augmentations de gages* in exactly the same way. A lay councillor in the Parlement of Paris paid a *droit annuel* of four hundred livres and had to buy a 'salary increase' of the same amount. The capital he owed depended upon the interest rate, as fixed by Colbert. In 1674, perhaps still unsure of himself, Colbert set a generous rate of 7.14 percent, or what was known as the 14th *denier*. Our magistrate multiplied his *paulette* of 400 livres by 14 and found that he owed 5,600 livres, which at interest of 7.14 percent generated an *augmentations de gages* of 400 livres. Although magistrates in the provincial parlements paid somewhat less in *augmentations de gages*, this approach permitted Colbert to collect almost as much money overall as the highest sums his predecessors had tried but failed to get for the *paulette* renewals of the 1620s and 1630s.[10]

Colbert's successors honoured his precedent and improved upon it. Every nine years, with the regularity of calendar intervals, in 1683, 1692 and 1701, the king renewed the *droit annuel* on the terms that Colbert had established, with one significant change. In 1683 the government raised the *denier* from fourteen to eighteen; and the 18th *denier* became the standard, applied in 1692 and 1701.[11] The new *denier* reduced Colbert's interest rate of 7.14 to 5.55 percent. With the *denier* 18, a magistrate surrendered more capital but received the same *augmentations de gages*. Our magistrate multiplied his *droit annuel* by 18 instead of 14 and paid 7,200 livres instead of 5,600; the *augmentations de gages* stayed at 400 livres. Obviously the king collected a lot more money with the 18th than with the 14th *denier*, at no extra cost to his treasury.

All the later renewals went very smoothly. When Colbert's hard-pressed successor, Claude Le Peletier, needed money in 1683, he unhesitatingly renewed the *paulette* in exchange for *augmentations de gages* capital, 'an immediate and considerable help', as he said himself. The parlements paid up even more quickly than in 1675, themselves forcing the few recalcitrant judges to disgorge.[12] The next controller general, Louis Phélypeaux de Pontchartrain, demanded a new round of *augmentations de gages* when the *paulette* expired in 1692, justifiably confident that it would produce money he could immediately use in the War of the League of Augsburg, then in its fourth year. He assured First President Harlay that the Parlement of Paris would find the new *augmentations de gages* 'very agreeable', rhetorically turning an exaction into something of a favour. By 1701, when the king next renewed the *paulette*, the parlements had become so compliant that Controller General Chamillart referred to *augmentations de gages* as 'one of the most reliable methods for obtaining funds'. No finance minister under Richelieu or Mazarin could have made that statement.[13]

Whatever they said to the contrary, Colbert and his successors understood that the fear of losing their offices, rather than any prospective advantages, drove the judges to surrender their money. The third Chambre des Enquêtes of the Parlement of Paris confessed that it was paying for the *augmentations de gages* of 1692 so as 'not to put our offices at risk', a realistic assessment shared by all the judges. A controller general memorandum of 1708 acknowledged frankly that this blackmail alone made *augmentations de gages* so lucrative all during the reign. The policies of Louis XIV had deliberately placed the venal offices of the magistrates 'in jeopardy', it said. So far from abandoning that policy, Louis XIV adopted it and improved upon it, scooping up the substantial sums displayed in Table 1.[14]

As the numbers in this table show, the magistrates in the parlements paid more than 4.2 million livres in *augmentations de gages* in 1674, when Colbert granted them a high rate of interest (7.14 percent). When Le Peletier reduced the interest rate to 5.55 percent in 1683, he increased the yield of *augmentations de gages* to almost 5.5 million. By 1692, the addition of new judges to the parlements carried the total to more than 6 million livres, the peak year. In 1701, *augmentations de gages* declined a little, to 5.67 million, for several reasons. The Parlement of Bordeaux, having proved financial distress, persuaded the government to lower its *augmentations de gages* obligation by 50 percent, causing a drop in the overall total. In partial compensation, the Parlement of Metz, which had more magistrates in 1701 than in 1692, paid a bit more; and a new parlement, at Besançon, paid for the first time. (The Parlement of Tournai, also new, pleaded poverty and obtained an exemption.) These sums represented the financial consequences of the political submission of the parlements.

In 1689, Le Peletier 'invited' the parlements to volunteer for an extra *aug-*

Table 1 Augmentations de gages *per parlement, 1674–1701 (£)*

Parlement	1674	1683	1692	1701
Paris	1,284,458	1,652,000	1,819,200	1,819,200
Bordeaux	581,042	747,200	869,600	340,000
Rennes	552,720	711,600	760,800	760,800
Rouen	514,192	661,600	745,200	745,200
Toulouse	380,324	489,600	521,600	521,600
Dijon	310,464	400,000	435,200	435,200
Grenoble	224,672	289,200	306,000	306,000
Aix	179,634	231,600	270,000	270,000
Metz	176,316	227,200	244,800	254,800
Pau	58,338	75,200	152,000	152,000
Besançon				71,225
Tournai				exempt
Totals	4,262,160	5,485,200	6,124,400	5,676,025

Source: This table is based upon BN, *Cinq Cents Colbert,* 259–260, 'États et évaluation par généralités, de tous les offices de judicature et finance (1665)', a general inventory of venal offices which enumerated the number and type of offices in each parlement and their *paulette* assessment. To produce Table 1, I simply multiplied the amount of the *paulette* each magistrate owed by the *denier* required for his *augmentations de gages* in the year indicated. This procedure assumes that each magistrate did pay his *augmentations de gages,* but this was overwhelmingly the case, as the AN, Series P, financial registers reveal. A study prepared in 1709 in the office of the controller general carried parlementary *augmentations de gages* of 1701 at 5,634,684 livres ('Estat général des offices . . .', AN, G7, 1325), which is virtually the same as my figure of 5,676,025 livres. For the Parlement of Bordeaux, see AN, E 1810: decree of 29 December 1681, no. 141; AD, Gironde, B Parl.Arrêts., 8–12 August 1682 and 12 September 1701.

mentatations *de gages* to help fund the onset of the War of the League of Augsburg. Since the current *paulette* ran through to 1692, Le Peletier could not connect the new *augmentations de gages* with the preservation of office and had to cajole rather than coerce the magistrates into submission. The precedents for voluntary loans offered little hope for success, but Le Peletier approached the Parlement of Paris optimistically, determined to improve upon the past. Negotiations elicited a promise of one million livres for the new *augmentations de gages,* another sign of First President Harlay's fealty to the government. As soon as the Parlement of Paris had agreed to pay, Le Peletier used its example to persuade the provincial tribunals that it was their turn to step forward.[15] Under Louis XIII, a finance minister would have found this a hard job, but times had clearly changed. Most provincial tribunals compliantly promised to pay from 200,000 to 300,000 livres, with tiny Pau settling on 54,000 livres. In sum, the controller general collected an unscheduled 3.15 million livres from the parlements with no more effort than it took him to get the client Harlay to cooperate and then to write a circular letter to the provincial tribunals. Table 2 shows how much each parlement contributed.

Table 2 Augmentations de gages *of 1689*

Paris	1,000,000
Aix	200,000
Bordeaux	300,000
Dijon	200,000
Grenoble	200,000
Metz	200,000
Pau	54,000
Rennes	300,000
Rouen	250,000
Toulouse	250,000
Besancon	100,000
Tournai	100,000
Total	3,154,000

Source: Paris: BN, *Fonds fr.*, 19,769: 'Estat des affaires extraordinaires . . .', f. 12r; Aix: Le Bret, first president, to Pontchartrain, controller general, 8 April 1693, AN, G7, 462; Bordeaux: Arguier, *commis*, to Chamillart, controller general, 7 March 1702, AN, G7, 139; Dijon: BM, MS 769 (Registres du Parlement): 28 January 1690, p. 2, and AN, E 1859: decree of 18 April 1690; Grenoble: AD, Isère, 2B4* ('. . . les finances du Parlement . . .'), f. 272rv; Metz: AD, Moselle, B 308 (Registres secrets): 17 August 1689 (f. 9r) and 13 September 1689 (ff. 19v–21v); Pau: AD, P-A, B 4541 (Registres secrets): 22 August and 19 September 1689 and 26 and 28 February 1690; Rennes: AD, I–V, IBb (Registres secrets) 273: 12 September 1689, f. 15; Rouen: Chamillart, intendant, to Pontchartrain, 21 December 1689, AN, G7, 493; Toulouse: Morant, first president, to Pontchartrain, 26 March 1692, AN, G7, 300; Besançon: AN, E 1860: 7 January 1690; Tournai: Bagnols, intendant, to Pontchartrain, 27 January 1691, AN, G7, 258.

In a *paulette* year the government also collected *augmentations de gages* capital from the seven chambres des comptes (3.9 million livres), the four cours des aides (660,000 livres), the two cours des monnaies (197,000), and the Grand Conseil (386,000). A study prepared for the controller general in 1709 showed that *augmentations de gages* collected in 1701 from all the superior courts came to almost 10.8 million livres, of which the parlements paid 52 percent. Other studies, prepared with a somewhat different statistical base, listed totals as high as 13.2 or 14.4 million livres. With contributions from the lower magistracy, the grand total for an *augmentations de gages* rose to about twenty million livres, a significant sum in an annual war budget of about one hundred million livres. One may reasonably suppose that when the parlements paid their *augmentations de gages*, it was easier for the government to collect them from everybody else.[16]

In 1683, 1692 and 1701, a *président à mortier* in the Parlement of Paris remitted 20,000 livres for *augmentations de gages* and a lay councillor, 7,200 livres; and many provincial judges paid almost as much. Until the government halved their obligations in 1701, the magistrates of Bordeaux paid at the levels of Paris: 18,000 livres for a *président à mortier* and 7,200 livres for a lay councillor. Also in the provincial upper ranks, at Rennes and Rouen, the *présidents à mortier* disbursed 10,800 and 14,400 respectively, and the councillors, 6,400 (Rennes) and 6,000 (Rouen). In the parlements in the financial middle, *présidents à mortier* spent 8,400 (Grenoble), 8,000 (Toulouse and Dijon), 7,200 (Aix) and 4,000 (Metz), while lay councillors laid out 4,800 (Dijon), 4,000 (Toulouse and Grenoble), 3,000 (Aix) and 2,400 (Metz) respectively.

But what did these sums mean to the private wealth of a particular judge? In the Parlement of Brittany, to begin with a provincial tribunal, the mean fortune of record was 283,800 livres, a figure derived from twenty-three fortunes reconstituted in full from among the 331 magistrates who held office in the reign. To be sure, the Breton judges included a couple of millionaires, and a few with fortunes of more than 500,000 livres. But the wealth of the majority ranged from 150,000 to 350,000 livres; and these fortunes congregated at the lower end of that scale. This spectrum of wealth seems valid also for Aix and Toulouse and probably applies to the provincial magistracy as a whole. Evidence for the wealth of the magistrates of the Parlement of Paris shows that most of their fortunes, though somewhat larger than those of the provincials, still fit within this range of 150,000 to 350,000 livres, with more of a bias towards the upper limit.[17]

Fortunes such as these provided a comfortable living standard, certainly in relation to that of the general population, but we should not think of the magistrates as an opulent group who could readily afford *augmentations de gages*. The wealthy elite aside, most judges had little financial room in which to manoeuvre. Since their wealth consisted largely of land and venal office, which generated returns of about 3 percent of capital, the majority of the judges had incomes of 4,000 to 9,000 livres. At 9,000 livres, judges could have supported their families without much difficulty in all the parlementary cities, including Paris. But most magistrates probably took in something closer to 5,000 livres, since income from venal office diminished sharply after about 1675 and income from land also suffered stagnation and then decline. Moreover, all their incomes, like those of the nobility in general, had to bear a variety of fixed expenses, such as the interest on debts incurred to pay for the office or portions owed to heirs as part of marriage or family settlements. Most judges found themselves financially encumbered all during their careers and needed to plan carefully to maintain themselves and their families in a dignified way. Since *augmentations de gages* payments ran from 2,400 livres for a councillor in Metz to 20,000 livres for a *président à mortier* in Paris, the majority could not pay for *augmentations de gages* from their annual incomes. They had to borrow.[18]

So great were their needs that they soon overwhelmed the traditional resources of patrons, family and colleagues and had to compete for funds on the credit market, with the mediating help of notaries. Notaries, familiar with the secrets of property settlements and inheritance, knew where to find money. They put the judges in touch with lenders for the *augmentations de gages* of 1683, 1692 and 1701.[19]

Sometimes an entire tribunal borrowed the money collectively, pleasing the controller general by paying everything it owed in a lump sum. In this case, a parlement appointed trusted magistrates to negotiate the loans; and these officials filed a *procuration*, or power of attorney, with one or more notaries in the parlement's seat and perhaps also with notaries in Paris. The Parlements of Aix and Dijon often proceeded this way, usually raising the capital they needed within months. As interest on their money, the lenders received the *augmentations de gages* of that parlement, year by year, directly from its paymaster (*payeur des gages*).[20]

More generally, however, magistrates borrowed as individuals, first seeking funds from family and friends before trusting themselves to notaries. Individual borrowing prevailed at Bordeaux, Grenoble, Metz, Rennes, Rouen, Toulouse and in some chambers of the Parlement of Paris. This method required each parlement to push individual magistrates to conclude their personal loans promptly in order to meet the *augmentations de gages* deadline, but all the tribunals lived up to that responsibility. For example, the Parlement of Rennes, once a rock of fiscal resistance, now wrote threatening letters to tardy magistrates to demand that they pay on schedule.[21]

The government ensured the confidence of lenders by providing them with sound collateral – the very offices of the judges. Under the *augmentations de gages* edicts of 1683, 1692 and 1701, a lender obtained a 'privileged mortgage' on the office of the borrower. Such a mortgage entitled the lender, in case of default, to be repaid in full, before all other claimants, because he or she had lent money for the sake of preserving the office, an obvious priority.[22] An edict of February 1683 reaffirmed the primacy of the privileged mortgage and laid out procedures by which creditors who held it could seize an office, instilling lenders with even more confidence.[23]

Foreclosure was already an occupational hazard for office-holders. Magistrates who had purchased their offices usually had to borrow heavily, and even judges who inherited their offices were likely to have inherited ancient debts too. Many walked a financial tightrope, and by no means all kept their balance. In the 1690s and early 1700s, creditors routinely seized offices of delinquent judges in the Parlements of Bordeaux and Rennes, among others. In 1709, Chancellor Pontchartrain, declaring that the 1683 edict must be 'executed to the letter', ruled in favour of creditors who wanted to seize the office of a debt-ridden councillor in the Parlement of Bordeaux, despite his many years of service. In assuming new debts in order to pay for their *augmentations de gages*, the magistrates therefore exposed their offices to creditors more than they had ever done.[24]

On a positive note, Louis XIV, in contrast with his predecessors, paid *augmentations de gages* faithfully, year by year and quarter by quarter, to the satisfaction of both the magistrates and their creditors. In the early 1660s, Colbert had repudiated some *augmentations de gages*, despite indignation in the Parlement of Paris; but when the Dutch War ended, he refunded the *augmentations de gages* of 1674 in full and in a lump sum. This permitted the magistrates to reimburse their creditors and increased the confidence of the latter in *augmentations de gages* loans.[25]

At the end of the War of the League of Augsburg, however, the king could no longer refund the capital paid for the *augmentations de gages* of 1683, 1689 and 1692 and did not wish to continue paying the loans at the full rate. Controller General Chamillart did not even consider repudiation, so numerous had the parlements' creditors become. To lighten royal expenses, he unilaterally reduced the interest on *augmentations de gages* from *denier* 18 (5.55 percent) to *denier* 20 (5 percent) and took the risk of an outcry in the parlements. But they all accepted this reduction in an apparent show of good will, utterly insincere since the king left the judges to pay their creditors the original interest rate. This reduction, however troublesome, was nevertheless considerably better than repudiation, apparently consigned once and for all to the past.[26]

In sum, Louis XIV repeatedly demonstrated his power to extract loans from the parlements as a requirement for admission to the *paulette*, a royal breakthrough on a previously vexed issue. As long as the magistrates could borrow money, however, and the king paid the *augmentations de gages* reliably, the judges suffered more politically than financially, a recurring sign of their subordination. It was only worrisome that at least every nine years they sank more deeply into debt, their offices more heavily mortgaged.[27]

The sale of offices

Offices in the parlements increased in value from the sixteenth into the middle decades of the seventeenth century. The price of a councillor office in the Parlement of Paris rose from about 11,000 livres in 1597 to 120,000 livres in 1637, an astonishing gain of some 1,200 percent in only forty years. In the Parlement of Rouen, the office of councillor shot up from 7,000 livres in 1593 to 84,000 in 1633, a proportionately similar increase. The office creations under Louis XIII may have slowed, but they did not stop this upward march, the fears of the magistrates notwithstanding. In Aix, the councillor office increased from a range of 3,000–6,000 livres around 1610 to 50,000 in 1633 and then pushed up to 81,000, as of 1659. In the Parlement of Rennes, the councillor office attained 100,000 livres in the 1630s and soared to a peak of 187,000 livres in the early 1660s. Office values probably rose comparably in the other parlements. When Louis XIV began to rule, offices formed the largest single component of the private wealth of many judges, making them more sensitive than ever to any changes in venality.[28]

Although Louis XIV might have emulated his predecessors and tried to create new offices in the parlements, suppressing as he could whatever opposition they proffered, instead he began his personal rule by trying to reform venality. In 1610, Loyseau had coined the satirical word 'archomania' to describe the maniacal quest for any sort of venal office, with little regard for its functions or inherent value. Authors, royal ministers and the Estates General in its periodic sessions had all condemned venality for absorbing investment capital to the detriment of economic growth. Monarchs from Charles VIII to Henry III pledged at least to reduce the number of venal offices, without ever living up to their promises. So Louis XIV inherited both an abundance of venal offices and an ongoing demand to get rid of them.[29]

An inventory commissioned by Colbert in 1665 listed 45,780 venal offices in the kingdom, carrying an estimated value of almost 420 million livres, with offices in the parlements among the costliest in the realm, the ripe fruit of archomania. This inventory served as the basis for proposals for the reform of venality, which Colbert brought to the king and the Council of Justice. In December 1665, the Council produced reform edicts for the Parlement of Paris and the provincial tribunals. Under these edicts, the king extended the *paulette* for only three years instead of the customary nine and announced his intention to terminate it in the future. He also imposed price controls on offices in the parlements, setting a *fixation* or ceiling that buyers and sellers were not to exceed, upon pain of losing the office. The edicts declared the king's intent to suppress venal offices as his finances permitted, redeeming them at *fixation* prices, set somewhat below market values. In sum, the edicts of December 1665 brought office prices down at once in order to make it cheaper to redeem offices in the future, meanwhile announcing the approaching end of the *paulette*. Although very different from forced loans and office creations, their traditional worries, the reforms posed an obvious threat to the venal interests of the magistrates.[30]

Colbert's inventory somewhat underestimated office prices in the parlements; and we can correct his list with real pre-1665 values in only a few cases. Figures for the *fixation* levels are also in short supply. Based on the information at hand, however, it is reasonably clear that Colbert intended to reduce prices in the parlements by about 15 to 20 percent, obliging office-holders to absorb the losses without compensation. Because prices were somewhat higher than he believed, he was actually threatening to reduce values by around 30 percent, all the harder to bear. This explains the hostile reception the *fixation* edict met in the parlements. Tensions in the Parlement of Paris rose steeply after the king registered it in a *lit de justice*. The Parlements of Rouen and Aix sent firm letters of protest, and the Parlements of Bordeaux and Rennes issued strongly worded remonstrances. All objected to the low values in the *fixation*, and the remonstrance of Rennes deplored what it saw as the impending socio-economic collapse of the entire magistracy. The reform edict alone makes clear that Louis XIV and Colbert had little concern for protecting the material interests of the parlementaires.[31]

In fairness, the immediate effects of the *fixation* edict were not as dire as the magistrates predicted. Sellers of office could escape the price limits by pressuring buyers to give them extra money under the table, a payment called a *pot de vin*. For example, Ormesson boasted in his journal that when he sold his office of master of requests he covertly received 84,000 livres above the *fixation* of 150,000 livres, a financial coup. When, in 1679, the Breton magistrate Berthou de Kerverzio purchased an office of *président aux Requêtes*, he noted privately that he paid 108,000 livres for it, well above the *fixation* of 90,000 livres stipulated in the contract. We can assume that many judges skirted the *fixation* in exactly the same way.[32]

Since buyers and sellers could evade the price ceilings, revisionist historians have concluded that the attempted reform did them little damage; but it must be noted that the government knew about evasions of the *fixation* and worked to curb them. An edict of March 1669 ordered the treasurer of the *parties casuelles*, the clearing house for venality, to approve office sales only when he knew that buyer and seller had obeyed the *fixation*. A successor declaration of November 1671 attempted to strengthen enforcement by requiring a buyer of office to deposit with the *parties casuelles* the sum he had agreed to pay the seller. When officials assured themselves that the negotiated price did not exceed the *fixation*, they paid the deposit to the seller, reducing the possibility that the latter could extract a *pot de vin*.[33]

Of course, the deposit requirement could not altogether suppress the private arrangements by which individuals circumvented the *fixation*, as Berthou proved in 1679; but it seems to have had some effect. Ormesson, who had triumphed earlier in the sale of his office, noted in 1671–1672 that the deposit had improved enforcement of the *fixation* significantly. The government's files refer to it through the 1680s, proving that it never wholly lapsed, like so many reform projects in the past. Nor should we assume that large numbers of buyers were anxiously eager to exceed the ceilings. In 1673, the heirs of the deceased Breton *président à mortier* Brie petitioned the royal council for more time to sell his office: no one had offered even the *fixation* price, they declared.[34]

Even more important, the *fixation* ended once and for all the price rise that had begun in the late sixteenth century. If immediately after 1665 a magistrate could still, through subterfuge, sell his office for more than its legal price, he could not reasonably hope that a regulated market, with its psychology of restraints and evasions, would generate the strong capital gains of the preceding decades. By 1690 prices had fallen in almost every parlement. It is logically possible, although empirically unlikely, that the halt in price increases and then the actual decline merely coincided with, and was not caused by, the price regulations of Louis XIV. But common sense tells us that the edict of December 1665 contributed powerfully to ending an era of capital appreciation upon which, significantly, the magistrates depended to make their offices profitable during their years in office.[35] However imperfectly obeyed in the short term, the reform edict ultimately damaged the interests of the magistrates.

The Dutch War obliged Colbert to abandon his plans to reform venality. The *paulette* could not be suppressed, since *augmentations de gages* depended upon it, nor could offices be redeemed. Like his predecessors, Colbert had to sell new venal offices in great quantity. He created clerks and minor officials in all the law courts and doubled the number of judges in the Châtelet, a civil and criminal tribunal in Paris. A vast number of small merchants found themselves, like solicitors in the 1660s, turned into holders of venal office. But Colbert seems never to have considered selling new offices of president and councillor in the parlements, which would have yielded more money than all of these. Some scholars have supposed that the parlements remained free of office creations all during the reign, which, if true, would have compensated the judges for the effects of the 1665 edict. However, their immunity on this point did not much outlive Colbert himself.[36]

The need to finance the War of the League of Augsburg (1689–1697) and the War of the Spanish Succession (1702–1713/1714) obliged Colbert's successors to create venal offices in the thousands and to extend venality into the recently acquired province of Franche-Comté. Not since the 1630s, under Richelieu, had new, and increasingly artificial, offices rained down upon the kingdom in such profusion. Venality, which Louis XIV had earlier tried to curtail, approached its extreme limits.[37] Inevitably the government resumed selling new offices in the parlements, abandoning what was left of Colbert's reform agenda. Just as they could not resist *augmentations de gages*, the tribunals could no longer ward off increases in their numbers. Freed from the restraints that had hobbled his predecessors, Louis XIV sold new offices in the parlements to the degree that the market would bear, with scarcely a trace of opposition.

In September 1689, Phélypeaux de Pontchartrain, the former first president of the Parlement of Rennes, replaced Le Peletier as controller general and lifted Colbert's ban on creating parlementary offices. He started with the Parlements of Rennes and Bordeaux, still suffering their respective exiles for a lack of zeal in suppressing the uprisings of 1675. In October, accepting Pontchartrain's advice, the king issued an edict creating in the Breton tribunal a new *président à mortier*, four *originaire* councillors, and two *non-originaire* councillors, for a total of 550,000 livres. Pontchartrain made clear that the tribunal would have to accept this package if it wanted to return home. The municipality of Rennes added about 500,000 livres, bringing the full ransom up to more than 1 million livres; but, having paid the price, the Parlement resumed work in Rennes in 1690, after an exile of more than fourteen years.[38] A similar pay-off returned the Parlement of Bordeaux to its capital, also in 1690. The Bordeaux tribunal agreed to the creation of a *président à mortier* and six councillors, all for 320,000 livres; and the city government accepted enough extra taxes to carry the total to the required 1 million.[39] These office creations, significant in their own right, prepared the way for a wave of new offices that soon swept over every other parlement in the realm.

In the Parlement of Paris, an edict of November 1690 created two *présidents à mortier*, sixteen councillors, and one *avocat général* – the largest sale of new offices in that tribunal in the century and the most lucrative, producing 2.85 million livres for the king. In 1691, office creations in Toulouse, Rouen, Dijon, Metz and Pau added thirty-five provincial judges, totalling another 2 million livres, while creations of four judges in Grenoble in 1692 and of nine in Aix in 1693 brought in 362,000 and 580,000 livres respectively. Follow-up sales took place in Metz in 1694 and 1695. The government sold the offices in the Parlement of Paris without the intercession of *traitants*, and thus netted all the 2.85 million livres that the new magistrates paid in. *Traitants* financed the sale of the provincial offices, collecting the conventional *remise en dedans*, or commission, of 16.7 percent (i.e. one-sixth the gross value); with that deduction, the provincial sales netted the government 3.35 millions. In summary, the government created 92 new judges in all these parlements between 1689 and 1692, increasing their numbers by 9.12 percent and gaining 6.2 million livres.[40]

During the Augsburg war, the king also 'converted' to venality the judges in the newly established Parlements of Besançon and Tournai, who had previously held their posts as royal appointees.[41] Except for the first presidents and the *procureurs généraux*, the forty sitting judges in Besançon and the twenty-five in Tournai had to purchase the offices that they currently occupied. The king also added eighteen new magistrates to the Parlement of Besançon and seven to the Parlement of Tournai, putting those offices for sale on the open market.

Adapting themselves to venality cost the sitting judges about 1 million livres, and the new magistrates together paid some 500,000 livres for their posts. Deducting the *remise* for the *traitants*, the net for the government was probably 1.28 million livres (see Table 5). These operations added another eighty-seven venality judges to the ranks of the parlementaires.

In total, Louis XIV and Pontchartrain increased the number of venality judges in the parlements by 179, a rise of 17.75 percent from the 1665 base of 1,008 magistrates, certainly the largest proportional increase in parlementary numbers since the reign of Henry III. The king earned almost 7.5 million livres from selling offices in the older parlements and by extending venality to Besançon and Tournai. This was probably the most profitable sale of new offices in the parlements that had ever taken place.

In contrast with their predecessors, the parlements of the 1690s did not protest, delay or obstruct registration of the office edicts and did nothing to interfere with the ensuing sales. The 1673 requirements for the registration of new laws all but ensured that everything would go well. For example, the edict creating new offices in the Parlement of Paris bore the date of November 1690; the Parlement registered it on 23 November. On 4 April 1691, the Parlement of Dijon registered the edict of March 1691 that created new offices there. The Parlement of Aix registered its creation edict, dated June 1693, on 19 June. Most first presidents could report, as did Morant from Toulouse, a 'perfect submission' in registering edicts for new offices. When the Parlement of Grenoble resisted a bit, Pontchartrain threatened to create a new subordinate law court, a *présidial*, and award it some of the Parlement's jurisdiction; the tribunal capitulated at once.[42]

In most parlements, the office sales proceeded smoothly and with reasonable speed. The new magistrates in the Parlement of Dijon took their seats between 13 June 1691 and 25 March 1692. The sales in Aix, Grenoble, Metz, Rennes and without doubt Paris also met with no obstacles. The sitting judges in Besançon and Tournai, who were obliged to purchase their offices, needed time to find the money; but the new offices in those parlements all found owners soon enough.[43]

Offices sold somewhat more slowly in the Parlements of Toulouse and Bordeaux, where economic conditions depressed the market; but the sitting judges offered no resistance to the newcomers. Of the five new offices created in Toulouse by the edict of February 1691, two remained unsold as of November 1693, despite the best efforts of Morant and the intendant Lamoignon de Bâville. Four of the six councillor offices created in Bordeaux sold rather quickly, as did the *président à mortier*; but it took more than a year before buyers for the last two councillor offices appeared.

Things went even more slowly in Rouen, where the edict of March 1691 created eleven new offices, including seven lay councillors, the largest expansion of any of the older provincial tribunals except Metz. Only three of the seven councillor offices sold by the end of 1691; and no buyers appeared for either of the two new *présidents à mortier*, which may not have sold until the late 1690s. Like Bordeaux and Toulouse, however, Rouen suffered from a scarcity of buyers, not from political obstruction.[44]

Indeed, the sitting judges had every reason to help sales along, since they suffered personally from any delay. When it created new offices, the government banned current owners from selling their posts and arrogated to itself the entire market, strong or weak. Otherwise the king would have found himself in a price war with local owners, an absurdity. Since a majority of the new offices sold within a year, the inconvenience did not last long; but it harmed the interests of would-be sellers of office while it was in place. If the new sales took more than a year, as they did in Bordeaux and Rouen, a growing number of magistrates experienced not only inconvenience but also financial distress. In Bordeaux, eight offices were already up for sale when the new offices appeared on the market; and those aspiring sellers had to wait many additional months before they could search for buyers, whereupon they found that the king's new offices had more than satisfied all demand. In Rouen, three or four offices normally changed hands annually; but because the sale of new offices proceeded slowly through the 1690s, a substantial backlog of old offices built up there, year by year, to the economic discomfort of established parlementary families.[45]

The king's sale of new offices came at an unfortunate time for all the tribunals. By the 1690s, office prices in the parlements had largely declined to, or fallen below, their *fixation* levels of 1665; and the new offices, by adding to the supply, kept prices down. Except for the office of *président à mortier* in the Parlements of Paris and Dijon, the venal market had softened everywhere. In 1690, the councillor office in Paris had descended to its *fixation* of 100,000 livres, as had the *président à mortier* in Toulouse, to 120,000 livres. The councillor offices in the provinces were sinking beneath the *fixation*, with declines of 15 percent in Rennes and Bordeaux and of almost 50 percent in Toulouse. Because Colbert had set the *fixation* below what he thought were true market values, the data in Table 3 somewhat understate the loss of capital since 1665.

In general, venal offices in these parlements had declined by 17 to 58 percent from the price levels in the inventory for 1665 and probably by another 10 to 20 percent from pre-1665 market prices. With the exception of Paris, all these parlements saw prices falling below Colbert's *fixations*. Other parlements had certainly suffered similar losses. Under Louis XIII, the parlements often complained, needlessly, that the appearance of new offices on the market would cause existing offices to decline in value. But this supply-and-demand truism applied in full to the economics of office under Louis XIV. Having saturated the markets, the new offices continued to depress prices for years to come, as Controller General Chamillart frankly acknowledged in 1702.[46]

Hoping to move office sales along, the government added the occasional sales incentive, in the form of one concession or another. But the controller

Table 3 *Office prices in selected parlements, 1665–1690s*

Parlement office	Inventory price	Fixation price	1690s price	Inventory/sale difference (%)
Paris				
PM	500,000	350,000	500,000	N/A
C (L)	120,000	100,000	100,000	−17
Rennes				
PM	180,000	150,000	140,000	−22
C (O)	120,000	100,000	80,000	−33
C (NO)	60,000	70,000	45,000	−25
Bordeaux				
PM	150,000	120,000	80,000	−47
C (L)	60,000	50,000	40,000	−33
Toulouse				
PM	150,000	120,000	120,000	−20
C (L)	83,000	60,000	35,000	−58

Abbreviations: PM: *président à mortier*; C: councillor; (L): lay councillor; (C): clerical councillor; (O) and (NO): *originaire*, or Breton, and *non-originaire*, or non-Breton, councillor, Rennes.
Source: The documentation for this table is in Table 4.

general yielded nothing of substance, nor did he find it necessary to appease the tribunals on all points. For example, magistrates of the Parlement of Paris recovered the privilege of nobility in the first degree, revoked by the king in 1669; but First President Harlay regarded this restoration as purely honorific. Most of his magistrates had already lifted themselves into the nobility, their fathers and grandfathers having held parlementary office before them, the standard two-generation ennobling procedure.[47] Moreover, the government did not extend the privilege to the provincial tribunals, even when they asked for it. The Parlement of Dijon requested first degree nobility along with financial and jurisdictional concessions: '. . . we have refused all the demands of the Parlement of Dijon', read a brusque note on the Parlement's supplicating letter to the controller general. When First President Faucon de Ris of Rouen also asked for first degree nobility for his tribunal, he met with an identical rebuff.[48]

As for modest concessions, a parlement might be allowed to revise its internal organization and procedures; or the government might promise that the royal council would show greater restraint in transferring lawsuits from one parlement to another, easing an old parlementary grievance. The king might also grant dispensations from the minimum-age requirements for office (twenty-five for councillors) or the restrictions on the number of judges in a tribunal who could be related by birth or by marriage. But it had always conferred these dispensations, upon petition by individuals, and kept general concessions to a minimum.[49]

The government might have revoked the *fixation*, to which the parlements had objected so strenuously when Colbert imposed it in 1665. After all, higher prices now served the king's financial interests. The creation edict of October 1689 for the Parlement of Rennes indeed terminated the *fixation* for that tribunal and restored the free market for offices there, and the Parlement of Bordeaux got the same concession. The controller general considered ending the *fixation* for the Parlement of Paris but chose instead to rescind only the deposit requirement, not the *fixation* itself, for reasons that he never explained. So Colbert's principle of price ceilings, although weakened, remained nominally in place except in Rennes and Bordeaux (where office prices declined anyway, all through the 1690s). Accommodation, even when it made sense, went only so far.[50]

Unlike most of the concessions to which Louis XIII had eventually agreed, those of Louis XIV did not deprive the government of any money it expected from the sale of office. If a parlement preferred, the government would create more or fewer councillor offices, as opposed to *présidents à mortier*, shuffling offices from one category to the other. But a parlement could not hope to reduce the final sum that Pontchartrain, in consultation with the intendants, had decided that the sale should produce. As he informed the Parlement of Rennes in 1689, '... the king has decided that he wants 500,000 livres ... [and] leaves it up to you to choose the means'.

A parlement could avoid an office creation only by paying the government the money it wanted in a lump sum, as a 'redemption'. The Parlement of Grenoble redeemed a few offices in this way; and the Parlement of Aix even scored a financial coup. In June 1693, the king created two *présidents à mortier*, six councillors and one *procureur général* at Aix; the sale was expected to gross 580,000 livres. But in July the king accepted a redemption offer of 440,000 livres from the Parlement, payable in three equal instalments over eighteen months. The difference between those sums was about equal to the commission of the *traitants*, a portion of which the Parlement also paid as a supplement, so the government lost nothing on the transaction and the *traitants* gained some compensation. The Parlement sold all the offices itself in one of the few markets where demand was still strong and made a profit of more than 100,000 livres, much of which it used to retire debt for the *augmentations de gages* of 1692! But while the Parlement of Aix actually profited from the sale of offices, no other tribunal enjoyed a comparable success.[51]

Summary

From the administration of Colbert through to that of Pontchartrain, the government steadily encroached upon the vested interests of the magistrates

Table 4 *Sale of new offices in parlements, 1689–1695*

Office	Judges 1665	New offices	Price per office (£)	Total sales (£)	Judges 1695	% Incr. from sales
Oct. 1689 Rennes						
PP	1				1	
PM	7	1	140,000	140,000	8	14.29
PE	4				4	
C(O)	40	4	80,000	320,000	44	10.00
C(N)	40	2	45,000	90,000	42	5.00
PR	2				2	
CR	10				10	
AG	2				2	
PG	1				1	
Totals	107	7		550,000	114	6.54
Sep. 1690 Bordeaux						
PP	1				1	
PM	7	1	80,000	80,000	9	12.50
PE	4				4	
CH	0				0	
C(L)	65	6	40,000	240,000	77	8.45
C(C)	7				7	
PR	2				2	
CR	8				8	
AG	2				2	
PG	1				1	
Totals	97	7		320,000	111	6.73
Nov. 1690 Paris						
PP	1				1	
PM	7	2	450,000	900,000	9	28.57
PE	10				10	
C(L)	162	16	100,000	1,600,000	178	9.88
C(C)	22				22	
PR	4				4	
CR	28				28	
AG	2	1	350,000	350,000	3	50.00
PG	1				1	
Totals	237	19		2,850,000	256	8.02
Feb. 1691 Toulouse						
PP	1				1	
PM	6	2	120,000	240,000	9	28.57

Table 4 (*cont.*)

Office	Judges 1665	New offices	Price per office (£)	Total sales (£)	Judges 1695	% Incr. from sales
Feb. 1691 Toulouse (*cont.*)						
PE	4				6	50.00
C(L)	93	2	35,000	70,000	93	
C(C)	6				6	
PR	2				2	
CR	11	1	25,000	25,000	12	
AG	2				2	
PG	1				1	
commissions of Pres. Enquêtes		2	30,000	60,000		
Totals	126	5		395,000	132	4.76
Mar. 1691 Rouen						
PP	1				1	
PM	7	2	150,000	300,000	9	28.57
C(L)	66	7	50,000	350,000	73	10.61
C(C)	17				17	
PR	2				2	
CR	12	2	30,000	60,000	14	16.67
AG	2				2	
PG	1				1	
Totals	108	11		710,000	119	10.19
Mar. 1691 Dijon						
PP	1				1	
PM	8	2	130,000	260,000	10	25.00
CH	2				2	
C(L)	51	3	66,000	198,000	54	5.88
C(C)	5				5	
PR	2				2	
CR	9	1	45,000	45,000	10	11.11
AG	2				2	
PG	1				1	
Totals	81	6		503,000	87	7.41
May 1691, Mar. 1694, Nov. 1695 Metz						
PP	1				1	
PM	10	2	50,000	100,000	12	20.00
CH	2				2	

Table 4 (*cont.*)

Office	Judges 1665	New offices	Price per office (£)	Total sales (£)	Judges 1695	% Incr. from sales
May 1691, Mar. 1694, Nov. 1695			Metz (*cont.*)			
C(L)	64	4	28,000	112,000	74	5.71
C(C)	6				6	
C(P)	6				0	
PR	0	1	25,000	25,000	1	N/A
CR	0	10	20,000	200,000	10	N/A
AG	2				2	
PG	1				1	
Totals	92	17		437,000	109	18.48
Nov. 1691 Pau[d]						
PP	1				1	
PM	3	1	45,000	45,000	7	33.33
C	22	6	30,000	180,000	46	27.27
AG	2				2	
PG	1				1	
Totals	29	7		225,000	57	24.14
Aug. 1692 Grenoble						
PP	1				1	
PM	3				3	
PE	6				6	
CH	1				1	
C(L)	47	3	?66000	?198000	50	
C(C)	4				4	
AG	2	1	?50000	?50000	3	
PG	1				1	
Totals	65	4		362,000	69	6.15
Jun. 1693 Aix						
PP	1				1	
PM	7	2	120,000	240,000	9	28.57
PE	3				3	
C(L)	49	6	50,000	300,000£	55	12.24
C(C)	1				1	
C(G)	1				1	
AG	2	1	40,000	40,000	3	50.00
PG	2				2	
Totals	66	9		440,000	75	13.64
Grand totals	1,008	92		6,792,000	1,128	9.12

Table 4 (*cont.*)

Abbreviations: PP: First (Premier) President; PM: *président à mortier*; PE: *président des enquêtes*; C(L): lay councillor; C(C): clerical councillor; C(O) and C (NO): *originaire* and *non-originaire* councillors in the Parlement of Rennes; CH: *chevalier d'honneur*: an office which existed in only a few parlements before 1702, when it became more general – it resembled that of councillor but was reserved for members of the old nobility, a concession to noble complaints against the social implications of venal office; PR: *président aux requêtes*; CR: *conseiller et commissaire aux requêtes*; AG: *avocat général*; PG: *procureur général*.

Notes:
a The 'Judges 1695' column also reflects the union to the Parlement in 1679 of the Chambre de l'Édit, a chamber previously reserved for Protestants.
b Explanations are necessary for the anomalies in the 'PM', 'PE', and 'C(L)' entries in the 'Judges 1695' column. At some point in the 1690s, a ninth *président à mortier* was created and took his seat; but I have no record of that creation and sale, so I do not associate it with the edict of February 1691. Two sitting councillors purchased the commissions of *président des enquêtes* created in 1691 and therefore moved from the 'C(L)' into the 'PE' category; but the creation of these commissions does not count as the creation of new offices.
c The 'C(P)' entry in 'Judges 1665' reflects the number of offices reserved for Protestant councillors; these were subsequently converted to 'C(L)' status and so appear in 'Judges 1695'.
d In addition to the office creations of November 1691, the government merged the Chambre des Comptes of Pau with the Parlement, thus requiring larger numbers in the 'Judges 1695' column than office creations per se would entail.
e Includes redemption of offices by Parlement
f (For the reasons given in the entries for Bordeaux, Toulouse, and Pau, the columns entitled 'Judges 1665', 'New offices' and 'Judges 1695' are not intended to total.

Sources: Rennes: BN, *Actes R.*, 23,614 (624): edict of October 1689; AN, P 3317: 'nouvelles créations' chapitre; Bordeaux: AN, P 3318: 'nouvelles créations' chapitre; Bezons, intendant, Bordeaux, to Pontchartrain, 10 February 1691, AN, G7, 135; Paris: BN, *Actes R.*, F. 23,614 (885): edict of November 1690; AN, P 3317 and P 3318: 'nouvelles créations'; Toulouse: AN, G7 1350: edict of February 1691; AN, P 3318 and 3319: 'nouvelles créations'; Rouen: AN, G7 493: edict of March 1691; AN, P 3318 and 3324: 'nouvelles créations'; Faucon de Ris, first president, Rouen, to Pontchartrain, 10 April 1691, AN, G7 493; Dijon: BM, Dijon, MS 769 (Registres du Parlement): 4 April 1691, p. 29: edict of March 1691; AN, P 3318: 'nouvelles créations'; Metz: BN, *Actes R.*, F. 23,614 (989): edict of May 1691; *ibid.*, F. 23,615 (497): edict of March 1694; *ibid.*, F. 23,615 (730): edict of November 1695; AN, P 3318, 3322, 3323, and 3326: 'nouvelles créations'; Pau: BN, *Actes R.*, F. 23,614 (1197): edict of November 1691; AN, P 3319 and 3324: 'nouvelles créations'. This edict also joined the Chambre des Comptes and the Parlement into a single tribunal, increasing the Parlement from 29 to 57 judges; Grenoble: BN, *Actes R.*, F. 21,776 (80): edict of August 1692. The Parlement redeemed a *président à mortier* for 90,000 livres and a *conseiller clerc* for 24,000 livres. The prices for the other offices are my estimates; Aix: BN, *Actes R.*, F. 23,615 (310): edict of June 1693.

Table 5 *Conversion to venality and sale of offices, 1692–1693: Parlements of Besançon and Tournai*

Office Aug. 1692, May 1693	Conver. 1692	Price office (£)	Conver. totals (£)	Sale 1693	Price office (£)	Sale totals (£)	Total offices	Total yield (£)
Parlement of Besançon								
PP	1	N/A					1	
PM	3	24,000	72,000	2	36,000	72,000	5	144,000
CH	2	9,000	18,000	1	(?)9000	9,000	3	27,000
C(L)	29	9,000	261,000	15	15,000	225,000	44	486,000
C(C)	2	9,000	18,000				2	18,000
AG	2	12,000	24,000				2	24,000
PG	1	N/A					1	
Totals	40		393,000	18		306,000	58	699,000
Mar. 1693 Parlement of Tournai								
PP	1	N/A					1	0
PM	2	37,500	75,000	1	40,000	40,000	3	115,000
CH	2	N/A					2	0
C(L)	16	25,000	400,000	6	30,000	180,000	22	580,000
C(C)	2	20,000	40,000				2	40,000
AG	1	25,000	25,000				1	25,000
PG	1	45,000	45,000				1	45,000
Totals	25		585,000	7		220,000	32	805,000
Grand totals, Besançon and Tournai							90	1,504,000

Abbreviations: See Table 4.
Sources: Besançon: BN, *Actes R.*, F. 23,615 (112): edict of August 1692; Boisot, *procureur général*, to Pontchartrain, 7 May 1693, AN, G7 277. See also AN, G7, 1342: MS 41, 'Mémoire d'Observations', c. 1704; Gresset, *Vénalité des Offices*, pp. 43–44. Tournai: BN, *Actes R.*, F. 23,615 (229): edict of March 1693, and Z. Thoissy 11 (ff. 366r–367v), edict of May 1689; AN, P 3321: 'nouvelles créations .'; AN, G7, 360: 'Soumission faite au Roy par les anciens conseillers au Parlement de Tournay', 1693–1694.

in their venal offices. In gratifying contrast with the past, these administrations proved strong enough to require the judges to pay forced loans, or *augmentations de gages*, to secure admission to the *paulette*. Pontchartrain even collected 'voluntary' *augmentations de gages*, which no other administration had done to any significant degree. Pontchartrain also created and sold new offices in the parlements and, for the first time, did so without incurring opposition, delay or the need to compromise. Putting his sums together, the 'voluntary' *augmentations de gages* of 1689 yielded 3.15 million livres, the regular *augmentations de gages* of 1692 produced 6.11 million livres, and the sale of offices of 1689–1695 brought in 7.48 million livres, a total of 16.74 millions (Tables 4 and 5). There can be no doubt that this was far more than any government had ever collected from the parlements in any comparable period of time. For the magistrates, this meant rising indebtedness, the mortgaging of their offices and the decline of office values. The government of Louis XIV, so far from respecting the venal interests of the parlements, as revisionist historians have argued, manipulated and exploited those offices to a degree that exceeded the abilities of its predecessors. It would be even more successful in the War of the Spanish Succession; and the financial difficulties of the judges would increase.

Notes

1 Mousnier, *Vénalité*, pp. 8–10, 95–116; Howell A. Lloyd, 'The Political Thought of Charles Loyseau (1564–1627)', *European Studies Review* 11 (January 1981), 53–82; Koenraad Walter Swart, *Sale of Offices in the Seventeenth Century* (The Hague, 1949).

2 AD, I-V, IBc 1 (Remonstrance of June 1666, Parlement of Rennes); AN, G7, 1342 (Remonstrance of Parlement of Besançon, 21 November 1702); BN, *Fonds fr.*, 16,524: representations of Parlement of Paris, 1704, ff. 69r–71r; Richelieu, *Testament Politique*, p. 238; BN, *Fonds fr.*, 7,009 ('Mémoire adressée à Louis XIV sur l'état politique . . . de France', 1688), f. 19; Ranum, *Fronde*, pp. 18, 76–77.

3 Lavisse, *Le Roi. Colbert*, pp. 361–364; Mousnier, *Vénalité*, p. 85; Moote, *Revolt of the Judges*, pp. 367, 374; Parker, *Making of Absolutism*, pp. 140–141, 148; Mettam, *Power and Faction*, pp. 111, 114–115, 155; Beik, *Absolutism and Society*, pp. 279–339 (by implication). Hamscher, *Parlement of Paris*, pp. 62–81, needs no emendation.

4 Glenn Joseph Ames, *Colbert, Mercantilism, and the French Quest for Asian Trade* (DeKalb, Ill., 1996), pp. 18–26; Cole, *Colbert and Mercantilism*, I, 478–501; BN, *Actes R.*, F.23,612 (769): declaration of 27 August 1664.

5 BN, *Actes R.*, F. 23,613 (15): declaration of 28 February 1669; Oppède, first president, Aix, to Colbert, 1 June 1669, BN, *Mél. Colbert*, 153, ff. 53rv–54v; *ibid.*, 151, ff. 81rv–82r (delinquents in the Parlement of Bordeaux); AD, I-V, IBb (Registres secrets, Rennes) 232: 2 and 9 April 1669 and 233: 16 December 1670; Mousnier, *Vénalité*, pp. 286, 658.

6 BN, *Actes R.*, F.23,613 (630): declaration of 27 October 1674.

7 Colbert to intendants, 18 December 1674, *Lettres*, II, pt. i, 368, and to d'Argouges, first president, Rennes, 28 December 1674, *ibid.*, p. 369.

8 BM, Aix, MS 955 (Délibérations du Parlement): 9 January 1675, ff. 112rv; BM, Dijon, MS 768 (Registres du Parlement): 10 January 1675, pp. 325–326; AD, Moselle, B 278 (Registres secrets, Metz): 17 January 1675, f. 82rv; AD, I-V, IBb 243 (Registres secrets, Rennes): 8 January 1675, f. 87rv; BM, Rouen, MS Y214/26 (Registres secrets): 18 January 1675, p. 274, and BN, *Fonds fr.*, 22,455 (Histoire du Parlement de Rouen), p. 359. The declaration is in BN, *Actes R.*, F. 23,613 (636); AN, P 3352 (Quittances des augmentations de gages . . . 1675): payments from the provincial parlements. For the Parlement of Paris, see AN, E 480/B: decree of 31 December 1674, no. 23, and E 485/B-486/A: decree of 31 May 1675, no. 33, and BN, *Mél. Colbert*, 249, 'Estat des augmentations de gages. 1676', ff. 33lr-397r. Colbert expressed his satisfaction with Rouen's *augmentations de gages* in his letter to Le Blanc, intendant, Rouen, 30 November 1675, BN, *Fonds fr.*, 8,751, f. 7rv.

9 Quoted in John Lough, ed., *France Observed in the Seventeenth Century by British Travellers* (Boston, 1985), p. 88.

10 Mousnier, *Vénalité*, pp. 284, 293, 300. (In 1638, the government increased its appraisals of office values by one-third, the first such change since the inception of the *paulette* in 1604.)

11 BN, *Actes R.*, F. 23,614, nos 134 and 138: edict and declaration of October 1683; F. 23,615, nos 143 and 151: edict and declaration of September 1692; F. 23,616, nos 845 and 853: edict and declaration of August 1701.

12 Mémoire présenté au Roy par M. le Pelletier . . . pour luy rendre compte de son administration', BN, *Fonds fr.*, 7750; AN, X1A 8402 (Conseil secret): 24 November 1683, f. 464v; BM, Aix, MS 955 (Délibérations du Parlement): 1 December 1683, ff. 288v–289r; BM, Dijon, MS 768 (Registres du Parlement): 1 December 1683, pp. 566–567; AD, Moselle, B 296* (Registres secrets, Metz), 28 December 1683, f. 47r, and 3 January 1684, ff. 50v–51v. For the compliance of the Parlements of Bordeaux, Grenoble and Rouen, see AN, P 3359 (Registre . . . des quittances d'augmentations de gages . . . 1683, 1684); and, for Pau, see P 3365. See also Brûlart, first president, Dijon, to Le Peletier, controller general, 20 December 1683, BM, Dijon, MS 542, ff. 198rv; Smedley-Weill, *Intendants de Louis XIV*, pp. 230–231.

13 Pontchartrain, controller general, to Harlay, first president, Paris, 30 August 1692, BN, *Fonds fr.*, 17,424, f. 29r; Chamillart, controller general, to Harlay, 26 April 1701, *ibid.*, 17,436.

14 Rachapt de l'annuel', memorandum, 1708, in AN, G7, 1325; AN, E 613: decree of 10 February 1693, no. 40 (the Enquêtes chamber); Moote, *Revolt of the Judges*, p. 44 and ff., treated the 'jeopardy' of venal office under Louis XIII.

15 Le Peletier, controller general, to intendants, 5 August 1689, AN, G7, 5; , *Actes R.*, F. 23,614 (585): edict of July 1689 for *augmentations de gages*.

16 Estat général des offices sujets au Rachat du prest et annuel', c. 1709, and 'Rachapt de l'annuel', 1708, in AN, G7, 1325; 'Mémoire touchant ce qui se peut faire pour les offices des compagnies supérieures . . .', c. 1700, BN, *Fonds fr.*, 16,524 (Harlay), f. 228r; and 'Estat des augmentations de gages', BN, *Fonds fr.*, 7,727, ff. 5r–6v. For the forced loans of other corporate groups, see E. Laurain, *Essai sur les présidiaux* (Paris, 1896), pp. 64–66; David D. Bien, 'The *secrétaires du roi*: Absolutism, Corps

and Privilege under the Ancien Régime', in *Vom Ancien Régime zur Französischen Revolution*, ed. Ernst Hinrichs (Göttingen, 1978), pp. 161–163.

17 John J. Hurt, 'The Parlement of Brittany in the Reign of Louis XIV' (Ph.D. diss., University of North Carolina, 1969), 198–240; Jean-Claude Paulhet, 'Les parlementaires toulousains à la fin du XVIIe siècle', *Annales du Midi* 76 (April 1964), 199–200; Maurice Virieux, 'Une enquête sur le Parlement de Toulouse en 1718', *Annales du Midi* 87 (1975), 47–49; Beik, *Absolutism and Society*, pp. 53, 79; Kettering, *Parlement of Aix*, pp. 231–232; Dewald, *Formation of a Provincial Nobility*, pp. 114–116, 125; F. Momplot, 'Recherches sociales sur les conseillers au Parlement de Paris, 1685 à 1690', (mémoire maîtrise, histoire, Paris IV, 1970); François Bluche, *Les magistrats du Parlement de Paris au XVIII siècle* (Paris, 1960), pp. 151–152, nn. 117, 128, 129, 131; Jean-Pierre Labatut, *Les ducs et pairs de France au XVIIe siècle. Étude sociale* (Paris, 1972), p. 324.

18 John J. Hurt, 'Les offices au Parlement de Bretagne: aspects financiers', *Revue d'histoire moderne et contemporaine* 23 (January–March 1976), 12, 23–24; Daniel Zolla, 'Les variations du revenu et du prix des terres en France au XVIIe et XVIIIe siècles', *Annales de l'école libre des sciences politiques* 8 (1893), 299–326, 439–461, 686–705; 9 (1894), 194–216, 417–432; Pierre Goubert, *Beauvais et le Beauvaisis de 1600 à 1730* (2 vols; Paris, 1960), I, 377–395, 411–419, 459–461, 493–512, 520–532; Emmanuel Le Roy Ladurie, *Les paysans de Languedoc* (2 vols; Paris, 1966), I, 511–533, 585–595, 637–638; Jean-Marc Moriceau, *Les fermiers de l'Île-de-France* (Paris, 1994), pp. 515–529, 549–555.

19 Jean-Paul Poisson, 'De quelques nouvelles utilisations des sources notariales en histoire économique (XVIIe–XXe siècle)', *Revue Historique* 249 (January–March 1973), 16–17. It is rightly argued that the financial services of the notaries reduced the need in France for a central bank modeled after that of England.

20 BM, Aix, MS 955 (Délibérations du Parlement): 1 December 1683, ff. 288v–289r; MS 977 (Délibérations), 31 March 1702, ff. 130v–132rv; BM, Dijon, MS 768 (Registres du Parlement): 1 December 1683, pp. 566–567, and 8 January 1684, p. 569; MS 769 (Registres), 22 September and 20 December 1692, pp. 64–65 and 76; AN, P 3379 (Augmentations de gages . . . 1692); BN, *Fonds fr.*, 16,524: notes, c. 1703, f. 214r, show the borrowing *en corps* of the Grand-Chambre of the Parlement of Paris.

21 La Tresne, first president, Bordeaux, to Chamillart, controller general, 17 September 1701, AN, G7, 139; AD, Isère, 2B4* (Livre rouge, Grenoble), f. 272rv; AD, Moselle, B 308 (Registres secrets, Metz), 13 September 1689, ff. 20r–21v; Picquet, *greffier en chef*, Rennes, to magistrates, 3 October 1692, AD, I-V (Rennes), B (Parlement) *Registre littéraire*, f. 22; BN, *Fonds fr.*, 22,455 (Rouen), 5 December 1692, p. 442; Morant, first president, Toulouse, to Pontchartrain, controller general, 24 September 1692, AN, G7, 301. The registers in AN, P 3359, 3361, 3381, 3386 and 3393 provide the names of the creditors of the judges, typically merchants, barristers, widows and 'bourgeois of Paris' (an elastic term), a social identity similar to that detected in Claude Michaud, 'Notariat et sociologie de la rente à Paris au XVIIe siècle', *Annales. E.S.C.* 32 (1977), 1154–1187.

22 BN, *Actes R.*, F. 23,614 (134): October 1683; F. 23,615 (143): September 1692; F. 23,616 (845): August 1701; Loyseau, *Cinq Livres*, Bk III, chs. vi, viii.

23 BN, *Actes R.*, F. 23,614 (87): edict of February 1683.

24 Pontchartrain, chancellor, to du Vigier, *procureur général*, Bordeaux, 4 August 1709, BN, *Manuscrits fr.*, 21,130; AD, Gironde, 1B 30 (Registre d'enregistrement), 1693–1710: examples of office seizures; Hurt, 'Parlement of Brittany in the Reign of Louis XIV', pp. 225–230.

25 See Colbert's circular letter to intendants in BN, *Clairambault*, 462, 14 July 1679; Hamscher, *Parlement of Paris*, pp. 65–66; Colbert, 'Mémoire pour l'instruction du Dauphin', *Lettres*, II, pt. i, 'Introduction', p. ccxv.

26 Controller General Chamillart to First President Harlay of Paris, 2 November and 3 and 6 December 1699: BN, *Fonds fr.*, 17,436; Chamillart's correspondence with the provincial first presidents is in AN, G7, 1769–1773.

27 David Bien, 'Offices, Corps, and a System of State Credit: The Uses of Privilege under the Ancien Régime', in *The Political Culture of the Old Regime*, ed. Keith M. Baker (Oxford, 1987).

28 Mousnier, *Vénalité*, pp. 360–362; Dewald, *Formation of a Provincial Nobility*, pp. 138–140; Kettering, *Judicial Politics*, pp. 221–224; André Germond, 'Les parlementaires Bretons de 1661 à 1720', (Diplôme d'Études Supérieures, Faculté des Lettres, Université de Haute-Bretagne, c. 1964, Rennes 2); La Roche-Flavin, *Treize livres*, Bk II, ch. xxii. The reform edict of December 1665 acknowledged that offices represented 'la meilleure partie' of office-holders' wealth.

29 William Doyle, *Venality. The Sale of Offices in Eighteenth-Century France* (Oxford, 1996), pp. 8–10; Salmon, *Society in Crisis*, pp. 152–154, 220–222; Davis Bitton, 'History and Politics: The Controversy over the Sale of Offices in Early Seventeenth Century France', in *Action and Conviction in Early Modern Europe. Essays in Honor of E.H. Harbison*, ed. Theodore K. Rabb and Jerrold E. Seigel (Princeton, NJ, 1969), pp. 390–403; Mousnier, *Vénalité*, pp. 35–36, 87–89, 645–662; Loyseau, *Cinq Livres*, Bk III, ch. i.

30 États et évaluation', 1665; BN, *Actes R.*, F. 23,612 (842): edict of December 1665 (also in Isambert, *Recueil général*, XVIII, 67–69); Hamscher, *Parlement of Paris*, pp. 157–164.

31 États et évaluation', 1665, lists estimated office prices. For true market prices in Rennes and Aix in the 1660s, see Germond, 'Parlementaires bretons', and Kettering, *Judicial Politics*, p. 224. For examples of *fixation* prices, see the edict of 1665 (Parlement of Paris); AD, I-V (Rennes), 1Ba 22, ff. 395–396: edict of December 1665; AM, Bordeaux, MS 795 (Registre secret): 16 January 1666, pp. 198–199; Eugène Lapierre, *Le Parlement de Toulouse* (Paris, 1875), p. 35. For the hostility of the Parlement of Paris to the reform edict, see ch. 1, this volume, pp. 21–22; for provincial opposition, see Hurt, 'Parlement of Brittany in the Reign of Louis XIV', pp. 122–124; BM, Aix, MS 975 (Délibérations du Parlement): 5 January 1666, f. 377r; AM, Bordeaux, MS 795 (Registre secret): 16–19 January 1666, ff. 196–201; AD, S-M (Rouen), IB 195 (Registres secrets): 7 January 1661, ff. 49v–50r; *avocats généraux*, Parlement of Rouen, to Colbert, 4 January 1666, BN, *Mél. Colbert*, 136, f. 7v.

32 Hamscher, *Parlement*, pp. 21–22; AD, I-V (Rennes), 2Eb (La Bourdonnaye) 25: Berthou de Kerverzio papers.

33 Mettam, *Power and Faction*, p. 260, incorrectly wrote that the *fixation* ceilings 'ipso facto lowered the amount which had to be paid for the *annuel*, the yearly payment under the terms of the *paulette*, because this was calculated on the basis of

one-sixtieth of the official value'. In fact, the *fixation* did not affect in any way the appraised value of offices upon which magistrates paid their *paulette*. See Mousnier, *Vénalité*, p. 161, and 'Mémoire sur l'évaluation des offices sujets aux Revenus Casuels', c. 1715, AN, G7, 1325. For the venal office legislation, see BN, *Actes R.*, F. 23,613 (21): edict of March 1669 and (237): declaration of November 1671.

34 Ormesson, *Journal*, II, 614–616, 627; AN, E 461/B-462/A: decree of 4 April 1673 in favour of the heirs of *président à mortier* de Brie. For enforcement of the deposit requirement, see BN, *Fonds fr.*, 7659 (Bienfaits du Roi, 1686), f. 5r, and Le Peletier, controller general, to Sève, first president, Metz, 25 June 1687, Arthur-Michel de Boislisle, ed., *Correspondance des contrôleurs généraux des finances avec les intendants des provinces* (3 vols; Paris, 1874–1897), I, 109.

35 Hurt, 'Les offices au Parlement de Bretagne', pp. 22–24, treats capital appreciation.

36 Clamageran, *Impôt*, II, 663–669; Doyle, *Venality*, pp. 23–24; Forbonnais, *Recherches et considérations*, III, 96–100; AN, P 3298: 'nouvelles créations'. Moote, *Revolt of the Judges*, p. 374, and Roland Mousnier, 'Conclusion', *Dix-septième siècle* 122 (1979), 77, suggested that Louis XIV never created offices in the parlements.

37 Doyle, *Venality*, pp. 26–37; Bonney, *King's Debts*, pp. 300, 317.

38 BN, *Actes R.*, 23,614 (624): edict of October 1689; AN, P 3317: 'nouvelles créations' chapitre (new offices in Rennes); Pontchartrain, controller general, to Bezons, intendant, Bordeaux, 31 October 1689, Boislisle, *Correspondance*, I, 200.

39 AN, P 3318: 'nouvelles créations', (edict of September 1690); Bezons, intendant, Bordeaux, to Pontchartrain, 10 February 1691, AN, G7, 135.

40 The increase of 9.12 percent is based on a corps of 1,008 parlementary judges in 1665, as established by Colbert's inventory. It is not clear whether the *traitants* also collected the *remise en dehors*, the surcharge of 10 percent (two *sols* per livre).

41 Louis XIV created the Parlement of Besançon in 1674–1676 and gave it jurisdiction over the newly conquered province of Franche-Comté: A. Estignard, *Le Parlement de Franche-Comté de son installation à Besançon à sa suppression* (2 vols; Paris, 1892), I, 30–100. The *conseil souverain* of Tournai became a parlement in 1686 with jurisdiction over Flanders: BN, *Fonds fr.* 16,873: 'Questions . . . qui regardent le Conseil Souverain de Tournay', ff. 299rv–301r. When the Treaty of Utrecht (1713) awarded the city of Tournai to the Austrian Habsburgs, Louis XIV moved the Parlement to Douai.

42 AN, X1A 8407 (Conseil secret): 23 November 1690; BM, Dijon, MS 769 (Registres du Parlement): 4 April 1691, p. 29; BM, Aix, MS 955 (Délibérations du Parlement): 19 June 1693, f. 424v; Morant, first president, Toulouse, to Pontchartrain, 7 March 1691, AN, G7, 300; (Brûlart gave a similar report for the Parlement of Dijon: letter to Pontchartrain, 5 April 1691, AN, G7, 157); for the Parlement of Grenoble, see BN, *Actes R.*, F. 21,776 (80).

43 BM, Dijon, MS 769 (Registres du Parlement): 4 April, 13 June and 18 July 1691; 13 February, 12 March and 25 March 1692; Metz: AN, P 3318, 3322, 3323, and 3326; BM, Aix, MS 976 (Délibérations du Parlement): 8 October 1693, f. 431r; Le Bret, first president, Grenoble, to Pontchartrain, 14 April 1693, AN, G7, 462; AD, I-V, IBb (Registres secrets, Rennes) 274: 13 May and 22 May 1690 and AN, P 3317; Maurice Gresset, *L'introduction de la vénalité des offices en Franche-Comté* (Besançon, 1989), pp. 57–61, 74, 113, 118; AN, G7, 260: 'Sousmission faite au Roy par les anciens Conseillers du Parlement de Tournay . . .'; AN, P 3321: 'nouvelles créations'

chapitre. The government screened candidates for *président à mortier* and *procureur général* for political reliability, but the other offices were not considered important enough for political scrutiny: Pontchartrain to Harlay, first president, Paris, 30 October 1690, BN, *Fonds fr.*, 16,524, f. 10v.

44 Morant, first president, Toulouse, to Pontchartrain, controller general, 26 March 1692, AN, G7, 300; Bâville, intendant, Toulouse, to Pontchartrain, 21 May 1692, *ibid.*; AN P 3318: 'nouvelles créations': 24 August 1691 and 5 January 1692, Parlement of Toulouse; Bezons, intendant, Bordeaux, to Pontchartrain, 24 November 1691, AN, G7, 724; Aulède, first president, Bordeaux, to Pontchartrain, 24 November 1691, Boislisle, *Correspondance*, I, 267; AN, P 3318: 'nouvelles créations': entries of 9 March, 6 April and 12 May 1691, Parlement of Bordeaux; Larcher, intendant, Rouen, to Pontchartrain, 5 September 1691, AN, G7, 493; Montholon, first president, Rouen, to Pontchartrain, 18 June 1692, G7, 494; Le Camus, lieutenant civil, Rouen, to Pontchartrain, 28 September 1694, AN, G7, 494; AN, P 3318: 'nouvelles créations': 26 and 30 June 1691; P 3324: 'nouvelles créations': 26 July 1697, Rouen.

45 Cambon, aspiring councillor in the Parlement of Toulouse, to Pontchartrain, 5 November 1693, AN, G7, 30; Bezons, intendant, Bordeaux, to Pontchartrain, 3 July 1691, AN, G7, 135; Larcher, intendant, Rouen, to Pontchartrain, 5 September 1691, AN, G7, 493.

46 Chamillart, controller general, to Harlay, first president, Paris, 28 November 1702, BN, *Fonds fr.*, 16,524.

47 BN, *Actes R.*, F. 23,614 (885): edict of November 1690; Harlay, 'Mémoire touchant ce qui se peut faire pour les officiers des compagnies supérieures', c. 1700, BN, *Fonds fr.*, 16,524, f. 229r; Bluche, *Magistrats du Parlement de Paris*, pp. 82–83.

48 Brûlart, first president, Dijon, to Pontchartrain, 15 February 1691, BM, Dijon, MS 542, ff. 326v–328r; 'Mémoire sur la proposition des nouvelles créations', *ibid.*, ff. 328r–329r, AN, G7, 157; Faucon de Ris, first president, Rouen, to Pontchartrain, 24 and 31 March 1691, AN, G7, 493.

49 The royal council transferred lawsuits from one parlement to another to preclude conflicts of interest between litigants and judges; but the latter still found such transfers, called evocations, offensive: Hamscher, *Conseil privé*, pp. 69–79.

50 BN, *Actes R.*, F. 23,614 (624): edict of October 1689 (Rennes) and *ibid.* (885): edict of November 1690 (Paris). For Bordeaux, see Bezons, intendant, to Pontchartrain, controller general, 10 February 1691, AN, G7, 135. See also Pontchartrain to Harlay, first president, Paris, 30 October 1690, Paris, BN, *Fonds fr.*, 16,524 (Harlay), ff. 10r–11r, and 'Mémoire sur la proposition des nouvelles créations' (Parlement of Dijon), AN, G7, 57.

51 Le Bret, first president, Grenoble, to Pontchartrain, 14 April 1693; BM, Aix, MS 976 (Délibérations du Parlement): 24 July 1693, ff. 426v–427v; undated letter from Pontchartrain, ff. 432v–433r; MS 977: 14 June 1695, ff. 5–6; Balthasar de Clapiers-Collonques, *Chronologie des officers des Cours souveraines de Provence* (Aix-en-Provence, 1909), pp. 24–25, 65–66, 117–118.

4

The ordeal of
the parlementaires

To fund the War of the Spanish Succession (1702–1714), Michel Chamillart, the controller general, increased current taxes, invented new taxes, borrowed heavily and manipulated the currency, the customary methods long called into use by hard-pressed finance ministers.[1] Like Pontchartrain, but with greater frequency, he also extracted large sums from the parlements; and his successor, Nicolas Desmarets, continued to pursue them financially. Long before the war ended, the magistrates had reached the limits of their financial endurance, with their offices heavily mortgaged and dwindling in value and office income drying up. On the subject of venality, the late reign of Louis XIV indeed subjected the magistrates to a grinding ordeal.

The *Augmentations de gages* of 1702–1703

In 1701, as preparations for the war began, the magistrates were busy paying the government 5.67 million livres in *augmentations de gages* for the renewal of the *droit annuel* (chapter 3, Table 1), their money going directly into various war-related treasuries. Based on past experience, they had reason to expect a financial respite of several years. But in late 1702 Chamillart surprised the tribunals when, in an unprecedented move, he demanded a new *augmentations de gages* in the same amount as in 1701 – another 5.67 million livres. To soften the blow, he set a higher rate of interest, the 16th *denier* (6.25 per cent), but the whole project took the parlements aback and led to somewhat mixed results.

Chamillart began by asking First President Harlay to persuade the Parlement of Paris to accept the *augmentations de gages* voluntarily, intending to use its example to induce the provincial parlements to fall into line. As a royal client par excellence, Harlay could be trusted, if anyone could, to serve the king's interests. Surprisingly, however, the first president protested strongly, his first demur on a financial issue, picturing his magistrates as destitute, having sold their 'silver plate and other movables' to satisfy the *augmentations de gages* of 1701. The first president countered with an offer to have the Parlement pay half of the sum it paid then.[2]

Chamillart rejected any compromise. The Parlement of Paris, he repeated, must provide as much money in 1702 as it had in 1701. When Harlay continued to object, the controller general told him curtly that if the magistrates did not pay in full, the king would create new offices to make up the shortfall. This, as he reminded Harlay, would damage their financial interests even more. On 28 November 1702, a defeated Harlay dutifully endorsed the *augmentations de gages* before the assembled chambers of the Parlement; and the magistrates accepted the *augmentations de gages* under the threat of a new office creation.[3]

Chamillart immediately set to work on the provincial tribunals, citing the nominal consent of the Parlement of Paris as an example to them all; and he repeated his threat to create new offices if the provincials did not agree to pay the new loan in full. Most agreed to pay the sums demanded soon after they received Chamillart's letter; those which demurred did so in vain, with the exception of Metz. Because the Treaty of Ryswick (1697) had taken away some of its territory, Metz obtained a reduction, bringing the anticipated yield of the new loan to 5.4 millions. Overall, the controller general had reason to be pleased. No finance minister before him had coerced the parlements into accepting an *augmentations de gages* of this size without the club of the *paulette* renewal.[4]

As favourable auspices, several tribunals paid for their *augmentations de gages* at once. The reliable magistrates of Aix borrowed their money within weeks and even helped the Parlement of Grenoble to find loans in Aix, permitting the latter also to settle its account swiftly. Similarly, the Parlements of Dijon, Metz, Besançon and Tournai all kept to reasonable schedules in raising their funds. But total collections in these six middle-sized parlements came to only 1.35 million, just 25 percent of the expected 5.4 millions.[5]

Four million livres had to come from the Parlement of Paris and the larger provincial institutions – Bordeaux, Rennes, Rouen and Toulouse; but all these fell short of the goals that Chamillart assigned them. The magistrates of Bordeaux, unable as a group to borrow their 340,000 lives, promised instead to pay a penalty of 750 livres apiece, one-fifth of an individual's *augmentations de gages* capital. In the end, they paid 51,000 livres of the 67,000 livres to which this amounted, a shortfall of 16,000 or 24 percent.[6] The Parlement of Toulouse, which owed 521,000 livres for *augmentations de gages*, paid 375,000, a deficit of 146,000 livres, 28 percent.[7]

The Parlement of Rennes needed 760,000 livres for its *augmentations de gages*, the largest sum among all provincial tribunals, but as *Président à Mortier* Bréquigny told Chamillart, not even six judges were financially able to pay their share. The Bretons had little success when they tried to borrow money in Rennes, Nantes and Paris, and they rejected Chamillart's proposal that they agree collectively to a penalty of 800 livres each. In the end, the Parlement allowed its magistrates to act as individuals, either paying the *augmentations de gages* or the 800 livres forfeit as they saw fit. But no one surrendered the 800 livres; and less than half took the *augmentations de gages*. Of the 760,000 livres that Chamillart wanted, only 300,000 livres came in – a deficit of 460,000, or 60 percent. The Parlement of Rouen did worse. As of 10 March 1703, it had paid almost none of its *augmentations de gages*; and an exasperated Chamillart called Rouen financially the slowest of all the superior courts. Vernouillet, the acting first president, was among those most embarrassed: he had sold his silver plate to pay the previous *augmentations de gages*, he said, and could do no more. In the end, Rouen probably paid about 178,500 livres, a shortage of 566,000 livres, or 76 percent.[8]

To add to Chamillart's displeasure, the Parlement of Paris failed to produce the 1.8 million livres that it had pledged. As of June 1703, the Paris judges had handed over some 1.2 million livres, but that left a balance of 600,000. An irate Chamillart demanded the names of the delinquent magistrates and threatened to strip them of their offices. After stalling as long as it could, the tribunal listed forty-six guilty judges, almost all of them the younger men in the Enquêtes and Requêtes chambers. Whether these judges were in real jeopardy is open to question. Chamillart had also warned delinquents in the Parlement of Bordeaux of severe consequences if they did not pay their *augmentations de gages*; and nothing happened to them. Under this pressure, however, some of the Paris offenders came up with another 200,000 livres, reducing the tribunal's deficit to about 400,000 livres. There, however, it stubbornly remained.[9] Table 6 summarizes the results of Chamillart's efforts to wrest forced loans from the parlements in 1702–1703.

Table 6 Augmentations de gages *of 1702–1703*

Parlement	Aug. gages owed (£)	Aug. gages paid (£)	Deficit (£)
Paris	1,819,200	1,400,000	419,200
Bordeaux	67,000	51,000	16,000
Rennes	760,800	300,000	460,800
Rouen	745,200	178,500	566,700
Toulouse	521,600	375,000	146,600
Dijon	435,200	435,200	
Grenoble	306,000	306,000	
Aix	268,000	268,000	
Metz	145,000	145,000	
Pau	152,000	152,000(?)	
Besançon	73,420	73,420	
Tournai	110,000	110,000	
Totals	5,403,420	3,794,120	1,609,300

Hard on the heels of the *augmentations de gages* of 1701, Chamillart had extracted nearly 3.8 million livres from the parlements without the leverage of the *paulette* renewal and therefore without the help of the 'privileged' mortgage. Although this result compared favourably with Pontchartrain's 'voluntary' *augmentations de gages* of 3.15 million in 1689, Chamillart was dissatisfied. He had assured the king that he would collect in full, and he had counted upon the 1.6 million that did not come in. The funds owed by the Parlement of Rouen, for example, had been promised to naval officials and to the war treasury at Lille.[10] Perhaps Chamillart also suspected the parlements of traces of political resistance, if not of a personal affront. Certainly it was the first time since the East India project of the early 1660s that they had cooperated less than fully in a financial affair. In any event, and whether as retribution or out of financial necessity, Chamillart immediately returned to the parlementaires for still more money, subjecting them to a third financial demand within the narrow span of three years.

The Chambres des Eaux et Forêts, 1704–1705

In an edict of February 1704, issued soon after the semi-failure of the *augmentations de gages*, the king created a new Chambre des Eaux et Forêts in every parlement in the realm. These chambers were to exercise final jurisdiction in all water and forest litigation, expediting the judicial process in these matters. The parlements already exercised appellate jurisdiction over *tables de marbre*, subordinate courts in which most water and forest lawsuits began; and they judged in first instance water and forest cases that affected the royal domain. But the 1704 edict abolished the *tables de marbre* and reassigned virtually all water and forest jurisdiction from the parlements to the new Chambres des Eaux et Forêts, without appeal. Though constituted as part of the parlements, the chambers would dispense water and forest justice in their place and at their expense.[11]

Water and forest issues aside, what the government really wanted was to sell the new offices that the chambers would hold. The edict created 154 presidents and councillors, an even larger contingent of new judges than had descended upon the parlements in the 1690s. The government expected to clear five to six million livres from the sale, about as much as from an *augmentations de gages*. Chamillart had more than made good on his threat to create more offices in the parlements as their punishment for not paying all their *augmentations de gages*. Already in February, even before publication of the edict, a group of financiers acting under the collective name of Charles Baudouin signed a lease for the sale; and twenty-four investors promptly joined in, eager to share the profits.[12]

The government primarily saw the Eaux et Forêts edict as a way to apply pressure to the parlements, whose interests dictated that they try to get the edict revoked. To do so, they would have to agree to the creation of other new offices or pay for a new *augmentations de gages* or accept a combination of the two. But whatever they chose, Chamillart expected the same amount of money as the sale of water and forest offices would produce. The treasury would profit either from the implementation of the edict or from its revocation.

Nicolas Desmarets, a director of finances and the future controller general, opened discussions with the parlements for the edict's revocation. Through the spring and summer of 1704, the postal service kept busier than usual with the exchange of letters and memoranda between Chamillart and Desmarets, on the one hand, and the parlements on the other.[13] Chamillart himself prodded any laggards. He was content merely to exhort Bordeaux and Toulouse, but he threatened Grenoble and Besançon, both more stubborn, with the creation of new Chambres des Requêtes, on top of the water and forest chambers, if they did not comply in full. As a result of this pressure, Chamillart and Desmarets obtained the appropriate commitments from all the parlements, and the Baudouin group felt confident enough to advance the king two to three million livres at the rate of about 250,000 livres every two or three months.[14]

The Parlement of Paris agreed to a creation of five new *présidents aux enquêtes* and two *présidents aux requêtes*, one for each of the *enquêtes* and *requêtes* chambers, and fifteen lay councillors. These 22 new offices would carry the Parlement to 278 judges, a gain of 8.59 percent from the 256 magistrates of 1695, and earn the treasury 2.45 million livres, considerably more than the *augmentations de gages* of 1702–1703. Like Pontchartrain in 1695, Desmarets sold these offices through the *parties casuelles*, all proceeds accruing to the king.

Confined to the provinces, the Baudouin partners nevertheless fared well enough, as the office sales recorded in Table 7 show. They achieved their biggest success with the Parlement of Rennes, selling 15 new offices there and increasing its judges to 129, a gain of 13 percent. That sale generated 725,000 livres overall and netted 604,000 livres for the crown, after the deduction of the Baudouin commission (*remise*). Sales of another 15 new magistrates in the Parlement of Besançon and of 13 in Tournai produced an additional 800,000 livres, for a net of 667,000 livres. The Parlement of Toulouse added seven new judges, with a gross of 245,000 livres and a net of 204,000. This carried Toulouse to 139 judges; it remained the second largest parlement in the realm. The office sales in Paris and the four provincial parlements thus added 72 new judges to the ranks of the parlementaires and netted the government 3.9 million livres. Although not nearly as large as the office creations of the 1690s, when 179 new venality judges took seats in all the tribunals, the sales of 1704–1705 carried the total magistracy from 1,218 judges in 1695 to 1,290 in 1705, an increase of almost 6 percent. Incidentally, these were the last office creations in the parlements for the rest of the Old Regime, the river of parlementary venality having at last run dry.

Table 7 *Sale of new offices in parlements, 1704–1705*

Office	Judges 1665	Judges 1695	New offices	Price per office (£)	Total sales (£)	Judges 1705	% Incr. from sales
Paris							
PP	1	1				1	
PM	7	9				9	
PE	10	10	5	200,000	1,000,000	15	50.00
C(L)	162	178	15	70,000	1,050,000	193	8.43
C(C)	22	22				22	
PR	4	4	2	200,000	400,000	6	50.00
CR	28	28				28	
AG	2	3				3	
PG	1	1				1	
Totals	237	256	22		2,450,000	278	8.59
Rennes							
PP	1	1				1	
PM	7	8	1	100,000	100,000	9	12.50
PE	4	4	2	72,000	144,000	6	50.00
C(O)	40	44	6	45,000	270,000	50	13.64
C(N)	40	42	2	30,000	60,000	44	4.76
PR	2	2	2	45,000	90,000	4	100.00
CR	10	10	2	30,000	60,000	12	20.00
AG	2	2				2	
PG	1	1				1	
Totals	107	114	15		724,131	129	13.16
Tournai							
PP		1				1	
PM		3	4	45,000	180,000	7	133.33
CH		2	1	20,000	20,000	3	50.00
C(L)		22	7	30,000	210,000	29	31.82
C(C)		2	1	25,000	25,000	3	50.00
AG		1				1	
PG		1				1	
Totals		32	13		435,000	45	40.63
Besançon							
PP		1				1	
PM		5	2	45,000	90,000	7	40.00
CH		3	1	20,000	20,000	4	33.33
C(L)		44	8	20,000	160,000	52	18.18
C(C)		2	1	16,000	16,000	3	50.00
PR			2	28,000	56,000	2	

Table 7 (*cont.*)

Office	Judges 1665	Judges 1695	New offices	Price per office (£)	Total sales (£)	Judges 1705	% Incr. from sales
Besançon (*cont.*)							
AG		2	1	20,000	20,000	3	50.00
PG		1				1	
Totals		58	15		362,000	73	25.86
Toulouse							
PP	1	1				1	
PM	6	9				9	
PE	4	6				6	
C(L)	93	93	3	30,000	90,000	96	3.22
C(C)	6	6				6	
PR	2	2				2	
CR	11	12	3	25,000	75,000	15	2.72
AG	2	2	1	80,000	80,000	3	50.00
PG	1	1				1	
Totals	126	132	7		245,000	139	5.30

Sources: Paris: BN, *Actes R.*, F. 23,617 (665): edict of May 1704; AN, P 3681: 'nouvelles créations'; AN, G7, 1366, MS 48: 'Chambres des Eaux et forests, Paris'; Rennes: BN, *Actes R.*, F. 23,617 (813): edict of October 1704; AD, I-V, IBb (Registres secrets) 303: 30 October 1704, ff. 31rv; Frédéric Saulnier, *Le Parlement de Bretagne, 1554–1790. Répertoire alphabétique et biographique* (2 vols; Rennes, 1909), nos 86, 323, 418, 558, 699, 851, 912, 981, 1019, 1035, 1056, 1082, 1188, 1201; Rouen: AD, S-M, 1B 223 (Registres secrets): 2 April 1704, f. 36v; BN, *Fonds fr.*, 22,455 (Parlement de Rouen), pp. 504, 514–516, 518–525; Toulouse: BN, *Actes R.*, F. 23,617 (951): edict of January 1705; AN, P 3395: 'nouvelles créations'; AN, G7, 1366: MS 89; Besançon: BN, *Actes R.*, F. 23,617 (723): edict of July 1704; AN, G7, 1366, MS 89; AD, Doubs, B 3768 (Délibérations): 26 May, 2 June and 3 June 1704; Tournai: AN, P 3681: 'nouvelles créations'; AN, G7, 261, 'Estat des offres & soumissions', 14 December 1704; G7, 1366, MS 89.

Some provincial tribunals met their Eaux et Forêts obligations by taking *augmentations de gages* instead of office creations, each paying from 60,000 (Pau) to 400,000 livres (Aix), for a total of 1.64 million. To escape the *augmentations de gages*, Bordeaux paid a forfeit of 40,000 livres, bringing this total to 1.7 million (Table 8). In addition, most parlements paid the Baudouin group the *deux sous pour livre*, a surcharge of a theoretical 10 percent, which could however be negotiated downwards.[15]

As the Eaux et Forêts affair progressed, the Baudouin group accepted various changes that reduced the scope of its lease, but the final audit in 1709–1710

Table 8 Augmentations de gages *in parlements, 1704–1705*

Parlement	Augmentations de gages (£)	Deux sous pour livre (£)	'Pure perte' (£)
Aix	400,000		
Bordeaux	200,000	10,000	40,000
Dijon	300,000	3,000	
Grenoble	220,000	(included in the 220,000)	
Metz	100,000	1,000	
Pau	60,000	2,000	
Rouen	248,000	10,000	
Toulouse	108,000		
Totals	1,636,000	26,000	40,000
Grand total	1,702,000		

Sources: Aix: BM, Aix, MS 956 (Délibérations du Parlement): 8 October 1704, ff. 187rv; Musée Arbaud, MS MQ 19: 18 May 1705, pp. 440–441; AD, B-R (Aix): B 3596: receipt for 400,000 livres; Bordeaux: Dalon, first president, to Desmarets, 20 June and 28 December 1705, AN, G7, 1337, MSS 152, 172; AM, Bordeaux, MS 797 (Registre secret): 17 June 1705, pp. 82–83; Dijon: Bouchu, first president, to Chamillart, 7 May 1704, AN, G7, 1341; BM, Dijon, MS 769 (Registres du Parlement): 15 June, 17 November and 12 December 1705, pp. 563–564, 586–588; Grenoble: BN, *Actes R.*, F. 23,618 (442): edict of April 1706; AN, G7, 1341, MS 144; Metz: AD, Moselle, B 338 (Registres secrets): 26 November 1704, f. 37rv; Pau: Parlement to Chamillart, 30 November 1704, AN, G7, 1337; Bertier, first president, to Chamillart, 26 January 1705, AN, G7, 116; AD, P-A (Pau), B 6017: edict of December 1705; Rouen: BN, *Actes R.*, F. 23,618 (750): edict of February 1707, and AN, G7, 1359, MS 243; AN, P 3956, 2 May 1708; Toulouse: BN, *Actes R.*, F. 23,617 (951): edict of January 1705.

showed that the partners extracted 3.48 million livres from the provincial tri-bunals, deducted a *remise* of one-sixth or 580,000, and paid 2.9 million to the treasury. Together with the returns from the sale of office in the Parlement of Paris, this meant that the government gained 5.35 million livres from issuing and rescinding the Eaux et Forêts edict, almost exactly the sum that Chamillart had fixed at the onset, in every way a better result than that of the *augmenta-tions de gages* of 1702–1703. Perhaps he had been right to suspect that the parlements had not done their best then.[16]

Although the government coerced the parlements into paying these sums, it did extend concessions to particularly cooperative tribunals. Chamillart promised the magistrates of Aix, Grenoble and Toulouse, among the first to agree to terms, that the royal council would exercise greater restraint in trans-ferring lawsuits out of their tribunals. The Parlement of Grenoble received an additional one thousand livres for firewood, candles and refreshments. The magistrates of Aix won a long-sought exemption from *lods et ventes*, transfer taxes on fiefs held from the royal domain.[17]

But Chamillart reserved these favours as rewards or incentives for financial cooperation: Rouen and Metz, where collections were slow, got nothing. Moreover, he identified these benefits in advance, offered them when he chose, and could not be pressed into giving anything more. The Parlement of Toulouse asked for the restoration of its privilege of nobility in the first degree, rescinded in 1669; and the Parlement of Dijon sought to recover jurisdiction over Burgundian towns and communities, lost to the intendant in the 1660s. The government refused both requests. From Bordeaux, First President Dalon recommended that the son of a *président à mortier* be accepted as a new *président des enquêtes*, although the son was only twenty-one and not thirty as the ordinance required. Desmarets turned him down. The Parlement of Besançon tried hard to reduce from eight to six the number of new councillors to be created there, but the government stuck to the higher number, all protests notwithstanding.[18] Whenever the issue arose, Chamillart also refused to allow *présidents des enquêtes* and *présidents à mortier* to shift their *augmentations de gages* burdens on to their junior colleagues.[19]

Only the Parlement of Aix, where First President Pierre Cardin Lebret negotiated skilfully, received any special favours. In return for the revocation of the Eaux et Forêts chamber, the magistrates promised to pay 400,000 livres for *augmentations de gages* and to accept that creation of a new Chambre des Requêtes which they had fiercely opposed on the eve of the Fronde. But the current version of the Requêtes chamber, unlike the one proposed before the Fronde, actually served the financial interests of the sitting judges. Lebret had arranged that they themselves would staff the Requêtes, in rotating shifts, fair compensation for the sums they paid in *augmentations de gages*. In addition, the Parlement got to keep the proceeds from the sale of clerks, receivers, payers and the like and won an increase of 1,100 livres in its housekeeping budget.[20] All the other tribunals, however, succumbed to strong-arm tactics and surrendered the funds that Chamillart demanded, without compensating gains of any substance.

Early in the War of the Spanish Succession, the parlements had therefore paid out some 15 million livres in the form of office creations and *augmentations de gages*. This compared favourably indeed with the 17 million that Pontchartrain had wrung from them over the longer term of the entire War of the League of Augsburg. Chamillart could also take pride in successfully asserting his authority after the somewhat disappointing *augmentations de gages* of 1702–1703, tightening up the already strict financial discipline that his predecessors had imposed. Paradoxically, however, his were the last financial affairs that succeeded in the tribunals, as the latter were approaching their financial limits.

Desmarets and the redemptions of the capitation and *paulette*

On 20 February 1708, Nicholas Desmarets, a nephew of Colbert, succeeded Chamillart as controller general and inherited the problem of funding the War of the Spanish Succession. Well qualified for his responsibilities,[21] and certainly experienced in dealing with the parlements, having administered the Eaux et Forêts project, he invented new ways to press the tribunals for money. But for the first time they showed signs of serious financial weakness, the depredations of Chamillart and Pontchartrain before him having taken a toll.

The first effort of Desmarets appeared in an edict of September 1708 for the 'redemption' of the capitation tax, introduced in 1695–1698 and revived by Chamillart in 1701, with an increase in rates. Under the new capitation schedule, the first president of the Parlement of Paris owed 3,000 livres per year, and the first presidents of the provincial parlements, 1,500 livres. The *présidents à mortier* of Paris were taxed at 1,500 livres, and those in the provinces, at 450 livres. The councillors of Paris bore a levy of 300 livres, those in the provinces, 225 livres. Paymasters deducted these sums directly from the *gages* of the judges, reducing their salary at its source.[22]

The *gages*, pensions and other emoluments of the first presidents ranged from 10,000 to 20,000 livres, so they could pay their capitation and still have a lot left over. But their capitation of 1,500 livres cost the *présidents à mortier* of Paris one-third of their *gages* of 4,500 livres, a considerable reduction; and most provincial *présidents à mortier*, who paid a capitation of 450 livres on *gages* of between 1,875 and 2,352 livres, suffered losses of between 20 and 25 percent, almost as bad. The councillors of Aix, Dijon, Grenoble and Rennes saw their salaries comparably reduced: they paid a capitation of 225 livres on *gages* ranging from 750 to 1,000 livres, losses of 25 to 33 percent. The tax virtually consumed the *gages* of 300 to 400 livres paid to councillors at Bordeaux, Metz, Pau, Rouen, Toulouse and even Paris, leaving most of them with net *gages* of little more than 100 livres.[23] It is worth noting that Chamillart had sold offices in, and extracted loans from, the parlements at a time when he was also taxing the magistrates' salaries at high rates.

The redemption edict required the judges to pay six years of capitation in advance, in a lump sum; and the government intended for them to pay in full. As Chancellor Pontchartrain put it to a grumbler, the judges could only 'submit . . . [and] suffer'.[24] The *présidents à mortier* of Paris had to pay 9,000 livres and those in the provinces, 2,700 livres; the councillors of Paris owed 1,800 livres, and those in the provinces, 1,350 livres. Together the parlements were to pay 2.16 million livres for the redemption, Paris leading the way with an obligation of 663,000 livres and Rennes coming first among provincials with 251,000. Most of the others owed between 90,000 and 180,000 livres.[25]

Although the capitation redemption was less than half an *augmentations de gages* and Desmarets promised interest of 5 percent on the capital advanced, the results disappointed him. Aix and Besançon alone redeemed their capitation promptly; the others lagged way behind. The Parlement of Dijon never paid in full, and the Parlement of Grenoble was still in arrears in 1712. Payments came in slowly from Metz and Toulouse. Rennes paid no more than 111,000 livres of its 251,000 total. Evidence suggests a very low yield in the Parlement of Rouen. A young magistrate of Bordeaux noted to himself that only a few of his colleagues could meet the capitation terms, and the intendant La Bourdonnaye said much the same thing.[26] The problem was that the credit market had softened markedly since the Eaux et Forêts affair. Potential creditors had diminished in number, and those who remained were losing their enthusiasm for the heavily indebted office-holders. The capitation redemption probably brought in only half what Desmarets expected, and his next financial operation also fared none too well.[27]

It is sometimes asserted that towards the end of his reign Louis XIV cancelled the parlements' *droit annuel* (or *paulette*) payments, as a sign of his respect for their importance and power;[28] but this view is incorrect. The parlements indeed put the *paulette* behind them, a milestone when viewed from an historical perspective. But so far from receiving a gift, the magistrates had to pay large sums to redeem the *paulette*. The redemption was just another fund-raising device, with Desmarets pushing the parlements hard for the money, citing the 'pressing needs of war'.

An edict of December 1709 announced that, as of 1711, office-holders would be able to enjoy the protective terms of the *droit annuel* without having to make their annual payments. Magistrates of the parlements would also be excused from *augmentations de gages* connected with the *paulette*. Regrettably, however, the king could not make these concessions as a gift. For the privilege of transmitting their offices to heirs or selling them to other parties, owners of office would have to redeem the *paulette* by paying it for sixteen years in advance. The king would reclaim the office of anyone who died without redeeming his *paulette*, with no compensation to the heirs. Mindful of the slow progress of the capitation redemption, Desmarets set a deadline of 31 December 1710, the day the current *droit annuel* expired.[29]

On a positive note, the *paulette* redemption, issued at the 16th instead of the 18th *denier*, cost less than an *augmentations de gages*. To calculate the sum he owed, the office-holder multiplied his *droit annuel* by sixteen instead of the customary eighteen. Moreover, the magistrate could pay up to one-third of this sum in *billets de monnaie*, paper instruments that had fallen to around 50 percent of face value and which the government wanted to remove from the market. The balance of two-thirds had to consist of specie, but one could deduct the *paulette* of 1710 from that balance. As another fillip, the edict ended Colbert's limits on office prices, the *fixation*; and buyers and sellers could again negotiate in a free market. In addition to favourable terms, the future prospect of enjoying the protection of the *paulette* without cost, once the sixteen years

Table 9 Droit annuel *redemption by parlements, 1709–1710*

Parlement	Droit annuel (£)	Total finance denier 16 (£)	One-third billets de monnaie (£)	Two-thirds specie (£)
Paris	112,696	1,803,138	601,046	1,089,396
Rennes	40,252	644,033	214,677	389,103
Toulouse	31,011	496,178	165,392	299,774
Bordeaux	23,593	377,493	125,831	228,068
Aix	23,530	376,480	125,493	227,456
Dijon	22,645	362,329	120,776	218,903
Grenoble	17,108	273,730	94,243	165,378
Metz	15,200	243,204	81,068	146,936
Rouen	13,928	222,862	74,247	134,685
Pau	7,780	124,492	41,497	75,214
Besançon	5,297	84,752	28,252	51,203
Totals	313,040	5,008,691	1,672,522	3,026,116

Source: AN, G7, 1325: 'Estat General des Officiers sujets au Rachat du prest et annuel';
François Veron de Forbonnais, *Recherches et considérations sur les finances de France*
(2 vols, Basel, 1758), II, 213. The 'one-third' and 'two-thirds' columns will not add up
to the 'total finance' because, as noted, the government deducted the *droit annuel* for
1710 from the two-thirds payable in coin. The Parlement of Tournai was exempted
from the redemption because it was in a war zone.

had elapsed, had to please the magistrates, who typically held their offices for
more than twenty years.[30] Desmarets had good hopes for the redemption,
expecting it to bring in 14.4 million livres, with the parlements supplying some
5 million livres, about the same as in an *augmentations de gages*. Table 9 records
their redemption obligations.

Despite the high hopes of Desmarets, however, only two parlements honoured the deadline of 31 December 1710. The Parlement of Pau, the first to
complete the redemption, had its money ready in June 1710, thanks to loans
from five noblemen, mediated by the intendant. The Parlement of Dijon followed close behind, redeeming its *droit annuel* as of 8 January 1711, only a little
late.[31] None of the others lived up to these examples. Desmarets reproached the
Parlement of Metz for being the slowest to redeem the *paulette*, but the usually
dependable Parlement of Aix could not raise its money either. The first president
himself advanced his Aix colleagues some 30,000 livres to purchase *billets de
monnaie*; but the judges could come up with very little coin. Besançon,
Bordeaux, Rennes, Toulouse and others also ran late in their payments, forcing
Desmarets to extend his deadline again and again.[32] We do not how much

Desmarets finally received from the *paulette* redemption, but the money came in so slowly it did not have the tonic effect he anticipated. The Parlement of Rennes eventually paid some 608,420 livres against its 644,000 livres, but that was over a long term indeed. Councillor Ferret disbursed only in 1714, and other magistrates were still paying in 1716.[33]

Judges who could not borrow money to redeem their capitation could also not find lenders for the *paulette*, no matter how good the terms. To make matters more embarrassing, the redemption edict awarded lenders that 'privileged mortgage' upon offices that up to now creditors had found so irresistible. When they did not rise to the bait on this occasion, they showed that they had begun to lose confidence in venality. In a dismaying turnaround, venal office now bore the taint of a bad investment; Chancellor Pontchartrain acknowledged as much himself. As the reign of Louis XIV dragged on, the economic foundations of parlementary venality began to crumble.[34]

Venal office in decline

In addition to their *gages*, which the king paid at quarterly intervals, the magistrates collected fees from litigants; these were known as *épices*. Originally a voluntary gift to judges, consisting of oriental spices or similar products, *épices* became obligatory money payments by the 1500s, assessed at the conclusion of a lawsuit by the presiding judges. Councillors ordinarily earned *épices* in several ways. A councillor could serve as a briefing judge (*rapporteur*), studying a case in advance and summarizing it in open court: this task earned him between one-fifth and one-half of the *épices* assessed in that case, depending upon the rules of a particular tribunal. The other judges collected a lump sum from the 'common fund', a pool made up of the *épices* remaining after the *rapporteurs* had drawn their shares. Magistrates who served in extra sessions convened to adjudicate complex litigation earned another type of *épices* called *commissaires*. Despite the protests of reformers that justice should be free, the magistrates saw *épices* as fair compensation for professional service, since *gages* were only interest paid on the capital invested in office. Colbert chose to regulate rather than to eliminate *épices*, in an edict of March 1673, which had little practical effect. *Épices* probably generated significant income in all the parlements well into the first half of Louis XIV's reign. In the 1660s a judge in the Parlement of Rennes could earn from one to three thousand livres per year, with little and sometimes even no effort.[35] By the late reign, however, everything had changed.

In 1692, the Parlement of Rennes fretted that its 'emoluments', i.e. *épices* and *commissaires*, had virtually disappeared; and the other parlements also reported big declines in office income. From 1700 to 1709, magistrates in Besançon, Toulouse and Rouen reported sharp drops in *épices*, by as much as 75 percent. To be sure, the parlements would resort to any excuse to explain why it took them so long to pay for *augmentations de gages* or other impositions. But this time they were telling the truth. The first presidents, who were of course royal appointees, confirmed that *épices* were falling. In 1702, Harlay noted that offices had grown financially sterile in the Parlement of Paris, no longer generating any profits at all, 'nothing'; and Lebret of Aix, writing in 1709, agreed that *épices* 'are not anything . . .' Chancellor Pontchartrain, receiving these reports from all the parlements, accepted the decline of *épices* as a fact of judicial life, as did controllers general, who had access to *épices* records.[36] The registers for Rennes, Besançon and Aix, the only ones we have, prove beyond doubt that a reduction in *épices* was indeed well under way.

Half the magistrates of the Parlement of Rennes served in a six-month semester convening in February, the other half in another six-month semester opening in August. In 1673–1674, *épices* and *commissaires* for the August and February semesters came to 91,000 livres but began to fall later in the decade. In 1692, the last year for which we have complete figures for both semesters, the total had dropped to 47,000 livres, a decline of almost 50 percent. In 1695, the August semester collected *épices* (there are no figures for *commissaires*) of only 17,000 livres, a drop of 62 percent from the *épices* of 45,000 livres it earned in 1673. Individual income from *épices* and *commissaires* diminished in proportion. In the Parlement of Besançon, the average *épices* payment for a councillor fell from 912 livres in 1676–1683 to 491 livres in 1695–1696, another drop of almost 50 percent; and the erosion worsened in the early 1700s.[37] From 1693 to 1705, the average common fund payment to the sixty magistrates in the Parlement of Aix was 306 livres per year, probably a much lower sum than it had been in the 1660s. Since the *rapporteur*'s portion, deducted in advance, was only one-fifth, most judges earned little more than their 306 livres. In 1706–1713, the common fund share slumped to an average of 234 livres, a loss of 23 percent.[38]

The first reason why *épices* declined is that the volume of litigation in the parlements had also gone down. In 1689, Aulède, first president at Bordeaux, confessed that half his magistrates were 'without employment', while the others had hardly anything to do. The first presidents of Toulouse, Rouen and Aix all said much the same thing. Metz, which like Rennes was divided into two semesters, declared that it was busy for only three weeks in either semester. The Parlements of Paris, Dijon and Grenoble reported low caseloads. In the Parlement of Rennes, which epitomized the trend, the average number of judicial decrees issued by the Grand-Chambre declined from 1,855 in 1664–1666 to 530 in 1714–1716, a fall of more than 70 percent.[39]

The causes of this decline have yet to be fully explained, but the government had to bear some responsibility for it. From the late seventeenth into the early eighteenth centuries, controllers general created *receveurs des épices* and similar officials, awarding them the right to tax *épices* at rates starting at 10 and rising to 25 percent. The parlements contended that the new taxes helped keep litigants from their chambers, an assessment which, while incomplete, necessarily contained some truth.[40]

As the value of *épices* tumbled, the magistrates also suffered a reduction in the market value of their offices, as buyers became aware of venality's financial problems. The recurrence of *augmentations de gages* certainly pushed office prices down, as markets froze up on the eve of the nine-year renewals of the *paulette*.[41] The office sales of the 1690s and early 1700s, by increasing the supply of offices, further reduced the demand for, and therefore the prices of, existing posts. The prices of many offices slipped below the levels of the *fixation* long before its ironic termination in 1709.

Bucking the trend, the offices of *président à mortier* in the Parlement of Paris maintained their *fixation* price of 350,000 livres; and in the provincial tribunals prices for these higher offices held more or less steady at the *fixations* of 120,000 to 150,000 livres. But the offices of councillor, by far the most numerous, suffered heavy losses in almost every parlement in the realm. In the 1665 *fixation*, Colbert had limited the price of a lay councillor office in the Parlement of Paris to 100,000 livres; and in 1690 Pontchartrain sold the sixteen new lay councillors for that very sum. This at least showed that the value of a councillor office, which before 1665 had exceeded 100,000 livres, had settled at the *fixation* level, since the government would have set higher prices if it could have done so. In 1703, however, First President Harlay lamented that the office of lay councillor had declined to 80,000 livres and was still falling. Offices of clerical councillor, he reported, sold at 50,000 livres, far below their *fixation* of 90,000. In 1704 the government priced new offices of lay councillor at 70,000 livres and did not try to sell clerical offices at all. In 1715, an analysis prepared for the controller general valued lay councillors at 56,000 livres, a slump of almost 50 percent in the twenty-five years since 1690.[42]

In the Parlement of Rennes, the *fixation* prices for the office of councillor were 100,000 livres for an *originaire* (Breton) and 70,000 for a *non-originaire* (non-Breton). But already in 1689 the government priced new *originaire* councillors at 80,000 livres, a decline of 20 percent. In the office sale of 1704, these offices sold at 45,000 livres, a drop of another 44 percent in fifteen years. The office of *non-originaire* councillor sold at 30,000 livres in 1704, a decline of more than 50 percent from the *fixation* of 1665. Similarly, the *fixation* price of a lay councillor at the Parlement of Toulouse was 60,000 livres; but the price sank to 35,000 livres in 1691 and to 30,000 in 1705, an overall decrease of 50 percent.[43] At Bordeaux the councillor office, with a *fixation* of 50,000 livres, fell to 28,000 livres by 1700 and to 18,000 in 1704, a loss of 65 percent, so low that Chamillart deemed it insufficiently profitable to create new ones. Even the venerable office of a Bordeaux *président à mortier* sank from a *fixation* of 120,000 livres to 75,000.[44]

The office of councillor in the Parlement of Grenoble, where the *fixation* was 66,000 livres, fell to 35,000 in 1704. In 1706, *traitants* appraised the councillor office at Pau, which had a ceiling of 36,000 livres, at 25,000 livres. In Metz, the office sold at its *fixation* of 36,000 livres in the 1680s but dropped to 28,000 livres in 1691. In Rouen, it sold at 50,000 livres in 1691, despite its *fixation* of 70,000 livres; and the government's decision not to sell offices there in the 1700s suggests that the decline had continued. From its *fixation* of 64,000 livres, the office of councillor in Aix fell to 45,000 livres in 1693 and to 38,000 livres in 1710.[45]

As lone exceptions to the rule, the new parlements at Besançon and Tournai actually posted increases in the prices of councillor offices. In 1692–1693, the lay councillor in Besançon sold for 18,000 livres, rose to 20,000 livres in the sale of 1704–1705, and went for 30,000 livres in 1714. In Tournai, the lay councillor climbed from 25,000 livres in 1693 to 30,000 livres in 1704. The other new offices in those parlements also gained. But only Besançon and Tournai resisted the otherwise universal decline in councillor prices in the late reign of Louis XIV.[46]

Buyers of parlementary office, fully aware of the adverse conditions, naturally increased the pressure on sellers, contributing to the earthward drift. In 1690, Guillaume La Grée instructed his notary to prolong negotiations for a councillor office in the Parlement of Rennes as long as possible. The delay, wrote La Grée, would erode the seller's asking price: '. . . the longer I wait, the more the offices . . . diminish in price'. His attitude, reversing the inflationary psychology of the 1660s, reflected the experience of magistrates all across France. In 1698, First President La Tresne of Bordeaux reported that the ever-diminishing bids for offices fed upon themselves, leaving no hope for an upturn in the near future.[47]

As the reign of Louis XIV neared its end, the economics of venal office thus shifted to the disadvantage of the judges. In the mid-1600s, when prices were rising and the income from *épices* had yet to fall, office in the Parlement of Rennes yielded an annual return of 3.45 to 3.66 percent, including capital gains. By 1705, with both prices and income trending downward, the return approached zero. The return on office investments in the other parlements was probably much the same. This downward trend in the economic fundamentals of venal office necessarily exerted a powerful effect on the magistrates, in both the long and short term, eroding wealth and status. Venal office, which had anchored family wealth in the sense of imparting stability, became a different kind of anchor, pulling wealth down.[48]

In 1711, Councillor Joachim Descartes was nearing the end of his thirty-year career in the Parlement of Rennes. He declared to his heirs that he had purchased his office for 90,000 livres in 1680 but that it had currently fallen to 45,000. This loss, which saddened him as a father, diminished his estate and reduced the inheritance shares that he would leave to his survivors. Such experiences, common enough, prompted René de La Bigotière, a Breton *président des enquêtes*, to call venal office an 'uncertain', 'insubstantial' form of property. A legist in the province, familiar with the Parlement, likened its offices to 'respectable poverty'.[49]

The *paulette* redemption edict acknowledged that economic conditions had deteriorated to the point where many office-holders had ceased to pay their *droit annuel*, a complete change from earlier decades, when it had been sacred. This was certainly the case in the parlements. The declines in *épices* and office values caused a number of magistrates, after doing their sums, to question the *paulette*'s value. In Bordeaux a councillor collected *gages* of 375 livres, but owed a *paulette* of 400 livres, a loss of 25 livres. With the 150–livre capitation of 1695–1698, the loss rose to 175 livres, and many ceased to pay the *droit annuel* at that point. As recommended by the first president, the government in 1700 reduced the Bordeaux *paulette* to 200 livres; but in 1701 the capitation rose to 225 livres, so the councillor still suffered a loss of 50 livres. Again, some judges preferred to forgo the *droit annuel* and to collect at least something in *gages*. Offices of deceased Bordeaux magistrates inevitably accumulated in the *parties casuelles*, lost to the heirs. In Rouen, the *gages* of a councillor came to 300 livres and his *paulette* to 333 livres. After paying a capitation of 225 livres, the councillor was out of pocket by 258 livres; and some Rouen judges also chose to do without the *droit annuel*. In 1706, the government reduced the Rouen *paulette* to 200 livres, but the remaining deficit of 125 livres still seemed too high.

It seems likely that more than a few magistrates in Metz, Pau, Toulouse and Paris, where the ratio of *gages* to *droit annuel* resembled that of Bordeaux and Rouen, were also skipping *paulette* payments. Even in Aix and Rennes, where respective *gages* of 1,050 and 750 to 1,000 livres more than offset the *droit annuel* of 166 and 355 livres, some magistrates still found it disadvantageous to pay. Where office had once combined income, capital, power and prestige, it had now become a source of anxiety and concern, unattractive to creditors and worrisome to owners. The financial and political policies of Louis XIV had largely brought about this disagreeable change and were about to deepen it.[50]

The crisis of 1709

As the war neared its climax, the government of Louis XIV fell into an economic and financial crisis, leading to a 'partial' or 'camouflaged' bankruptcy, like that of 1661. Overburdened by taxes, the economy faltered and the tax base shrank. The severe winter of 1708–1709, besides causing deaths in the hundreds of thousands, dealt a heavy blow to agriculture, commerce and industry, and further diminished the fiscal yield. A crisis erupted on the money market of Lyons, where the international financier Samuel Bernard defaulted on the promissory notes he had issued on behalf of the king. The government faced its worst financial dilemma since the Fronde. In his High Council, Louis XIV showed unaccustomed anxiety on the subject.[51]

The king had to suspend payment on all debts and obligations, including the *gages*, *augmentations de gages*, pensions, capitation interest and any other remuneration owed to the magistrates of parlements. Although this stoppage was in the nature of things, it came as a rude shock to the judges and to their creditors. To be sure, the wars, civil wars and upheavals that had afflicted France from the reign of Henry III through to the regency of Anne of Austria had often led to just this result.[52] But from early in the administration of Colbert, the government had disbursed with the regularity of a solstice, never missing a payment, convincing the magistrates and their creditors that *gages* and *augmentations de gages* had become as solid as the floor beneath their feet. When the government did suspend payments, everything gave way, quite literally in the case of First President Le Peletier of Paris. On the eve of the stoppage, his dining room floor collapsed as he sat at table with family and guests, tumbling the whole party into the basement, an accident that served as metaphor and as omen.[53]

Starting in late 1708 for some, and then throughout 1709 for the rest, the parlements found that they could no longer collect their *gages* and *augmentations de gages*. These payments probably amounted to between 1.5 and 2 million livres per year, with *augmentations de gages* accounting for upwards of 750,000 of the total. The Parlements of Rennes and Aix calculated their annual losses at more than 200,000 livres apiece. With so much money involved, the parlements began to flood Desmarets with demands for payment.[54] The loss of *gages* might not have meant much for some judges, but the failure of *augmentations de gages* put all their debt-encumbered offices at risk.[55]

Creditors holding privileged mortgages threatened to confiscate offices or other properties in the Parlements of Toulouse, Dijon and others. From Aix, Lebret warned that the 364 (!) creditors to whom his magistrates owed 1.8 million livres 'will inevitably move to seize their personal properties', a prediction which soon came true. The Parlement of Grenoble came under legal pressure from its formerly eager lenders in Provence and the Comtat d'Avignon. Bordeaux magistrates began selling whatever they could to appease their creditors, but four of them lost their offices and their careers. It was not without reason that their First President Dalon said that the magistrates needed their *gages* and *augmentations de gages* 'to live'.[56] The magistrates of Aix angrily described their plight as 'the worst ever' and alarmed Lebret with their 'vivacity'. In 1705, he had earned their gratitude for the favourable terms of the Eaux et Forêts affair, but now they scorned him and made him think they were ready to rebel.[57]

The Parlement of Rennes tried to do something about the common plight. As the Bretons suffered one payless quarter after another, Desmarets unwisely pressed them for the money that they owed for the capitation redemption, not even half complete. In a surprisingly harsh letter of 28 May 1709, he demanded a list of all the Parlement's magistrates, not just the delinquents, and threatened to have the royal council double the capitation of each judge. The magistrates would have to pay this double sum collectively, the solvent judges expending funds on behalf of those who could not disburse. In retaliation, the Parlement addressed a circular letter to all the tribunals condemning

Desmarets' efforts at intimidation and attaching a duplicate of his provocative capitation letter, the better to heighten collective wrath. This effort to rally the parlements failed when the royal postal service intercepted the letters and handed them over to intendants. Both Lamoignon de Courson, at Rouen, and Lebret, who was also intendant of Provence, found the letter far too inflammatory for the addressees to read. Desmarets, who had his own copies, accused the Parlement of trying to 'incite all the other Parlements in order to end the good will that they have shown in redeeming their capitation'.[58]

The financial pressures on the parlements now resembled those that precipitated the Fronde[59] – office sales, forced loans, suspended payments – only worse, given the heavy debt load and the decline in office values. The bold letter from Rennes might conceivably have revived the spirit of parlementary opposition and provoked not another Fronde, since the government of Louis XIV is not to be confused with that of the unpopular regency of Anne of Austria, but some sort of political crisis nevertheless. But Desmarets did not think so, and he was right. Once he had received an apology from the Parlement, he treated the affair as a misunderstanding, alleging that a careless clerk had somehow sent that threatening letter to the wrong law court, and let the matter drop, anticlimactically. The controller general never worried that the other parlements would respond to the Breton cues. He was confident that the kingdom would remain politically stable, as he showed in a general letter of 19 November to the parlements about their *gages* and *augmentations de gages*.

In this letter, Desmarets candidly blamed the whole problem on the ongoing economic and fiscal crisis, which had deprived the king of revenue. But the default was only temporary, he alleged, driven by the current exceptional circumstances. The controller general promised to resume payments as soon as possible, without predicting when that would be, and commended those parlements (Aix and Dijon) that, at his request, had ceased legal action against financial officials. He told the tribunals that he fully expected them all to submit to the king and to bear their losses on his behalf, as long as necessary. This letter brought no comfort, aside from its realism and vague promises about the future. But all the parlements accepted these assurances as though they believed them, all except Aix, which could no nothing alone.[60]

This is all the more revealing because we know that Desmarets understood the financial predicament of the magistrates very well. In a grim assessment of the kingdom's finances, written on 26 August 1709, three months before his letter to the parlements, he recognized that the judges had depleted their personal resources for the sake of the war. They had paid 'immense sums', he admitted, and many had mortgaged their offices to the limits, exposing themselves to creditors again and again. But even so, the controller general did not fear that the parlements would turn against the government, despite the difficulties of the moment. The long reign of Louis XIV told him that he could take them for granted, and he was almost right.[61]

Remonstrances and *augmentations de gages* to 1715

As the reign neared its end, the parlements for the most part stayed within the political boundaries that the king had long since assigned them. On the subject of registering laws and issuing remonstrances, they continued to observe, but if necessary the government enforced, the requirements about registration procedure from the ordinance of 1667 and the declaration of February 1673. Infractions occurred rarely, on issues of no importance, and remonstrances became few in number.

The new Parlements of Tournai and Besançon were understandably slow to master the rules of 1673. In 1699, the Tournai tribunal registered an edict subject to future remonstrances, the sort of qualified registration that the 1673 declaration forbade. With the chancellor as *rapporteur*, the royal council quashed the decree with a sharp rebuke; and Tournai fell into line with an unqualified registration. Similarly, the Parlement of Besançon registered the Eaux et Forêts edict 'under the reserve of remonstrances', reviving a constitutional phrase and shocking the council, which ordered an immediate, pure and simple registration. Besançon also yielded.[62]

Only on rare occasions did one of the older tribunals step out of line; and those parlements always got caught and scolded. In 1706, the Parlement of Dijon disobeyed Chamillart and twice declined to register a declaration that awarded the new office of *conseiller garde des sceaux* to the *président à mortier* Fuyot on the grounds that it violated precedent for him to hold two positions. Rather than register the declaration, the Parlement remonstrated against it, a breach of the 1673 requirements. But when the Royal Council of Finances rejected the remonstrance and admonished the judges, the Parlement registered the declaration without further delay; and Fuyot kept the office. When it registered a declaration of 1712 on property transfers, the Parlement of Toulouse remonstrated, declaring that it would ignore the new law in favour of local precedents. Chancellor Pontchartrain condemned any 'illusion on your part' that parlements could disregard that law or any other. Toulouse promptly surrendered.[63]

The majority observed the regulations about issuing remonstrances all the way to the end of the reign. The Parlement of Pau remonstrated against an edict of 1691 which united it with the Chambre des Comptes of Béarn and against the Eaux et Forêts edict of 1704. But the Parlement registered those edicts on the schedule that the 1673 rules established and forwarded its remonstrances, as it said, 'in accordance with the ordinance'. In 1709, both Bordeaux and Rouen remonstrated against declarations that regulated grain farming in that famine year, but they submitted their registration decrees along with their remonstrances, just as the law required.[64]

In both form and content, then, the discipline of the 1670s held firm into the last years of the reign; but the king put the parlements to a severe test when he defaulted on *gages* and *augmentations de gages*. As we have seen, the default threw the tribunals into confusion; it also made remonstrances more numerous and, within limits, more pointed in their defence of vested interests. Without throwing off the shackles of 1673, the parlements grew more restless and took the first steps to reassert themselves.

This became clear in late 1710 when the king created a 10 percent tax on income called the *dixième*. Except for members of the clergy and the indigent, everyone was to pay one-tenth of his or her income from land, pensions, rentals, *rentes*, fees, salaries, etc. Although most taxpayers understated income in the declarations they submitted, depriving the *dixième* of its full effect, it still produced much-needed revenue for the treasury. In one significant respect, the magistrates found the new tax impossible to evade. With the *dixième* declaration, the government had in effect reduced the magistrates' *gages* by the stated 10 percent. Given the current default on *gages*, the chief result, disagreeable enough, was to reduce future claims for salary arrears, a writing down of the royal debt owed them.[65] By another declaration, issued soon after the *dixième*, the king unilaterally lowered the interest rate on *augmentations de gages*. The *augmentations de gages* of 170l and 1702–1703 paid 5.5 and 6.25 percent, respectively; but in 1710 the king reduced them both to 5 percent. This unilateral reduction, the first since early in the administration of Colbert, in effect repudiated capital. It inflicted a loss of between 10 and 15 percent of the money paid for *augmentations de gages*, and the magistrates had to bear the loss alone. Their creditors retained the legal right to receive payment at the original rates.[66]

This combination of financial issues explains why the *dixième* provoked remonstrances from virtually all the provincial parlements – Dijon, Rouen, Toulouse, Metz, Pau, Douai (formerly Tournai) and perhaps others, the first show of widespread protest since the 1670s. The Parlement of Paris submitted no written remonstrances, but perhaps its first president remonstrated orally. For the time being, however, all this protest took a somewhat muffled form, as the parlements for the most part exercised restraint in what they said. But the more forthright remonstrance of the Parlement of Toulouse showed that beneath the surface dissatisfaction was growing.[67]

Toulouse used its *dixième* remonstrance to draw a vivid picture of the social and economic misery of a province still suffering from the crisis of 1709. Everywhere the Parlement saw 'sadness and consternation' and the new tax was 'painful and onerous' to all, including the parlementaires themselves. Here the remonstrance got to its point, a comprehensive lament for the financial losses the judges had suffered in their venal offices during the last twenty years:

> It seems moreover that it is Rigorous to exact the . . . [*dixième*] . . . from officers of justice and of finance who are [already] ruined by the diminution of the price of their offices, who are deprived of their *gages*, who are without *épices*, without function and incapable of paying the sums that are required of them for the redemption of their capitation and for that of the *paulette*.[68]

This terse sentence summarized all the growing parlementary grievances over venal office: dismay over the decline of *épices* and office prices, anxiety about the capitation and *paulette* redemptions, resentment at the recent stoppage of *augmentations de gages* and opposition to a new tax on top of these ongoing afflictions. Any parlement could have said the same thing, and some began to adopt the same tone. On 19 August 1715, as his final illness overtook the king, the Parlement of Dijon issued an equally vivid remonstrance against a declaration which prolonged the *dixième* and restored the capitation.[69]

Reinforcing their remonstrances, the parlements also sent deputations of magistrates to Paris to apply more or less continuous pressure for the resumption of their *augmentations de gages*. In March 1709, the Parlement of Dijon commissioned Councillor Bouhier to advance its 'affairs' at Paris. The Parlement of Aix sent a magistrate to the city for the sole purpose of obtaining money. In 1714, the Parlement of Rennes named Councillor Robin d'Estréans as its permanent deputy to the controller general, with the blunt instruction to 'get us paid our *augmentations de gages*'. Deputations from Bordeaux arrived in the capital in 1714, 1716 and 1718 for much the same purpose. As late as 1722, the Parlement of Grenoble had representatives in Paris, also seeking back payments. The deputies and the remonstrances signalled a growing determination in the parlements to defend their investment in venal office, but they produced only modest results at the time.[70] They were more important as a sign of things to come in the approaching regency.

The declaration that reduced interest on *augmentations de gages* promised that the government would resume paying the judges on 1 January 1711. This promise turned out to be somewhat misleading as payments, rather than resuming as a matter of course, depended upon a parlement's negotiating skills and influence at court. Thus, the Parlement of Aix, where the capable Le Bret was still the first president, was among the first to receive some *augmentations de gages*, whereas the Parlement of Dijon, scolded by Chancellor Pontchartrain for being too outspoken, had to wait until the end of the year. In 1711 and 1712, most although not all parlements received a partial payment for 1709, but little more after that. The government also began to pay the magistrates their *gages* with a bit more regularity, after deducting the *dixième* in advance. But from 1711 to 1715 the parlements complained frequently about the continuing lag in their *gages* and *augmentations de gages* and the steadily accumulating arrears. Thus, in 1715, Dijon and Toulouse were owed up to three years of payments, while the Parlement of Rennes and others had fallen even farther behind.[71] The issue remained unresolved.

When Louis XIV died on 1 September 1715, he left the magistrates with their offices taxed, yielding scant income, reduced in value, heavily mortgaged, exposed to creditors and with unpaid *augmentations de gages*. The defences with which the parlements had once protected their venal interests had collapsed altogether, and the two recent wars had taken a heavier toll of property in office than even their apprehensive predecessors could have imagined. These depredations served as denouement to the political subservience that began with Colbert in the 1670s. When the king died, however, his political regimen was beginning to show the first signs of wear and tear, brought on by unrest over the alarming state of venal office. Whether the incoming regency government could hold the line against the newly aggrieved parlements remained to be seen.

Notes

1 Richard Bonney, 'The Eighteenth Century. II. The Struggle for Great Power Status and the End of the Old Fiscal Regime', in Richard Bonney, ed., *Economic Systems and State Finance* (Oxford, 1995), pp. 320–325; Paul Harsin, 'La finance et l'état jusqu'au système de Law', in Fernard Brandel and Ernest Labrousse, eds *Histoire économique et sociale de la France*, II (Paris, 1970), 267–276.

2 Harlay, first president, Paris, to Chamillart, controller general, 25 September 1702, BN, *Fonds fr.*, MS 16,524 (Harlay), f. 161r; the king also created two offices of *chevaliers d'honneur*, offices reserved for nobles, in each provincial parlement, but most tribunals paid up to 50,000 livres to avoid having to accept these offices: BN, *Actes R.*, F. 23,617 (139): edict of July 1702: AN, P 3681: 'nouvelles créations'.

3 Harlay to Chamillart, 11 November 1702, f. 168r, and 28 November 1702, f. 177r, in BN, *Fonds fr.*, 17,424 (Harlay); Chamillart to Harlay, *ibid.*, 8 November, f. 163v; 18 November, f. 174r; 26 November, ff. 175v–176r; and 29 November 1702; BN, *Actes Royaux*, F. 23,617 (no. 235): edict of 1702.

4 BM, Aix, MS 977 (Délibérations du Parlement): 14 December 1702, f. 145rv; BM, Dijon, MS 769 (Registres du Parlement): 7 December 1702, p. 454; AD, Moselle, B 334 (Registres secrets, Metz): 28 December 1702, f. 43v, and B 336: 27 January 1704, ff. 61v–64v; AD, P-A, B 4545 (Registres secrets, Pau): 11 December 1702, f. 111v; AD, I-V, IBb (Registres secrets, Rennes) 299: 5 December 1702, ff. 60–61; BN, *Fonds fr.*, 22,455 (Parlement de Rouen), pp. 496–497; Parlement of Tournai to Chamillart, 13 December 1702, AN, G7, 260; AD, Isère, 2B5* (Parlement of Grenoble): 6 February 1703, ff. 245v–246r; Chamillart to Morant, first president, Toulouse, 2 December 1702, Boislisle, *Correspondance*, II, 133.

5 Lebret, first president, Aix, to Chamillart, 15 January and 2 July 1703, AN, G7, 466; BM, Aix, MS 977 (Délibérations du Parlement): 2 January 1704, ff. 165v–166v; AD, Isère, 2B5* (Grenoble): 7 March to 30 July 1703, ff. 247r–249v; BM, Dijon, MS 769 (Registres du Parlement): 14 August 1703, p. 495; and Bouchu, first president, to Chamillart, 24 March 1704, AN, G7, 1341. For Metz, see AD, Moselle, B 336 (Registres secrets): 27 January 1704, ff. 61v–64v; Boisot, first president, Besançon, to Chamillart, 20 April 1703, AN, G7, 1342; AN, P 3395 (Augmentations de gages, 1701–1702).

6 AD, Gironde, B (Parlement) Arrêts (April–June 1703): 23 May 1703; Dalon, first president, to Desmarets, *directeur des finances*, 26 December 1705, AN, G7, 1337; Desmarets to Dalon, 21 January 1706, AN, G7, 10.

7 Fieubet, deputy of the Parlement, to Desmarets, 9 October 1704, AN, G7, 1350, MS 145; 'Les officiers du parlement de Toulouse', c. 1704, AN, G7, 307.

8 Bréquigny, *président à mortier*, Rennes, to Chamillart, 8 December 1702, AN, G7, 182; IBc (Parlement) 1: 'augmentations de gages'; AD, S-M, IB 222 (Registres secrets, Rouen): 10 March 1702, ff. 29–30; BN, *Fonds fr.*, 22,455 (Parlement de Rouen), pp. 497–498, 501; AN, G7, 1775, MS 247–248.

9 BN, *Fonds fr.*, 16,524 (Harlay): Chamillart to Harlay, 15 June and 11 December 1703, ff. 188rv and 199v; Harlay to Chamillart, 22 June 1703, ff. 189r–190r; 192r; 200r; 207rv–209rv; AN, X1A 8420 [Conseil secret], 13 December 1703. For identical pressure against Bordeaux, see Dalon, first president, to Desmarets, 3 May 1704, AN, G7, 140; Desmarets to Dalon, 21 January 1706, AN, G7, 10.

10 Chamillart to Herbigny, intendant, Rouen, 7 March 1703, AN, G7, 497, and Boislisle, *Correspondance*, II, 133; Chamillart to Harlay, 15 June 1703, BN, *Fonds fr.*, 17,439 (Harlay), f. 41v; for Rouen, see AN, G7, 1775, MS 247: 14 July 1703; *ibid.*, 1366, MS 97.

11 BN, *Actes R.*, F. 23,617 (552): edict of February 1704; Guyot, *Répertoire*, XVI, 660–664; Mousnier, *Organs of State and Society*, pp. 287–296. See the parlements' protests over this loss of jurisdiction in AN, G7, 1337, 1351.

12 AN, G7, 1366 (Eaux et forêts, divers, 1703–1715), nos 66 and 100; G7, 1330, 'Offices des chambres des Eaux et forêts'.

13 Desmarets to d'Aguesseau, *procureur général*, Parlement of Paris, 29 February 1704, AN, G7, 9 (1704).

14 Correspondence and memoranda in AN, G7, 9, 1330, 1342, 1350–1351, 1366; Aix, Musée Arbaud, MS MQ 19, August 1704, f. 418; AD, Doubs, B 3768 (Délibérations, Parlement de Besançon): 26 May and 2 June 1704; AM, Bordeaux, MS 797 (Registre secret): 4 April 1704, p. 33; BM, Dijon, MS 769 (Registres du Parlement): 14 August 1704, pp. 536–537; AD, Moselle, B 337 (Registres secrets, Metz): 21 April 1704, ff. 30rv; AD, I-V (Rennes), IBb (Registres secrets) 303: 5 and 22 August 1704, ff. 2rv, 9rv, and Brilhac, first president, Rennes, to Desmarets, 16 April 1704, AN, G7, 184.

15 AN, G7, 1337, 1349–1351, 1366.

16 AN, G7, 1366, MS 96, 'Bordereau sommaire . . . des Chambres des Eauex et forests', and MS 120, 'Traité des chambres des eaues et forestz', 1709–1710. As a supplement to this treaty, the provincial tribunals had each had to pay 24,000 livres to purchase four dispensations for nobility in the first decree.

17 Aix: BN, *Actes R.*, F. 23,618 (15): edict of April 1705; Besançon: BN, *Actes R.*, F. 23,617 (723): edict of July 1704; Grenoble: BN, *Actes R.*, F. 23,618 (442): edict of April 1706 and AN, G7, 1341, MS 144; Rennes: BN, *Actes R.*, F. 23,617 (812): edict of October 1704; Toulouse: BN, *Actes R.*, F. 23,617 (951): edict of January 1705; and Paris: BN, *Actes R.*, F. 23,617 (665): edict of May 1704. In addition, the government made office sales easier by releasing purchasers of new offices from the kinship restrictions, as between father and son or uncle and nephew, and the minimum age requirements set by the venality edicts of 1665 and 1669.

18 Toulouse: 'Projet de création pour le Parlement de Toulouse', AN, G7, 1350, MS 146; Dijon: 'Les gens tenans la cour de Parlement de Dijon' to Desmarets, 5 June 1704, AN, G7, 1341, MS 48; Bordeaux: Dalon, first president, to Chamillart, 20 December 1704, AN, G7, 1337, MS 21, and Parlement to Chamillart, 4 May 1705, *ibid.*, MS 149; Besançon: AD, Doubs, B 3768 (Délibérations): 3 June 1704, and B 394 (Correspondance), Parlement to Chamillart, n.d.

19 AN, G7, 1337: 'Mémoire pour Messieurs des Enquestes du Parlement de Bordeaux . . .', c. November 1704, and AM, Bordeaux, MS 797 (Registre secret): 18 March 1705, pp. 67–74; AN, G7, 1350: 'Mémoire pour le Parlement de Toulouse', c. August 1704; 'Mémoire de Messieurs les présidents à mortier au parlement de Toulouse', 3 August 1704; *présidents à mortier* to Desmarets, 10 December 1704.

20 Aix, Musée Arbaud, MS MQ 19: August 1704 (f. 418), 4 October 1704 (ff. 420–421), 18 May 1705 (ff. 440–441); BM, Aix, MS 956 (Délibérations du Parlement); BN, *Actes R.*, F. 23,618 (15): edict of April 1705; AN, G7, 1351: MS 86; AD, B-R (Aix), B 3596: balance, 22 August 1712.

21 On Desmarets, see the favourable impressions of Jean-Baptiste Colbert, marquis de Torcy, *Journal inédit* (Paris, 1884), pp. 75, 94; Adolphe Vuitry, *Le désordre des finances et les excès de la spéculation à la fin du règne de Louis XIV* (Paris, 1885), pp. 19–24; Abel Poitrineau, 'Desmarets', in François Bluche, ed., *Dictionnaire du Grand Siècle* (Paris, 1990), pp. 465–466.

22 François Bluche and Jean-François Solnon, *La véritable hiérarchie sociale de l'ancienne France. Le tarif de la première capitation (1695)* (Geneva, 1983), pp. 17–18, 30–38, 95; Marion, *Dictionnaire*, pp. 69–71; capitation memoranda in AN, G7, 1134, 1138–1139; BN, *Fonds Fr.*, 16,524 (Harlay), f. 219r.

23 BN, *500 Colbert*, MSS 259–260. Some *présidents à mortier* and councillors received royal pensions over and above their *gages*.

24 AN, AD+, 678: edict of September 1708; Pontchartrain to Huchet de La Bédoyère, *procureur général*, Parlement of Rennes, 10 June 1709, BN, *Manuscrits Fr.*, 21,129 (Recueil des lettres), f. 502r. For official pressure, see BM, Dijon, MS 769 (Registres du Parlement): 10 December 1708, p. 710; AD, Moselle (Metz), B 346 (Registres secrets): 19 November 1708, f. 32r.

25 Aix: AN, E 801/B: decree of 26 February 1709; Besançon: Boisot, first president, to Desmarets, 29 March 1709, AN, G7, 283; Dijon: 'Estat . . . pour le rachat de la capitation', AN, G7, 163; Grenoble: notation in AN, G7, 1134; Metz: La Porte, first president, to Desmarets, 10 February 1709; Rennes: AD, I-V, IBb (Registres secrets) 314: 12 May 1710, ff. 36–37; Parlement of Toulouse to Desmarets, 8 December 1709, AN, G7, 312; 'Capitation du Parlement', Paris, BN, *Fonds Fr.*, 16,524 (Harlay), f. 219r.

26 BM, Aix, MS 977 (Délibérations du Parlement): 10 June 1712, ff. 431r–433r; Parlement of Besançon to Desmarets, 6 February 1710, AD, Doubs, B 396; BM, Dijon, MS 769 (Registres du Parlement): 5 December 1710, p. 816; AD, Isère (Grenoble), 2B4*, ff. 326r–327v; AD, Moselle (Metz), B 348 (Registres secrets): f. 42rv; AD, I-V (Rennes), IBb (Registres secrets) 319: 27 January 1713, f. 51; BN, *Fonds fr.*, 22,455 (Parlement de Rouen), p. 530; Bautot, unidentified, Rouen, to Desmarets, 29 January 1709, AN, G7, 499; Montbrun, *président à mortier*, Toulouse, to Desmarets, 23 January 1709, AN, G7, 311; Savignac, *Mémorial général de Mr. de Savignac* (Bordeaux, 1931), p. 12; AM, Bordeaux, MS 797 (Registre secret), 23 January 1709, pp. 143–144; La Bourdonnaye, intendant, Bordeaux, to Desmarets, 23 February 1709, AN, G7, 143.

27 AD, Isère (Grenoble), 2B 1046: 'Sommes empruntées pour le rachat de la capitation'; La Porte, first president, Metz, to Desmarets, 10 February 1709, AN, G7, 382; AD, I-V (Rennes), IBb (Registres secrets) 311: 11 January 1709, ff. 61–62; Montbrun, *président à mortier*, Toulouse, to Desmarets, 23 January 1709, AN, G7, 311.

28 As in A. Lloyd Moote, 'Law and Justice under Louis XIV', in *Louis XIV and the Craft of Kingship*, ed. John C. Rule (n.p., 1969), p. 234; Ford, *Robe and Sword*, p. 113.

29 BN, *Actes R.*, F. 23,619 (687), edict of December 1709; and BN, N.a.f., 9,807 ('. . . parties casuelles . . . 1709'): ff. 24r–25r.

30 On *billets de monnaie*, see Lüthy, *Banque protestante*, I, 191–195; AN, G7, 1138–1139, MS 226, c. 1708, and AN, E 810/A: decree of 19 November 1709.

31 Le Camus, intendant, Pau, to Desmarets, 7 June 1710, AN, G7, 118; AD, P-A (Pau) B 4547 (Registres secrets): 13 January and 6 June 1710; Parlement of Dijon to Desmarets, 8 January 1711, AN, G7, 163.

32 Desmarets to Parlement of Metz, 1 April 1710, in AD, Moselle, B 349 (Registres secrets), f. 51rv; J.L.H. D'Esmivi de Moissac, *Histoire du Parlement de Provence, 1501–1715* (2 vols; Aix, 1726), II, 474; BM, Aix, MS 977 (Délibérations du Parlement): 23 December 1710, ff. 391v–392r; AD, B-R (Aix), B 3596: 'Quittance du Rachat de l'Annuel'. On extensions of the redemption deadline, see BN, *Actes R.*, F. 23,620 (no. 59): declaration of 28 April 1711; (no. 502): declaration of 8 August 1713; F. 23,621 (no. 270): declaration of 18 January 1716; (no. 573): declaration of 5 December 1716.

33 Desmarets to Parlement of Bordeaux, as reported by First President Dalon, AM, Bordeaux, MS 797 (Registre secret): 10 June 1711, p. 176; see Savignac, *Mémorial*, pp. 100, 113 for his problems in paying for the redemption; Parlement of Besançon to Desmarets, 18 February 1710, AD, Doubs, B 396, and first president, *procureur général* and *présidents à mortier* to Desmarets, 22 March 1712, Boislisle, *Correspondance*, III, 432; *présidents à mortier*, Toulouse, to Desmarets, 12 May 1715, AN, G7, 323; payments of Parlement of Rennes, 1709–1716, AN, G7, 197; Saulnier, *Parlement de Bretagne*, I, 357 (Councillor Ferret).

34 Pontchartrain to La Bigotière de Perchambault, *président des enquêtes*, Rennes, 18 November 1702; Depping, *Correspondance*, II, 360.

35 Mousnier, *Vénalité*, pp. 75–76; Poitrineau, 'Gages, Épices, Vacations', in Bluche, *Dictionnaire du Grand Siècle*, p. 632; La Roche-Flavin, *Treize livres*, Bk I, ch. xxii, pt. ix; Loyseau, 'Cinq Livres', Bk IV, ch. viii.

36 Harlay to Chamillart, 25 September and 11 November 1702, BN, *Fonds Fr.*, 16,524 (Harlay), ff. 161, 168, and d'Aguesseau, *procureur général*, Paris, to Chamillart, 10 January 1708, AN, G7, 435; Lebret, first president, Aix, to Chamillart and Desmarets, 8 April 1693, AN, G7, 462; 1 November 1704, Boislisle, *Correspondance*, II, 207; 22 July 1709, AN, G7, 473; remonstrances of Parlement of Besançon, 21 November 1702, AN, G7, 1342; Bezons, intendant, Bordeaux, to Chamillart, 12 January 1700, AN, G7, 139; Brûlart, first president, Dijon, to Pontchartrain, 8 December 1689, AN, G7, 157; 'Mémoire pour le parlement de Dauphiné', 1704, AN, G7, 1351, MS 99; La Porte, first president, Metz, to Chamillart, 11 March 1704, AN, G7, 1330; Parlement of Brittany to Lefevre de La Falluère, first president, 24 September 1692, AD, I-V (Rennes), IBb, *Registre littéraire*, f. 21v; Bernières de Bautot, unidentified, Rouen, to Chamillart, 29 January 1709, AN, G7, 499; 'Mémoire pour le Parlement de Toulouse', August 1704, AN, G7, 1350.

37 Hurt, 'Les offices au Parlement de Bretagne', pp. 9–19; Gresset, *Gens de justice*, I, 324–325, 330.

38 AD, B-R (Aix dépôt): B 3601 (Registres de la comptabilité). There are no solid figures for *épices* and *commissaires* for the parlements of the eighteenth century: Bluche,

Magistrats, pp. 169–170; Jean Egret, *Le Parlement de Dauphiné et les Affaires Publiques* (2 vols; Grenoble, 1942), I, 29.

39 Aulède, first president, Bordeaux, to Pontchartrain, 22 December 1689, AN, G7, 134; and Bezons, intendant, Bordeaux, to Chamillart, 12 January 1700, Morant, first president, Toulouse, to Pontchartrain, 1 December 1689, AN, G7, 299; Faucon de Ris, first president, Rouen, to Pontchartrain, 31 January 1691, AN, G7, 493; Lebret, first president, Aix, to Pontchartrain, 8 April 1693, AN, G7, 462, and to Desmarets, 1 November 1704, Boislisle, *Correspondance*, II, 207; La Porte, first president, Metz, to Chamillart, 11 March 1704, AN, G7, 1330; Brûlart, first president, Dijon, to Pontchartrain, 8 December 1689, AN, G7, 157; 'Mémoire pour le parlement de Dauphiné', 1704, AN, G7, 1351; Le Peletier, first president, Paris, to Desmarets, Boislisle, *Correspondance*, III, 166; Hurt, 'Les offices au Parlement de Bretagne', p. 19; Colin Kaiser, 'The Deflation in the Volume of Litigation at Paris in the Eighteenth Century and the Waning of the Old Judicial Order', *European Studies Review* 10(1980), 309–336.

40 Hamscher, *Conseil privé*, pp. 90–91, especially n. 32, summarizes historical opinion on the causes of the decline; BN, *Actes R.*, F. 23,614 (926): edict of February 1691, creating *receveurs*; F. 23,617 (857): edict of November 1704, other officials; with implementing decrees in AN, E 599/A: decrees of 28 August 1691; d'Aguesseau to Chamillart, 10 January 1708, AN, G7, 435; remonstrances of Parlement of Besançon, 21 November 1702, AN, G7, 1342; 'Mémoire . . .', Parlement of Grenoble, c. 1705, AN, G7, 1341, MS 111; Parlement of Tournai to Chamillart, 13 December 1702, AN, G7, 260.

41 Morant, first president, Toulouse, to Pontchartrain, 22 November 1691, AN, G7, 300.

42 See the *fixation* levels in BN, *Actes R.* F. 23,612 (842): edict of December 1665. The *président à mortier* and councillor prices from the 1690 sale are in AN, P 3317–3318: 'nouvelles créations'; BN, *Fonds Fr.* 16,524 (Harlay), f. 212v, and Harlay to Chamillart, 25 September 1702, *ibid.*, MS 161; 'Mémoire sur l'évaluation des offices sujets aux Revenus Casuels', c. 1715, AN, G7, 1325.

43 Rennes: office prices in AN, P 3317 (1690 sale) and 3955 (1704 sale). Toulouse: the *fixation* prices are in Lapierre, *Parlement de Toulouse*, p. 35. For the prices and sales of the 1690s, see Bâville, intendant, to Pontchartrain, 22 December 1690, AN, G7, 299; Morant, first president, to Pontchartrain, 22 November 1691 and 2 January 1692, and 'Mémoire sur la nouvelle crue . . . au Parlement de Toulouse', AN, G7, 300; AN, G7, 1350, MS 110 (councillor price, Toulouse).

44 Bezons, intendant, Bordeaux, to Pontchartrain, 10 February 1691, AN, G7, 135, and AM, Bordeaux, MS 795 (Registre secret): pp. 198–199 (16 January 1666); AN, P 3318: 1690s prices; Bezons, Bordeaux, to Pontchartrain, 12 December 1699, AN, G7, 135. The 1704 evaluation of 18,000 livres is in AN, G7, 1337, MS 53, and Dalon letter, 11 June 1704, AN, G7, 1337. See also William Doyle, *The Parlement of Bordeaux and the End of the Old Regime, 1771–1790* (New York, 1974), pp. 27–29.

45 Grenoble: 'Instruction sur les emprunts', 1703, AN, G7, 245, and undated Baudouin memorandum, c. 1704, AN, G7, 1351; Pau: 'Propositions faites pour procurer un secours au Roy', 1702, AN, G7, 116, and Saint-Maclary, subdelegate, to Chamillart, 21 November 1706, AN, G7, 117; Metz: Emmanuel Michel, *Histoire du Parlement de Metz* (Paris, 1845), p. 274; AN, P 3318: 'nouvelles créations'; Sève, intendant, to

Pontchartrain, 31 January 1695, AN, G7, 377; 'Mémoire pour le Parlement de Metz', c. 1703, AN, G7, 382; Rouen: Faucon de Ris, first president, to Pontchartrain, 10 April 1691, AN, G7, 493; AN, P 3318: 'nouvelles créations'; Aix: Kettering, *Judicial Politics*, p. 224; AN, P 3320: 'nouvelles créations'. The councillor office of Elzéar d'Antoine of the Parlement of Aix was valued at 38,000 livres at his death in 1710, well below the 50,000 livres the tribunal found acceptable: Monique Cubells, *Le Provence des Lumières. Les parlementaires d'Aix au 18eme siècle* (Paris, 1984), p. 119; Brûlart, first president, Dijon, to Pontchartrain, 15 March 1691, AN, G7, 157.

46 AN, P 3318: 'nouvelles créations'; Gresset, *Gens de justice*, I, 326–327.

47 Saulnier, *Parlement de Bretagne*, II, 615 (La Grée); La Tresne, first president, Bordeaux, to Pontchartrain, 8 July 1698, AN, G7, 135.

48 Hurt, 'Offices au Parlement de Bretagne', pp. 22–26.

49 Sigismond Ropartz, *La famille Descartes en Bretagne, 1586–1762* (Rennes, 1877), p. 206 [see Raymond A. Mentzer, Jr., *Blood and Belief: Family Survival and Confessional Identity among the Provincial Huguenot Nobility* (West Lafayette, Ind., 1994), p. 64, for a similar example from the Parlement of Toulouse.]; René de La Bigotière, *Commentaires sur la coutume de Bretagne*, 2nd edn (Rennes, 1702), p. 348; Noël du Fail, *Les plus solennels arrests et règlements donnéz au Parlement de Bretagne*, ed. Michel Sauvageau (2 vols; Nantes, 1715–1716), I, 49 (the assessment of the jurist Sauvageau).

50 Bordeaux: La Tresne, first president, to Pontchartrain, controller general, 8 July 1698, Boislisle, *Correspondance*, I, 484, and Bezons, intendant, to Pontchartrain, 12 December 1699, AN, G7, 135; Bezons, intendant, to Chamillart, 12 January 1700, and La Tresne to Chamillart, 14 October 1701, AN, G7, 139; and Dalon, first president, to Chamillart, 19 December 1705, AN, G7, 177; Rouen: Lamoignon de Courson, intendant, to Desmarets, 22 May 1705, AN, G7, 497; 'Recette du droit annuel, année 1706', AN, G7, 1359, and 'Mémoire sur l'évaluation des offices . . .'; BN, *Fonds fr.*, 22,455 (Parlement de Rouen), p. 521; BM, Aix, MS 976 (Délibérations du Parlement): 22 March 1706, ff. 208v–209r, and 'Mémoire pour le Parlement de Toulouse', August 1704, AN, G7, 1350.

51 Lüthy, *Banque protestante*, I, 105–106, 188–228; Dessert, *Argent, pouvoir, et société*, pp. 210–220. Torcy, *Journal inédit*, p. 94, recorded the financial anxiety Louis XIV showed in a council session.

52 Mousnier, *Vénalité*, pp. 460–462; Bonney, *King's Debts*, pp. 26, 46; Kettering, *Judicial Politics*, p. 225.

53 El Annabi, *Parlement de Paris*, p. 63 and n. 54; Mêmes, *président à mortier*, to Chamillart, 6 March 1712, AN, G7, 439 (a similar episode).

54 Desmarets to Lebret, first president, Aix, 1 July 1709, BN, *Fonds Fr.*, 8890; BM, Dijon, MS 769 (Registres du Parlement): 23 February 1709, p. 715; 'Gages et augmentations de gages . . . parlement de Provence', BN, *Fonds fr.*, 8,906, ff. 20rv–28r; 'État général . . . parlement de Bretagne', AN, G7, 199; AD, I-V, IBc (Parlement of Rennes) 2bis.

55 Lebret, first president, Aix, to Desmarets, 22 July 1709, AN, G7, 475; Parlement of Aix to Desmarets, 27 May 1709, AN, G7, 473; Dalon, first president, Bordeaux, to Desmarets, 6 August 1709, AN, G7, 143; Parlement of Dijon to Desmarets, 16 November 1709, AN, G7, 162; Bertin, first president, Pau, to Desmarets, AN, G7, 118; Parlement of Toulouse to Desmarets, 8 December 1708, AN, G7, 312.

56 Parlement of Toulouse to Desmarets, 8 December 1709, and Bâville, intendant, to Desmarets, 8 October 1709, AN, G7, 312; Parlement of Dijon to Desmarets, 16 November 1709, AN, G7, 162; Lebret, first president, Aix, to Desmarets, 23 June, 12 and 30 July 1709, and Parlement of Aix to Desmarets, 27 May 1709, AN, G7, 473; Dalon, first president, Bordeaux, to Desmarets, 29 July 1709, AN, G7, 143. For seizures of office by legal writ in Bordeaux in 1709–1710, see AD, Gironde, 1B (Registres d'enregistrement) 30; and Savignac, *Mémorial*, p. 17.

57 Parlement of Aix to Desmarets, 27 May 1709, and Lebret, first president, to Desmarets, 23 June, 9, 12 and 19 July 1709, AN, G7, 473; La Garde, *procureur général*, to Lebret, 8 July 1709, AN, G7, 473.

58 Desmarets to Parlement, 28 May 1709, AD, I-V (Rennes), IBb: *Registre littéraire*, f. 33; Parlement to Desmarets, 5 June 1709, *ibid.*, f. 34; Desmarets to Brilhac, first president, Rennes, 21 July 1709, in Boislisle, *Correspondance*, III, 174–175; Lamoignon, intendant, Rouen, to Desmarets, 6 July 1709, *ibid.*, 180; Le Bret, first president and intendant, Aix, to Desmarets, 9 and 12 July 1709, AN, G7, 473. See Pierre-Joseph Marchand, *Un intendant sous Louis XIV, étude sur l'administration de Lebret en Provence* (Paris, 1889).

59 Mousnier, *Vénalité*, pp. 283–308, 645–661; *idem.*, 'The Fronde', pp. 143–146; Moote, *Revolt of the Judges*, pp. 54–62, 78–84.

60 Controller general to first presidents of superior courts, 19 November 1709, AN, G7, 14, and Boislisle, *Correspondance*, III, 239–240. Contrast the cooperative letter from Le Peletier, first president, Paris, to Desmarets, 27 November 1709, AN, G7, 436, with the still agitated reactions of Lebret, first president, Aix, to Desmarets, 25 November 1709, AN, G7, 474.

61 Mémore de M. Desmaretz au Roi', 26 August 1709, in Boislisle, *Correspondance*, III, 603–604, and his retrospective analysis of this period: 'Compte rendu au Régent', 1716, *ibid.*, 677.

62 Bagnols, intendant, Tournai, to Pontchartrain, controller general, 13 June 1699, and petition of the Parlement of Tournai, 2 June 1700, AN, G7, 259; Boisot, first president, Besançon, to Chamillart, controller general, 11 April 1704, with marginal note by Desmarets, 11 April 1704; and Doroz, *procureur-général*, to Desmarets, 22 April 1704; Bernage, intendant, to Chamillart, 16 May 1704, AN, G7, 279. The Besançon remonstrance is in AN, G7 1342.

63 BM, Dijon, MS 769 (Registres du Parlement): 28 July and 12 August 1706; 11 March 1707; AN, E 1938: 11 September 1706, ff. 121r–124r; Pontchartrain to Parlement of Toulouse, 19 July 1712, AD, H-G (Toulouse), 51B/29.

64 AD, P-A (Pau), B 4541 (Registres secrets): 30 August 1689, ff. 21v–24v, and 18 December 1691, ff. 163v–167v; B 4545: 10 June 1704, ff. 201v–202r; Parlement to Pontchartrain, controller general, 29 December 1691, AN, G7, 113. For Aix, see Pontchartrain to Parlement, 30 January 1707, AD, B-R (Aix depot), B 3688 (Correspondance); 'Remonstrances du Parlement de Provence', A.A.E., *Petit Fonds*, 1731, ff. 22rv–35rv; Dalon, first president, Bordeaux, to Desmarets, controller general, 10 August 1709, Boislisle, *Correspondance*, III, 200; AD, S-M (Rouen), 1B 228 (Registres secrets): 8–9 July 1709, ff. 45v–48r.

65 Clamageran, *Impôt*, III, 92–99; Richard Bonney, "Le secret de leurs familes': The Fiscal and Social Limits of Louis XIV's *Dixième*', *French History* 7 (December 1993), 383–416.

66 BN, *Actes R.*, F. 23, 619 (907): Declaration of 7 October 1710. The reduction of interest rates also applied to government *rentes*.

67 Antoine, 'Les remontrances', pp. 107–108, did not list all the parlements that remonstrated; for remonstrance texts, see BM, Dijon, MS 769 (Registres du Parlement): 22 and 29 November 1710, pp. 811–813; AD, S-M (Rouen), 1B 230 (Registres secrets): 24 November 1710, ff. 4r–6r, and 15 December 1710, ff. 8v–9r.

68 BN, *Fonds fr.*, 6557, ff. 144rv–146r.

69 BM, Dijon, MS 770 (Registres du Parlement): 7 August 1715, pp. 234, 241–242; Parlement to Desmarets, 22 August 1715, AN, G7, 165.

70 BM, Dijon, MS 769 (Registres du Parlement): 15 March 1709, p. 733; BM, Aix, MS 977 (Délibérations du Parlement): 7 November 1710, f. 389r; AD, I-V (Rennes), IBb 323: 12 September 1714, f. 18; Parlement to Robin d'Estréans, 13 March 1715, *ibid.*, *Registre littéraire*; AM, Bordeaux, MS 797 (Registre secret): 21 November 1714, pp. 328–329, and 1 April 1718, p. 819; AD, Gironde, series B, *Parl. Arrêts.*, 18 March 1716; AD, Isère, 2B4*, 26 March 1722, f. 345r, for the Parlement of Grenoble.

71 Le Bret, first president, Aix, to Desmarets, 3 May 1711, AN, G7, 477, and BM, Aix, MS 977 (Délibérations), 7 December 1711, ff. 410v–4llr; Parlement of Dijon to Desmarets, 8 January 1711, AN, G7, 163, and Pontchartrain, chancellor, to Parlement of Dijon, 17 February 1711, Brûlart, *Choix de Lettres*, II, 321–322; AD, Moselle, B11 (Parlement of Metz); Parlement of Rennes to Desmarets, 10 January 1712, AD, I-V, IBb (Registre littéraire), and Robin d'Estréans to Parlement, 6 May 1716, *ibid.*, f. 56; Desmarets to Parlement of Toulouse, 1712, AD, H-G, 51B/36; AD, B-R (Aix, Annexe), B 3610–3611; AD, Isère, 2B 1046, 'Sommes empruntées', Parlement of Grenoble.

5

The regent and the parlements:
the bid for cooperation

On 2 September 1715, the Parlement of Paris recognized Philippe, duc d'Orléans, a grandson of Louis XIII and the nephew of the late Louis XIV, as regent of France, with the exercise of sovereignty until Louis XV, five years old, came of age. In so doing, the tribunal set aside the political articles of the testament of the late king who, distrusting Orléans, had denied him the title of regent and merely named him chief of a Regency Council, where he could be outvoted by rivals and enemies. Although the magistrates had followed the dictates of public law, they also did Orléans a favour, which he promptly repaid.[1]

By the Declaration of Vincennes, issued on 15 September, the regent restored to all the parlements the right to submit remonstrances before they registered new laws, that part of registration procedure that allowed them the most influence upon legislation. The tribunals thus recovered some of the leverage and bargaining power taken from them in 1673, and even those historians most sympathetic to Orléans have faulted him for what they see as a political mistake.[2] Indeed, one can well ask why the regent, as one of his first official acts, chose to blur the sharp, clear lines within which Louis XIV had confined the once unruly tribunals.

The answer is that he wanted to make the magistrates of the Parlement of Paris, and by extension those in all the tribunals, into friends and allies. In an effort to win their affection, he cajoled, courted and occasionally capitulated to the very judges whom Louis XIV had tethered. In 1718, when Orléans finally broke with the Parlement, he described his earlier attitude towards it as one of 'deference' and 'friendship'. The duc de Saint-Simon, his lifelong friend and a member of the Regency Council, condemned it as irresolute fawning, born of an exaggerated sense of the Parlement's importance. But Orléans was not alone in believing that the tribunal could trouble his regency unless he got it on his side.[3]

Well before 1715, high-level officials anticipated that all the parlements would emerge from their political cocoons once the reign ended. Already in 1709, d'Argenson, the lieutenant general of police for Paris, had cautioned the government about the prospects for a future revival of the Parlement of Paris. In a memorandum of 1712, Achille de Harlay, the retired first president, predicted that the tribunals in general would become much more powerful once the regency began. Between 1710 and 1715, moreover, intendants notified Controller General Desmarets of the reappearance of opposition hotheads in the Parlements of Bordeaux, Rennes and Toulouse and foresaw a difficult time ahead. In 1714, the Parlement of Paris lent substance to these warnings when some magistrates sharply criticized, and proposed remonstrating against, the Bull *Unigenitus*, by which Pope Clement XI, at the request of Louis XIV, condemned the rigorous Christianity of Jansenism. Some judges sympathized with Jansenism, and they all supported the independence of the French church, which the bull threatened. In the summer of 1715, as he prepared to convene an unprecedented national council to reinforce the bull and to issue a declaration imposing it throughout the realm, a defiant king considered holding his first *lit de justice* since 1673, to suppress growing *Unigenitus* opposition in the Parlement. Although his death soon thereafter removed any prospect of a crisis, Orléans must have concluded from these episodes, as well as the earlier warnings, that he needed to pacify the magistrates by relaxing Louis XIV's regimen.[4]

The regent also tried to befriend influential judges in the tribunal. He named several magistrates to his new administrative councils, taking them into his service and thus honouring a promise he made on 2 September. The councils took the place of the high officials through whom Louis XIV had largely governed, the secretaries of state and the controller general. Henri d'Aguesseau, the respected *procureur-général* of the Parlement, and Guillaume Joly de Fleury, its senior *avocat-général*, who had both supported Orléans on 2 September, won appointments to the Council of Conscience, along with the staunchly Jansenist abbé Pucelle, a clerical councillor in the Grand-Chambre. The Parlement welcomed the creation of the Council of Conscience, which would treat *Unigenitus* issues, and admired d'Aguesseau and Joly de Fleury, who had opposed the bull. D'Aguesseau was also known for his character and learning and as an advocate for the Parlement's right to remonstrate. In addition, the regent named Charles Dodun, a *président des enquêtes*, to the Council of Finances, and Councillors Goislard de Montsabert and Menguy, the latter another abbé and Jansenist, to the Council of the Interior. When Orléans created a Chambre de Justice in March 1716 to investigate charges of fraud against financiers and revenue farmers, he made sure that twelve of its thirty members were magistrates of the Parlement – two *présidents à mortier*, Chrétien de Lamoignon and Antoine de Portail, and ten councillors.[5]

The new president of the Council of Finances, the most important administrative council, was Adrien-Maurice, duc de Noailles, also known for his good relations with the judges, especially d'Aguesseau and Joly de Fleury, already his clients. Chancellor Voysin died of a stroke on 1 February 1717, whereupon

Noailles rushed to the Palais Royal before dawn and prevailed upon Orléans to name d'Aguesseau to the post, making his client the head of the judiciary, a personal coup but one that the Parlement received with the greatest enthusiasm. Orléans appointed Joly de Fleury as the new *procureur-général*, completing the circle, so to speak. As if all this were not enough, the regent lavished money upon First President Mesmes, hoping to draw him into his circle of loyal judges.[6]

With the appointments of these magistrates and the publication of the Declaration of Vincennes, Orléans had made his bid for the friendship and support of the Parlement of Paris. Affable, approachable and hardworking, newly popular for his attempt through the councils to govern differently from Louis XIV, the regent had reason to believe that he could make the Parlement an ally and more reason to think that he needed its support.

In the first years of his regency, Philippe had to cope with a well-placed rival, his brother-in-law Louis de Bourbon, duc du Maine, the legitimized son of Louis XIV and the marquise de Montespan. The late king had made Maine and his younger brother, the comte de Toulouse, into princes of the blood, stretching precedent, and declared them eligible to succeed to the throne, a breach of fundamental law.[7] He had also named them to the Regency Council, the new governing council that had replaced the High Council, the Council of Dispatches and the Royal Council of Finances. Two of Maine's closest friends, Marshals Villeroy and d'Harcourt, sat there too, reinforcing him and Toulouse. His wife, the diminutive, ambitious Anne de Condé, a granddaughter of the Great Condé, aggressively pushed Maine forward. This group belonged to an 'old court' faction that had long opposed Orléans and now feared him, since he stood an outside chance of becoming the monarch, if the ailing Louis XV died and if the allies could bar the late king's surviving grandson, King Philip of Spain, from asserting his right to the French throne.[8] Moreover, Maine himself had clients in the parlements and numbered First President Mesmes, who took Orléans's money but played a double game, among his closest friends.[9] In these circumstances, the regent needed all the personal support he could muster.

Despite his careful attentions, the magistrates found reasons to be dissatisfied with the regent, starting with the very Declaration of Vincennes issued to appease them. For all the significance of permitting remonstrances before registration, the declaration scarcely altered other aspects of title I of the ordinance of 1667 or of the declaration of 1673, both of which retained their standing as law. Like the ordinance, the new declaration imposed time limits on the use of remonstrances, giving the Parlement of Paris one week in which to submit a remonstrance, starting from the day that it voted to issue one, and setting six weeks as the term for the provincial tribunals. Like the ordinance and the declaration, Vincennes avoided the word remonstrances and perpetuated the circumlocution, 'what it [the Parlement] judges a propos'. It also held the parlements responsible for registering laws once the government had answered

127

any remonstrances, the monarchy's essential demand since the sixteenth century. However much he desired to placate the tribunals, the regent had no wish to usher them on to the centre stage of politics, as the limited scope of the Vincennes declaration showed.[10] As time passed, judges even alluded intemperately to the 'tyranny' and oppression that they believed they had suffered under Louis XIV, reflecting the literary and philosophical criticism directed against the king before he died.[11] They thus pushed for a broad interpretation of Vincennes, hoping to reclaim all their traditional functions of registration and remonstrance and perhaps even to set the political clock back a century or so, ambitions that Orléans could not possibly satisfy. The issue of *augmentations de gages* posed an additional problem. Like the deposed Desmarets, the new government had to deal with the parlements on a financial issue that it could not resolve in their favour. All during his tenure Noailles allowed them to hope for a satisfactory resolution of their *augmentations de gages* claims; but the parlements had about run out of patience with his promises when the regent abruptly dismissed him from office, in January 1718.

What followed was one of the sharpest conflicts between the government and the parlements in the Old Regime, a clash of principles and personalities so intense that the words *Fronde* and *frondeur* came back into use, with all the associations that they conveyed. Observers in Paris tried to match events and personalities with those of 1648, an indoor diversion stimulated by the recent publication of the memoirs of Cardinal de Retz and Guy Joly, leading figures in the Fronde. However farfetched, such comparisons became less implausible as tension rose to a high point. Although only the Parlements of Paris and Rennes involved themselves openly in the struggle, others, such as Rouen, watched and waited, close to the sidelines. In any case, Paris and Rennes made a potentially formidable coalition.[12]

The issues were whether the parlements, in remonstrating before registering the laws, would recover their full registration powers and their capacity to influence government policy, especially financial policy, and, secondarily, whether they could induce the government to restore their *augmentations de gages* and other payments, thus reclaiming some of their recent losses in socio-economic ground. A larger question was whether Orléans, once he had failed in his bid for the cooperation of the parlements, would return to the authoritarian measures of Louis XIV in their regard and validate those methods as an example for future kings – whether with regard to the parlements the reign of the Sun King would bequeath a legacy or become an episode.[13]

Orléans, Noailles and *augmentations de gages*

As president of the Council of Finances, the duc de Noailles, who had no particular financial expertise, benefited from the services on the Council of nine proven administrators – four councillors of state, four masters of requests and a *président aux enquêtes* from the Parlement of Paris. Some of these veterans had quite a future before them, three rising to the office of controller general, another becoming lieutenant general of police for Paris, and a fifth (Pierre Gilbert de Voisins) the most respected member of the mid-century council of Louis XV. The senior member, Hilaire Rouillé du Coudray, had laboured under Chamillart and Desmarets and had long since attached himself to Noailles. Although the Council of Finances reported to the Regency Council, which always had the last word, it acted with reasonable autonomy. Its responsibilities included supervising the provincial intendants and keeping an eye on the parlements, and it inherited the job of paying the latter what they were owed.[14]

The royal debt consisted of loans taken out as *rentes* and *augmentations de gages*, unfunded obligations to pay the *gages* of new offices, and a swollen river of promissory notes issued in the recent war by treasurers, receivers and suppliers of *matériel*. Modern authorities estimate this debt at 1.739 billion livres, more than ten years of state income, far too much for the new government to repay or even to service. In addition, Noailles faced a budget deficit of 77 million livres, almost half the king's annual income, a gap so large that all government agencies, along with the army, had run out of funds. Two years later, Noailles still shuddered at the memory of his first trying weeks in office.

When the regent decided that he would not, as he put it, dishonour Louis XV by declaring bankruptcy at the onset of the reign, he left it to Noailles and the Council of Finances somehow to close the gap between income and expenditure. Noailles lowered interest on the debt, suppressed recently created offices, and increased the value of gold and silver coin in terms of livres, the money of account, making the treasury's specie last longer and stretch further at least for a while. He also launched a judicial persecution of financiers and revenue farmers to force them to return some of their profits to the regent. In other words, Noailles proceeded down a path already worn smooth by Colbert and others, hoping that, given time, he would shrink the debt and balance the budget. Perhaps he would have done, eventually, but in the near term he presided over a de facto, partial bankruptcy, not much different from the real thing.[15]

The parlements preferred almost anything to a declared bankruptcy and an outright repudiation of *augmentations de gages*; but what they wanted most was to collect their arrears in full, in specie, and in the near future, none of which was likely to happen. In late 1715, the government owed the Parlement of Paris two years of *gages* and *augmentations de gages*; and the arrears due to the provincial parlements, treated less favourably, ran from five to seven years. The Parlements of Aix and Rennes placed their annual arrears at more than 100,000 livres; those of the Parlement of Paris were probably twice as high. There being no present hope of paying the tribunals their money, Noailles and the Council decided to reduce its liabilities by arbitrarily dropping the interest on *augmentations de gages*. On 14 January 1716, the Council drafted an edict to lower interest to 4 percent from the 5 percent set by Desmarets in 1710. The Regency Council approved the edict on 18 January. Five years after it had last reduced these rates, writing off 10 to 15 percent of the capital invested, the government repudiated another 20 percent. Although Noailles told the parlements, apologetically, that sheer necessity had forced him to take this step, he presented it to the Regency Council as a personal triumph, part of his overall effort to reduce government spending.[16]

But Noailles obviously risked making enemies of the parlements, which neither he nor Orléans wanted to do; and they therefore tried to dampen the natural resentment of the judges as the reduction went into effect. Orléans himself promised First President Mesmes that the new rate would make it possible to resume paying all *augmentations de gages*, at an early date. Noailles made the same pledge to the provincial tribunals. In various communications to the judges, both Orléans and Noailles accepted the validity, including the moral validity, of their financial claims and repeatedly pledged to find them their money.[17] In 1716, Noailles even managed to pay most tribunals a portion of their arrears, as a show of good faith. Decrees of council awarded the Parlement of Paris arrears of about one year of *augmentations de gages*, and most provincial parlements also received a year's payment.[18] These sums, along with the promises of more to come, helped to calm the parlements for a while.

As before 1715, the parlements also complained that their *augmentations de gages* creditors were threatening to confiscate their heavily mortgaged offices and other forms of their property. Seeking royal protection, the judges reminded the government that they had incurred their debts in the service of the late king. Moreover, they had borrowed at 5.5 percent and were now to be paid, if ever, at 4 percent, another argument in favour of royal protection. On 12 June 1716, members of the Council of Finances admitted to themselves that the parlements had justice on their side; but, as always, the question was what the government could do. In theory, the Council could order the creditors to accept the same 4 percent interest rate now promised to the judges. Fearing a hostile reaction from a wide range of creditors, including members of the great nobility, however, the Council decided to temporize a while longer. Noailles instructed the intendants to persuade creditors to suspend their lawsuits against office-holders until 1717, postponing the day of reckoning.[19]

In August 1717, Noailles indeed offered to pay the Parlement of Rennes its *augmentations de gages* in full – but in *billets d'état*, certificates that he had created in 1716 to replace the various paper instruments left over from the recent war. But the sceptical Bretons insisted on specie and showed no interest in yet another example of insecure government paper. They not only declined the offer, they spurned it, and disavowed the deputy, Robin d'Estréans, who had negotiated the arrangement. This rejection all but doomed Noailles's plan to pay the other tribunals in *billets d'état* also; and his ire, to which he gave immediate expression, confirmed the Breton view that the offer would have advantaged the government more than themselves. After two years in office, the duc de Noailles, for all his promises, had made no headway in his effort to resume regular payments of *augmentations de gages* and very little in paying the arrears.[20]

As the months passed, the parlements, pursued by their lenders, renewed their complaints; and on 4 December 1717, Noailles summarized the issue at a session of the Regency Council. He acknowledged that Louis XIV had required the parlements, as well as other law courts, to borrow heavily for their *augmentations de gages*; that their creditors were demanding that the judges pay the original interest rate on these loans; and that the magistrates could not do so. They needed relief so badly that they could not be fobbed off with more assurances, Noailles declared, and they could well become enemies if the government made them wait any longer. Noailles recommended that the Regency Council set 4 percent as the interest rate for all new loans, permitting the magistrates and other debtors to refinance their outstanding debts.[21]

For reasons that went unrecorded, the Regency Council declined to act upon his recommendation, a blow foreshadowing his dismissal, now less than two months away. Noailles had spent two years promising the parlements to solve the problem of their *augmentations de gages*; except for the partial payments of 1716, he had failed to do so. On his analysis, the regency could expect a resurgence of political agitation in the parlements in the near future. Indeed, the Parlement of Paris had already shown some recent signs of life, having just got the better of Noailles in the first serious dispute over a fiscal edict since the early reign of Louis XIV.

Noailles and the Parlement of Paris

At four long sessions of the Regency Council held between 19 and 26 June 1717, Noailles reported on his progress in reducing the state debt and balancing the budget. Equipped with a huge folio volume on current finances, he impressed the Council with his command of fact, quoting figures from memory and offering a *tour d'horizon* of the subject. But he also conceded that it would take years of additional effort and sacrifice to restore the financial health of the state; and this sober assessment, although apparently well received, undermined his standing with the regent in ways that he did not then perceive. Orléans had already turned to the Scottish financier John Law for more imaginative solutions. Unaware that the ground was shifting beneath his feet, Noailles forged ahead.[22]

In August, the regent approved Noailles's 'great edict', the name it acquired from its seventeen lengthy articles intended to reform royal finances and to stimulate the national economy. It was also called the *dixième* edict, since it exempted real property, but only real property, from the *dixième* tax, part of an effort to return fiscal burdens to their pre-war levels. To make up for lost *dixième* revenue, the edict, among other economies, shifted the cost of maintaining lanterns and cleaning streets in Paris from the royal to the city budget. It also established procedures by which the holders of the venal offices that Noailles had recently abolished could obtain the repayment that he had promised them. Additional articles, amplified by accompanying legislation, announced that the government would no longer pay interest on *billets d'état* and other state paper in order to induce owners to exchange it for shares in John Law's new Company of the West. Everything was to take effect on 1 January 1718, after which the government promised to simplify tax collections and to study new measures of financial reform.[23]

Whatever its merits, however, the edict appeared inopportunely, since the magistrates, after two years of Noailles's financial administration, had begun to turn against him, the regent's conciliatory efforts notwithstanding. Against the wishes of First President Mesmes, the judges had just reinstated the 'cabinet', a commission of magistrates appointed from each chamber to scrutinize new legislation before it came to the full Parlement for a vote. The cabinet increased the influence of the younger, more assertive magistrates in Enquêtes and Requêtes and diminished that of the cautious, veteran judges in the Grand-Chambre. Tension between the junior and senior judges had already surfaced; and the first president could not control his junior colleagues. Indeed, no individual or group – no factions representing either Maine or Noailles – had the upper hand among the magistrates as a whole; their alliances shifted back and forth.[24]

The presidents of the Enquêtes and Requêtes chambers took the lead in the deliberations on the *dixième* edict. On 28 August, President Nicolas Lambert of Requêtes brusquely demanded that the government open its financial registers and allow the judges to see for themselves the amount of the king's income and the size of his debts. President Frizon de Blamont of Enquêtes, who was to enjoy rising influence in the weeks to come, supported the idea of disclosure and, with the warm approval of excitable, younger judges, condemned the 'despotic' character of the preceding reign. But the *présidents à mortier* and the Grand-Chambre magistrates resisted the intemperate rhetoric and demands of their junior colleagues. In the end, a compromise between the two groups sent First President Mesmes off to the regent with a request, not a demand, for financial information. When he appeared at the Palais Royal, however, Mesmes unexpectedly cited a precedent from the turbulent regency of Anne of Austria, causing Orléans to lose his temper. The regent heatedly vowed to stand against any 'cabal' in the Parlement, an apparent reference to Lambert, Blamont and the younger judges and a disparaging interpretation of their motives. With the *dixième* edict off to a bad start, several *présidents à mortier*, meeting privately with Orléans a bit later, tactfully persuaded him that he had spoken too harshly at his meeting with the Parlement's deputies. Still clinging to his policy of seeking the tribunal's friendship, the regent accepted the rebuke in good temper and acted to make amends.[25]

Orléans invited another deputation from the Parlement to the Palais Royal where, restored to serenity, he dispensed compliments all around and invited Noailles to speak. Occasionally consulting account books and memoranda ostentatiously spread before him, but also quoting figures from memory, Noailles overwhelmed the deputies with five hours of financial data, a star turn that benefited from his earlier performance at the Regency Council. The magistrates returned to their tribunal with a favourable report on the way Orléans and Noailles had treated them.[26]

However, the Palais Royal session did not altogether smooth the passage of the 'great edict', when the Parlement began to consider it line by line. Although the judges approved most of its seventeen articles, they denounced the article that required owners and renters in Paris to pay for street cleaning and lantern maintenance, since Parisians had redeemed street-cleaning and lantern taxes in 1704. They also argued that, on principle, the government should not try to compel holders of *billets d'état* and other notes to convert their paper into shares in the unknown Company of the West. The government's failure to reimburse holders of suppressed venal offices also drew fire. So the Parlement decided to submit a remonstrance on these grievances, completing the document on 9 September.[27]

Noailles learned where the Parlement stood well before this date, having been kept informed by his official and unofficial sources in the tribunal, which throughout the dispute leaked information through the windows and under the doors. He convened his Council of Finances to discuss an appropriate response and then attended a session of the Regency Council on the issue. Since Noailles's reform plan depended in part upon budget savings from those contentious articles, the government faced a difficult decision – whether to use coercion to register the edict or whether to back down. The first option implied taking a strong line towards the parlements, a change in policy that the regent was not ready to make, while the second option, however embarrassing, fitted the conciliatory political attitudes that had shaped the regency to this point.

The Council of Finances, no doubt following the wishes of Noailles himself, recommended that the Regency Council satisfy the Parlement on all counts. The Regency Council accepted this proposal after a long discussion, about which we are ignorant but which may not have been altogether harmonious. In the end, the regent issued a revisionary declaration that excused Paris from paying for lantern and street maintenance and promised to continue interest payments on *billets d'état* and other notes until such time as the holders, at their discretion, chose to convert them. The Parlement registered the *dixième* edict and the interpretative declaration on the same day, 10 September, ending the two-week dispute. The tribunal emerged with a victory that, if not of overwhelming importance, nevertheless impressed observers as a sign of its impending revival, as the barrister Matthew Marais, a sensible witness, noted.[28] But the roots of the victory traced to Orléans's policy of cultivating the Parlement, not from any independent political strength of its own.

After a few months, however, the judges renewed their questions about state finances, making the efforts to conciliate them appear to have been doomed from the start. On 14 January 1718, claiming that the receivers general had abruptly ceased to pay the interest on notes they had issued, contrary to the promises of Noailles, the more assertive judges persuaded the majority to begin work on a general remonstrance on financial issues and, by implication, on his financial administration. In this remonstrance, prepared over the next two weeks, the Parlement began with the complaint that Noailles had failed to reimburse former office-holders after he had abolished their offices. It also denounced the untimely way the government paid interest on *billets d'état*, notes of the receivers general, and even the once reliable *rentes* on the Hôtel de Ville.

This led to a sober homily on the duty of the reigning monarch to repay subjects who had entrusted the late king with their gold and silver and now held government paper of uncertain value and yield. An allusion to that unwelcome drop in interest rates, or Noailles's 4 percent, also made its way into the remonstrance. Although it concluded by condemning John Law's new bank, which seemed about to become a national bank with control of state revenues, the remonstrance drew no distinction between Noailles and Law. If anything, it damaged Noailles more than Law, not least in the forthright language that it employed. His client group had failed to protect him.[29]

Although these grievances ostensibly reflected the interests of all state creditors, the remonstrance permitted the judges to press their claims, indirectly, on the subject of *augmentations de gages*, their private concern. One of the unwritten protocols of a remonstrance barred the Parlement from acting too obviously on its own behalf. If it transgressed, it suffered ridicule and loss of prestige, since a written remonstrance was virtually a public document, sometimes even printed in the form of a pamphlet. But the judges kept their venal interests very much in mind, even if they did not put these interests into the plain text. On that 14 January when the magistrates began to itemize the financial issues that the remonstrance would take up, one of the younger councillors, Antoine de Nicolaÿ of Enquêtes, sought to include *augmentations de gages*, correctly seeing no difference between them and the other financial instruments the judges were citing. His colleagues hushed him up, not because they disagreed with him but because they wished to disguise the self-interest that lay behind the remonstrance. For political reasons, then, the remonstrance took shape as a defence of all the king's creditors, even though it also applied, in a particular but hidden way, to the magistrates themselves. The Parlement finished it in late January.[30]

The judges probably expected Orléans and Noailles, who had retreated in the face of the September remonstrance, to make new concessions, perhaps even to the point of paying *augmentations de gages*. Instead, the regent's anger with the

Parlement, suppressed the preceding August, rose to new heights as he learned that the Parlement, by its remonstrance, had virtually censured his financial stewardship. Saint-Simon found him pacing the long gallery of the Palais Royal, tense and wary. When, at the head of a deputation, the first president presented the remonstrance on 26 January 1718, and declaimed it in a booming voice, as though he were a tribune of the people, the Parlement wounded the regent more than it knew. That night he consulted the letters patent of February 1641, by which Louis XIII had excluded the Parlement from political and financial affairs; pleased with its contents, he arranged for the law to be reprinted.[31]

As a further complication, Law and Noailles had begun to clash over financial policy and to work against each other, a breach which the regent had tried but failed to mend. Rumour held that Noailles had sent his client d'Aguesseau to write those parts of the remonstrance that condemned Law, even though the final document drew no distinction between the two rivals. At any rate, the regent had to choose between Noailles, with whom he had allied, and Law, whose economic ideas beckoned alluringly. He also had to choose between conciliating the Parlement, a policy identified with Noailles and d'Aguesseau, and a new, firmer approach. Since the two problems, without being precisely the same, overlapped and impinged, he had to determine which was the more important, deserving priority. No wonder he paced the gallery of his palace.[32]

On 28 January 1718, two days after receiving the remonstrance of the Parlement, Orléans astounded the political world when he abruptly stripped the respected d'Aguesseau of the seals of office and banished him to his rural property. Evidently, the regent had decided that relations with the Parlement troubled him most of all and that d'Aguesseau, an ally of the tribunal, had somehow contributed to this problem. Indeed, d'Aguesseau had just promised to support a new fiscal remonstrance from the Parlement of Rennes, suggesting that he also supported, or would support, the remonstrance of Paris. So he had to go.

Orléans's intentions towards Noailles were less clear. Possibly he hoped that the fall of d'Aguesseau would turn Noailles, after a private interview, into a supporter of Law, as he had been before. If so, the regent met with disappointment, for Noailles, appearing unexpectedly at the Palais Royal, did not hide his anger at d'Aguesseau's disgrace, making it impossible to continue him in office. The regent permitted Noailles to resign as president of the Council of Finances rather than suffer the indignity of dismissal, and as a palliative, appointed him to the Council of Regency. Even so, the fall of the esteemed d'Aguesseau reverberated in the capital and in the Parlement for weeks to come.

The regent's choice to replace the Noailles–d'Aguesseau team set off additional tremors. As the new president of the Council of Finances, Orléans appointed Marc-René de Voyer, marquis d'Argenson, the lieutenant of police for Paris, hitherto without financial experience. Even more surprising, the regent made d'Argenson keeper of the seals, giving him the functions of the disgraced d'Aguesseau, to whom in character and public standing he bore so little resemblance. In his person, d'Argenson now united both financial and judicial administration, an unusual combination; and the regent clearly expected him to use these powers to good purpose. Unlike Noailles, d'Argenson was to protect rather than obstruct John Law; he was also to bring the Parlement to heel. The prospect that he could deal with the Parlement, an old personal enemy, and by extension all the parlements seemed d'Argenson's chief qualification for his new offices. In this respect, he had work to do. In addition to the need to answer the remonstrance of the Parlement of Paris, he inherited from Noailles a sharp conflict with the Parlement of Rennes, which in January 1718 was nearing its climax.[33]

The revival of the Parlement of Rennes

Although most provincial parlements exercised political restraint early in the regency, several tribunals did manage to assert themselves to some degree, usually without much success, excepting only the Parlement of Rouen. In 1716, that Parlement, prompted by First President Camus de Pontcarré, arrested local revenue farmers and took their money to pay for the tribunal's household expenses and the annual pension of Pontcarré himself. The Regency Council, upon the recommendation of Noailles and the Council of Finances, decided to make a public example of the Parlement. But Pontcarré, summoned to Paris, paid court to Orléans and to all members of the Regency Council and shifted the blame to the revenue farmers themselves. In the end, the Council, although voiding the tribunal's decrees, cleared Camus of blame and expelled the revenue farmers from Rouen, a turnaround due not only to the first president's negotiating skills but also to the regent's policy of conciliation.

Even so, the Council of Finances, in the absence of personal interventions by the regent, frequently sanctioned parlements if they trespassed into royal finances. When, for example, the Parlement of Toulouse in 1716 jailed the city's receiver of *gabelles* and seized his cash reserves because he owed the tribunal some 55,000 livres in unpaid *gages*, the Council of Finances immediately ordered the magistrates to release the man and to return any money that they had pocketed. It also summoned to Paris the presiding judge, the marquis de Ciron, a famous name in the Parlement, to upbraid him for interfering with royal finances. The Parlement of Metz, which tried to free its litigants from the obligation to purchase stamped paper, incurred a strong reprimand for this clear attempt at tax evasion. In addition, the Parlements of Grenoble and Dijon met with flat refusals when they submitted strongly worded requests and remonstrances to demand financial concessions with regard to their *gages* and capitation.[34]

Those parlements that transgressed and got caught became more obedient thereafter, and the incidents they created had no further consequences. The Parlement of Rennes, however, showed much more determination. Step by step and piece by piece, Rennes set about dismantling parts of the fiscal machine built up in Brittany since the 1670s. The Parlement, ruling in favour of plaintiffs in one tax-related lawsuit after another, issued decrees that impeded or made it impossible to collect taxes of many years standing. By the end of 1716, the Council of Finances and the Regency Council had on seven occasions annulled or set aside one or more financial decrees of the tribunal, far more than for any other parlement.

The Bretons began by threatening officials of the tobacco farm with some sort of judicial assault, but Noailles, apprised of the danger, managed to protect them. Undiscouraged, the Parlement shifted its focus to the revenue farm for the *contrôle des actes*, one of the innovations of Colbert, and ordered the arrest of all nineteen of the farm's collectors. Some fled the province, and others went into hiding; but eleven found themselves in the tribunal's lock-up, accused of embezzlement and fraud. To counteract this mischief, the finance and regency councils annulled the Parlement's decrees and transferred the accused to the Chambre de Justice in Paris, the special court that Noailles created in 1716 to examine the conduct of the financiers. But the Parlement simply expanded its horizons and began harassing a variety of financial underlings. In threatening these officials with judicial sanctions, the Parlement encroached upon the jurisdiction of the provincial intendant, appointed on a permanent basis as recently as 1689. In 1716, the intendant of Brittany was Paul Feydeau de Brou, who must have seemed vulnerable, since he was new to the province, having taken up his duties in February.[35]

Feydeau reacted slowly to the Parlement's forays, and his lethargy encouraged the tribunal to push ahead. On 20 August 1716, the Parlement declined to register letters patent awarding a financier, Nicolas des Nouveaux, the right to sell in Brittany new judicial offices called *greffiers, gardes conservateurs des minutes*, i.e. clerks who were to take over the storage and retrieval functions of the sitting clerks in all the law courts of the province. The Parlement rejected the letters patent, alleging concerns over procedure, and issued a decree forbidding the collection of *gardes conservateurs* taxes, which it then sent it to all the lower courts in Brittany. In addition, the Parlement voted to remonstrate against the *gardes conservateurs* law and against the frequency with which the Regency Council had overridden its recent decrees. Feydeau failed to report these actions to Noailles; not until December did the latter learn what had happened, from the revenue farmers themselves. Once he was informed, he promptly brought the issue to the Council of Finances, which quashed the Parlement's decree of 20 August. He then took the affair to the Regency Council, which summoned to Paris the *président à mortier* who had presided at the session, the *procureur-général* and the *rapporteur*. All were to depart for the capital within forty-eight hours of receiving the summons. Noailles sent

Nicolas Denis, a council *huissier* (bailiff), to deliver the summonses to the offending magistrates. Finally, he reprimanded Feydeau for not informing him of all these events and commanded him to pay closer attention to what the Parlement did with future legislation and council decrees.[36]

On 7 November 1716, the magistrates had voted to issue still another remonstrance, against a fiscal edict of August 1716. That edict suppressed subordinate judicial offices created and sold between November 1689 and December 1712 and reduced the taxes that they collected by about one-third, promising to use the proceeds to refund the capital of these former officeholders. This solution caused much resentment, because the taxes, though reduced, continued to exist and because the former owners of office did not, even so, receive their money. The remonstrance, completed on 18 December, contended that declarations of 1715 had already suppressed some offices listed in the August edict, so that the taxes created with those offices should have already expired.[37]

Plausible though this argument was, it arrived in Paris too late for a hearing. The same council sessions that condemned the Parlement for failing to register the *gardes conservateurs* law also censured it for its treatment of the August edict. From Paris it looked as though the Parlement, having waited until November to vote for a remonstrance, had exceeded the six-week time limit as reaffirmed in the Declaration of Vincennes. So the councils issued *lettres de jussion* for immediate registration of the edict of August 1716 and, in addition, summoned the presiding magistrates and the *rapporteur* to Paris for a formal reprimand – like their colleagues in the *gardes conservateurs* affair. The *huissier* Denis also carried these decrees to Rennes and served the additional summonses on all the magistrates that they named.

As things worked out, the Parlement capitulated to the government and warded off whatever humiliation lay in store. The guilty magistrates in the *gardes conservateurs* dispute apologized to Noailles and promised to behave themselves in the future. In its collective defence, the Parlement noted that its remonstrance on the August edict had in fact observed the six-week restriction in the Vincennes declaration, since it had not begun its deliberations until November. (The declaration started the six weeks on the day a parlement began to deliberate on a new law.) Then it registered the August edict on 29 December, without waiting for an answer to its remonstrance; the intendant Feydeau did not even have to present the *lettres de jussion*. The government accepted these excuses and revoked its summonses to the responsible magistrates. In the end, therefore, the Parlement of Rennes yielded or lost on every point for which it had contended during the year. Wisely, however, Noailles instructed Feydeau to redouble his political surveillance of the magistrates and to keep the government fully informed about their future conduct.[38]

As if to justify this precaution, the Parlement immediately resumed its efforts to undermine royal taxes. Feydeau, now reporting more frequently, accused the tribunal of concocting legalisms to obstruct general fiscal administration. In April 1717, for example, the Parlement excused a litigant from paying *droits de contrôle* on legal documents, a clear violation of law and precedent, as the councils noted, in quashing the decree. Unfazed, the Parlement released merchants from paying levies on salt, tin and alcoholic beverages, prompting the Council of Finances to demand the grounds for such presumptuous decrees. In November, the councils dealt with a fresh attack by the Parlement upon the revenue farmer of the *contrôle des actes*. The tribunal had not only liberated a solicitor from paying *contrôle* duties on summonses; it had also opened criminal proceedings against the farmer's chief clerks, forcing them to suspend all their collections. All over the province, litigants followed the lead of the Parlement, threatening and intimidating clerks and collectors of the *contrôle des actes*. Upon the recommendation of the Council of Finances, the Regency Council annulled the Parlement's decree on the *contrôle*, upheld the jurisdiction of the intendant, and forbade all tribunals in Brittany to render any similar judgements in the future. Despite these acts of council, it seems likely that the Parlement did real damage to the revenue farms in 1717 and merited a punishment for that reason alone, as well as for encroaching upon the jurisdiction of the intendant.[39]

The tribunal escaped serious retribution because the government had become more concerned about rising opposition in the Estates of Brittany, the biennial session of which the king had just convened. Already in December 1715, when the Estates held its first assembly after the death of Louis XIV, discussions over finances had taken on a scope and an intensity not seen since the 1660s. The Estates of 1715, while granting the free gift by acclamation and without discussion, in accordance with the precedent set by Colbert, reasserted the claims of the province to fiscal autonomy. In response, the administration permitted the Estates to establish various commissions to oversee tax collections. These commissions promptly exceeded their mandate and began to obstruct or impede the work of tax collectors throughout the province. Of particular importance, capitation commissions administered that tax in each of the nine dioceses of Brittany, without the participation of the intendant, an extraordinary concession. In 1717, the Estates wanted to renew and to extend the powers of these bodies, especially the capitation commission.

Since 1715, the Estates, like the Parlement, had thus acted against revenue farmers in a parallel effort to slow the gears of the Breton fiscal machine. The nobles of Brittany, who sat by personal right in the second estate, took the lead in this struggle. Prominent nobles met secretly in their chateaux and read, wrote, and circulated lively pamphlets denouncing the capitation and the *dixième* and commenting enviously on the fiscal powers of the Parliament of England. Some openly refused to pay the *dixième*, concealed livestock and harvests, and mobilized peasants armed with muskets to discourage officials from searching their property. Magistrates of the Parlement could not sit in the

Estates, but they all belonged to the nobility; and many were related, sometimes closely related, to the very nobles who led the Estates in its anti-fiscal struggle. When the Estates of 1717 opened at Dinan on 15 December, the Parlement and the Estates nobility had never been more united, nor more determined.[40]

Noailles knew all about the agitation in Brittany – the secret meetings, the discussions, the published memoirs and pamphlets – and worked out a strategy to deal with it. On 6 November, the Regency Council endorsed his approach, in the form of instructions to Marshal Pierre de Montesquiou, the new *commandant en chef*, a surrogate governor who acted in place of the absentee governor, the comte de Toulouse. Montesquiou had won his marshal's baton at the celebrated battle of Malplaquet (1709), where he commanded the army's right wing with commendable valour; and he distinguished himself again at Denain (1712), a great victory over the formidable Prince Eugene of Savoy. Although loaded with honours and distinctions, the new *commandant* offended Bretons with his irascible, imperious manner, apparently a hold-over from his military career.

Breton historians have laid at his feet much of the blame for the upheaval that marked his tenure; but in the Estates of 1717, he only followed his instructions, however arrogant he may have seemed. These instructions began with significant concessions to the province, in keeping with the broadly conciliatory policy of the regent. The *dixième* on property, which had provoked so much opposition, would expire on 1 January, in accordance with Noailles's 'great edict' of August 1717. Moreover, the government had reduced its demand for a 'free gift' from the current 3 million livres to 2 million, payable as usual over the next two years. These concessions, Noailles noted, amounted to a liberal tax reduction of 1.6 million livres per year.

On other matters, the government intended to stand firm. It wished to subordinate the nine capitation commissions to the intendant, and it wanted the Estates to start protecting revenue farmers and their subordinates throughout Brittany. Most of all, Noailles, alerted to the rising dissidence, wanted to maintain the precedent by which the Estates voted its 'free gift' on the first day of the session, without preliminary discussion of any kind, let alone any consideration of provincial grievances.[41]

This last demand led to an uproar. The Estates, influenced by activist nobles, waited until the second day of the session to consider the 'free gift' and then only to declare that the deputies must first examine Brittany's financial condition before it agreed to any sum at all. Montesquiou and Feydeau de Brou argued against this demand for two days, without success. On 18 December, only the fourth day of the Estates, Montesquiou dissolved the session, to all appearances peremptorily but in keeping with his precise instructions from Noailles, his abrasive manner aside. Since the Estates had accomplished none of its financial business, the authority for all the taxes peculiar to Brittany – the Breton *fouage*, for example, took the place of the royal *taille* – would expire on 1 January, 1718.

The dissidents looked upon impending financial disarray as a weapon in their hands.[42]

Hard-riding couriers from Dinan took only two days to bring the dispatches of Montesquiou and Feydeau de Brou to Noailles. When the Regency Council, speedily convened, met in extraordinary session on 21 December, it determined to confront the crisis head-on. The regent and his Council members approved a recommendation from Noailles to levy all future taxes in Brittany on the authority of the king, without the consent of the Estates that law and tradition demanded. To this end, the Council issued a robust decree castigating the behaviour of the Estates dissidents, defending the stance of the government, and enumerating all the taxes – *fouage*, duties upon spirits, etc. – that Bretons must continue to pay, Estates or no Estates.

Having decided upon what he himself called 'authoritative measures', Noailles dispatched nine battalions of infantry, ten squadrons of cavalry and eight squadrons of dragoons – a small army of perhaps eight thousand soldiers. Fewer troops ('a lot less') would have done just as well, as he admitted to his brother-in-law, a Breton nobleman; but the councils wanted not merely to suppress actual dissent but also to uproot any tendency whatsoever to obstruct the government. Since historians have emphasized the authoritarian methods of d'Argenson, into whose administration as Noailles's successor this affair continued, it is only fair to note that Noailles first adopted a firm approach.[43]

He next focused his attention upon the Parlement of Rennes, which doubled as a Cour des Aides, or tax dispute tribunal, all the more relevant to the current situation. The Regency Council issued the decree of 21 December as letters patent, which it expected the Parlement to register and thus to confer the public standing the new measures needed. On the orders of Noailles, Feydeau de Brou pointedly warned influential magistrates that if the Parlement did not submit, it could expect an unfavourable decision on a serious jurisdictional dispute with the Chambre des Comptes of Nantes. Moreover, its *augmentations de gages* would go unpaid for a long time to come, and the magistrates who had entered the Parlement in the *Eaux et Forêts* creation would lose their offices, with only a hollow prospect of future reimbursement.

Finally, the intendant underlined the gravity of an article in the letters patent that provided, in case of resistance from the Parlement, for the creation of a new law court to take over its jurisdiction – to be composed of outsiders under the supervision of the intendant. The regent also ordered the irascible Montesquiou to issue identical threats to many of these same judges. At bottom, the strong-arm tactics of Noailles resembled those of Colbert in 1673: to confront the Parlement with the stark choice of obeying or disobeying the king and eliminating any middle ground between the alternatives. Feydeau de Brou even sent Noailles copies, taken from the Parlement's registers, of the proceedings in the forced registrations of 1672–1673, the last time that the government had resorted to authoritarian methods in the tribunal.[44]

Everything now depended upon the attitude of the Parlement of Rennes; and for all his apparent confidence, Noailles became apprehensive as the wait began. Feydeau advised him that at the very least the Parlement would act only towards the end of the six weeks provided by the Declaration of Vincennes, and then issue a remonstrance. Not until the Regency Council had rejected the remonstrance would anyone know whether the magistrates would obey the government or not. So an early resolution, which was what the government most wanted, seemed out of reach. In the event, however, the Parlement displayed more political acumen than anyone had expected.

On 3 January 1718, it indeed voted to issue a remonstrance, but it completed the document on 10 January, far in advance of the Vincennes deadline, probably a bid for favour. The remonstrance, firm but respectful, entreated the government to reconvene the Estates, respect traditional prerogatives, and recall the soldiers. In a move that took everyone by surprise, the Parlement also appointed a deputation of six leading magistrates to make the difficult midwinter journey to Paris to plead its case in person. Noailles felt unable to forbid the judges to send a deputation, but he did warn them that much depended upon the character and standing of the deputies. On that point, he had no cause for complaint. Of the six deputies, two were *présidents à mortier* and a third was dean of the Grand-Chambre. The leader of the deputation, the *président à mortier* La Bourdonnaye de Blossac, represented a family long noted for its devotion to the government: his brother Jacques-Renaud, a respected *conseiller d'état*, had been intendant at Bordeaux, and his brother-in-law was Feydeau de Brou! The magistrates had put their best foot forward.

The deputies arrived in Paris on 18 January and paid courtesy calls on all the people with influence – La Vrillière, the secretary of state, charged with provincial affairs; the comte de Toulouse, governor of Brittany; Chancellor d'Aguesseau; other members of the Regency Council; and the duc d'Orléans himself. Everyone received them cordially. Toulouse expressed his sympathy and offered his good offices. The chancellor approved of the deputation and promised to support its remonstrance with all his prestige ('*crédit*'), a promising development. A long session with Noailles, who was also cordial, induced hope for a settlement. Quarrelsome nobles from the Estates, summoned to Paris for reprimands, were also making progress with Noailles. All in all, a compromise in keeping with the conciliatory tendencies of the regent appeared likely, perhaps even a turnaround similar to the one engineered by Camus de Pontcarré on behalf of the Parlement of Rouen.

It only remained to obtain an audience with the young king in order to present the remonstrance and then to await a reply. On the morning of 28 January, after ten days of salutations and visits, the deputies arrived at the chancellor's house on the Place Vendôme to fix a date for the audience. There they sat, in his anteroom, when someone astonished them with the news that d'Aguesseau had just lost his place in the government and relinquished the seals of office. A short time later, to their further surprise, they learned that Noailles had resigned and that the regent had made d'Argenson both keeper of the seals and president of the Council of Finances. This turn of events meant that they would have to start all over with a new administration. La Bourdonnaye fell ill with gout and did not recover for several weeks. So the issues posed by the Parlement of Rennes, like those of Paris, would have to wait longer to be resolved.[45]

This chapter has argued that in the first two years of his regency the duc d'Orléans made a conscious effort to win the friendship of the parlements and to make them his allies in his struggle with his rival, the duc du Maine. Although never formally enunciated, this bid for cooperation lay beneath the blandishments, inconsistencies and reversals that he showed in his treatment of the tribunals. But the grievances of the parlements, above all the disappointing inability of the Noailles administration to satisfy their financial claims, made it hard for such an alliance to take root. When the Parlements of Paris and Rennes put the regent to the test, they unintentionally brought about a change in the government and created the conditions for a change in policy. As of January 1718, Orléans had pulled back from his politics of accommodation, without as yet deciding what to do next. If he chose to return to the authoritarian methods of the government of Louis XIV, d'Argenson stood ready to help.

Notes

1 Dom Henri Leclercq, *Histoire de la Régence pendant la minorité de Louis XV* (3 vols; Paris, 1921–1922), I, 103–126; Michel Antoine, *Louis XV* (Paris, 1989), pp. 20, 30–37; James D. Hardy, *Judicial Politics in the Old Régime. The Parlement of Paris during the Regency* (Baton Rouge, La., 1967), pp. 35–44; J.H. Shennan, *Philippe, Duke of Orléans, Regent of France, 1715–1723* (London, 1979), pp. 1, 29–31; *idem*, 'The Political Role of the Parlement of Paris, 1715–23', *The Historical Journal* 8 (no. 2, 1965), 179–200.

2 Leclercq, *Régence*, I, lxviii–lxix; II, 79; Antoine, *Louis XV*, p. 33.

3 Flammermont, *Remontrances du Parlement de Paris*, I, 74; Louis de Rouvroy, duc de Saint-Simon, *Mémoires de Saint-Simon*, ed. Arthur de Boislisle (41 vols; Paris, 1879–1928), XXIX, 43, 211–212; XXX, 86,167, 178–179; XXXIII, 25; XXXV, 28; E. de Barthélemy, comte, ed., *Gazette de la Régence* (Paris, 1887), pp. 10, 61 Barthélemy attributed these informative letters to Jean Buvat, a copyist in the royal library and the author of the *Journal de la Régence*, ed. Émile Campardon (2 vols; Paris, 1865); Hardy, *Judicial Politics*, p. 137, and Shennan, *Regent*, pp. 31–32, 77, only noted the regent's attempt to befriend the Parlement of Paris, without giving it due interpretative weight.

4 El Annabi, *Parlement de Paris*, p. 112; 'Mémoire sur la Régence, par Mrs. De Harlay et le Chancelier Voisin', BN, *Fonds fr.*, 10,362, f. 24v; Bâville, intendant, Toulouse, to Desmarets, 10 June 1710, AN, G7, 313; Courson, intendant, Bordeaux, to

Desmarets, 7 September 1715, AN, G7, 146; and Ferrand, intendant, Rennes, to Desmarets, in Henri Fréville, *L'intendance de Bretagne (1689–1790)* (3 vols; Rennes, 1953), I, 159. On *Unigenitus* and the Parlement, see Antoine Dorsanne, *Journal de M. l'abbé Dorsanne* (2 vols; Rome, 1753), I, 99–103; AN, U 221: 15 February 1714, pp. 226–235; and, for background, Torcy, *Journal inédit*, pp. 158, 212. It is not true, as some accounts have it, that the Parlement, in registering *Unigenitus*, inserted on its own initiative a modification clause guaranteeing Gallican liberties, in defiance of the king and thus in violation of the 1673 rules. In fact, the royal council, after learning of magistrates' opinions, issued the changes itself.

5 Saint-Simon, *Mémoires*, XVII, 59–63, 80; Leclercq, *Régence*, I, 149–151; Hardy, *Judicial Politics*, p. 54; Shennan, *Regent*, p. 39; see the entries for these magistrates in François Bluche, *L'origine des magistrats du Parlement de Paris* (Paris, 1956); Glasson, *Parlement de Paris*, II, 18; Dessert, *Argent, pouvoir, et société*, pp. 242–244.

6 Antoine, *Conseil du roi sous Louis XV*, pp. 78–85, *passim*; Saint-Simon, *Mémoires*, XXVII, 168, 176–177, 193–199; Noailles to d'Aguesseau, 13 January 1717, AN, E 3647; Shennan, *Regent*, p. 29; Francis Monnier, *Le chancelier d'Aguesseau* (1863; reimpression, Geneva, 1975), pp. 167–170; Isabelle Storez, *Le chancelier Henri François d'Aguesseau* (Paris, 1996), pp. 239–244, 357–404; d'Aguesseau, 'Fragmens sur . . . remontrances', *Oeuvres complètes*, X, 4–31. In 1717, the regent arranged for an early payment of 500,000 livres on Mesmes's *brevet de retenue*, a certificate recording the sum he had paid to his predecessor when he assumed office and which he had the right to claim from his successor: AN, E 3651: decree of 20 May 1717, f. 329r, and E 2004: decree of 3 February 1719, ff. 304rv–306rv.

7 Labatut, *Ducs et pairs*, pp. 341–350.

8 Shennan, *Regent*, pp. 22, 38, 43–44; Saint-Simon, *Mémoires*, XXIX, 81–93.

9 Hardy, *Judicial Politics*, p. 33; Saint-Simon, *Mémoires*, XXVII, 297; XXIX, 200; XXXIII, 21–22; Philippe de Courcillon, marquis de Dangeau, *Journal de Dangeau* (19 vols; Paris, 1854–1860), XVII, 445, noted the clients of Maine in the Parlement of Toulouse.

10 BN, *Actes R.*, F. 21,275 (91); Isambert, *Recueil général*, XXI, 40–41. See citations of the declaration of 1673 in AN, E 2033: decree of 5 July 1722, ff. 12rv–13rv, and Boutaric, *Explication de l'ordonnance*, p. 7. Hardy, *Judicial Politics*, p. 48, and Shennan, *Parlement of Paris*, p. 286, exaggerated the degree to which the Parlement recovered its political powers in the early regency.

11 Élie Carcassonne, *Montesquieu et le problème de la constitution française au XVIIIe siècle* (1927; reprint, Geneva, 1978), pp. 27–29; Keohane, *Philosophy and the State in France*, pp. 312–357.

12 Saint-Simon, *Mémoires*, XXX, 86–87, n. 7; Leclercq, *Régence*, II, 157–158. Leclercq made a pioneering effort to synthesize the crises involving the Parlements of Paris and Rennes; but recent scholars have more or less ignored the connection, generally focusing upon the Parlement of Paris alone, as is the case with Hardy and Shennan, or upon the Parlement of Rennes, as in Jean Meyer, *Le Régent* (Paris, 1985), pp. 188–219.

13 The Jansenist issue did not become prominent in the parlements until the 1730s. See Peter R. Campbell, *Power and Politics in Old Regime France, 1720–1745* (London and New York, 1996), pp. 195–221, 237–274, and Dale K. Van Kley, *The Damiens Affair and the Unraveling of the Ancien Régime, 1750–1770* (Princeton, NJ, 1984), pp.

99–165, and idem, *The Religious Origins of the French Revolution. From Calvin to the Civil Constitution, 1560–1791* (New Haven, 1996), pp. 15–134.

14 Ordonnance . . . pour le conseil des finances', E 3640, ff. 10rv–18r; Isambert, *Recueil général*, XXI, 61–66; Albert Esslinger, *Le conseil particulier des finances à l'époque de la polysynodie (1715–1718)* (Paris, 1908).

15 Bonney, 'The Eighteenth Century. II', p. 325; Noailles to abbé Guillaume Dubois, councillor in the Council of Foreign Affairs and ambassador to England, July 1717, AN, E 3648; AN, E 3640 (Council of Finances): 20–21 September 1715, ff. 19rv–21rv; AN, E 3641: 24 October 1715, f. 240r; Marcel Marion, *Histoire financière de la France depuis 1715* (5 vols; Paris, 1927–1928), I, 87–89; Lüthy, *Banque protestante*, I, 287; Edgar Faure, *La banqueroute de Law* (Paris, 1977), pp. 90–97.

16 AN, E 3641: 8 November 1715, f. 96rv; 14 January 1716, ff. 102v–103r; BN, *Fonds fr.*, 22,672 (Conseil de Régence): 18 January 1716, f. 12r; Noailles, 'Mémoire pour les finances', June 1717, BN, *Fonds fr.*, 7769, f. 163; AD, I-V (Rennes), 1Bc 2bis; BN, *Fonds fr.*, 8906, 'Gages et augmentations de gages . . . parlement de Provence', 1716, ff. 20rv–28r; BN, *Actes R.*, F. 20,974 (52).

17 AN, E 3641: 8 November 1715, f. 96v; Buvat, *Journal*, I, 125; Noailles to intendants, 30 April 1716, AN, E 3645, f. 414rv; BN, *Fonds fr.*, 23,672 (Régence): 13 June 1716, f. 68v; Noailles to La Vrillière, secretary of state, 15 June 1716, AN, E 3645, ff. 553v–554r, and to the Grand Conseil, Cour des Monnaies, and the masters of requests, 11 September 1716, AN, E 3646, ff. 719r–720r; AN, E 3649, ff. 211v–212v (remonstrance, Parlement of Dijon), ff. 253r–254v (remonstrance, Parlement of Aix).

18 AN, E 1983: 29 February 1716, f. 349rv; E 1984: 7 March 1716, ff. 286r–300rv; E 1985: 16 May 1716, ff. 239rv–255rv. Only the Parlement of Rennes failed to benefit from this general round of payments, for reasons unknown.

19 AN, E 3641: 12 June 1716, f. 105rv; Noailles to intendants, 22 June 1716, AN, E 3645, ff. 574rv–575v; to Bertier, first president, Aix, 22 July 1716, *ibid.*, ff. 636v–637v; and to *lieutenant-général*, Aix-en-Provence, 6 November 1716, AN, E 3646, f. 829rv (protecting the Parlement of Grenoble); Dodun, councillor of the Council of Finances, to Parlement of Aix, 9 August 1717, 9 and 15 January 1718, AD, B-R, B 3688.

20 AN, E 3642: 11 June 1717, f. 174v, and E 3652: 31 July 1717, ff. 166rv–169r; Noailles to Bourgneuf de Cucé, *président à mortier*, Rennes, 2 August 1717, AN, E 3648, ff. 297v–298rv; Parlement of Rennes to Orléans, 18 August 1717, AD, I-V, IBc 2bis.

21 AN, E 3643: 3 December 1717, ff. 427v–428r; E 3653: 4 December 1717, ff. 124rv–128v.

22 Saint-Simon, *Mémoires*, XXXI, 341; for Noailles's report, see BN, *Fonds fr.*, 7769 ('Mémoires sur les finances') and AN, E 3652, ff. 141rv–146r (19 June), 146v–154r (21 June), 153r–158v (23 June) and 158v–161r (26 June).

23 Édit du Roy portant suppression du dixième des biens' (August 1717), BN, *Actes R.*, F. 23,621 (781); Regency Council sessions on this edict in BN, *Fonds fr.*, 23,672 (Régence): 19 June 1717, f. 174r; *ibid.*, 23,673: 21 August 1717, ff. 32v–33r, 35v–36r.

24 Délibérations du Parlement au sujet des trois Édits du mois d'Aoust 1717 et de la

Déclaration du 21 dud. mois', in BN, *Fonds fr.*, 10,231, item 93a (internal evidence suggests that the author of this document, obviously a government informer, was Roger Gilbert de Voisins, the newly appointed *greffier en chef* of the Parlement and brother of the Gilbert de Voisins who served on the Council of Finances); El Annabi, *Parlement de Paris*, pp. 65–75 (on public access to the Palace of Justice); Mathieu Marais, *Journal et mémoires*, ed. de Lescure (4 vols; Paris, 1863–1868), I, 225.

25 Délibérations du Parlement'; Marais, *Journal et mémoires*, I, 231–232. For biographical information on these magistrates, see Bluche, *L'origine des magistrats*.

26 Délibérations du Parlement'; BN, *N.a.f.*, 9,771: unsigned notes, 6 September 1717, ff. 46rv–47r; Buvat (?), *Gazette de la Régence*, pp. 202–203.

27 Flammermont, *Remontrances*, I, 50–55; BN, *N.a.f.*, 9,771, f. 46v; Hardy, *Judicial Politics*, pp. 83–87. Although Hardy thought that the Parlement broke new constitutional ground by registering some articles and rejecting others, it was only taking preliminary votes on the various sections ('chefs') of the edict before a final vote on the whole, a normal procedure for complex legislation.

28 AN, E 3642, 7 September 1717, ff. 320rv–321r; BN, *Fonds fr.*, 23,673 (Régence), 8 September 1717, ff. 40v–41rv; Marais, *Journal et mémoires*, I, 237 (a common-sense assessment). This episode was neither the 'major victory' for the Parlement, as Hardy believed, *Judicial Politics*, p. 88, nor a 'compromise' either, as depicted in Shennan, *Regent*, p. 82, since the tribunal got its way on the contested points.

29 Hardy, *Judicial Politics*, pp. 89–94; Shennan, *Regent*, pp. 83–84; Flammermont, *Remontrances*, I, 57–65; Noailles to Mesmes, first president, 13 January 1718, AN, E 3648.

30 AN, U 416: 14 January 1718; U 420: 15–19 January 1718; BN, *Fonds fr.*, 23,673 (Régence): 22 January 1718, ff. 75v–76rv. U 416, a helpful 'Journal du Parlement', was kept by Delisle, an obscure *épices* clerk in the Grand-Chambre, on the orders of First President Mesmes. U 420 (1718) and U 421 (1719–1722) contain the informative preliminary notes of Gilbert de Voisins, the chief clerk, who used these notes to compile the secret register. He probably doubled as a political spy for the government (see n. 24), which would explain why Mesmes asked Delisle to keep a special record. Shennan, *Regent*, pp. 83–84, understated the self-interest that lay behind this remonstrance.

31 Buvat (?), *Gazette de la Régence*, pp. 225, 228; Saint-Simon, *Mémoires*, XXXI, 27–31.

32 Leclercq, *Régence*, II, 135–138; Saint-Simon, *Mémoires*, XXXIII, 2–10, 31–34; BN, *N.a.f.*, 9,640, ff. 131rv–136r (unsigned note attacking Noailles). For a well-informed defence of John Law, see the anonymous 'Histoire des finances pendant la Régence', in *John Law. Oeuvres Complètes*, ed. Paul Harsin (3 vols; Paris, 1934), III, 324–327. Harsin, I, lxxiv–lxxxviii, believed that Law himself wrote this document, possibly in collaboration with others, a hypothesis he repeated, with further observations, in Faure, *Banqueroute de Law*, p. 695. Antoin E. Murphy rejected this notion: *John Law. Economic Theorist and Policy-Maker* (Oxford, 1997), pp. 9–10. But the issue remains unresolved.

33 Faure, *Banqueroute de Law*, p. 141; Buvat (?), *Gazette de la Régence*, pp. 220–223; AN, U 416: 28 January 1718; Saint-Simon, *Mémoires*, XXXIII, 38.

34 For Toulouse, see BN, *Fonds fr.*, 23,672 (Régence): decree of 11 January 1716, f. 8rv; for Rouen, AN, E 3641: 28 February 1716, f. 245rv; E 3649: 29 February 1716, ff. 97r–99v, and AD, S-M, 1B 235 (Registres secrets): 7 March 1716, ff. 32r–36r, and

8 May 1716, ff. 56v–63r (reports of Camus de Pontcarré); for Metz, see AN, E 3642, f. 276v, and BN, *Fonds fr.*, 23,673 (Régence), f. 43r: decrees of 13 August and 8 September 1717; AN, E 3640: 11 July 1716, ff. 27v–28r (Grenoble), and BN, *Fonds fr.*, 23,672: 16 May 1716, f. 62rv (Dijon).

35 Le Moy, *Parlement de Bretagne*, pp. 87–107; AN, E 3645, ff. 504v–505v (tobacco farm); E 3649, decree of 4 July 1716, ff. 305rv–306r (*contrôle des actes*); E 3641, decrees of 3 and 17 July 1716, f. 249r (*contrôle des actes* and *greffiers des experts*), 13 and 20 October 1716, f. 250r; BN, *Fonds fr.*, 23,672 (Régence), decrees of 24 October and 14 November 1716, ff. 12r and 117rv (*receveurs des consignations* and *receveurs des épices*); AD, I-V, IBc 2bis (remonstrance on the *receveurs*); Noailles to Brilhac, first president, 31 May 1716, E 3645; Fréville, *Intendance de Bretagne*, I, 170–172.

36 Le Moy, *Parlement de Bretagne*, pp. 99–100, n. 5; AD, I-V, IBb 657 (Registres secrets): 20 August 1716; AD, I-V, IBc 2bis (drafts of the remonstrance); AN, E 3641: decree of 15 December 1716, f. 251r; BN, *Fonds fr.*, 23,672 (Régence): decree of 19 December 1716, f. 126r; Noailles to Feydeau de Brou, intendant, 20 December 1716, AN, E 3646, ff. 905rv–906r. Denis is listed as a *huissier ordinaire du Conseil d'État et Privé du Roy* in the Almanach Royal of 1718.

37 AD, I-V, IBb 657 (Registres secrets): 7 and 13 November, 29 and 31 December 1716; IBc 2bis: remonstrance of 28 December 1716; Le Moy, *Parlement de Bretagne*, pp. 98–99; BN, *Actes R.*, F. 23,621 (480): 'Édit du Roy Portant Suppression de différens Offices', August 1716.

38 Noailles to Denis, *huissier*, 29 December 1716, f. 916rv; to Feydeau de Brou, 29 December 1716, ff. 917rv–919r; to Cornulier, *président à mortier*, 29 December 1716, f. 920rv, all in AN, E 3646; to Feydeau de Brou, 9 January 1717, ff. 8v–9rv; to Cornulier, 8 January 1717, f. 7rv; to du Poulpry, councillor, 8 January 1717, ff. 6v–7r, all in AN, E 3647; Parlement to Chancellor Voysin, 24 December 1716, AD, I-V, IBc 2bis (in defence of its remonstrance).

39 AN, E 3642: 15 June 1717, f. 179rv, and E 3651: 26 June 1717, ff. 414rv–416rv (*droits de contrôle*); E 3642: 20 August 1717, f. 283rv, and 19 October 1717, f. 360v, for the Parlement's decrees on merchant taxes; E 3643: 9 November 1717, f. 379v, and E 3653: 13 November 1717, ff. 46v–48v (*contrôle des actes*).

40 Rebillon, *États de Bretagne*, pp. 249–253; Barthélemy Pocquet, *La Bretagne Province*, vol. vi of *Histoire de Bretagne* (1914; reimpression, Mayenne, 1985), pp. 4–7, provide the background; for the government's condemnation of the efforts of the new Estates commissions to impede revenue farmers, see AN, E 3649: decree of 9 May 1716, f. 199rv; 'Extrait des proces verbaux faits par les huissiers pour quelques gentilshommes de Bretagne de payer leur dixième', 28 August 1717, AN, E 3652, ff. 325r–327r. Christophe Rosnyvinen de Piré, a leader of the second estate dissidents, was the father of a councillor in the tribunal: Maurice Montigny, *Guillemette de Rosnyvinen de Piré* (Paris, 1923), pp. 19–20. Feydeau de Brou emphasized the importance of these family ties, in a letter of 26 December 1717, to Noailles, in Le Moy, *Parlement de Bretagne*, p. 111, n. 5.

41 Rebillon, *États de Bretagne*, pp. 253–254; Fréville, *Intendance de Bretagne*, I, 187–191; AN, E 3653, ff. 1rv–9r: 'Mémoire . . . pour . . . Maréchal de Montesquiou', 6 November 1717; Noailles's letter of 28 December 1717, to Malo-Auguste, marquis de Coetquen, his Breton brother-in-law, shows that he knew a lot about the activities of dissident nobles: AN, E 3648, ff.531rv–533v.

42 Rebillon, *États de Bretagne*, p. 255.
43 BN, *Fonds fr.*, 23,673 (Régence), ff. 67v–68rv (21 December 1717); AN, E 3653, ff. 227v–229r; AN, E 1993, ff. 560rv–566r (decree of 21 December). AN, E 3648, contains letters from Noailles to explain the Council's actions to friends, supporters, and high officials in Brittany; Le Moy, *Parlement de Bretagne*, pp. 110–111; Rebillon, *États de Bretagne*, pp. 256–257; Fréville, *Intendance de Bretagne*, I, 191–193.
44 Noailles to Feydeau de Brou, 21 December 1717, ff. 508rv–512v, and 11 January 1718, ff. 558v–559rv, AN, E 3648; Feydeau to Noailles, 26 December 1717, in Fréville, *Intendance de Bretagne*, I, 193; Noailles and Orléans to Montesquiou, 21 and 29 December, E 3648, ff. 505rv–507rv.
45 AD, I-V, IBb (Registres secrets) 329: 3 and 10 January 1718, ff. 48v–49r and 52v; AD, I-V, IBc 2bis (remonstrance of 10 January 1718); BN, *N.a.f.*, 9,640, ff. 197rv–199rv, and 9771, ff. 43rv–46v; Arthur Le Moy, ed., *Remontrances du Parlement de Bretagne au XVIIIe siècle* (Paris, 1909), pp. 1–5. For Noailles's views of the Parlement's deputation, see his letters in AN, E 3648, to Montesquiou, 5 January, ff. 538rv–539r, 7 January (no pagination), 16 January; ff. 568rv–569r, and 24 January 1718, ff. 581v–582r, and to Feydeau de Brou, 7 January (no pagination) and 16 January; 1718, f. 569rv; Noailles to Montesquiou, 16 January 1718, AN, E 3648, ff. 568rv–569r (on the Breton nobles). For the adventures of this deputation, see La Bourdonnaye's final report to the Parlement: AD, I-V, IBb 660 (Registres secrets): 28 April 1718.

6

Confronting the Parlement
of Paris, 1718

The menacing appearance of d'Argenson, the new keeper of the seals and president of the Council of Finances, so frightened contemporaries that they called him Rhadamanthus, a judge of the underworld in Greek mythology known for his stern sense of justice. But d'Argenson's efficiency as chief of police for Paris, his talent for making rapid decisions and his ability, even at the age of sixty-five, to work through the day and into the night, or vice versa, also won their respect. Experienced in government and an early supporter of John Law, he seemed fully capable of overcoming the Parlement of Paris, as though born for the moment. He had clashed with the tribunal over jurisdiction and assembled embarrassing personal files on some of its magistrates, as they had reason to know. In 1716 the Parlement, seeking its revenge, attempted to try him for embezzlement and fraud, a fate from which the regent providentially rescued him; but the experience naturally made him more hostile than ever towards the judges.

In the summer of 1718, d'Argenson assumed the key role in the regency's decisive confrontation with the Parlement and worked hard to achieve the final victory. Perhaps most important, he defined the central issue of the dispute as the question of legislative sovereignty, adding to it an important ideological dimension. His son René-Louis, who watched d'Argenson at work, likened him to Richelieu, although he might have adopted Pussort and Colbert as the better comparison.[1]

The magistrates took d'Argenson's new appointment as an affront and did not even consider registering the letters patent appointing him keeper of the seals, an unfavourable augury for their relationship. When, on 21 February 1718, d'Argenson responded formally to the Parlement's recent remonstrance, he added to its discontent. It was not that their old enemy, on his first encounter with the tribunal, displayed Rhadamanthine severity. On the contrary, as he stood in the Tuileries palace before a deputation from the Parlement and in view of the royal court, anxiety and clumsiness overcame him. He fumbled with his notes, dropped them twice and stammered as he read aloud. Bring the keeper of the seals a bit of candle, someone quipped from the rear; he cannot see what he is saying. His brief statement, to which he finally gave voice, also failed to impress. It merely reaffirmed the government's promise to pay interest on all its notes and loans, a bland, halting response that answered none of the substantive points in the remonstrance.[2]

At a divisive plenary session on 4 March, the Parlement appointed commissioners to examine d'Argenson's remarks but assigned them no deadline upon which to report. This tabled things until further notice – although not, as it turned out, permanently. For the time being, however, the Parlement's remonstrance of 26 January, which had so troubled the regent, became moot. D'Argenson, if inelegantly, had won a victory of sorts. All the same, the deliberations of 4 March made clear that the tribunal contained scores of magistrates eager to take him on.

Two presidents from the Enquêtes chambers led a drive to confront the keeper of the seals with new, stronger remonstrances, which would have been the Parlement's first *itératives remontrances* since the Fronde. President Frizon de Blamont, prominent in earlier deliberations, urged the magistrates to remonstrate in defence of the fundamental laws of the realm, even if the Declaration of Vincennes did not seem to permit such a general remonstrance. But Frizon cited supporting precedents dating to 1561 and condemned the 'blow' dealt to remonstrances by ministers of the late king. In his person the ideas of sixteenth-century constitutional theorists, buried since the administration of Colbert, returned to the political surface.

For his part, President Henri Feydeau de Calende attacked the General Bank of John Law which, founded in 1716, had become a state-sanctioned central bank. All the kingdom's problems, he alleged, began with the Bank and the way its suspect paper notes endangered the royal debt. Where Blamont had defined the political issue, Feydeau concentrated upon the financial question, which happened to include unpaid *augmentations de gages*. When in his discourse he cited a precedent from 1648, he thrilled his political friends but drew a warning from the first president, whom the regent had earlier scolded for making just such a reference. Feydeau also alluded to recent council decrees that, as he put it, had overturned traditions in the provinces, an unmistakable reference to Brittany, the deputies of whose Parlement lingered in Paris and had surely contacted their counterparts in the capital's tribunals. When their proposal for iterative remonstrances came to a vote, the Enquêtes presidents fell just six ballots short of victory. Such a close defeat showed that the government had aroused a lot of opposition in the tribunal.[3]

D'Argenson dealt with the deputies from the Parlement of Rennes on 17 February, when he responded to the remonstrance that they had delivered in January. Although he performed less awkwardly than at the Tuileries a few days later, he nevertheless surprised the Bretons with his curious reaction. The keeper of the seals declared that the regent would allow the Parlement to remonstrate for a new session of the Breton estates and for the recall of the soldiers, but the judges would have to rewrite their current remonstrance. Its language showed a lack of respect for the king, making it unacceptable as it stood. Bewildered, since they believed that their remonstrance observed the norms, the Bretons repeatedly asked d'Argenson to show them the actual words that had given offence, which, almost comically, he seemed unable to do.

The Parlement finally revised its remonstrance, excising in a puzzled way what it had to guess were the more argumentative passages, and sent it back to Paris, not much changed. Evidently satisfied, d'Argenson on 13 March agreed to transmit the bowdlerized version to the king. The regent's final answer, which d'Argenson handed the deputies on 15 March, was not very helpful. The government promised nothing about the Estates or the soldiers and left matters in the province where they had stood since December. It continued to collect taxes on its own authority, and the troops settled into indefinite occupation duty. D'Argenson did drop Noailles's insistence that the Parlement register the council decree of 21 December that had ordered the collection of those taxes; since some of the taxes were being paid anyway, he may not have seen the point. But this still left the province without its estates and under political tutelage.[4]

The rest of the winter and most of the spring slipped by anticlimactically, without much friction between the government and the tribunals. D'Argenson, however hostile to the Parlement of Paris, did not try to provoke it, now that the January remonstrance was no longer at issue. The Parlement, although still irate over the dismissal of d'Aguesseau, held its peace. The crisis that broke this undeclared truce took both sides by surprise and grew steadily in intensity, like a thunderstorm.

At the recommendation of d'Argenson and the Council of Finances, the regent in May 1718 issued an edict devaluing the livre by one-third in terms of specie. The government thus wrote up the value of its gold and silver stock and could pay its bills, denominated in livres, with less coin. The May edict also ordered the French to have their coin recast into smaller, lighter pieces bearing a higher face value. Finally, it encouraged holders of *billets d'état* to hand in some of these notes along with their specie, on the promise that the government would destroy the *billets* and thus shore up the value of those remaining in circulation. In a recent precedent, Noailles had also resorted to devaluation, although not to this degree and against the reservations of the Parlement of Paris. D'Argenson, anticipating strenuous opposition there, had the May edict registered by stealth in another superior court, the Cour des Monnaies, which had jurisdiction over currency disputes.[5]

The Cour published the new edict on 1 June, giving the Parlement no time to react, since the long Pentecost observance began almost at once. But in the ensuing hiatus the magistrates concluded that John Law, using d'Argenson as his proxy, was chiefly to blame. They saw the edict as resembling Law's Bank in its assault upon regular financial procedures and private family interests. They resented the fact that under its terms the government now owed them less gold and silver for their *augmentations de gages*, a development from which debtor magistrates, who now also needed less coin to pay their creditors, for some reason took little solace. By sending it to the Cour des Monnaies instead of the Parlement, moreover, the judges believed that Law and d'Argenson had intentionally circumvented proper procedure, preventing them from exercising their constitutional role of examining new law. But despite what the magistrates saw as his schemes to undermine the economy and constitution of France, Law stayed busy running his Bank and his new Company of the West and nothing else. The idea of devaluing the livre originated with d'Argenson, who saw the edict purely in financial terms. As president of the finance council, he simply needed the additional money to fund his budget.

Nevertheless, the assumption of malice lay behind everything the Parlement did throughout 1718; it believed that it was defending the whole constitutional and social order against dangerous innovations. On the other hand, d'Argenson, who also defined ideological issues starkly, began to accuse the Parlement of encroaching upon the king's rightful authority. Financial issues and constitutional ideas thus opened a gap between the two sides, and it widened steadily through the summer.

Commissioners appointed by the Parlement, having met continuously in the Pentecost interval, recommended that the tribunal join forces with its sister law courts in Paris, the Chambre des Comptes, the Cour des Aides and the Cour des Monnaies. In a plenary session on 14 June, the magistrates voted enthusiastically to invite deputies from these tribunals to meet with their deputies that very afternoon in the Chambre Saint-Louis of the Palais de Justice. The deputies would deliberate on how to wage a joint struggle against the May edict.

An assembly in the Chambre could only heighten widespread interest in the way current events matched those of the Fronde. In 1648 the Chambre Saint-Louis, composed of representatives from these very tribunals, had attempted to dismantle the machinery of absolute government; and several magistrates, President Feydeau and others, drew explicitly upon this precedent. Mesmes, who supported the idea of a joint meeting, nevertheless disliked any such allusions: 'Please God that no one speaks of a junction of the companies as was done in 1648.' The first president had no wish to rekindle the wrath of the regent on this sensitive point, but few magistrates shared his caution.

Since the keeper of the seals did not want to relive the Fronde, he ordered the Cour des Aides, Chambre des Comptes and Cour des Monnaies not to participate in any such meeting. Similar orders had done no good in 1648, but this time the three tribunals, more easily frightened, complied. A new Chambre Saint-Louis did not therefore take place. As this was the best occasion for any concerted action on the part of the superior courts of Paris, d'Argenson might have counted this non-event as a personal triumph; but he never stopped worrying that such a session would convene in the near future. Throughout the summer, indeed, the three other tribunals modelled their political behaviour on that of the Parlement and looked to it for leadership. D'Argenson believed that this association, even if it did not progress to a joint meeting, itself endangered the monarchy and so argued in council sessions through the summer.[6]

As the dispute continued, First President Mesmes took an increasingly active role in the struggle against devaluation, which he called the most important issue to come before the Parlement in a long time. He probably hoped to advance the cause of his patron, the duc de Maine, and likely acted under the latter's supervision, even if this connection is not altogether provable. In any event, he presided over a tribunal that wanted to be led in the very direction that he was increasingly prepared to indicate. Mesmes began to work closely with the presidents and magistrates of the Enquêtes chambers whom he had previously tried to rein in, meeting with them in his home and seeking their advice. Prominent *présidents à mortier* also joined the discussions, notably Chrétien de Lamoignon, the grandson of the first president who had held office early in the late king's reign. With the leadership lining up against the May edict, the internal discipline associated with the Parlement of Louis XIV had clearly dissolved.

Once they received the old coins, the royal mints had thirty days in which to turn out new ones; as they did so, the May edict would take effect, whatever the magistrates might do. On 17 June, the Parlement therefore asked the regent to suspend execution of the recoinage edict and to send it to the Parlement for a vote by *liberté des suffrages*. The first president told the *gens du roi*, who were to convey this request, to report back quickly, 'as soon as you can, that will be best, because the affair is very important and urgent'. Orléans naturally rejected the plea, calling it 'extraordinary', and said the Parlement should simply issue a remonstrance. But remonstrances took time to write, occasioning delay that, given the Parlement's habitual use of that tactic, ironically worked in the government's favour at this point.

On 19 June, moving the process along, the Parlement condemned the edict with 'representations', which, being less formal, it could issue more quickly than remonstrances. The representations, reflecting virtually unanimous opinion, defended the Parlement's jurisdiction over the currency and argued that the edict would harm the French by costing them gold and silver in the reminting process and by subjecting them to inflation, the latter also damaging to the state. Orléans rejected all these points on the spot and the mints began to turn out the new coins, just as Mesmes had feared.[7]

On 20 June, in an extraordinary decree, a frustrated Parlement authorized oral and written remonstrances for the revocation of the May edict. Since the regent intended to dispose of this issue through remonstrances, this in itself gave no offence. But the decree went on to forbid anyone within the Parlement's jurisdiction to use reminted coins in any way and commanded notaries not to write contracts that listed the new values for the livre. Although the Parlement could cite precedents for these orders, none challenged royal legislation to this degree. Law charged that the Parlement had brazenly tried to impose its authority upon the regent, a claim that reflected loyalist opinion and showed the rise of ideological tension.

In order to rally the public, the magistrates intended to publish their decree before the Regency Council could annul it. They ordered the *gens du roi* to print the decree, to post it throughout Paris, and to send copies to all the subordinate tribunals within the Parlement's jurisdiction, more than half of France. But in the late afternoon of 20 June, within hours after the magistrates had concluded their session, the government closed their print shop and commanded all the city's printers to refrain from publishing their decree. Undeterred, the Parlement had it copied by hand and posted the copies in the Palais and throughout Paris, where the decree attracted public attention the next morning and for days thereafter. These measures took the tribunal well beyond the bounds of conventional resistance.[8]

Soon after the Parlement had finished for the day, d'Argenson, kept up-to-the-minute by private spies, described its actions at an extraordinary session of the Regency Council and asked for authority to punish the judges. Deliberations in the Council took several hours, lasting until 7 p.m., and the magistrates did not lack for supporters at the highest levels, then or in the days to come. Evidently, the duc du Maine spoke on their behalf, as did others, reportedly Marshals Villeroy and Villars, the core group of Orléans's opponents. The regent thus had to contend with a divided Council that, moreover, he had enlarged from its original twelve members to seventeen, making it even more unwieldy than before. Despite the dissent, Orléans got this conflicted Council to accept the recommendations of d'Argenson and to quash the Parlement's decree with a decree of its own. The competing decrees of Council and Parlement, each bearing the date of 20 June, appeared all over Paris the next morning, point and counterpoint.

But when the *gens du roi* brought the Council decree under seal to the tribunal, Mesmes was prepared for them, probably forewarned by Maine and his friends. The first president ostentatiously refused to receive the decree and sent it back to the government, unread, the seal not even broken. He declared that the king could only send the Parlement open legislative acts in the form of letters patent, edicts or ordinances, not sealed decrees, a fine point that d'Argenson interpreted as yet another affront to royal authority.

In retaliation, the Council on 21 June evoked from the Parlement all legal disputes involving the coinage, temporarily voiding its competence in this important sphere. Three days later, the regent discharged from his administrative councils three of the five magistrates of the Parlement who had served there from the beginning – Councillor Pucelle from the Council of Conscience and Councillors Ferrand and Menguy from the Council of the Interior. They returned to full-time service in the tribunal, but now as the regent's opponents.[9]

On 22 June, the duc d'Orléans, telling the *gens du roi* that he wished above all to preserve royal authority, ordered the Parlement to submit its remonstrance on 27 June, intending to end the coinage dispute then and there. This early deadline meant the magistrates had to work rapidly and in effect prevented them from issuing any more obstructive decrees, like that of 20 June. Increasing the pressure, the regent demanded that the Parlement register new letters patent that contained the evocation decree of 21 June, presumably his revenge upon the first president for having refused to open the nullification decree of 20 June. The magistrates decided that their remonstrance would include an article against the letters patent, which they boldly declined to register.

First President Mesmes, at the head of a deputation of magistrates, read the remonstrance aloud to the king, the regent and the court at the Tuileries on the morning of 27 June. Restating the key points in the representations of 19 June, the remonstrance asserted the Parlement's competence over all edicts involving the value of coins, as an issue of general importance and beyond the normal authority of the Cour des Monnaies. The tribunal again opposed the May edict on the grounds that a weaker livre harmed French economic interests abroad, eroded the resources of individuals through inflation and damaged the finances of the state.

Despite the haste in which they had worked, the authors of the document made a strong, clear argument, one that aroused much favourable comment. In tone and substance, the remonstrance was more moderate than might have been predicted, unequivocally affirming the magistrates' devotion to royal authority and justifying their opposition to the May edict by citing eight precedents back to 1571. Many judges ordered copies for their private use; and the Chambre des Comptes and the Cour des Aides, which presented remonstrances of their own, decided that their arguments would conform to those of the Parlement.[10]

The Regency Council met on the afternoon of 27 June and again on 30 June to decide how to answer the remonstrance. These turned out to be the crucial Regency Council meetings on the subject of the Parlement, the last at which a free exchange of opinion took place. Once again, the supporters of the tribunal attempted to shield it from retribution. The duc du Maine and the comte de Toulouse, along with Marshals d'Huxelles, Villeroy and Villars, all spoke in favour of their remonstrance and for the revocation of the edict, arguing for an overall change in policy. But d'Argenson opposed any compromise with the judges, the regent sided with him, and together they prevailed over Maine and his group. The Council, although still divided, voted to uphold the May edict and to condemn the Parlement for opposing it, leaving it to d'Argenson to compose a strong reply to the tribunal's remonstrance. He delivered this reply on 2 July at the Tuileries before the king, the members of the Council and the same deputation of judges who had presented the remonstrance six days earlier.[11]

If those judges, again led by Mesmes, anticipated another lacklustre performance by an inept keeper of the seals, they experienced a rude shock. On this occasion, d'Argenson displayed all the intellectual energy for which he had long been known. But his personal performance, however effective, was the least of things. It was his 900-word rebuttal that shocked the magistrates and sent them back to the Parlement in disarray.

D'Argenson disposed of the recoinage edict, the main topic of the remonstrance, in about two hundred words, bluntly upholding the new law and taking little note of the arguments against it. Then he changed the subject. The crucial issue, said the keeper of the seals, was not the edict but the Parlement's treatment of the king's legislative authority and what he called its misguided attempt to share or limit that authority. D'Argenson was only thirteen when, in 1665, Louis XIV presided at the Council of Justice; but from what followed it was as though he had attended the Council's sessions, so closely did his arguments resemble those of the councillors who wrote title I of the ordinance of 1667. Indeed, he had most likely studied the government's minutes of those sessions, still available today, and absorbed their contents.

Like the royal councillors of 1665, d'Argenson attributed legislative authority in its entirety to the king and all but excluded the Parlement from the whole process by which law was made and took effect. The king merely proclaimed his laws through 'the courts', said d'Argenson, avoiding the word 'Parlement'. These courts registered the laws as a sign of their 'indispensable' obedience to the monarch and not, he implied, to validate or to certify the legislation. The kings sent their laws to the superior courts merely from convenience; the laws could easily go to lower tribunals instead. It made no legal difference which courts received them first. All laws, in the resonating opinion of the keeper of the seals, existed entirely as the expression of the sovereign's will.

Although d'Argenson did not openly challenge the principles of *vérification* and *liberté des suffrages*, his manifesto in effect dismissed those ideas altogether. He all but said, and clearly meant, that the courts did not and could not verify, sanction, or assess the laws. Adopting the ideas and to some degree the language used in 1665 in the Council of Justice, he reaffirmed the absolutist concept of legislative power. Indeed, he took a step beyond where his predecessors had left off. Unlike title I of the ordinance or the declaration of 1673, the keeper of the seals in 1718 did not even admit that the parlements had a passive legislative role.

In addition to setting the Parlement straight on theory, d'Argenson condemned its recent plan to convene the other superior courts of Paris in the Chambre Saint-Louis. He must have feared that its sister tribunals would heed some new attempt by the Parlement to assemble the Chambre, for his statement adventitiously forbade it ever to do so. The king alone, d'Argenson proclaimed, held power in its entirety; and he used this power as he chose. He had chosen to delegate discrete portions to particular tribunals. But each tribunal, created separate and distinct, could not share delegated authority with the others, unless the king, the source of all their authority, permitted it. The tribunals could not join together by means of 'unions, invitations, or associations'. They did not represent the nation or speak for the parts of which it was composed; any such principle endangered the very foundation of the kingdom. D'Argenson's unexpected condemnation of the Chambre Saint-Louis and any claim by any institution to represent the nation, neither of which the remonstrance included, must have stemmed from unrecorded discourses or private expressions of opinion. In either case, his unanticipated denunciation came as another shock.

D'Argenson also surprised the magistrates when he made a brief but emphatic reference to the Fronde. The precedents cited in the remonstrance did include a currency decree from the Fronde year of 1652. D'Argenson might have ignored this citation, which the Parlement placed in a judicial not a political context; but he chose to single it out when he ordered the Parlement never again to refer to a period whose 'memory should be entirely abolished'. This unwonted stricture applied directly to those recent parlementary discourses which had evoked the events of 1648 and thus the Fronde itself. Finally, the keeper of the seals gratuitously insulted the magistrates by suggesting that their opposition to the May edict stemmed from their self-serving desire to free themselves from paying their share of the state debt. Of all his crisp judgements about the Parlement, this one struck closest to home.[12]

To sum up, the regent through his keeper of the seals had not only condemned the recent behaviour of the magistrates, he had also affirmed the principles of absolute government in language not heard since the 1660s. This resort to principle added an ideological dimension to the quarrel, raising the stakes by challenging the Parlement on theory. For this reason, the dispute could only grow more intense, involving not only policy but constitutional principle as well. It also began to attract unwelcome attention in the provinces, raising the prospect that other tribunals might join the fray.[13]

As Mesmes told the Parlement on 4 July, when he had the diatribe read aloud in a plenary session, d'Argenson's words appeared 'important' in the sense that they enunciated principles which, if left unchallenged, would undermine the whole body of constitutionalist thought and confer an inestimable psychological advantage upon the government. The magistrates agreed at once, from the most senior to the youngest among them, on the grounds that d'Argenson had attacked 'maxims as ancient as the Parlement' in favour of principles 'of great consequence' which 'it would be difficult to prove'. Cochet, a veteran *président aux requêtes* normally inclined to moderation, endorsed these assessments completely. 'The more one studies this matter', he concluded, 'the more one finds that it is important.' All agreed that they had to defend their constitutional traditions. On 8 July, the Parlement voted overwhelmingly to submit its third remonstrance of the year, in part against the recoinage edict but largely a full-fledged constitutionalist rebuttal to the absolutist theses of d'Argenson. Magistrates flooded the drafting committee with helpful memoranda – some quite extensive in their arguments, evidence and citation of precedent.[14]

The vote in favour of a new remonstrance meant that d'Argenson had failed to silence the Parlement; indeed, the regent complained to the *gens du roi* that the tribunal was now submitting remonstrances too frequently, as though to wear him down. So the government temporized on the date when it would receive the remonstrance and then, having fixed that date, abruptly postponed it by a week. As his excuse, the regent cited the extreme heat that oppressed Paris all that summer and supposedly threatened the health of the young king, who would have to endure another long session when the Parlement brought its remonstrance to the Tuileries. By no coincidence, however, the delay gave the mints additional time to turn out new coins, making the recoinage portions of the remonstrance increasingly pointless. Even so, the magistrates worked away at their document, which grew steadily in size.

On the morning of 26 July, the first president took all of forty-five minutes, so long had the remonstrance become, to read it to his assembled colleagues. The magistrates approved it with apparent unanimity and then considered whether or not, at the ceremony set for the Tuileries later that morning, the first president should read it aloud and in full, as a 'long sermon', in the words of Mesmes himself. Acting at the request of the regent, and thus relapsing into his consistent inconsistency, the first president proposed that he merely deliver the document in order to spare the king on a warm day. Probably he also wanted, by avoiding a public reading, to diminish its éclat, reinsuring himself with the government. But the magistrates voted overwhelmingly, 126 to 25, for a full reading, no matter what the regent or the first president preferred; and with those instructions, Mesmes and a deputation set off for the Tuileries. It took more than an hour to present the remonstrance to Orléans, the Regency Council and the assembled court; but Louis XV withstood the experience without visible strain.[15]

The fresh remonstrance reasserted constitutionalist principles on the registration of laws, in studied opposition to d'Argenson's absolutist manifesto of 2 July. If the keeper of the seals had echoed Louis XIV's councillors from 1665, the Parlement drew heavily upon Pasquier and his constitutionalist successors. The old mentors might have written the tribunal's final text, so closely did it adhere to their tenets. Like their ancestors, the judges of 1718 accepted, to all appearances, the legislative sovereignty of the king, who, they acknowledged, wielded 'the only legitimate power in France, from which all others derive'. This unqualified confession attempted to discredit d'Argenson's charge that the Parlement intended to diminish royal authority. In another sixteenth-century convention, the remonstrance argued that all past kings had expected the Parlement to examine new legislation to ensure that it did not violate the fundamental laws of the realm. To honour this historic command and to fulfil their oath of office, the magistrates of the Parlement (not the judges of sister or subordinate tribunals) must obviously receive the laws, deliberate upon them, and vote with *liberté de suffrages*. This was the irreducible meaning of registration; and registration, 'a necessary condition of the law', was an integral part of the monarchy, not to be separated from it. The magistrates stated all these theses with as much emphasis as possible.

They thus set precedent, tradition and constitutionalist theory in direct opposition to the absolutist principles of the keeper of the seals and underlined the theoretical distance between them. Recent scholars have treated both man-ifestos as reflecting only the fringes of French political thought, so extreme as to be almost outside the spectrum. In fact, the contrasting statements clearly stated, for the benefit of a new generation, the ideological tension between princes and parlements that had originated in the sixteenth century, survived for most of the seventeenth, and had inevitably reappeared, now that Louis XIV was dead. Such a collision of ideas and principles was in the nature of things, as the Introduction to this study argued.[16]

Although the government chose not to answer the remonstrance, wishing to break off the verbal duel now that the mints were producing the new coins in quantity, the tribunal, resilient as always, took up another financial issue. Summoning Charles Trudaine, the *prévôt des marchands* of Paris, over whom it had administrative jurisdiction, the Parlement learned from him that the government was selling more *rentes* on the Hôtel de Ville than it had funds to pay for. This fresh excursion into finances, consuming the first weeks of August, may have been intended, as Saint-Simon charged, to win the political support of the *rentiers* of Paris, whose interest payments the government could not meet.

The magistrates decided to issue yet another remonstrance, this time on general financial policy, and to include in it a critique of d'Argenson's meaning-less answer to their remonstrance of 26 January. The commissioners appointed in February to study that response now got to work. What would have been the fourth remonstrance of the year targeted John Law and his Bank, which included in its deposits tax revenues that in principle belonged under the control of regular financial officials. The magistrates resented this interference in financial administration and saw his overall plans as a vast confidence scheme, perpetrated by a disreputable foreigner. The problem, said President Feydeau bluntly, was how to 'bring this man down'.

After a heated discussion on 12 August, in which the magistrates denounced Law by name or as 'that foreigner', the tribunal issued a decree that compared in audacity with its decree of 20 June on the coinage. The Parlement ordered the Bank reduced to its original status as a private institution, instructed it to return state funds to regular fiscal officials, and banned all foreigners, meaning Law, from the administration of finances. President Feydeau, who proposed the decree and condemned John Law by name, saw it pass by an overwhelming margin, 130 to 29, supported by both junior and senior magistrates, including half the *présidents à mortier*.

The next question was in what manner the Parlement would publish its decree. The first president and the dean, Le Nain, urged their colleagues to show moderation. But on 18 August, after another overwhelming vote, 139 to 40, the Parlement issued the decree as conspicuously as it could – by having it read aloud at a plenary session, with the doors and windows flung open, in the full view and hearing of the crowds that thronged the galleries of the Palais de Justice. It also ran copies off its printing press, sent them to subordinate tribunals, and posted them in Paris. The diarist Barbier saw people reading the decree all over the city.

The new decree appeared at a bad time for the financial health of Law's Company of the West, which was closely related to the Bank. After a six-month suspension, Law had just resumed selling Company shares. Since its prospects appeared bright, a perception heightened by its acquisition of the tobacco revenue farm, the Company saw its stock rise nicely in value into the summer of 1718. When the Parlement published its decree of 12 August, the run-up ended, and prices fell off sharply. Law placed the losses at 100 million livres and derided the magistrates as financial simpletons.[17]

Most important, the decree of 12 August, which went well beyond anything that the Parlement had previously done, appeared to have serious constitutional implications. Loyalists like Saint-Simon saw it as a frontal attack upon royal authority and a near revolutionary effort to insinuate the Parlement into affairs of state, an assessment shared to a degree by some modern scholars. The judges themselves, as we have seen, believed that they were upholding tradition, precedent and the laws of the realm against unprincipled innovations. One of those infrequent but inevitable breakdowns in the French system of government therefore loomed ahead.

The magistrates made a malicious interpretation of their intentions even more believable when, on 22 August, they demanded that the regent allow them to inspect his financial registers, seeking proof that the government had in fact destroyed, as it had promised, the *billets d'état* acquired in the recoinage process and by other means. The Parlement also began to deliberate on the government's failure to pay its creditors the interest that it owed them, with the full intention of exploiting this issue as well. When the *gens du roi* presented these concerns to the duc d'Orléans, he turned and walked away, astonished at the tribunal's presumption.[18]

On the afternoon of 19 August, as Saint-Simon met in his Paris mansion with a frightened John Law (more dead than alive, said the memoirist), he received two unexpected visitors – Henry Jacques de Caumont, duc de La Force, and Louis Fagon. The former was vice-president of the Council of Finances and was about to be named to the Regency Council, the latter a junior councillor of state. They had just come from the regent who, alarmed by the Parlement's decree against John Law, had ordered them to confer with both Law and Saint-Simon and advise him what to do. For the first time, Saint-Simon dared hope that Orléans, whom he regarded as politically careless, at last understood that he faced a real crisis. Unknown to Saint-Simon, Orléans was in fact working fourteen hours a day in an effort also to solve international problems. He had just negotiated the Quadruple Alliance with England, the United Provinces and Austria, agreeing to provide money to his allies in any future war with Spain. This pledge made the financial interference of the Parlement all the more troublesome.[19]

Saint-Simon and his fellow conspirators decided that Orléans should try to impose his will in a *lit de justice*, the logical next step now that the Parlement was ignoring the annulment decrees of the Regency Council. But if the friends of Orléans raised this idea in Council, they risked seeing the duc du Maine and his group change the mind of the regent, possibly by contending that a trip to the Parlement would endanger the health of Louis XV, given the oppressive heat. As Maine was superintendent of the king's education and saw him daily, even occupying an apartment in the Tuileries, such an objection could not be dismissed out of hand. Besides, Maine would inevitably alert the magistrates as to what they should expect, allowing them to plan the most effective rejoinder. Finally, the conspirators did not believe that the regent, known for equivocation, would persevere for very long.

At length Saint-Simon hit upon the solution: they would hold the *lit de justice* in the Tuileries itself, making it unnecessary for the king to travel the streets of Paris, and they would keep everything secret until the very day of the ceremony. To this end, they would have the regent convene the obligatory Council session on the morning of, and just before, the *lit de justice*, catching Maine and the Parlement by surprise. So, indeed, it was to be, once the regent agreed to everything.

D'Argenson, informed of the plan, supported it at once, although he insisted that he needed several days in which to prepare new laws for the *lit de justice*. The abbé Guillaume Dubois, the former tutor of the regent and soon to be his secretary of state for foreign affairs, also joined in; but he seems to have wavered, possibly hoping to mediate some compromise with the Parlement. A more important, less hesitant recruit was the young Louis-Henri de Bourbon-Condé, duc de Bourbon, titular chief of the Regency Council and head of the powerful Condé family, princes of the blood. Law had shrewdly conferred shares of Bank and Company stock upon 'Monsieur le Duc', making him wealthier than ever; the regent now promised to appoint him superintendent of the king's education in place of the duc du Maine, still another reward. Meanwhile, Saint-Simon quietly attended to the *lit de justice* paraphernalia, the benches, podiums and draperies. He also fortified Orléans with frequent visits; but it was not until the Parlement took its initiative on the *billets d'état* and threatened further action on the *rentes*, that he dared believe the regent would execute the plan in full.[20]

At a session of the Regency Council on 21 August, d'Argenson presented a masterly summary of what he regarded as the Parlement's recent challenges to royal authority. He then read the tribunal's new decree against John Law and the

General Bank and took immediate issue with it, refuting the precedents that it had cited and its overall theme. In words which he again drew from absolutist thought, and likely from the Council of Justice of 1665, the keeper of the seals defined the current issue as to whether the king's subjects were to obey the monarch or the Parlement, 'and which of the two has legislative power'. Once the question was put that squarely, the Council had little choice but to quash the Parlement's decree. The regent announced that the Council would reconvene in the near future to approve the full text of an annulment decree and to decide what else to do. Just as Saint-Simon had feared, however, word leaked out that the Council intended to void the Parlement's decree, and a rumour began to circulate that the king would soon hold a *lit de justice*; but that rumour could not have come from the Regency Council, where the matter had not been discussed.[21]

Tension, like the heat, became oppressive, spawning anxious speculation and feverish, contradictory rumours. Foreign ambassadors predicted turmoil; Saint-Simon and his friends weighed the prospects of civil war. The regent's mother, Elisabeth Charlotte, despaired of her son's life. The friends of Maine, also pondering an uncertain future, feared that cells in the Bastille awaited them. John Law hid out in the Palais Royal, frightened by reports that the Parlement intended to hang him. When at last he returned home, several judges paid him an unexpected courtesy call, anxious to reinsure themselves should Law win out after all.[22]

Orléans scheduled the next meeting of the Regency Council and the *lit de justice* both for Friday, 26 August; although bedridden by a worrisome attack of fever, he issued the necessary orders into the early hours of that morning. At 5 a.m., drumbeats reverberated in the city, as more than thirty companies of cavalry, dragoons, guardsmen and musketeers, all newly paid, took positions in and around the Tuileries, the rue de Richelieu, and the Saint-Germain market, the key points for crowd control. Messengers notified members of the Regency Council that it would meet at 8 a.m. At 6 a.m., the master of ceremonies, Michel Desgranges, arrived at the Parlement, where barely a handful of magistrates had begun to assemble.

Since the first president was still at home, Desgranges informed the senior *président à mortier*, Lamoignon, that the king would hold a *lit de justice* that day. In the event of any resistance, the master of ceremonies had orders to command the judges to leave the Palais de Justice and to cease exercising their offices. But Lamoignon merely sent for Mesmes who, arriving hurriedly, convened an immediate plenary session, where the *gens du roi*, having seen the regent at the Palais Royal, announced that the *lit de justice* would take place at 10 a.m. in the Tuileries. Saint-Simon and his friends had planned well; everything moved with machine-like precision.[23]

As the magistrates pondered how to react, the members of the Regency Council arrived at the Tuileries for their meeting. Orléans, as Saint-Simon noted with relief, seemed fully recovered from his fever, and an unusual resolution illuminated his face and worked its way into his posture. In a surprise, the regent took the comte de Toulouse aside and induced him to leave the meeting and to take the duc du Maine with him. By departing, Orléans persuaded Toulouse, they would spare themselves humiliation and anguish; their absence, he did not need to explain, would also make the session go more smoothly.

When the meeting began, the princes having exited quietly, the regent revealed that he was holding a *lit de justice* short notice to register the Council's annulment of the Parlement's decree of 12 August. If he were to send the decree to the Parlement in the ordinary way, he explained, this would only hand the judges another occasion to disobey the king and further compromise royal authority. The keeper of the seals, who spoke next, expanded upon his ongoing charge that the Parlement was using remonstrances to claim a role in affairs of state and finances. The Council's new annulment decree, he declared, included regulations on remonstrances, 'in the manner of a code', to curtail this abuse. This, of course, went well beyond what the Council had agreed to on 21 August.

D'Argenson then read his annulment decree, which included the new restrictions on remonstrances, and letters patent that restated everything for purposes of public law. The severe language in these documents astonished the Council members, and the regent astounded them with the forthright way that he endorsed the texts. No one had imagined that he would ever adopt so harsh a tone or take so firm a line with the Parlement. Silence descended upon the Council session; Saint-Simon said that one could have heard a mite walk. When Orléans asked for the votes, everyone approved – the duc du Bourbon, with enthusiasm; the friends of Maine, grudgingly. Most members said little or nothing, except the duc de Noailles, who, chagrined at the humiliation of his protégés, spoke at some length, without effect.

Having surprised his Council, the regent truly stunned it when he declared that he would also strip Maine and Toulouse of their status as princes of the blood and reduce them to their original rank of dukes and peers. On legal grounds, as well as from social envy, most peers, especially Saint-Simon, had taken offence when the late king, advancing his legitimized sons, made them princes of the blood. Politics now spurred the regent to diminish his rivals, returning them to their previous status. As a junior peer, the duc du Maine had no claim to oversee the king's education, so the regent awarded the superintendent dignity to Bourbon, who glowed with pleasure in his seat. Marshal Villeroy, perhaps Maine's closest supporter, deplored the unhappy state of his friend, but Orléans heatedly denounced Maine as an 'enemy revealed', voicing the resentment that he had felt for at least the three years of his regency.[24]

Meanwhile, the magistrates, enveloped in their heavy red robes and numbering some 150, a substantial complement, left the Parlement at 9.30 and made their sweltering way along the Quai des Orfèvres, across the Pont Neuf, and up the Rue Saint-Honoré towards the Tuileries. Few onlookers lined the streets, dashing any hopes for public intervention. At the Tuileries, where soldiers filled the courtyard, an escort guided them into a great antechamber on the first floor, where they found Saint-Simon's benches and paraphernalia set up much as they would have been in their own Grand-Chambre. Taking their places on the lower benches, while peers and dignitaries filed into tiers of seats along the sides, some magistrates, especially Mesmes, noted with dismay the unexpected absence of Maine and Toulouse, whose seats Saint-Simon and the duc du Sully, the senior peers in attendance, triumphantly occupied. The king appeared, preceded by Orléans, Bourbon and the prince de Conti, and made his way to a throne on a platform in a corner.

D'Argenson took his seat in an armchair beneath the throne, a small desk and papers before him, the royal seals at hand. After the preliminaries, an uncomfortable silence descended, as the keeper of the seals sat motionless and menacing, savouring the moment, his enemies helpless before him – Rhadamanthus, true to life. At last he rose and began to speak, so firmly that his voice carried across the vast chamber and into the public area where spectators crowded round. His words surged through the magistrates, leaving them visibly shaken. When he had finished, d'Argenson had the clerk Gilbert read aloud the annulment decree and the letters patent that the Council had just approved. As these texts – the discourse, the decree and the letters patent – all came from the pen of d'Argenson and dealt with the Parlement in similar ways, we may treat them as a single document. They represented the strongest assertion of the principles of absolute government in more than fifty years.

D'Argenson castigated the Parlement for trying to usurp royal authority, arrogating to itself power that belonged to the king alone, his main thesis during the entire clash. He had said as much on 2 July, but he now elaborated on the charge and embellished it with concurrent accusations. By its recent decrees, d'Argenson declared, the tribunal had tried to lift itself above the other superior courts of Paris, claiming authority over financial issues that lay outside its sphere. It had abused remonstrances by issuing too many and had attempted by remonstrances to coerce the king. Its decrees of 20 June and 12 August proved that the Parlement believed that it could issue orders contradicting the king's very words, no matter how precisely chosen. It thought itself able to do what it wished over and against the king who, relegated to second place, could no nothing without its assent. This could only mean the Parlement considered itself to be the superior legislator of the kingdom. Today's *lit de justice*, as d'Argenson put it, would redress the tilting balance between the monarch and the Parlement, the paramount issue of the day.

The keeper of the seals addressed the issue of remonstrances, to which the annulment decree and the letters patent devoted their first six articles. These articles reaffirmed that fundamental concession of the Declaration of Vincennes by which the Parlement could issue remonstrances before it registered laws, provided that it took no more than one week to do so. But in reaction to recent events, the articles imposed new restrictions upon remonstrances, more in the spirit of Colbert and Louis XIV. The decree and letters patent ordered the Parlement never to make remonstrances or representations about, and certainly not to deliberate upon, laws that the king did not send it, a restriction obviously prompted by its claim to jurisdiction over the recoinage edict.

If, in the absence of remonstrances, the Parlement did not register a law within one week of deliberating upon it, then that law would be deemed registered and sent down to subordinate tribunals as though it had been. This provision restated article 5 of title I of the ordinance of 1667 and served notice that, although Louis XIV had never invoked this authority, the regency government might well choose to do so. If the Parlement did not produce its remonstrance on time, then the law in question would, again, be treated as registered. Once the government had answered a remonstrance, the Parlement must register the new law without delay. In addition, the government, not the Parlement, would decide whether a remonstrance would take oral or written form.

These articles permitted the royal administration to set the complete schedule under which remonstrances would be written, delivered, answered and ended. They also enabled ministers to influence the topics of remonstrances, by restricting them to laws sent directly to a tribunal. They permitted the government to choose whether remonstrances would be presented with greater or lesser éclat, orally or in writing. Finally, it seems likely that d'Argenson intended to use these new powers to edit future remonstrances, as he had done with the January remonstrance of the Parlement of Rennes. In sum, d'Argenson revoked the spirit and narrowed the scope of the Declaration of Vincennes, upholding, in his view, the rightful legislative authority of the king.

After dealing with remonstrances, the articles shifted to other issues. Article seven commanded the Parlement never to invite other courts to any association, union, confederation or assembly, without royal permission. Obviously d'Argenson had not forgotten the tribunal's earlier attempt to rally its sister courts against the recoinage edict. The next article renewed a command of Francis I, periodically restated, that the Parlement refrain from deliberating upon any financial issues whatsoever or, indeed, upon any affairs of state. All the tribunal's recent decrees, deliberations, and other acts concerning finances and the state were overturned. The concluding articles vigorously quashed its financial decree of 12 August as inconsistent with royal authority. That decree, together with the equally offensive decree of 20 June and any documents that had contributed to them, were to be ripped from the Parlement's registers and archives and the Regency Council's decree inserted in their place, as a permanent reminder of the king's authority. (This last punishment, however, did not take place.)

After Gilbert read the Council decree and the letters patent, d'Argenson turned to the *avocat-général* Guillaume de Lamoignon, the brother of the *président à mortier*, for the recommendations of the *gens du roi*. Lamoignon, having been warned that the government would seize his property if he did not cooperate, obediently advised the Parlement to register the legislation. First

President Mesmes, also invited to speak, asked for time in which the Parlement might deliberate upon the new laws, the stalling tactic that the magistrates had selected in their hurried discussions earlier that morning. But d'Argenson paid no attention. He strode purposefully along the benches where sat the peers, dignitaries and magistrates, and pretended to listen to their opinions. Then he approached the king, paused briefly before him, turned and declared, with a whiplash in his voice, 'The king wishes to be obeyed and on the spot'. At this, all the judges, presidents and councillors alike, seemed to collapse into themselves, bowing their heads in despair, Mesmes's chin falling almost to his knees.

Under traditional procedure, the *lit de justice* would have been at its end, the king having issued his orders and making ready to depart. But in an unprecedented move, d'Argenson registered the new laws on the spot, the royal seals at hand, the burner for sealing wax glowing with flame, and Gilbert standing by with the Parlement's register. Since six legislative acts were involved, it took time to get the job done. The *lit de justice*, which began at 10 a.m., concluded around 2 p.m. A dejected company of magistrates finally made its way back across the Seine, leaving only the first president behind. After the *lit de justice*, the duc du Maine summoned Mesmes to his apartment at the Tuileries where, with guards at his doors, he had languished through the entire ceremony. There the duchesse, in a rush of her Condé blood, abused the first president for an hour and finally mounted a stool (since she was small of stature), seized his cravat and slapped him hard.[25]

Only in the days after a *lit de justice*, no matter how formidable, could a government know for sure if it had succeeded in its effort to intimidate a parlement, as the Introduction to this study has argued. In this case, the apparently vanquished magistrates recovered overnight and, in a plenary session on 27 August, began to plan their comeback. For the next forty-eight hours it appeared that this *lit de justice*, like so many before 1661, had failed. First President Mesmes, obviously invigorated by his encounter with Maine, led the way, this time unequivocally. As the first president told it, the *lit de justice* had dealt the Parlement the hardest blow that it had ever suffered in its long history, and it must rise to this unprecedented challenge.

Also stung by the *lit de justice*, his colleagues rushed to agree, in one angry discourse after another. D'Aligre, a *président à mortier*, said the only question was whether the Parlement should be rigorous or prudent in its new struggle. For the moment, the magistrates decided, prudently, to compose a full written record of the ceremony, intending to discredit the new legislation by establishing that they had neither deliberated nor been heard on it. Twenty-four deputies, ten from the Grand-Chambre and two each from the seven Enquêtes and Requêtes chambers, were to assemble on Sunday, 28 August, in the Chambre Saint-Louis to draw up the Parlement's account of the *lit de justice*. The Parlement would meet on Monday, 29 August, to approve the document.

Much more significantly, the tribunal also charged the deputies to consider what it could do *against* the *lit de justice* and the new laws registered therein. In his opening remarks, the first president had proposed that the magistrates read all the laws in their next session to decide what to do about them. This invited the Parlement to find ways to undermine the legislation, much as it had done after the *lit de justice* of January 1648. In addition, Mesmes identified d'Argenson as a good subject for a judicial investigation in his own right. *Président à mortier* Le Peletier proposed that some deputies visit Chancellor d'Aguesseau at Fresnes, his rural home and place of exile, to ask if he had surrendered the seals voluntarily, as d'Argenson's letters of provision alleged. Another magistrate revived the idea of interrogating John Law. In short, the judges who had prudently agreed to document the *lit de justice* did not intend to stop there. They were prepared to deepen the crisis and to challenge d'Argenson and, by implication, the regent with every political and judicial weapon at their disposal.

On 28 August, the deputies met for almost five hours in the Chambre Saint-Louis. Their number included such leading activists as the outspoken *président aux enquêtes* Frizon de Blamont; Councillor Henri-Charles Feydeau, the son of another fiery Enquêtes president; Armand de Saint-Martin, an Enquêtes councillor known for his combative instincts; and Councillors Pucelle and Ferrand, still smarting from having been booted off the administrative councils of the regency. Mesmes himself was a deputy. By themselves, the deliberations on 27 August and the session of the deputies on 28 August violated d'Argenson's order to the Parlement not to discuss affairs of government. We can only assume that the deputies would have brought strong recommendations to the Parlement on 29 August, a further infraction. Thanks to his informants, d'Argenson must have known for sure.[26]

The keeper of the seals struck first and stopped the Parlement before it could intensify this clash. During the night of 28–29 August, he sent armed musketeers to arrest three of the most prominent Chambre Saint-Louis deputies – Frizon, Feydeau and Saint-Martin. Twenty to thirty musketeers arrived between 2 and 3 a.m. to arrest them at their homes. When Saint-Martin's porter refused to open the door, the musketeers hacked through with axes and took the judge into custody anyway. Masters of requests searched the houses for incriminating documents, filling two cartons with suspicious papers belonging to Frizon. Their searches complete, the musketeers bundled the magistrates into two large carriages and drove them to the city of Orléans, en route to far-flung prisons on the periphery of France.

When the Parlement assembled early that morning, the magistrates naturally clamoured for the release of their unfortunate colleagues. A deputation of sixty-three judges, almost a third of the full Parlement and drawn from all its chambers and ranks, proceeded to the Tuileries that afternoon to plead their case en masse before the king, the regent and the assembled court. Although the large deputation was meant to impress, an unmoved d'Argenson replied coldly that affairs of state, which had caused the arrests, belonged to the king alone and thus fell outside the jurisdiction of the tribunal. What happened to the prisoners, d'Argenson declared, would depend upon the future behaviour of the magistrates as a group. Contemporaries recorded his terse reply as a further humiliation for the deputies who, despite their numbers, came away empty-handed, their plans for further resistance to the *lit de justice* definitively quashed.[27] This last episode, no more than an empty gesture intended to preserve appearances, provided the denouement to the long confrontation of 1718 and marked the final defeat of the Parlement, in terms of the regency of Philippe d'Orléans.

For 1718, the expression *lit de justice* should be used, in the manner of synecdoche, one part standing for the whole, to designate all the related events that occurred in the four days from 26 to 29 August, before and after the ceremony itself. In this extended sense, we can agree with the gazeteer Buvat that the *lit de justice* changed everything.

It handed the Parlement a stinging defeat and boosted the political authority of the regent. Because of the *lit de justice*, the Parlement ceased to resist d'Argenson, Law and the policies of Orléans. The deputies to the Chambre Saint-Louis never reported, and the Parlement abandoned any further thought of undermining the laws registered on 26 August. The arrest of the three judges, by no means the only opposition spokesmen, stood as a warning to others. Those magistrates who had been the most vocal throughout the disputes of 1717 and 1718 fell silent; and First President Mesmes fell ill, suffering an apparent stroke.

The influence of the faction of the duc du Maine waned; he and the duchesse withdrew to their property at Sceaux and did not receive visitors. In September, the regent terminated his experiment with administrative councils, with the exception of the Marine Council, and began to govern, like Louis XIV, through ministers and secretaries of state. D'Argenson naturally emerged stronger than ever. 'The Parlement wanted to ruin him', Buvat observed, 'and he ruined the Parlement'. In a way roughly comparable to the initiatives of Chancellor Maupeou in the 1770s, the *lit de justice* rearranged political forces to the advantage of the government.[28]

New appointments in the Parlement underlined the point. On 5 December 1718, Germain-Louis Chauvelin, an *avocat-général* who had supported d'Argenson, rose to the dignity of *président à mortier*; and Pierre Gilbert de Voisins, who had served with distinction on Noailles's Council of Finances, replaced him as the new *avocat-général*. The regent thus placed loyal supporters on the *gens du roi* and among the presidents. In addition, André Potier de Novion, a loyalist *président à mortier* who out of disgust had scarcely attended Parlement sessions in 1718, resumed his service.[29] These magistrates formed the nucleus of a new loyalist faction, which would steadily grow.

In a narrow sense, it had all come down to the effective use of force, as the diarist Barbier noted, comparing d'Argenson favourably with Mazarin, in another reference to 1648. The keeper of the seals apparently shared this view. Weeks before the *lit de justice*, d'Argenson put it bluntly to his son, a junior councillor in the tribunal, 'My son, does your Parlement have any troops? We have 150,000 men. That's what this comes down to.'[30] Intimidation and coercion do not, of course, tell the full story. The regent's opponents in, and outside the Parlement, turned out to lack the daring, skill and strength that he and Saint-Simon imputed to them. The *lit de justice* surprised the government's opponents and gave it a psychological advantage, while the arrests of their colleagues sapped the courage of the judges. Irresolution and weakness in one's adversaries often lead to a good result.

On the other hand, these adversaries, especially the judges, yielded not only to physical strength but to the vitality of the ideas of absolute government and the legacy of Louis XIV, itself far from moribund. A small but determined circle of the regent's advisers, who still believed in absolute government, fortified the regent's inclination to defend it. Personalities, character and ideas made the difference in 1718, turning back the Parlement's efforts to reassert constitutionalist ideas and to restore them to registration procedure, depriving it even of that 'victory in defeat' with which it emerged from the Fronde.[31]

Notes

1 Frédéric d'Agay, 'Argenson', in Bluche, *Grand Dictionnaire*, pp. 102–103; Saint-Simon, *Mémoires*, XXXIII, 34–36; Buvat (?), *Gazette de la Régence*, pp. 230–232, 236; Dangeau, *Journal*, XVI, 194 (18 September 1715). For d'Argenson's prior disputes with the Parlement, see El Annabi, *Parlement de Paris*, pp. 102–103, 282, 341–342. D'Argenson's son René-Louis de Voyer was a young councillor in a *chambre des enquêtes* of the Parlement. See his celebrated *Journal et mémoires du marquis d'Argenson*, ed. E.J.B. Rathery (9 vols; Paris, 1859–1867), I, 41.

2 Flammermont, *Remontrances*, I, 65; AN, U 416: 22 February 1718; Buvat [?], *Gazette de la Régence*, p. 237; U 416: 31 January 1718 (noting the Parlement's aversion to registering d'Argenson's letters of appointment to be keeper of the seals).

3 AN, U 416 and 420: 4 March 1718. The ambiguous role of Mesmes, the friend of the duc du Maine, is noted in Buvat [?], *Gazette de la Régence*, p. 233.

4 La Bourdonnaye, *président à mortier*, Paris, to Parlement of Rennes, 19 February, 14 and 15 March 1718, AD, I-V, IBc 2bis; IBb 330 (Registres secrets): 23 February, ff. 7v–8v; 17 March, ff. 17rv–18r; and 8 April 1718, ff. 25v–28v; IBb 660 (Registres secrets): 28 April 1718 (final report of La Bourdonnaye on the Parlement's deputation to Paris). See also Le Moy, *Parlement de Bretagne*, pp. 117–121; idem, *Remontrances*, pp. 6–8.

5 Faure, *Banqueroute de Law*, pp. 143–145; Frank C. Spooner, *The International Economy and Monetary Movements in France, 1493–1725* (Cambridge, Mass., 1972), pp. 249, 290, 329–330; Edmond-Jean-François Barbier, *Journal historique et anecdotique du règne de Louis XV* (4 vols; Paris, 1847–1856), I, 6.

6 AN, U 416 and 420: sessions of 2, 13, 14 and 15 June 1718; Saint-Simon,

Mémoires, XXXV, 347–349, contains the accounts in the Parlement's secret register, AN, X1A 8435; Law [?], 'Histoire des finances', 333; Buvat [?], *Gazette de la Régence*, p. 263. In 1655, the Parlement of Paris also strongly resisted the principle of devaluation and challenged the competence of the Cour over a coinage edict: Hamscher, *Parlement of Paris*, pp. 91–93. Hardy, *Judicial Politics*, pp. 102–104, and Shennan, *Parlement of Paris*, pp. 287–288, failed to note the interaction of the Parlement with the other superior courts of Paris.

7 AN, U 416 and 420: sessions of 17–19 June 1718; Barbier, *Journal historique*, I, 8; Buvat (?), *Gazette de la Régence*, p. 263; Flammermont, *Remontrances*, I, 69–74 (the representations and the regent's rejection of them).

8 AN, U 416 and 420: 20–21 June 1718; Flammermont, *Remontrances*, I, 74–75; Law (?), 'Histoire des finances', 333; Buvat, *Journal*, I, 279. Scholars tend to accept Glasson's verdict that on this occasion the Parlement encroached upon royal authority: Glasson, *Parlement de Paris*, II, 31; Leclercq, *Régence*, II, 152; Shennan, *Parlement of Paris*, p. 289; Hardy, *Judicial Politics*, p. 106.

9 BN, F. 23,673 (Regency Council), f. 89v: 20 June 1718; BN, *N.a.f.*, 9,771, ff. 63r, 138r; AN, U 416 and 420: 21 June 1718; U 416: 24 June 1718; AN, E 1994, f. 79rv (20 June 1718) and f. 82rv (21 June 1718); Buvat [?], *Gazette de la Régence*, p. 265; Saint-Simon, *Mémoires*, XXXV, 352–353. Dodun, a *président des enquêtes*, stayed in the Council of Finances, and Councillor Goislard remained in the Council of the Interior; but they no longer attended sessions in the Parlement.

10 AN, U 416 and 420: 19, 22, 25, and 27 June 1718; AN, X 1B 8899 (Minutes. Conseil): 27 June 1718; Flammermont, *Remontrances*, I, 77–84; Buvat, *Journal*, I, 280. The accounts in Hardy, *Judicial Politics*, p. 108, and Shennan, *Parlement of Paris*, pp. 288–289, are incomplete.

11 BN, F. 23,673 (Regency Council): sessions of 27 and 30 June 1718, ff. 92rv, 93r; AN, U 416: 1 July 1718; Buvat (?), *Gazette de la Régence*, p. 269.

12 Flammermont, *Remontrances*, I, 85–87; BN, *Fonds fr.*, 9771, ff. 102rv–103rv; and AN, U 420. For mid-century issues of representation, see Keith Michael Baker, 'Representation Redefined', in idem, *Inventing the French Revolution. Essays on French Political Culture in the Eighteenth Century* (Cambridge, 1990), pp. 231, 233. Hardy, *Judicial Politics*, pp. 111–112, Shennan, *Regent*, pp. 87–88, and idem, *Parlement of Paris*, p. 289, do not give d'Argenson's statement the attention it deserves.

13 An unknown witness took notes on d'Argenson's statement and sent a transcript to First President Camus de Pontcarré of the Parlement of Rouen: AD, S-M, 1B 5446.

14 AN, U 416 and 420: 4, 8 and 12 July 1718. The quotations are from notes taken on the spot by the *greffier* Gilbert, in U 420. As a recent retiree, with more than twenty years of service, President Cochet held *lettres d'honneur*, by which he still attended sessions and enjoyed the right to speak and to vote.

15 AN, U 416: 12, 13, 14, 18, 26 and 27 July 1718; U 420: 14 and 26 July 1718; U 226 (Conseil secret): 14 and 27 July 1718, ff. 427rv–428r, 472v–473r. Most of the *présidents à mortier* supported the first president's preference for a brief presentation of the remonstrance; but obviously the government had little support among the councillors.

16 Flammermont, *Remontrances*, I, 88–105; BN, *N.a.f.*, 9,771, f. 136rv ('Projet de Réponse aux Remontrances'); Dangeau, *Journal*, XVII, 351 (31 July 1718). Shennan, *Regent*, pp. 88–89, found the remonstrance 'extreme', as, in effect, did

Hardy, *Judicial Politics*, p. 114. The Parlement published its representations and remonstrances in pamphlet form, along with the collateral remonstrances of the other superior courts of Paris, in 'Recueil des Remontrances faites au Roy en M.DCC.XVIII. par ses cours souveraines . . .', AN, U 416, 18 August 1718, and University of Delaware, Special Collections, K.F815/P252re.

17 AN, U 226 (Conseil secret): 1 August, ff. 478r–479rv; 6 August, ff. 493v–494r; 9 August, ff. 507v–508r; 11 August, ff. 508rv–509rv; and 12 August, ff. 513v–515r; U 416: 1, 6, 9, 11–12, 17–20 August; and U 420: 6, 11 and 12 August 1718; Law [?], 'Histoire des finances', 330–336; Faure, *Banqueroute de Law*, pp. 117–119, 126–128, 132–133, 147–149; Barbier, *Journal historique*, I, 8; Dangeau, *Journal*, XVII, 357; Flammermont, *Remontrances*, I, 106–107; Marion, *Histoire financiére*, I, 93–95; Lüthy, *Banque protestante*, I, 304–310.

18 AN, U 226 (Conseil secret): 22 August 1718, f. 560r, and U 416 and 420: 22 August 1718; Saint-Simon, *Mémoires*, XXXV, 17, and Law [?], 'Histoire des finances', 336, assessed the decree as an assault upon royal sovereignty, a view implicitly adopted by Leclercq, *Histoire de la Régence*, II, 157–158, and explicitly by Shennan, *Parlement of Paris*, p. 290.

19 Saint-Simon, *Mémoires*, XXXV, 30–31; Michel Antoine, *Le Gouvernement et l'Administration sous Louis XV. Dictionnaire biographique* (Paris, 1978), pp. 99 (Fagon), 138–139 (La Force). Negotiations for the Quadruple Alliance concluded on 2 August; its financial clauses made the regent all the more anxious about the Parlement: Faure, *Banqueroute de Law*, p. 164.

20 Saint-Simon, *Mémoires*, XXXV, 26–82; Leclercq, *Histoire de la Régence*, II, 159–166.

21 BN, *Fonds fr.*, 23,673 (Regency Council): 21 August 1718, ff. 97v–98r; Saint-Simon, *Mémoires*, XXXV, 82; BN, *N.a.f.*, 9,771, ff. 158v–159r, which includes the d'Argenson quotation, is a memorandum upon which he based his report to the Council. Dangeau, *Journal*, XVII, 361–362 (21 August), shows that some Council members talked about what happened at this session. The Council's annulment decree, backdated to 21 August, is in AN, E 1994, ff. 113rv–121r, and Isambert, *Recueil général*, XXI, 159–162. D'Argenson did not bring this decree to the Council for approval in its final form until 26 August, the day of the *lit de justice*. The Parlement did not, therefore, 'ignore' the decree on and after 21 August, despite the assertions in Hardy, *Judicial Politics*, pp. 120–121, 125.

22 Saint-Simon, *Mémoires*, XXXIV, 202; XXXV, 103, 137, 140; d'Argenson, *Journal et mémoires*, I, 39, 41. Orléans's mother was Elisabeth Charlotte, duchesse d'Orléans (1652–1722), known in Germany as Liselotte von der Pfalz and in France as Madame or Madame Palatine. See her letters of 27 and 30 August, and 21 September 1718, in Elisabeth Charlotte Orléans, duchesse d', *A Woman's Life in the Court of the Sun King. Letters of Liselotte von der Pfalz, 1652–1722*, trans. Elborg Forster (Baltimore, 1984), pp. 216–218.

23 Leclercq, *Histoire de la Régence*, I, 168–170, drew upon Saint-Simon, *Mémoires*, XXXV, 142–163. For details, see Barbier, *Journal historique*, I, 9; Buvat [?], *Gazette de la Régence*, p. 279. The clerk Delisle, already at work at 6 a.m., wrote 'Jour Remarquable' at the top of the page which began his transcription of the events of 26 August, 1718: U 416.

24 BN, *Fonds fr.*, 23,673 (Regency Council): 26 August 1718, ff. 98v–99rv; Saint-Simon, *Mémoires*, XXXV, 170–210, provides a more complete, if biased, account of

this Council session. At the request of Saint-Simon, a friend of Toulouse, Orléans restored Toulouse to his princely honours for the duration of his life only, without the capacity to transmit them to heirs.

25 For the *lit de justice*, see especially AN, U 416: 26 August 1718 (which contains the d'Argenson quotation); a *procès-verbal* signed by Mesmes and d'Argenson; AN, X 1B, 8900: another *procès-verbal*; BN, *Actes R.*, F. 21,290 (69), the official version; Flammermont, *Remontrances*, I, 108–111, offers another official account; Saint-Simon, *Mémoires*, XXXV, 210–235, is the classic eyewitness account, despite its bias; see also Dangeau, *Journal*, I, 370–372 (26 August 1718); Barbier, *Journal historique*, I, 9–11; the best secondary treatments are Leclercq, *Régence*, II, 161–187, and Hardy, *Judicial Politics*, pp. 125–134. For an analysis of the documents which provide accounts of this *lit de justice*, see Boislisle's note in Saint-Simon, *Mémoires*, XXXV, 224–225, n. 1, and Hardy, *Judicial Politics*, p. 130, n. 1. The *lit de justice* legislation consisted of the original letters of provision for d'Argenson's office of keeper of the seals, the council decree and the letters patent for the Parlement of Paris, and three edicts concerning Maine, Toulouse and Bourbon. The minutes of the Parlement's decrees of 20 June and 12 August 1718 were not, after all, ripped from its registers, as seen in AN, X 1B 8899–8900. Mesmes's encounter with the duchesse du Maine is described in Saint-Simon, *Mémoires*, XXXV, 266–267, and in BN, *Dossiers bleus*, 445 ('De Mesmes'), f. 5r.

26 AN, U 226 (Conseil Secret), f. 575v (27 August 1718); AN, U 416 (for the charge to the Chambre Saint-Louis deputies and the names of the deputies) and U 420: 27 August 1718.

27 AN, U 416: 29 August and 14 November 1718; Saint-Simon, *Mémoires*, XXXV, 365–372, reproduces the Parlement's secret register entries for its sessions of 29–31 August and 3, 5 and 7 September 1718; Flammermont, *Remontrances*, I, 116–118 (Parlement's entreaty of 29 August); Barbier, *Journal historique*, I, 13–16; Dangeau, *Journal*, XVII, 373–375; and Saint-Simon, *Mémoires*, XXXV 290–291. The authorities took Feydeau to the Ile d'Oléron and Saint-Martin to the Ile de Ré, both off the coast of La Rochelle, while Frizon was relegated to the Sainte-Marguerite island fortress on the Mediterranean.

28 Buvat [?], *Gazette de la Régence*, pp. 275, 286; Saint-Simon, *Mémoires*, XXXV, 271 (a good analysis of the Parlement's defeat); Leclercq, *Régence*, II, 189, endorsing Saint-Simon's view. Hardy quixotically minimized the importance of the *lit de justice*, in *Judicial Politics*, p. 137, and Shennan gave it scant attention in *Parlement of Paris*, p. 291, and *Regent*, p. 90 (mistakenly locating it in the Louvre).

29 AN, U 416: 5 December 1718. Chauvelin became keeper of the seals in 1727, Gilbert rose to high rank in the councils of the king, and Potier became first president of the Parlement in 1723.

30 Barbier, *Journal historique*, I, 14–15; d'Argenson, *Journal et Mémoires*, I, 23.

31 Moote, *Revolt of the Judges*, p. 375 ('victory in defeat'). Louis XVI found no comparable ideological stalwarts upon whom he could rely; see Munro Price, *Preserving the Monarchy. The comte de Vergennes, 1774–1787* (Cambridge, 1995).

7

Sequels

The regent's victory in the *lit de justice* came opportunely, as his government still faced two troublesome, leftover issues. The first involved the Parlement of Rennes. Lethargic in the first half of 1718, the Breton tribunal roused itself that summer in sympathy with the Parlement of Paris and opened another political front, so to speak. Had the Bretons prevailed, they might have cancelled the advantages accruing to the government from the *lit de justice*, setting a bad example for other provincial tribunals and possibly inspiring the Parisian magistrates to try again. To prevent this, d'Argenson had to reach quickly into a far corner of the realm and silence the Bretons once and for all.

The second problem was how to deal with the national debt and, more specifically, what to do about the *augmentations de gages* of the judges. John Law inherited this problem, as after the *lit de justice* he set about reconstructing the economy and finances of the realm. The foreigner whom the magistrates of Paris had so grievously antagonized ended up with the power to pay, or not to pay, their *augmentations de gages*. On the other hand, Law did not yet know whether he could impose his idea of a financial settlement on the tribunals or whether he would have to compromise with them. It remained to be seen whether the benefits of the *lit de justice* would carry over into these additional areas of controversy.

D'Argenson and the Parlement of Rennes, 1718–1720

Six deputies from the Parlement of Rennes stayed in Paris from January to April 1718 and, beyond a doubt, contacted judges in the Parlement of Paris, exchanging information, sharing views and establishing personal ties. Once the deputies returned to Rennes, the whole Parlement closely followed the struggle waged by the Parisian judges against the recoinage edict. That episode led to the idea, which apparently originated with the Bretons, of joining forces with the senior tribunal, another 'association' for d'Argenson to apprehend and to disapprove.

In 1709, the Parlement of Rennes had distributed a circular letter to all the parlements in an apparent effort to rally them in mutual opposition to the financial demands of the government, so the idea of a broad association had already taken shape and needed only to be revived. In August 1718, an anonymous Breton magistrate revived it with emphasis when he tried to persuade an Enquêtes judge in Paris to get that Parlement to propose a 'general union', on the basis of which both tribunals would fight the new coins. Unfortunately for the Bretons, d'Argenson's agents intercepted the letter, and the idea of general union did not make it to the Parlement of Paris after all.[1]

News of the *lit de justice*, in which the king forbade all such associations, arrived in Rennes on 30 August. Senior judges, especially the *présidents à mortier*, had by now shifted their support to the government and welcomed this sign of its revival. But virtually all the Enquêtes judges and even some in the Grand-Chambre rushed to defend the beleaguered Parlement of Paris, with all the greater determination once they learned that three Paris judges were in prison. On 3 September, the Parlement of Rennes, despite the efforts of the senior magistrates, voted to remonstrate in support of the Paris tribunal and to seek clemency for the prisoners. It also wrote the Parlement of Paris a letter of solidarity expressing its eagerness to profit from its 'wise' deliberations. The letter, with a copy of the remonstrance enclosed, arrived at the Parlement in the evening of 6 September, conveyed thither by a special, unidentifiable courier, the use of whose services showed that the Bretons understood that their correspondence might otherwise be intercepted. The intendant Feydeau, alerting the government to what was coming, condemned the remonstrance and the letter as leading to 'a kind of association' in violation of the orders of the king.[2]

In the aftermath of the *lit de justice*, however, the Parlement of Paris wished to avoid even the appearance of political alliances and therefore proceeded with a caution that the Bretons had not expected. First President Mesmes, charged with framing a reply, kept his pen under control and wrote nothing to encourage associations and unions. He may indeed have obtained the regent's approval of his answer before he sent it to Rennes. While thanking the Bretons for their good wishes, Mesmes told them that the Parlement had now submitted to the king and the laws that he had 'imposed'. This disappointing response could not lead to the solidarity for which the Rennes magistrates had hoped; for that they would have to wait until the 1750s, when the idea of parlementary union revived and attracted wide support. But the Parlement of Rennes, even without outside help, soon clashed with the regency on another matter.[3]

Once again, difficulties began in the provincial Estates, which the government reconvened on 1 July 1718, again at Dinan. The contract between the Estates and the government having expired on 1 January, d'Argenson was still collecting taxes in Brittany with the help of the soldiers who, under the *commandant en chef*, Montesquiou, patrolled the province. Scholars have contended that the Bretons, withholding their taxes in support of the Estates, forced the government to call a new session in order to restore the revenue stream. But the instructions that d'Argenson gave the royal deputies to the Estates showed no sign that he felt any such pressure. It seems clear that the intendant Feydeau, who oversaw tax collections, had done well enough to dispel any tendency to panic.

Before the Estates reconvened, Montesquiou, taking his precautions, excluded those nobles who had been particularly strident in the preceding session. The government more or less controlled the first estate, consisting of up to three score prelates and abbots, who depended upon the king for their livings and advancement. The government also exerted considerable influence upon the third estate or commons, since it chose their deputies from the small urban oligarchies and paid their expenses and emoluments. As a result, the preliminary purge of the second estate helped ensure a harmonious opening session, as did Montesquiou's soldiers, standing conspicuously about the streets. On 1 July, the Estates voted the free gift immediately and without any preliminary discussion of financial grievances, thus complying with the government's primary demand.

On 14 July, however, controversy erupted over the *droits d'entrées*, a surtax upon the highly remunerative *impôts et billots* and *devoirs*, duties which Bretons paid on alcoholic beverages, including cider. The Estates, growing restless despite the government's influence, refused to renew the lease for the *droits d'entrées*, scheduled to expire on 1 October. D'Argenson promptly obtained a council decree renewing it on the authority of the king, and Montesquiou browbeat the first and third estates into registering this decree, against the staunch opposition of the nobles. He then expelled sixty-two particularly dissident noblemen, who retaliated by publishing a widely-read manifesto of protest. The prospect that the *droits d'entrées* would continue indefinitely, together with the strong-arm tactics of Montesquiou, so infuriated the nobles that, once again, they sought the help of the Parlement.[4]

As chapter 5 showed, nobles in the Parlement and in the Estates had worked together since the death of Louis XIV to obtain financial relief for the province; and their joint efforts continued throughout 1718. The Parlement's deputies to Paris had no doubt compared notes with the four prominent Estates nobles also summoned to the capital for a rebuke, one of whom, du Groësquer, spent time in the Bastille. Another Estates dissident happened to be the father of a judge. In March, as the Parlement's deputation prepared to return to Rennes, Montesquiou induced the government to summon two additional magistrates to Paris for a scolding, *président à mortier* Larlan de Rochefort and a councillor, Lambilly. Their presence in the capital afforded further occasions for talks between opposition judges and hardliners from the Estates.

Pressed by the Estates, the government in July permitted all these notables to return home. Rochefort and Lambilly somehow found their way to the

Estates at Dinan, only thirty-five miles from Rennes, and enjoyed a tumultuous reception from members of the second estate. Du Groësquer and his colleagues, barred from the Estates, set up headquarters at Rennes itself and received visits from the judges. A 'committee' of magistrates and Estates nobles took shape, and judges wrote discourses for the nobles to deliver at Dinan and visited Dinan themselves. Long before they attempted to ally with the Parlement of Paris, the magistrates of Rennes were working in harmony with nobles in the Estates of Brittany.[5]

Those nobles continued to denounce the way that the Estates had registered the recent council decree, declaring it null and void on the grounds that, in fiscal matters, the three estates had to be unanimous. On 13 August, the nobles sent the *procureur syndic* of the Estates, Coëtlogon, a member of a prominent parlementary family, to ask the tribunal to register and endorse a statement declaring the *droits d'entrées* illegal. The Parlement issued the degree the Estates wanted that very day and appointed a bailiff to take it to Dinan, where it had a bracing effect, although Montesquiou exiled Coëtlogon and three other nobles. He put the bailiff in leg-irons.

On 7 September, responding to another request from the noble order, the Parlement issued a second decree in this affair, comparable in its way to the extraordinary decrees published by the Parlement of Paris in July and August. This new decree forbade the levy of taxes of any kind without the consent of the Estates. This meant that if the government dissolved the Estates again, before the deputies had approved taxes, Bretons could cite the Parlement's decree as legal grounds for refusing to pay. Villeguérin, an *avocat-général* loyal to the government, predicted serious damage to the capitation and other levies if the decree went into effect. To make matters worse, the Parlement allowed nobles in the Estates to make copies of the decree and to distribute them throughout the province. It also sent the decree to all its subordinate tribunals. When another bailiff brought the 7 September decree to Dinan, several gentlemen volunteered to escort him, lest he suffer the fate of his predecessor.[6]

On 12 September, the Parlement remonstrated in support of the Estates and especially of the noble order. This new remonstrance, the strongest of the regency, scolded the government for using troops in Brittany, collecting taxes without consent, and trying to coerce Estates deputies. It naturally sided with the nobility in condemning the *droits d'entrées* and the council decree that perpetuated that levy. The Parlement also denounced the exile of Coëtlogon and the others as a breach of their rights. All these issues, the remonstrance noted in a provocative side comment, called the legitimacy of the Estates of 1718 into question. After reading this remonstrance, the intendant Feydeau feared that the Parlement would declare the revenue farms illegal, making it all but impossible for him to renew their leases.[7]

In July, before he had subdued the Parlement of Paris, d'Argenson attempted to placate the Breton judges with an offer to pay them 100,000 livres in arrears on their *augmentations de gages*, using some of the new money generated by recoinage at the mint in Rennes. No doubt he made this gesture in an effort to mollify the tribunal during the new session of the Estates. His proposal appealed to a handful of the judges, but a large majority opposed it, noting that the deval-uation of the livre had diminished its appeal. D'Argenson's effort to bribe the Parlement came to nothing, and Feydeau and Villeguérin informed him that activist judges had taken over the tribunal, a sign of more disorder to come. So d'Argenson, like Noailles before him, had to consider what he should do about the Parlement.

He began by resuming negotiations with the Estates, signing a two-year con-tract and concluding the Dinan session on 23 September. To his immense satis-faction, d'Argenson rid himself of the diocesan bureaux, returned the administration of the capitation to the intendant, and dealt the cause of pro-vincial fiscal autonomy a setback. But he had to abandon the controversial *droits d'entrées*, which indeed expired on 1 October, and agree that Bretons would pay only the traditional beverage taxes, the *devoirs* and *impôts et billots*. Although Feydeau favoured surrender on this point, arguing rightly or wrongly that the traditional revenue farms would yield more money without the surtax burden, the administration clearly gave up on one of the main points with which it had begun the Estates session. In all probability, d'Argenson decided to compromise with the Estates, ending that year-long dispute, so that he could deal with the Parlement by itself.[8]

On 24 September, the day after the Estates session ended, the government considered what to do about the Parlement's decrees of 13 August and 7 September and its remonstrance of 12 September. The main question, as a working document put it, was whether the regent should discipline the entire tribunal or only those magistrates guilty of 'irregular conduct'. In the end, d'Argenson decided to do both. As a first step, a stinging council decree of 29 September quashed the Parlement's decrees of 13 August and 7 September in the most emphatic way.[9]

After summarizing the Parlement's decrees, the Council voided them as a 'reprehensible' and 'damaging' attack upon the king's authority. The nobles who obtained the decrees had no legal right to approach the tribunal, and the Parlement lacked the authority to hear them. The *avocat-général* Joseph de Francheville, who had endorsed the decree of 13 August, had 'forgotten' his duties. (This censure augured badly for Francheville's professional future.) On pain of disobedience, the Parlement was forbidden to assume any further juris-diction over, or to issue any decrees concerning, the affairs of the Estates. All copies of the Parlement's decrees were to be turned over to the intendant, and copies of the council decree were to be posted on the premises of the Parlement and in all the subordinate courts of Brittany. Moreover, the Parlement's decrees of 13 August and 7 September were to be stripped from its registers, cut into pieces and the council decree inserted in their place, 'word for word', a permanent reminder of royal authority. This latter stipulation recalled what d'Argenson, at the *lit de justice*, had in mind for the Parlement of Paris.

D'Argenson commissioned Nicolas Denis, the royal bailiff who had served decrees on the Parlement in 1717, to carry this new decree to Rennes and to see to its execution. Denis left Paris on 3 October and arrived in Rennes at the *hôtel* of the intendant Feydeau on 8 October, having suffered a delay when his carriage broke down. Fortuitously, Montesquiou appeared almost at once, and the three began preparing for what they had to do. Feydeau had the local printer, Vatar, run off copies of the council decree and arranged a meeting with the *président à mortier* La Bourdonnaye de Blossac, his brother-in-law, and Huchet de La Bédoyère, the *procureur-général*, whose loyalties were uncertain. When he learned of Denis's mission, Huchet indeed tried to excuse himself. But Montesquiou insisted, and the *procureur-général*, however reluctantly, then carried out his duties to the letter.

In 1673, the last time such an intervention had occurred, Chamillart, the intendant at Caen, had convened a plenary session of the Parlement and torn a refractory decree from its register in full view of the magistrates. But either d'Argenson did not look this precedent up, or he judged that tensions in the Parlement made such an open confrontation inadvisable. He ordered Denis to register the council decree not in a plenary session but, more quietly, at the tribunal's archive (*greffe*). The Feydeau group decided to wait until the afternoon of 10 October, after the long morning session of the Parlement, when they would have the best chance of escaping detection. Everything worked out just as they planned.

At 1 p.m. on 10 October, Denis served the council decree on the Parlement's clerk, Gerbier, and instructed him to report to his archive at 3 p.m. At 2.30 p.m., he served the same decree, with identical orders, on Picquet de La Motte, the chief clerk, at his apartment in the Palais de Justice. At 3 p.m., the appointed time, Denis arrived at the *greffe*, clad in his black satin robe of office and wearing around his neck a golden chain with a pendant, also in gold, bearing the likeness of the king on one side and that of the regent on the other, signifying that the bearer embodied the will of the sovereign. Huchet joined Gerbier and Picquet, so that Denis had all the Parlement's papers and registers at his disposal.

Picquet handed Denis two heavy folders stuffed with the documents from the Estates upon which the Parlement had based its decrees of 13 August and 7 September. Denis removed the papers and cut them into shreds, which he left behind in a sack, as part of the record. At this point in its judicial year, the Parlement's minutes consisted of notebooks in which the clerks set down in preliminary form the information that they would later use to draw up the 'secret register', the final record. Denis took the notebooks and located the entries for 13 August and 7 September. When he saw that those pages contained ordinary judicial decrees, along with the political decrees involving the Estates, he put his scissors away and merely defaced the political decrees, drawing heavy vertical and lateral lines across them, still visible today. In the margins he noted that the council decree of 29 September had voided and superseded these decrees; and he placed the council decree on top of them.

The Parlement's clerks, after perfunctory objections, did not interfere; and Denis left Rennes peacefully, his mission accomplished. On 11 October, however, when Huchet informed the magistrates in a plenary session what Denis had done, they responded with a surge of anger and almost sanctioned the *procureur-général* and the clerks for not defending the archive. In the end, the Parlement contented itself with a vigorous remonstrance against the 'vile' Denis who had profaned its registers.[10]

D'Argenson harboured no illusion that the council decree by itself would make the Parlement of Rennes bow to the regency government once and for all. Even as he had the Parlement's decrees overturned in council, he was arranging to punish those judges who had most offended, relying upon Feydeau to identify miscreants. Before Denis arrived in Rennes, eight magistrates received *lettres de cachet* exiling them to such distant provinces as Burgundy and Languedoc. Montesquiou added two more names to the list, bringing the total to ten, a purge of about 15 percent of the magistrates of this semester. Even so these banishments, important as they were, did not quell the spirit of opposition in the tribunal: Feydeau wrote that the exiles took their *lettres de cachet* as 'badges of honour'. But d'Argenson had not finished.

On 6 October, as Denis was making his way to Rennes, the keeper of the seals decided to order the Breton *présidents des enquêtes* to let the intendant inspect all the documents involving their purchase of office – their *lettres de provision*, decrees of reception, and all their receipts and contracts. This requirement subjected the four serving *présidents* to a long, uncomfortable scrutiny and caused them to fear, not without reason, that the government intended to suppress their offices and to reimburse them with depreciated *billets d'état*. Villeguérin reported that such a prospect, even it concerned only the four presidents, sobered the other judges considerably more than had the exiles of their colleagues. In the end, the Enquêtes presidents escaped the suppression of their offices; but it took some time for anxiety on this point to dissipate.

As for the exiles, long months passed before they could return to Rennes; and they had first to apologize to Montesquiou, whom they had always blamed for their misfortunes, and obtain his support, another humiliation. Moreover, two never returned at all, having been required to resign. One of these unfortunates was Francheville, the *avocat-général* denounced in the council decree for neglecting his duties. Meanwhile, d'Argenson rejected the Parlement's remonstrance of 23 October and, in his letter on that subject, scornfully boasted to the judges that he knew everything about their most secret deliberations, a warning that they were all under political surveillance.[11]

At the beginning of this uproar, Noailles had said that he wanted to extinguish even the inclination of the Bretons to oppose the government. The exiles of individual judges, the threats to strip magistrates of their offices, and the two resignations under pressure considerably dampened that dissidence. But even as the government asserted its authority, some judges began to sympathize with, and a few became involved in, the eponymous 'Pontcallec conspiracy' that soon troubled the peace of the province. Only the royal victory over this conspiracy ended any lingering tendency among the magistrates to oppose the government.

After the Estates concluded in September 1718, hostile nobles, still angry with Montesquiou for his authoritarian rule, drafted an 'Act of Union', a statement of their grievances, and over the next few months obtained signatures from several hundred nobles who shared their views. For the most part, these nobles, in signing the Act, merely pledged their devotion to provincial privileges and did not intend to take things any further. But a small group of hardliners, many of them war veterans, set up an armed camp on the property of Clément de Guer, marquis de Pontcallec, whose château occupied a defensible site in a dense forest not far from the town of Vannes on the Gulf of Morbihan. When war between Spain and France began, an emissary of the Pontcallec group made his way to Spain and negotiated an alliance with Philip V, who sent a warship to the coast of Brittany to support the impending revolt. But Montesquiou marched on the Pontcallec redoubt, which the defenders, their numbers and enthusiasm declining by the day, abandoned without a fight. The marshal tracked most of them down over the winter and took them to the royal prison at the old ducal château in Nantes, by which time the Spanish warship had sailed away, the nobles' alliance with Spain having come to nothing.

On 26 March 1720, the Chambre Royale at Nantes, a hand-picked royal tribunal, condemned twenty noblemen to death, including sixteen who had fled to Spain or other sanctuaries and were executed in effigy. But the remaining four nobles, notably Pontcallec, the most reluctant in the face of death, perished beneath an executioner's adze on the Place du Bouffay, the centre of justice in Nantes. Several dozen conspirators, imprisoned along with them, eventually obtained amnesty and release, d'Argenson having concluded that the four deaths would suffice to subdue the province and frighten any of its remaining sympathizers in Paris.[12]

As an institution, the Parlement of Rennes took no part in the conspiracy and, once it disintegrated, condemned it as irresponsible and lawless. But many of its magistrates, embittered by their struggle with d'Argenson, sympathized with the plot; and some actively supported it. Among the latter was Councillor Pierre-Joseph de Lambilly, a firebrand from 1718. He openly joined the Pontcallec insurgency, and he was among those whom the Chambre Royale ordered executed in effigy. Had he not escaped to Spain, where he died around 1730, he would have shared the fate of Pontcallec on the Place du Bouffay, for all his status as a parlementaire. In fleeing, he unfortunately took with him what he knew about the involvement of other judges, leaving it to future historians to fill in the blanks as best they can. This has made our task more difficult, but we are not altogether reduced to speculation.

In December 1719, the Chambre Royale had Councillor Louis Saint-Pern du Lattay arrested on the very premises of the Parlement, an affront which the tribunal forcefully protested, to no effect. Saint-Pern, like Lambilly one of the moving spirits of 1718, spent at least six months in prison in Nantes, until the amnesty of 1720–1721 permitted him to return home. After Lambilly, he was the magistrate most implicated in the conspiracy, although others surely participated in one way or another. *Président à mortier* Larlan de Kercadio attended clandestine meetings at Pontcallec, obviously incriminating behaviour. Then, too, relatives of the judges, close relatives at that, got involved.

For example, both the brother and the brother-in-law of Huchet de La Bédoyère, the *procureur-général*, were among those hauled before the Chambre Royale, as was a nephew of a *président à mortier*, Robien. Indeed, the surnames of many Pontcallec sympathizers who filled the prison at Nantes belonged to families of long standing in the Parlement: Andigné de La Chasse, Becdelièvre du Boëxic, Boisbaudry, Bourgneuf, Lantivy du Coscro, Talhouët, and others. In all likelihood, these names designated relatives of the magistrates – younger sons and younger brothers, nephews and cousins, to say nothing of relations by marriage. Since their kinfolk manifestly supported the Pontcallec conspirators, this can only mean that a number of judges, in addition to Lambilly, Saint-Pern and Larlan, had some involvement too. How far their support might have carried them no one can say. The regent, who was not vindictive, broke off the investigation once the Chambre Royale had imposed its death sentences.

In any event, when the government crushed the conspiracy, it also destroyed the Parlement's morale, already weakened by the banishments, threats and forced resignations. As was the case with the Parlement of Paris, the recourse to authority, as opposed to negotiation and compromise, had the desired effect. The sense of grievance among the magistrates gave way to an instinct for self-preservation. The senior judges recovered their control over the tribunal, and the younger magistrates lost interest in political controversy. The period of calm that descended upon the Parlement of Rennes in 1720 lasted into mid-century.[13]

As events unfolded in Brittany, the Parlement of Paris stood by unable to help. Only once did the magistrates in Paris try to repay their Breton colleagues for the letter of support and the sympathetic remonstrance of September 1718. In December, after one of its imprisoned judges had returned to his duties, the Parlement sent the *gens du roi* to ask the regent to release the other two. At the suggestion of two colleagues, First President Mesmes instructed the *gens du roi* to add 'a little word on behalf of our colleagues in Brittany'. Someone in the Parlement of Paris alerted a magistrate in Rennes about this coming intervention, raising hopes in Brittany that the reciprocal interests of the two tribunals might yet unite them. The regent told the *gens du roi* amiably that they could hope for an early return of their two judges, only one of whom was still in prison, the other having been sent to his rural property. But as for the Parlement of Rennes, he declared, his manner changing and his voice rising sharply, that affair did not concern them in any way, now or in the future. He would never permit the two questions to be linked. Once again, d'Argenson's views had carried the day; this government would brook no association between tribunals, certainly not in the aftermath of its successes.[14]

D'Argenson *fils*, the memoir writer, penned the epitaph to the opposition movements in the Parlements of Paris and Rennes. How, he asked rhetorically, had his father closed the breaches in the wall of government that, if left open, would have led (in his opinion) to revolution? By *coups d'autorité*, of course: 'we cut off heads in Brittany . . . and [we] held the *lit de justice* in the Tuileries'.[15] Again, that succinct reply oversimplified things, but it captured the essence of what had happened, the resort on the part of the regency government, when challenged, to authoritarian methods. Such methods, as Saint-Simon had warned, risked disagreeable consequences in the event of failure. But in the France of 1718, with the administrative and military structures of Louis XIV still intact and opposition movements inexperienced and disorganized, a government could hope to overcome its opponents by coercing them.

John Law, *augmentations de gages* and venal office

After the *lit de justice* of 26 August 1718, the regent permitted John Law to pursue his ambitious plans for the revival of French economy. Starting in September 1718 and continuing into 1720 when, having converted to Catholicism, he became controller general, Law attacked what he regarded as the twin aspects of the economic dilemma, a financial crisis consisting of an inability to service the debt and a monetary crisis characterized by an oversupply of dubious state paper and the disappearance of coin.

Law's System, as it came to be called, dealt with these problems as though they formed twinned parts of a whole. The System began with the Company of the West, renamed the East India Company and known colloquially as the Mississippi Company once Law awarded it a monopoly of international trade, expected to flourish with the peace. The Company also collected direct and indirect taxes and deposited the proceeds in Law's General Bank, which soon became a state-owned Royal Bank, with the power to fix the monetary value of specie. The Company and the Bank merged, and Law started to pay the state debt with Bank notes and shares of Company stock, thus converting the debt into equity. When Bank notes became paper currency and Law moved to demonetize gold and silver while lowering interest rates, the System neared completion, having grown far beyond the gravest anxieties of the Parlement of Paris.[16]

The Parlement, subdued in the *lit de justice*, confined itself to passive disapproval of the System, whenever it received the laws that the government issued on the subject. When, for example, the edict for the Royal Bank came to the Parlement on 16 December 1718, the judges withheld their approval, still opposed to making Bank notes into currency. Rather than issuing a remonstrance, however, or adopting some hopeless judicial ploy, they merely asked the regent to find other financial methods to serve his purposes. Similarly, the Parlement disapproved of awarding the East India Company exclusive rights to commercial empire; but, again, it merely implored the regent to consider the disadvantages of monopoly. These supplications took the place of outright opposition and remonstrances, as in the recent past; and no one in the Parlement renewed the attack upon John Law or made any further references to the Fronde.

Although d'Argenson and Law took offence when the Parlement declined to register the laws that created the System, they did not allow the tribunal to delay or impede its growth. Citing the authority that it had assumed in the *lit de justice*, the Regency Council issued decrees and letters patent declaring the laws registered for want of action by the Parlement. As we have noted, Louis XIV never used the power provided by the ordinance of 1667 to register laws purely by act of council. On behalf of the regent, d'Argenson did so routinely, even on matters that did not concern the System. Indeed, he no longer bothered to issue *lettres de jussion* or otherwise to attempt to coerce the Parlement into registering contentious laws. He simply treated the magistrates as irrelevant to the legislative process, and the System took shape in the form and on the schedule that John Law ordained. Even without the approval of the Parlement, it enjoyed public acceptance and acclaim. Rarely had the tribunal been less consequential in public affairs.[17]

Council decrees of 27 and 31 August 1719, authorized the Company to reimburse the state's lenders up to 1.6 billion livres, the estimate for the remaining state debt, paying the creditors in Bank notes or shares of stock, a step that brought the System to the height of its power and influence. The first debts so retired consisted of the paper issued by revenue farmers and treasury officials, surviving *billets d'état*, and outstanding claims from the owners of venal offices suppressed by Noailles. However, decrees of 26 October and 26 November ordered that *augmentations de gages*, capital and interest, would be reimbursed in the same way. The worst fears of the magistrates thus came true. Instead of the specie that they had originally paid out they would receive paper certificates invented by their old enemy. In March 1720, specialists on the Finance Council began clearing *augmentations de gages* from the king's registers and providing the magistrates with Bank notes, since Law, a devout believer in paper currency, had also demonetized gold and greatly reduced the use of silver as money.[18]

Law wanted all reimbursed creditors to use their Bank notes to buy shares in the Company. To turn creditors into shareholders, he issued more stock in 1718 and 1719, setting a unit price of 5,000 livres but allowing purchases with a down payment of 500 livres. He then drove market values into the range of

9,000 to 10,000 livres, a price that he hoped to maintain, now that he had made his original investors, who included the regent and the duc de Bourbon, very rich. From the narrow Rue Quincampoix in the heart of commercial Paris, brokers took their cues from Law and encouraged the rise in stock prices, which grew into a boom, as Law fed the market with new shares. In principle, the magistrates could have purchased Company shares with their notes and ridden the wave of rising prices, benefiting from the System like many others. But since the reimbursement commission began work only in March 1720, the judges did not receive their notes at the opportune moment for investing, even had they been so inclined. Law probably inflicted this delay to punish them for their opposition to him and his policies; he knew very well that creditors had to invest early in order to obtain the best returns.

Believing that low interest rates would also favour stock prices, Law next attacked constituted *rentes*, which he blamed for immobilizing capital and keeping it out of the hands of merchants and entrepreneurs. In March 1720, he obtained an edict that reduced all future *rentes*, those contracted by the state, the Company, or private individuals, to 2 percent. This interest rate brought the rate of return on *rentes* into line with the dividends paid on shares, even at the peak prices of 10,000 livres.[19]

At this reduction of interest rates, however, the Parlement of Paris and the provincial parlements finally made an effort to bar the way. There can be no doubt, of course, that the judges viewed the Bank notes as an unsuitable reimbursement for *augmentations de gages*. But the unwritten ban against self-interested remonstrances obliged them to maintain a public silence on that grievance. When Law dropped interest rates to 2 per cent, however, he created an issue that involved the whole kingdom and gave the parlements an occasion to protest. On 17 April 1720, the Parlement of Paris broke what it called a 'respectful silence' and issued a remonstrance, its first since the *lit de justice*. The Parlements of Besançon, Dijon, Rouen and Toulouse joined in, apparently spontaneously, without any sign of collusion.

These remonstrances protested that the interest rate edict did more harm than good, threatening to ruin individuals and institutions who, hitherto dependent upon *rentes*, now faced a sharp drop in this income. The unfortunates allegedly included retired domestic servants, orphans, individuals in religious orders and the religious orders themselves, all of whom lived from fixed revenues. For them, argued the remonstrances, interest at 2 percent would generate so little income that it would condemn investors to consume their capital, leaving them penniless in the end. Since debtors could use Bank notes to repay old *rentes*, creditors risked further losses, if and when the notes declined in value. According to the Parlement of Paris, paper instruments had already done more injury to family wealth than twenty years of war taxes. This new assault could only complete the destruction. Well-founded rumours that Law intended to drop interest all the way to 1 percent added to the concern.

When Guillaume Menguy, the *rapporteur* for the interest rate edict in the Parlement of Paris, recommended against it, he had warned that, 'All the fortunes of respectable people will be ruined.' The magistrates made this into the central theme of their remonstrance and conspicuously included themselves among interest-rate victims. Dropping at last any reluctance to evoke their private affairs in public, they charged in their remonstrance that the edict threatened 'the entire ruin of all the magistrates of the kingdom'. The provincial parlements made the same claim. None of the parlements openly protested against Law's idea of repaying *augmentations de gages* with Bank notes, but this concern surely spurred them into remonstrating against 2 percent interest, in hopes of damaging the System in one way or another.

Such strong remonstrances from so many parlements on such a contentious issue might have deterred the regency, earlier in its history, from going ahead. Indeed, Armand de Saint-Martin, one of the magistrates arrested in 1718, had originally welcomed the 2 percent edict as affording a good opportunity for the tribunal to recover its political standing. Events proved him wrong. The government simply rejected the remonstrances, starting with that of Paris, and continued on its way. When the Parlement voted to remonstrate again, ignoring the new ban on iterative remonstrances, d'Argenson obtained letters patent to implement the edict anyway: it took effect at once. The *lit de justice* therefore continued to produce political results; Law's System stood beyond the reach of the parlements.[20]

Ironically, the System began to collapse soon thereafter, not as a result of opposition from the parlements but because an overconfident Law pushed Bank notes and Company shares to unsustainable heights, making them vulnerable to speculators. To defend the System, a council decree of 21 May 1720 ordered a reduction of about 50 percent in the value of the shares. But this unexpected change of policy created panic among investors and cost Law his popularity, almost immediately. On 27 May, Orléans, bowing to public pressure, rescinded the decree and relieved Law of his post of controller general, although he kept him on the Regency Council. Hoping to stage a comeback, Law took aim at d'Argenson, who had recently become an enemy. He visited Chancellor d'Aguesseau at his rural exile at Fresnes and restored him to the government, sending the unfortunate d'Argenson into embittered retirement. The return of d'Aguesseau, its old friend, together with the upheaval over the System, unexpectedly brought the Parlement back on to the political scene.[21] Emerging from the shadows, the tribunal entertained its last hopes for the full payment of *augmentations de gages*.

On the morning of 27 May, the Parlement, seeing its warnings about John Law abundantly fulfilled, voted to issue an immediate remonstrance against the 21 May decree. Since Orléans, under pressure from all sides, was at that moment rescinding it, he promptly informed the Parlement of his new stance, sparing himself the tribunal's inevitable reminder that he had established Bank notes by 'authority'. To the magistrates' surprise, the regent also invited them to advise him on financial policy. On 8 June, a hopeful deputation from the Parlement joined the regent and members of his government in a long meeting about finances, d'Aguesseau acting as spokesman for Orléans. It seemed as though, once again, the regent would seek the cooperation and friendship of the Parlement.

Each side wanted something from the other. For the first time since the *lit de justice* the government thought it needed the Parlement to register a new law –-an edict to create twenty-five million livres in *rentes* at 2.5 percent interest, for a capital of one billion livres. The money was to be used to redeem notes on the Bank and thus to liquidate the System. Although the government had been legislating for two years without the Parlement's sanction, it now sought its seal of approval to calm public fears. The Parlement's deputies could accept the conversion of notes into *rentes*, a step that, after all, repudiated at least one of the principles of John Law. But they wanted a 5 percent interest rate, 3 percent at least.

Although he said he might increase interest rates in the future, Orléans declined to pay the new *rentes* at more than 2.5 percent. On the other hand, he agreed to certain textual changes in the edict in order to satisfy the deputies on minor points and, more importantly, acceded to their request to take their *augmentations de gages* receipts in payment for the *rentes*. The latter concession remained a private understanding between the regent and the Parlement; but for the moment it appeased the magistrates considerably, since the new *rentes* offered some promise of retaining value, which could not be said for Bank notes, let alone *augmentations de gages*. This bargain also shows once again that the judges had kept *augmentations de gages* in mind all during their opposition to the System. The Parlement registered the edict on 10 June, having wrung its first concessions since the administration of Noailles.[22]

Within a month, however, the government reneged on that agreement and virtually ceased to exchange Bank notes for even modest amounts of silver, another violation of a private undertaking. This led to tense meetings between the chancellor and deputies from the Parlement on a range of financial issues, including *augmentations de gages*. Like Law and d'Argenson, however, Chancellor d'Aguesseau made no headway with the tribunal and began to lose standing with the regent, the magistrates and the general public. When the regent sent the Parlement an important new law to reorganize the East India Company and permit it to absorb 600 million livres in Bank notes, the magistrates subjected the plan to a withering scrutiny. Fearing that the Company would depreciate the notes, the fate of the *billets d'état* before them, the Parlement on 17 July declined to register the edict.

This uncooperative reaction shocked Orléans, who regarded the East India edict as crucial to his plan to shore up what was left of the System, all the more urgent as street disturbances, near riots, had just occurred. Another impasse in relations with the Parlement had thus arrived, somewhat unexpectedly. Once again, the regent had to decide what to do about foot-dragging and outright opposition in the tribunal. In a fresh display of resolve, Orléans banished the tribunal to Pontoise, a small town about twenty miles north-east of Paris (where, in 1652, near the end of the Fronde, Queen Anne had established a loyalist rump parlement). Orléans issued these orders on 21 July 1720, and the magistrates set up at Pontoise two days later. There they stayed until December, disgraced for the second time in two years.

Saint-Simon, always the hardliner, said contemptuously that the *lit de justice* was a much more severe punishment than the Pontoise exile, a sign in his opinion that the will-power of the regent had flagged once again. On the surface, he had a case. Although Pontoise lacked the comforts of Paris, few magistrates suffered much hardship. Orléans privately subsidized ample daily buffets for their benefit at the elegant river-front home rented by the first president. He also extended loans to (presumably cooperative) judges who needed help with other expenses. These facts led Saint-Simon to his low opinion of Orléans's backbone.

On the other hand, the regent seems to have understood, better than his friend, that the Parlement of 1720 no longer posed the threat that it had in 1718 and, in its weakened state, did not need to be treated so harshly. Visiting Pontoise, the *avocat* Barbier found the magistrates shrinking from real conflict and anxious to comply with orders. They wanted to stay within 'the rules'. The *lit de justice* and the arrests of their colleagues had no doubt impressed them, but there was more to it than that.

When Frizon de Blamont, one of the opposition leaders arrested on 30 August 1718, returned to the Parlement in 1719, his colleagues had treated him to a hero's welcome. But they did not know that, during his time in prison, Frizon had become a paid spy for Orléans, whom he now kept well informed. According to Barbier, who as an employee of d'Argenson was in a position to know, other magistrates performed the same clandestine service, all no doubt confident that this time they had chosen the winning side. Apparently First President Mesmes joined in too. A council decree of 28 June 1720 reinforced his authority over the tribunal, suggesting that the chief magistrate now belonged to Orléans. This would explain why the regent paid for his buffet and lodging. Whatever Saint-Simon thought, Orléans had neutralized the Parlement of Paris as a source of significant opposition and infiltrated it with his agents. When the magistrates registered unaltered a new *Unigenitus* declaration in December, the regent allowed them to return to Paris.[23] Meanwhile, the government exercised its authority and imposed its own *augmentations de gages* settlement.

Le Peletier des Forts, now acting controller general, obtained a decree on 25 August 1720 that transformed all unrefunded *augmentations de gages* into *rentes*, much as the Parlement had wanted; but the decree also reduced the interest rate to the dreaded 2 percent, the target of the April remonstrances. In January 1717, Noailles had lowered *augmentations de gages* from 5 to 4 percent, in effect repudiating capital; this new reduction repudiated 50 percent of what remained. With this act, the government had made its last decision on the question of *augmentations de gages*, one more or less in keeping with the ideas of John Law, who soon left France forever amid the final crack-up of the System. Although he had wanted to abolish *rentes*, Law had long favoured 2 percent as a general interest rate applying throughout the kingdom, despite the petitions against it by the tribunals.[24]

Perhaps surprisingly, this settlement most damaged the upper strata of magistrates, those rich enough to purchase *augmentations de gages* out of their own pockets and to keep for themselves the income thus generated. For example, a *président à mortier* of the Parlement of Rennes, Le Meneust de Bréquigny, purchased *augmentations de gages* in 1701 and 1702 and drew 1,275 livres in annual income from them. When in 1710 Desmarets dropped the interest rate to 5 percent, he reduced Le Meneust's potential *augmentations de gages* income to 1,040 livres; and in 1716 Noailles, by imposing a 4 percent interest rate, lowered it to 864 livres. In the reduction of 1720, Le Meneust's return on *augmentations de gages* fell to 432 livres, a decline of two-thirds from the 1,275 livres with which he began. A councillor in that Parlement saw his income from those two *augmentations de gages* fall by the same two-thirds, from 755 livres to 256 livres. These sums, although usually unpaid as a result of the financial crisis, still counted as assets in calculating private wealth; they now counted that much less. Some magistrates lost even more, those who from friendship or other reasons had purchased the *augmentations de gages* of their colleagues, investing more money than they were obliged to do, tens of thousands of livres.

In every parlement in France, this same upper rank of magistrates, those able to purchase their own *augmentations de gages* and perhaps those of their colleagues, naturally suffered along with the Bretons this two-thirds drop in capital and promised income. We cannot be sure what proportion of the some 1,200 magistrates of the parlements fell into this upper group, but a reasonable estimate would be around 25 percent. These wealthier judges, those whose interests the government of Louis XIV has been thought most anxious to protect, actually suffered the heaviest losses in *augmentations de gages* assets.

Under the decrees of 1719–1720, all judges could accept Bank notes as their reimbursement, both on their capital and their arrears, or they could convert their *augmentations de gages*, including the arrears, into *rentes* at 2 percent. How many chose which option is uncertain, but the profusion of decrees issued by the Council to implement the conversion into *rentes* suggests that some adopted the latter course, grudgingly accepting the loss in income. But even this did not mean that the magistrates were at long last collecting their annual interest. In 1725, the Parlement of Rennes complained once again about the continuing failure of the government to pay magistrates the interest they were owed from their former *augmentations de gages*; and the Parlement of Grenoble had the same lament. In the end, it is uncertain how much money the wealthier magistrates actually received in *augmentations de gages* interest. It is only too likely that they had to write off most of their capital as a total loss.[25]

Indebted magistrates fared better. Law intended to clear the debt not only of the king but also of the king's subjects, using low interest rates and Bank notes to do so. As a result of the System, the majority of the judges, those who out of necessity had borrowed for their *augmentations de gages*, could repay their creditors with the Bank notes that they received from the government, cancel their debts, and liberate their offices from the burdensome 'privileged' mortgages. The notes remained legal tender through most of 1720, and the government forced reluctant creditors to accept them. When, for example, *augmentations de gages* creditors of the Parlement of Grenoble refused to take the notes, the Royal Council ruled in favour of the magistrates and imposed the notes upon its lenders, as it did in all such cases.

All during 1720, before and after the fall of Law, debtor judges in the parlements had the opportunity to free themselves of their *augmentations de gages* debts. Most likely, they all did so, either through the mechanism of Bank notes or by negotiating interest down to 2 percent. After 1720, we no longer hear their worried complaints about the harassing demands of their creditors; that issue, at least, had been resolved, one of the few benefits of the Law System. Ironically, the great majority of the magistrates, distrusting paper money, had treated Law as their common enemy, whereas he primarily injured the upper ranks of their corps. The System, in addition to the social and economic damage that it inflicted, did bring relief to debtors, including debtor judges.[26]

But this relief, welcome as it was, did not otherwise improve the financial health of the magistrates and cannot be treated as evidence that the government wished to take any special care for their interests. The decline and virtual collapse of office prices remained the most important socio-economic legacy of the reign of Louis XIV, so far as the magistrates were concerned. It will be remembered that by 1715 the price of the office of lay councillor in the Parlement of Paris had fallen from above 100,000 livres in 1665 to 50,000 livres, while in Rennes the councillor office had dropped from above 100,000 to 45,000 livres, in Toulouse from 60,000 to 30,000 livres, in Bordeaux from 50,000 to 18,000 livres, and so on. Inevitably, the price of venal office continued to decline under the duc d'Orléans, partly because the regency failed to resume paying *augmentations de gages*. In 1716, Joly de Fleury, the senior *avocat-général* of Parlement of Paris, lamented that prices for councillor offices had fallen to between 30,000 and 40,000 livres and that at least thirty offices in the Parlement, then vacant, could find no buyers at even basement prices. He believed that many of his colleagues would sell their offices if they could; but potential buyers would not return to the market. These dismal conditions also prevailed in the provincial parlements and in other corporations. Early in the regency, the company of *secrétaires du roi* declared that 27 of its 340 offices were vacant and that more than 60 secretaries would sell their offices if buyers ever

turned up. Confidence in the institution of venality dropped to steadily descending points.[27]

Thirty years after his death in 1683, Colbert had prevailed on the issue of the price of venal office. The decline of office prices, which he had attempted to achieve by his regulations of 1665, had occurred as an unintended by-product of the fiscal exactions that, if perfected by his successors, he had nevertheless launched. It only remained to revive his plan to suppress venal offices as their prices declined and as finances permitted. With office prices at their lowest level in a century and the magistrates, the leading office-holders, once again under the government's control, the regency had a historic opportunity to shrink the institution of venality in a dramatic way.

D'Aguesseau, while he was *procureur-général*, had urged the regent to reduce the offices created by Louis XIV, as a matter of judicial reform. In 1716, Joly de Fleury joined in, if from different motives. He urged the government to reimburse dozens of offices, as a way to shore up the personal finances of the remaining officials. In 1719 and again in 1720, John Law gave the regent a revolutionary plan to suppress all offices in the Parlement of Paris, to reimburse their holders with Bank notes and to replace the magistrates with appointees who would serve one-year terms, renewable at the king's pleasure. In the end, nothing came of these ambitious proposals; but their very existence exposed the depths to which venal office, burdened by *augmentations de gages* and other exactions, had sunk.[28]

As he suppressed the last traces of dissidence in the Parlement of Rennes, kept his thumb on the Parlement of Paris, and settled *augmentations de gages* on terms of his choosing, the regent resolved the political and financial questions left over from the preceding reign. At every key point involving these intertwined issues, he got his way by resorting to coercion and overriding the wishes of the majority of the judges, damaging their constitutional and socio-economic interests along the way. The coercive measures, like the issues themselves, stemmed from the policies of the past reign, so that Orléans, after trying to win the parlements over, ended up where Louis XIV had left off, embracing the policies and methods of the late king. On the most important issues involving the parlements, the past reign flowed into its successor, after the brief interlude in which Orléans had vainly practised conciliation. Thus the regency not only benefited from the gains Louis XIV made at the expense of the parlements; it ratified and perpetuated those gains, passing them down the century.

Notes

1 Le Moy, *Parlement de Bretagne*, p. 129. AN, G7, 199, contains a copy of the letter of 26 August 1718 from an unidentified magistrate of the Parlement of Rennes to Pomereu, a member of the first Enquêtes chamber at Paris.

2 Bourgneuf de Cucé, *président à mortier*, to d'Argenson, 30 August 1718, AN, H1, 429; Villeguérin, *avocat-général*, to d'Argenson, 4 September 1718, *ibid.*, testified to the loyalty of the senior magistrates and the restless activism of the younger judges; AD, I-V (Rennes), IBb 331 (Registres secrets): 2 and 3 September 1718, f. 9r; Feydeau, intendant, to d'Argenson, 3 September 1718, AN, H1, 429. The Parlement's letter and remonstrance are published in Saint-Simon, *Mémoires*, XXXV, 373–375; the remonstrance is also in Le Moy, *Remontrances*, pp. 11–13.

3 AN, U 416 and 420, record how the Parlement of Paris went about drafting a reply to the Parlement of Rennes. Dangeau may have been right to say that the first president had the regent approve the letter in advance: *Journal*, XVII, 382 (repeated in Saint-Simon, *Mémoires*, XXXV, 291), even though the registers of the Parlement do not mention this. The letter is in U 416 and AD, I-V (Rennes), IBc 2bis. Roger Bickart saw the initiative of the Parlement of Rennes as a harbinger of the collective manifestation of solidarity among the parlements in 1753: *Les parlements et la notion de souveraineté nationale au XVIIIe siècle* (Paris, 1932), pp. 148–151.

4 Pocquet, *Bretagne province*, pp. 18–32; Rebillon, *États de Bretagne*, pp. 257–260; Fréville, *Intendance*, I, 200–205. See also AN, G7,1859, 'Instructions Générales', 22 May 1718, for the instructions to the royal deputation; AN, E 1999, ff. 338rv–340r, 346rv–348v: two decrees issued on 30 July 1718, which quashed the *délibération* of the Estates of 14 July and added a surtax to the capitation to pay for the extra troops that entered Brittany in January.

5 Pocquet, *Bretagne province*, pp. 27–28. Feydeau de Brou, intendant, Dinan, 16 August 1718, and Villeguérin, 4 September 1718, AN, H1, 429, wrote to d'Argenson about the close relationship between the nobles in the Parlement and the Estates. The 'Apologie de la Noblesse et du Parlement de Bretagne', BN, *N.a.f.*, 9,640, ff. 211rv–221r, is a well-informed declaration of the joint grievances of the second estate and the Parlement, upon which they surely collaborated. On its importance, see Pocquet, *Bretagne province*, p. 123.

6 Pocquet, *Bretagne province*, pp. 28–31; Le Moy, *Parlement de Bretagne*, pp. 127–132; AD, I-V (Rennes), IBb 331 (Registres secrets): 13 August and 7 September 1718, ff. 4rv and 10rv; Villeguérin to d'Argenson, 7 and 14 September 1718, AN, H1, 429, and 26 October 1718, AN, G7, 199; Feydeau de Brou, intendant, Dinan, to d'Argenson, 8 September 1718, AN, G7, 199.

7 AD, I-V (Rennes), IBb 331 (Registres secrets): 12 September 1718 (approval of the remonstrance), f. 11v; Feydeau, intendant, Dinan, to d'Argenson, 13 September 1718, AN, H1, 429, which also contains the remonstrance.

8 For the Parlement and *augmentations de gages*, see the letters to d'Argenson from *président à mortier* Cornulier, 8 July 1718, AN, G7, 199, and Feydeau, 27 August 1718, AN, H1, 429, and the Parlement's letter to the regent, 22 March 1719, A-D, I-V, IBc 2bis. D'Argenson explained his strategy regarding the Estates in his letter to Feydeau, 18 September 1718, H1, 429. For this session of the Estates, see also Rebillon, *États de Bretagne*, pp. 261–263, and Fréville, *Intendance*, I, 209–212.

9 See 'États de Bretagne . . . quatre points sur lesquels il y a à délibérer', 24 September 1718, which despite its heading dealt with the Parlement, in AN, H1, 429, and the decree of 29 September 1718 in AN, E 2000, ff. 274rv–276v.

10 'Instructions' to Nicolas Denis, *huissier*, 3 October 1718, AN, G7, 199; Denis to

d'Argenson, 9 October 1718; Feydeau to d'Argenson, 9 October 1718; and Huchet de La Bédoyère to d'Argenson, 12 October 1718, all in *ibid.*; 'Procès-verbal', Denis, 10 October 1718, AD, I-V (Rennes), IBc 2bis; AD, I-V, IBb 661 ('Registres secrets sur papier'): 10 October 1718. Le Moy, *Parlement de Bretagne*, p. 134, and Pocquet, *Bretagne province*, pp. 33–34, treat this episode briefly. For the reaction of the Parlement to the mission of Denis, see AD, I-V, IBb 331 (Registres secrets): 11, 13 and 24 October 1718, ff. 15rv–16r, 18v–22r (these pages contain the remonstrance, also published in Le Moy, *Remontrances du Parlement de Bretagne*, pp. 14–24). The intendant Feydeau had already identified Francheville as the magistrate most responsible for the decree of August 13: letter to d'Argenson, AN, H1, 429. Huchet de La Bédoyère had to apologize for neither preventing the Parlement from issuing its decrees of 13 August and 7 September nor informing the government about them; see his letters of 2 and 8 October 1718 in AN, G7, 199. On the role and dress of a *huissier du Conseil*, also called a *huissier de la chaine*, see Antoine, *Conseil sous Louis XV*, p. 555.

11 For the names of the judges exiled from Rennes, see: AD, I-V (Rennes), IBb (Registres secrets) 331: 11 October 1718, ff. 15rv; Montesquiou to d'Argenson, 2 October 1718, AN, H1, 429; preliminary lists of magistrates deemed worthy of banishment are in *ibid.* and BN, *N.a.f.*, 9,640, f. 200r ('Noms des officiers du Parlement de Bretagne qui ont esté exilez'); Villeguérin to d'Argenson, 16 and 21 October 1718, AN, G7, 199; Feydeau to d'Argenson, 23 October 1718, AN, H1, 429; AN, E 2000: decree of 6 October 1718, ff. 310rv–311r. See Feydeau's memoranda concerning the offices of the four *présidents des enquêtes* in AN, H1, 430. For the government's rejection of the remonstrances of the Parlement, see the letters of La Vrillière, secretary of state, 6 November 1718, and d'Argenson, 9 November 1718, in AD, I-V, IBc 2bis. See also Le Moy, *Parlement de Bretagne*, pp. 135–139, and Pocquet, *Bretagne province*, pp. 33–34.

12 Pocquet, *Bretagne province*, pp. 35–158, is the best treatment, although he understated the conspiracy's potential to harm the regency. Meyer, *Régent*, pp. 188–219, provides an incisive re-examination. See also Pierre de La Condamine, *Pontcallec. Une étrange conspiration au coeur de la Bretagne* (3rd ed; Mayenne, 1988).

13 Pocquet, *Bretagne province*, pp. 116–121; La Condamine, *Pontcallec*, pp. 325–352, provides a 'Liste des Inculpés'. For the magistrates and their families, see Saulnier, *Parlement de Bretagne*, II, 557–558 (Lambilly), 790 (Saint-Pern); and the entries in P. Potier de Courcy, *Nobiliare et armorial de Bretagne* (Nantes, 1862) and Henri Frotier de La Messelière, *Filiations bretonnes (1650–1923)* (5 vols; Saint-Brieuc, 1912–1924). La Vrillière noted the possible family connections between the accused and members of the Parlement in his letter of 7 October 1719, AD, I-V (Rennes), IBc 2bis, as did d'Argenson, 28 December 1719, *ibid.*

14 BN, *N.a.f.*, 9,771, 'Députation du Parlement au Régent', f. 168r; AN, U 416 and 420: 5 and 12 December 1718; Feydeau, intendant, to d'Argenson, 11 December 1718, AN, H1, 430.

15 D'Argenson, *Journal et mémoires*, I, 41.

16 Murphy, *John Law*, pp. 164–230, who is well disposed to the System; Faure, *Banqueroute de Law*, pp. 154–228, more critical. See also Paul Harsin, *Les doctrines monétaires et financières en France du XVIe au XVIII siècle* (Paris, 1928), pp. 162–179, and Lüthy, *Banque protestante*, I, 308–316.

17 See, for example, the *greffier*'s notes on the Parlement's deliberations on the Royal Bank, AN, U 420, 16 December 1718, and the registration decree by the Regency Council, AN, E 2001: 27 December 1718, ff. 494rv–497r; the deliberations of 17 June 1719 on the creation of the East India Company, U 421, and the Council's registration decree of that day, E 2006, f. 409rv. When, on 27 June 1719, the Parlement declined to register an edict creating new offices to fund the military order of Saint-Louis, a matter unrelated to the Law System, the Council simply issued the king's registration decree on 1 July: U 421: 27 June 1719; and E 2002: 1 July 1719, ff. 289rv–290r. See also the extracts from the Parlement's registers published in Saint-Simon, *Mémoires*, XXXVI, 463–466. For the irritation of the regent on even this ineffective opposition, see *ibid.*, pp. 42, 301–305. It is hard to see how it can be argued that the Law episode strengthened the tribunal's claim that it should always register the laws: Shennan, *Parlement of Paris*, p. 293. The Parlement's failure to register the legislative components of the System had nothing to do with the System's ultimate demise.

18 AN, E 2007: 31 August 1719, ff. 514rv–518r; E 2008: 26 October 1719, ff. 384rv–387r; E 2009: 26 November 1719, ff. 211rv–213r; E 2017: 4 March 1720, ff. 37rv–38r. AN, P 3389, is an example of an *augmentations de gages* register showing the cancellation of *augmentations de gages* by virtue of the council decree of 26 October 1719; Faure, *Banqueroute de Law*, p, 223.

19 Murphy, *John Law*, pp. 188–230, especially Table 14.1; Faure, *Banqueroute de Law*, pp. 201–205, 220–401; Harsin, *Doctrines monétaires et financières*, pp. 171–182; Law (?), 'Histoire des finances', pp. 339–342. For the edict setting the 50th *denier*, or 2 percent, for constituted *rentes*, see BN, *Actes R.*, F. 23,622 (200): edict of March 1720. Thomas E. Kaiser, 'Money, Despotism, and Public Opinion in Early Eighteenth-Century France: John Law and the Debate on Royal Credit', *Journal of Modern History* 63 (March 1991), 1–28, explores Law's efforts to support the prices of Company shares by manipulating public opinion.

20 Murphy, *John Law*, pp. 200–201, and Law (?), 'Histoire des finances', 350–356. The deliberations of the Parlement of Paris on the March edict are in AN, U 421: 10 and 22 April 1720; the Menguy quotation is from 10 April. See the remonstrance of 17 April in BN, *Fonds fr.*, 7,013, ff. 428rv–440rv, and Flammermont, *Remontrances*, I, 126–140. For the remonstrances of the provincial parlements, see BN, *Fonds fr.*, 7,547, ff. 112rv–122rv (Toulouse); *N.a.f.*, 9,711, ff. 208rv (a reference to a forthcoming remonstrance from Dijon); AD, Doubs, B 2,840: Parlement of Besançon, 17 April 1720; AD, S-M, IB 239: Parlement of Rouen, 27 April 1720. Letters patent of 24 April 1720, addressed to the Parlement of Paris and its subordinate tribunals, cited the council decree registered in the *lit de justice* of 26 August 1718, as authority for implementing this edict, 'à peine d'interdiction': BN, *Actes R.*, F. 23,622 (203). Faure was wrong to believe that the provincial tribunals, unlike Paris, received the edict favourably: *Banqueroute de Law*, p. 402.

21 Law (?), 'Histoire des finances', 375–380; Saint-Simon, *Mémoires*, XXXVII, 314–333; Dangeau, *Journal*, XVIII, 292–293 (23 May 1720); Faure, *Banqueroute de Law*, pp. 428–455.

22 Dangeau, *Journal*, XVIII, 294–295 (27 May 1720); AN, U 421: 27 and 29 May, 10 June, and 3 July 1720 (the secret arrangement about *augmentations de gages*); BN, *Actes R.*, F. 23,622 (256): edict of June 1720 for twenty-five million livres in *rentes*

on the Hôtel de Ville, at *denier* 40. The minutes of the 8 June meeting are also in Saint-Simon, *Mémoires*, XXXVII, 476–477.

23 AN, U 421: 3, 5, 9, 17 and 21 July 1720; Dangeau, *Journal*, XVIII, 321 (15 July 1720), 322–323 (17 July 1720); Saint-Simon, *Mémoires*, XXXVI, 210, 395 (the perfidy of Frizon de Blamont); XXXVII, 349–362; Barbier, *Journal historique*, I, 39–43, 53–54; Hardy, *Judicial Politics*, pp. 180–184. A council decree of 28 June 1720, issued as letters patent on 17 October 1720, awarded the first president alone the right to convene a plenary session and to allocate *épices* and overturned internal regulations of the Parlement in these matters: BN, *Fonds fr.*, 7,220, ff. 181v–183r. The Parlement, after dragging its heals on the *Unigenitus* declaration, succumbed to threats and coercion, as seen in Hardy, *Judicial Politics*, pp. 182–201.

24 AN, E 2019: decree of 25 August 1720, ff. 443r–446v, and U 421: 30 August 1720.

25 AN, G7, 199, 'État général des augmentations de gages dues au Parlement de Bretagne', 20 July 1718. Hubert de Lasse, a councillor in the Parlement, purchased not only his own *augmentations de gages* in 1701 but also those of Councillor Sanguin and *président à mortier* Marbeuf, a total investment of 22,400 livres in that year alone: AD, I-V, IBe: *Livre des comptes*, f. 11. Implementing decrees on the reduction of *augmentations de gages* to 2 percent, or the *denier* 50, are in AN, E 2020: 10 September 1720, ff. 143rv–144r; E 2027: 18 March 1721, ff. 145rv–147r; E 2028: 6 May 1721, f. 35rv; and E 2029: 2 August 1721, f. 313rv. For the fate of the Bank notes, see Faure, *Banqueroute de Law*, pp. 501–515. For the 1725 remonstrance of the Parlement of Rennes, see BN, *Fonds fr.*, 7,013, f. 424r.

26 AN, E 2015: 17 September 1720, ff. 126rv–130v (in favour of the Parlement of Grenoble). Additional creditors of the Parlement had already accepted a reduction of their interest rate to 2 percent: AD, Isère, 2B 1046: 1720. See the similar rulings of the Council in favour of the company of royal secretaries, who had also borrowed to purchase *augmentations de gages*: E 2012: 22 March 1720, ff. 91rv–93r; 17 June 1720, ff. 193rv–195r; and E 2013: 30 August 1720, ff. 41rv–44r; and in favour of the master of requests Monet de La Salle, E 2012: 8 April 1720, f. 106rv; Faure, *Banqueroute de Law*, p. 402. For pessimistic judgments on the socio-economic effects of the System, see the pioneering articles of Earl J. Hamilton, 'Wages and Prices at Paris under John Law's System', *The Quarterly Journal of Economics* 51 (1937), 42–70, and 'Prices and Wages in Southern France under John Law's System', *Economic History (A Supplement to the Economic Journal)* 3 (1934–1937), 441–461. Faure, *Banqueroute de Law*, pp. 536–552, and Meyer, *Régent*, pp. 233–235, offer more nuanced assessments. For the debtor relief under the Law System, see Jean-Paul Poisson, 'Introduction à une étude quantitative des effets socio-économiques du Système de Law', in idem, *Notaires et Société* (Paris, 1985), pp. 309–356, and Emmanuel Le Roy Ladurie, *The Peasants of Languedoc*, trans. John Day (Urbana, Illinois, 1974), pp. 260–261.

27 BN, *Fonds fr.*, 7,760, ff. 205rv–213rv: 'Mémoire sur les différentes créations d'offices qui ont été faites dans le Parlement . . . Remise à la fin de 1716' (by Joly de Fleury); *ibid.*, 7,765, ff. 271rv–272rv: 'Mémoire de l'état présent de la compagnie des secrétaires du Roy', c. 1716.

28 Doyle, *Venality*, pp. 53. 55; Saint-Simon, *Mémoires*, XXXVI, 304–311; Faure, *Banqueroute de Law*, p. 403; Ford, *Robe and Sword*, pp. 121–122.

Conclusion

As previously noted, revisionist historians view the royal state as ruling Old Regime France by means of compromises with national and regional elites, sharing authority with them and protecting their interests in return for their loyalties. This study has tried to show that the administration of Louis XIV had after all an authoritarian core, especially in its relations with the parlements. Absolute government, whatever ornate compromises decorated its multiple facades, rested on an authoritarian foundation.

With respect to our topic, the critical period was 1671–1673. As a result of their resistance to the fiscal demands of the Dutch War, the king imposed upon the tribunals those rules about registration procedure that deprived them of any influence upon new laws, relegating them to the margins of political life for the duration of the reign. Viewed from the perspective of constitutional thought and parlementary precedent, both dating from early in the sixteenth century, this was a big step in a new direction, a daring break with precedent. It was at once inherent in the claims long advanced by sympathizers with absolute government but also contingent upon the events of the 1670s and the personal decisions of Louis XIV.

Nothing ensured that the king would subject the parlements to such a stern regimen; he might have stopped with the rules he established in 1667, more in line with those of his predecessors, and avoided a showdown, as they always did. Instead, he put the parlements in their place and kept them there until he died. When the regent Philippe d'Orléans, after a brief conciliatory period, enjoyed a fresh success with authoritarian methods, he demonstrated once again the hard realism that lay at the heart of absolute government. This is not to deny that in other areas, notably in their spheres of judicial and administrative competence, the royal administration treated the parlements favourably, even leniently. But this was because the king already occupied the political high ground, controlling the strategic terrain. Strong where it counted most, he could afford to relax pressure in areas where issues of supreme authority did not come into play.

If this sterner view of Louis XIV's absolutism proves convincing, the political subjugation (not too strong a word) of the parlements should bulk larger in our assessments of the Sun King's reign. All the current general treatments, along with recent biographies, have underestimated the depth and significance of this achievement. It is time to give it due interpretative weight.

Arguably, the victory won by Louis XIV was of such consequence that it influenced the government's relations with the tribunals into the middle of the eighteenth century. Until about 1750, the behaviour of the Parlement of Paris is described as 'restrained' and 'passive' and its remonstrances as 'moderate', the occasional fracas over *Unigenitus* aside. Much the same has been said for the provincial tribunals. Recent scholarship has attributed this relative calm to the skill with which the ministers of Louis XV, especially his prime minister, Cardinal Fleury, bribed key magistrates and outmanoeuvred others, knowing when to compromise and when to stand firm. On this reading of things, 'management' took precedence over coercion, manipulation overshadowed issues, and the influence of personal relationships outweighed that of ideas.[1] But we should not forget that duress could be effective too, when applied in memory and in the style of Louis XIV.

All the royal officials who served the regent began their careers under the late king, and many continued to serve after Orléans died in 1723, carrying the absolutist tradition forward. On 8 June 1725, when the government held a *lit de justice* in the Parlement of Paris, the keeper of the seals, Fleuriau d'Armenonville, one such veteran, explicitly threatened the Parlement with a return to all the rules and regulations of Louis XIV, invoking that name to good effect.[2] More significantly, Louis XV, like his predecessor, did not hesitate to coerce the tribunals into registering taxes during the War of the Austrian Succession (1741–1748).[3]

As late as 1766, with the old coercive methods more or less forgotten, a mature Louis XV had one more occasion to remember them. With the Parlements of Rennes and Pau in upheaval and attracting worrisome support from the Parlement of Paris, the king faced the sort of concerted resistance that had so troubled d'Argenson. On 3 March 1766, Louis XV marched into the Parlement of Paris and addressed the magistrates in the famous *séance de la flagellation*. In ringing tones, the king reaffirmed the theory and practice of royal sovereignty just as d'Argenson had done, using the latter's defiant clarity and repeating his very arguments, ideas and language.

This could not have been pure coincidence. The primary author of Louis XV's address may well have been the distinguished *conseiller d'état* Pierre Gilbert de Voisins, who began his career under Noailles and d'Argenson. Voisins assisted d'Argenson in the struggle with the Parlement in 1718 and attended the *lit de justice*, providing a living link with that emphatic recourse to authority. D'Argenson's files on the Parlement, compiled then and periodically consulted thereafter, still existed in 1766, available for further study. Since d'Argenson, in preparing for the *lit de justice*, had most likely examined the Council of Justice files from 1665, the *séance de la flagellation*, in drawing upon him, drew upon Louis XIV as well. In this sense, Louis XIV and Colbert joined Louis XV in the flagellation session, together with Pussort, Philippe d'Orléans and d'Argenson himself.[4]

Revisionist historians, as we have also seen, have treated venal offices as a barrier to absolute government, contending that the king could not tamper with this quintessential vested interest lest he endanger his rule by provoking the wrath of the magistrates. Under Louis XIV the contrary was true, as we have demonstrated, with the parlements suffering recurring forced loans and repeated sales of new offices up to the default of 1709, with all its disagreeable consequences. Things could hardly have been otherwise, given the historic link between the parlements' political powers and the magistrates' investments in venal office. Once the king broke the former, the latter stood defenceless before him. In the event, Louis XIV not only exploited venality to the full, turning the judges into sources of ready money, he also damaged their economic interests severely, given the central role that venal office played in their overall wealth.

If this second argument also wins adherents, it would force a reconsideration of the social and economic condition of the magistrates of the parlements in the early eighteenth century. Rather than seeing them as emerging more or less undamaged from the reign of Louis XIV, poised to take advantage of the new century,[5] we should understand them as a weakened, almost endangered group, reeling from the depredations of the late king. A good way to assess this conclusion is to consider the fate of office prices in the eighteenth century.

These eventually rose somewhat from the low points of the late reign and the regency, but they never returned to the levels of the 1690s, let alone those of the 1660s. By 1750, for example, the price of a councillor's office in the Parlement of Paris had climbed from below 35,000 livres, its low point after 1715, to above 40,000 livres. It then rose to around 50,000 livres in the mid-1750s, where it seems to have stabilized, at about the levels of 1715, considered a bad year for venality. The Parlements of Aix, Besançon, Bordeaux, Dijon, Grenoble, Metz, Rennes and Toulouse continued to suffer low prices for councillor offices until late in the reign of Louis XV, after which a modest recovery began in at least some tribunals and lasted into the 1780s. But such increases as did take place, starting as they did from such a low base, could not make up the ground lost while Louis XIV was king and Philippe d'Orléans was regent. This is all the more meaningful when we recall that in 1722, the regent restored the *droit annuel*, the redemption of which had been ordered in 1709, and reimposed the annual *paulette* payments upon venal office-holders, with the single but important exception of the judges of the parlements and other superior courts. In other words, these magistrates alone could henceforth transmit their offices to heirs or buyers, without having to pay for the privilege. This benefit should have boosted office prices; its failure to do so shows how weak the demand for them remained. The damage that the Sun King inflicted upon their venal offices stayed with the judges until the end of the Old Regime.[6]

In 1749, the ongoing, visible decline of venality prompted fresh plans for suppressing offices in the parlements. The new reformers actually took 'the great Colbert' as their model and admiringly glossed his celebrated reform edict of 1665. Their Colbert-inspired memoranda likely contributed to the actual suppression by Louis XV in 1756 of seventy-nine councillor offices in the Parlement of Paris, two whole *chambres des enequêtes* – about one-third of the tribunal's complement. In telling contrast to their staunch defence of office a century earlier, this suppression actually met with the approval of the magistrates, so anxious were many to divest themselves of an investment gone wrong. Louis XV promised to reimburse the offices at 50,000 livres, one-half the value that Colbert had set, further proof of the long-term decline. Even so, many offices in the Parlement remained vacant, and the volume of litigation, and therefore *épices*, also stayed low, as under Louis XIV.[7]

Had the parlements struggled with any success against Louis XIV and the regent, they might have retained some political powers and spared themselves most of the financial reverses that they suffered in their venal offices. The magistrates would then have advanced into the eighteenth century with real political and social strength and enhanced prestige. No one can tell how such an Old Regime, with an invigorated upper magistracy, would have functioned; but it would have been rather different from the Old Regime that we actually have. As it was, the parlements and their magistrates emerged grievously weakened from the reign of Louis XIV,[8] their political functions virtually abolished and their venal offices stripped of the capital gains built up in the past century. As the preface to this study suggested, historians who wish to generalize about absolute government will have to decide, in light of the evidence presented by revisionists, how heavily to weigh this new material and determine whether it belongs in a main or in a subordinate clause.[9]

Notes

1 The adjectives describing the tribunal's behaviour are those of Shennan in *Parlement of Paris*, pp. 298–308; for the political weakness of the parlements in the first half of the century, see also Ford, *Robe and Sword*, pp. 82, 97–98, and Egret, *Louis XV et l'opposition parlementaire*, pp. 25–49. Campbell, *Power and Politics*, pp. 259–264, 276, 292–295, credits the ability of the government and especially Cardinal Fleury to 'manage' the Parlement in the 1730s and the 1740s. Similar views are expressed for the 1750s in John Rogister, *Louis XV and the Parlement of Paris* (Cambridge, 1995), pp. 22–23, 58, 187, 257–258.

2 BN, *N.a.f.*, 9,750, ff. 217rv–219v, 'Précis de ce qui s'est passé au Parlement au lit de

justice le 8 juin 1725'. Along the same lines, Shennan, *Regent*, pp. 134–145, makes the regency a retrospective triumph for the bureaucracy of Louis XIV.

3 Rogister, *Louis XV and the Parlement of Paris*, pp. 33–35, 47–49, 52, 75, 94.

4 Compare d'Argenson's statements of 5 July 1718, and 26 August 1718, in Flammermont, *Remontrances*, I, 85–87, 109–110, with that of Louis XV at the *séance de la flagellation*, 3 March 1766, in *ibid.*, II, 555–560. Bickart, *Parlements et la notion de souveraineté*, p. 71, first noted the textual similarity. Of course, Louis XV himself held the *lit de justice* of 1718; and although he was only eight and a half, he may have remembered something about it. While a committee produced the *flagellation* statement, traditional scholarship names Gilbert de Voisins as the primary contributor: Antoine, *Louis XV*, pp. 853–854; but Julian Swann, *Politics and the Parlement of Paris under Louis XV, 1754–1774* (Cambridge, 1995), pp. 269–270, dissents. Campbell, *Power and Politics*, p. 260, shows d'Argenson consulting his father's papers in 1732. Bickart, *ibid.*, pp. 151–153, and Swann, *ibid.*, pp. 131, 147–148, 163, 168, 198–199, 226–227, 268–270, are good introductions to the coordination of parlementary opposition in mid-century called the 'union des classes'.

5 As in Ford, *Robe and Sword*, pp. 3–76.

6 Doyle, *Venality*, pp. 211–215, is the best treatment and replaces earlier efforts to grapple with the problem of office prices, e.g. Ford, *Robe and Sword*, pp. 148–150. As Doyle notes, it is problematic to compare prices before and after 1726, when the livre stabilized, a task made more difficult by the often violent fluctuations of the livre from 1680 to 1720. On the other hand, it is not altogether clear that currency edicts had much influence on prices: James C. Riley, 'Monetary Growth and Price Stability: France, 1650–1700', *Journal of Interdisciplinary History* 15 (Autumn 1984), 235–254. For prices in the Parlement of Paris, see Bluche, *Magistrats*, pp. 166–167, and BN, *Fonds fr.*, 7,760, ff. 199v–200rv. The overall decline of office prices in the eighteenth-century provincial parlements is documented in Egret, *Parlement de Dauphiné*, I, 18–19; Jean Meyer, *La noblesse bretonne au XVIIIe siècle* (Paris, 1966), II, 938–941; Doyle, *Parlement of Bordeaux*, pp. 28–30; and Albert Colombet, *Les parlementaires bourguignons à la fin du XVIIIe siècle* (2nd edn; Dijon, 1937), p. 62. However, the offices of *présidents à mortier* resisted much of this downward pressure. For the restoration of the *droit annuel*, see BN, *Actes R.*, F. 23,621 (no. 640; declaration of 9 August 1722), and Doyle, *Venality*, p. 50.

7 BN, *Fonds fr.*, 7,760, ff. 214rv–254rv (the reform memoranda); Doyle, *Venality*, pp. 102–103; Swann, *Politics and the Parlement of Paris*, p. 15. Although the reimbursement terms are unclear, it seems doubtful that a magistrate could have obtained 50,000 livres for an office that he had purchased a few years earlier for, say, 30,000 to 40,000 livres. Ford, *Robe and Sword*, p. 53, n. 35, notes that many offices in the parlements were unoccupied in 1789.

8 For the intellectual impoverishment of the magistrates, see William F. Church, 'The Decline of French Jurists as Political Theorists, 1660–1789', *French Historical Studies* 5 (Spring 1967), 1–40.

9 Recent studies featuring the inherent power of absolute government are: T.J.A. Le Goff, 'Monetary Unification in France under the Monarchy', *The EURO in Comparative Context*, Workshop, York University, 4–5 March 1999, forthcoming; John A. Lynn, *The Wars of Louis XIV, 1667–1714* (London and New York, 1999).

Select bibliography

MANUSCRIPT SOURCES

Archives des Affaires Étrangères

Petits fonds
1511 (Brittany, 1671–1710), 1549 (Dauphiné, 1658–1696), 1639 (Languedoc, 1658–1699), 1731 (Provence, 1704–1715)

Archives Nationales

Series E. *Conseil du Roi*
I have examined eighty-seven volumes in the collection entitled *Minutes d'arrêts. Collection formée par les secrétaires du conseil*, which contains decrees issued by the financial components of the royal council. I concentrated upon the periods in which financial issues assumed prime importance and consulted volumes ranging from E 396b (21–30 April 1667) to E 754a (3–10 March 1705). A manuscript inventory, E 1683/22–432, provided assistance. The *Collection formée par les secrétaires d'état* consists of *arrêts en commandement* issued by the governing sections of the council. I inspected ninety-five registers in this series, from the onset of the reign of Louis XIV through the succeeding regency of the duc d'Orléans, volumes E 1716 (1662) to E 2073 (1726). For the years up to 1710, a note-card inventory is available under E 1684–1962; and for the regency, Michel Antoine's *Inventaire des arrêts du Conseil du Roi. Règne de Louis XV (arrêts en commandement)* (2 vols; Paris, 1968–1974) is indispensable.
Also:
3640–3643: Deliberations of the Royal Council of Finances, 1715–1718
3644–3653: Royal Council of Finances, 1715–1718

Series G7. *Contrôle Général des Finances*
5–22: memoranda and copies of the Controller General's correspondence
For letters from the intendants involving the parlements, I read liasses 113–123 (Béarn, Parlement of Pau); 134–135, 138–147 (Parlement of Bordeaux); 157–158, 160–170 (Burgundy, Dijon); 171–198 (Brittany, Rennes); 241–242, 245–248, 250–251 (Dauphiné, Grenoble); 258–265 (Flanders, Tournai); 276–285 (Franche-

Comté, Besançon); 299–301, 304–323 (Languedoc, Toulouse); 374–384 (Metz); 426–443 (Paris); 461–462, 465–466, 473–474, 477–478, 480–481 (Provence, Aix); 493–494, 497, 499–505 (Rouen); and 532, 536, 537–540 (various)

Also:

1132–1141, 1317,1323–1328: Capitation, *dixième*, stamped paper, office sales, etc.

1330, 1335, 1337, 1341–1343, 1350–1351, 1359, 1366: Eaux et Forêts affair

1755, 1756–1758, 1769–1773: Correspondence relative to parlements and other superior courts

1775–1777: Extraordinaire des Guerres

1849: Conseil de Finances, 1718–1719

Series H1. *Pays d'états. Pays d'élections. Intendances*
429–430: Administration provinciale. Parlement de Bretagne, 1718–1724

1691–1692: Correspondence with d'Aguesseau, intendant of Bordeaux and Toulouse, 1671–1673

Series P. *Chambre des Comptes et comptabilité*
Registers 3290–3291, 3295, 3298–3299, 3317–3328, 3351–3353, 3359–3361, 3364–3365, 3377, 3379–3382, 3384, 3386, 3389, 3392–3395, 3398, 3401, 3595, 3681, 3797–3800, 3955–3956: *quittances du receveur des revenus casuels du Roi* and *quittances des augmentations de gages*

Series U. *Extraits, copies et mémoires intéressant diverses juridictions*
28: *Extraits de registres du Conseil secret du Parlement* (1645–1648)

156 (1560–1562), 159 (1572–1576), 160 (1576–1583), 162 (1583–1591), 163 (1591–1598), 221 (1713–1714), 222 (1714–1715), 226 (1718), 227 (1718–1719): *Extraits du Conseil et du Conseil secret du Parlement*

336: 'Débats du Parlement de Paris pendant la minorité de Louis XIV . . '. (1648)

416: 'Journal du Parlement, par Delisle' (1718)

420–421: 'Premières minutes des séances du Conseil secret, redigées par le greffier Gilbert' (1718–1722)

591: 'Répertoire chronologique du Conseil secret du Parlement de 1678 à 1691'

768–770: 'Recueil des remontrances des parlements'

Series X. *Parlement de Paris*
X 1a. Civil. Registres. Conseil secret

Registers 8395 (1666–1668), 8396 (1668–1671), 8397 (1671–1673), 8398 (1673–1674), 8399 (1674–1676), 8402 (1681–1683), 8406 (1689–1690), 8407 (1690–1691), 8409 (1692–1693), 8416 (1699–1700), 8417 (1700–1701), 8419 (1702–1703), 8420 (1703–1704), 8426 (1709–1710)

X 1a. Civil. Registres. Letttres Patentes, Ordonnances

Registers 8665 (1666–1667), 8667 (1669), 8669 (1671–1672), 8670 (1672–1674), 8671 (1674–1675)

X 1b. Minutes d'arrêts. Conseil

Folders 8868 (1669–1670), 8899 (1717–1718), 8900 (1718–1719), 8901 (1719–1720), 8902 (1721–1722), 8903 (1722–1723)

Bibliothèque Nationale

Manuscrits français

6,652–6,654: *Registres du secrétariat du cabinet du roi*, 1670–1673

    6,657: *Pièces historiques*

    6,819: *Parlements et Chambres des Comptes de province*

    6,899–6,900: *Papiers d'état de Michel Le Tellier*, 1669–1678

    7,009: 'Mémoire adressée à Louis XIV sur l'état des finances de la France . . .'

    7,013: *Recueil de pièces concernant les princes légitimés, les parlements et la Cour des Aides*

    7,216–7,217: *Procès-verbal de l'ordonnance du mois d'avril mil six cens soixante sept*

    7,220–7,221: *Recueil . . . en forme de dictionnaire des édits, déclarations et principaux arrests rendus sur les affaires de finances . . .*

    7,547: *Mémoires et états concernant les parlements*

    7,548: *Establissement du Parlement de Paris . . . de M. de Harlay Premier Président*

    7,549: *Mémoire dressé par le garde des sceaux de Marillac principallement contre l'authorité du Parlement*

    7,654: *Des Bienfaits du Roi qui traite des officiers du Robe . . .*, 1684

    7,655–7,658: *Dictionnaire . . . des Bienfaits du Roi*, 1685–1687

    7,659: *Bienfaits du Roi*, 1686–1690

    7,660–7,666: *Bienfaits du Roi*, 1691–1702

    7,727: *Estat général des dépenses dont les fermes unies sont chargées*

    7,749: *Estat des finances de la France depuis l'année 1600, jusqu'à l'année 1786*

    7,750: *Mémoires de la finance*, 1600–1715

    7,753: *Recueil de pièces sur les finances*

    7,760: *Recueil de pièces relatives à la création et suppression de diverses charges au début du règne de Louis XV*

    7,765: *Recueil de mémoires sur la réforme et rétablissement des finances*, 1715–1717

    7,766: *Projets de mémoires sur les revenus de l'État*, 1715–1717

    7,769: *Mémoires pour les finances, adressés au Régent*, 1715–1717

    8,690: *Establissement du Parlement de Metz*

    8,750: *Correspondance des ministres avec M. Le Blanc, intendant de . . . Rouen*, 1675–1678

    8,890–8891, 8,906: *Intendance de Lebret*, 1709–1710, 1716

    10,231–10,232: *Mémoires sur les charges de la cour du conseil*, 1699–1732

    10,362: *Mémoire sur la Régence, par M. de Harlay et le Chancelier Voisin*

    16,524; 16,582: *Papiers du président Achille III du Harlay, concernant l'histoire du Parlement de Paris*

    16,871: *Parlements de Toulouse, Bordeaux, Grenoble*

    16,872: *Parlements de Provence, Rouen, Dijon*

    16,873: *Recueil de pièces sur les parlements (Rennes, Metz, Tournai)*

    17,413; 17,436; 17,437: *Correspondance de Achille III de Harlay, procureur-général, puis premier président du Parlement de Paris*

    19,582: *Correspondance . . . premier président de Harlay*, 1699–1701

    21,129; 21,132–21,134: *Recueil des lettres écrites par le chancelier Louis Phélypeaux,*

comte de Pontchartrain
    22,455: *Abrégé. Histoire du Parlement de Rouen, II partie. Règne de Louis XIV*
    22,816: *Lettres à M. de Harlay*, 1707–1715
    23,672–23,673: *Registres des procès-verbaux des séances du Conseil de Régence*

Nouvelles acquisitions françaises
1,360: *Recueil de pièces historiques et juridiques . . .*
    1,431: *Histoire des finances pendant la Régence de 1715*
    3,373: *Lettres originales de rois Louis XIV et Louis XV*, 1673–1716
    3,497: *Provence: Offices, 1704–1716*
    8,432: *Recueil de remontrances des parlements*, 1720–1753
    9,640: *Règne de Louis XV*
    9,750: *Extraits imprimés sur les lits de justice. Extraits des lits de justice, notes manus-*
crites
    9,771: *Remontrance (sic) sur les parlements*
    9,807: *Mémoire abrégé pour connoître les parties casuelles . . . année 1709*
    10,652: *Histoire du Parlement de Franche-Comté*

Cing Cents Colbert
259–260: *États et évaluation, par généralités, de tous les offices de judicature et finance*, 1665

Mélanges de Colbert
I have read Colbert's correspondence with officials in the parlements in volumes
102–103, 105–109bis, 114–176bis; these volumes begin in 1661 and end in 1677.
    248: *Estat des charges assignées sur les domaines et amendes*,1675
    249: *Estat des gabelles de France*, 1676

Clairambault
461–468: *Copies des dépêches de Colbert avec commissaires départis dans les provinces,*
1679–1683
    613: *Mémoires. Conseil de Justice*
    759: *Pièces concernant les parlements de province*

Cabinet des Titres
Carrés de d'Hozier: 31, 131, 444
    Dossiers bleus: 30, 43, 128, 132, 141, 203
    Pièces originales: 91, 489–490

Provincial parlements

Parlement of Aix
Archives Départementales, Bouches-du-Rhône
Series C. *États de Provence*. 43 (1666–1668), 45 (1669–1672), 47 (1672–1676)
Archives Départementales, Dépôt annexe, Aix-en-Provence
Series B. Parlement. 3363 (*Actes constitutifs*), 3596 (*Liquidations des offices du Parlement*),
3601 (*Registres de la comptabilité*), 3610–3611 (*États des pensions et des dettes*), 3669
(*Délibérations et remontrances du Parlement*), 3688 (*Correspondance du Parlement*)

Bibliothèque Méjanes, Aix-en-Provence, Manuscrits
945–946: Thomassin, François, *et al.*, 'Histoire du Parlement de Provence', 2 vols
 975–977: *Délibérations du Parlement de Provence*, 1653–1715
Musée Arbaud, Aix-en-Provence, Manuscrits
MQ 19, 'Journal du Parlement . . . par Balthazar de Rabasse de Vergons et André de la Garde, procureurs généraux', 1677–1708

Parlement of Besançon
Archives Départementales, Doubs
Series B. Parlement. 394 (*Correspondance*); 396 (*Correspondance*); 2,840 (*Remontrances*), 3,768 (*Délibérations*); 3,834 (*Délibérations*)

Parlement of Bordeaux
Archives Départementales, Gironde
Series B. *Parlement Bordeaux. Arrêts. Chambres diverses.* Several liasses, notably for 1669, 1671–1672, 1682, 1701–1703, 1716
 Series B. *Fonds 1B. Registres d'enregistrement.* 1B 29–34 (1644–1702)
Archives Municipales, Bordeaux, Manuscrits
722–732: *Recueil de lettres autographes adressées aux présidents au Parlement*
 794–797: *Registre secret du Parlement de Bordeaux*, vols 38–41 (1658–1718)

Parlement of Dijon
Archives Départementales, Côte-d'Or
Series B. *Parlement de Bourgogne. Enregistrement des édits et lettres patentes*, 12,108 (1663, 1669–1679); 12,109 (1676–1676)
 Series C. *États du Duché de Bourgogne. Décrets originaux des États*: 2,997–2,998 (1662–1679). *Décrets des États et Délibérations des élus*: 3,107–3,120 (1662–1675). *Cahiers des remontrances des États de Bourgogne*: 3,238–3,329 (1524–1698)
Bibliothèque Municipale, Dijon, Manuscrits
541–542: *Lettres, monseigneur Brûlart, premier président au parlement de Dijon, 1661–1692*
 767–770: *Registres du Parlement de Dijon, 1652–1722*

Parlement of Grenoble
Archives Départementales, Isère
Sub-Series 2B. *Parlement de Dauphiné. Enregistrement*, 2,355**–2,357 (1665–1673). 2B3*: *Ordonnances, arrêts, déclarations et délibérations importantes du parlement, 1526–1760.* 2B4*: *Transcriptions de lettres, réception de princes, lettres de remontrance, délibérations du Parlement . . ., etc., 1556–1767.* 2B5*: *Délibérations du Parlement . . . concernant la vie interne . . ., 1646–1762.* 2B 1,046: *Livre des créanciers du Parlement, 1712–1757*

Parlement of Metz
Archives Départementales, Moselle
Series B. *Parlement de Metz. Registre des délibérations ou registres secrets.* 264* (1667–1668), 275*-276 (1673–1674), 278*-279 (1674–1675), 296*-297 (1683–1684), 308* (1689–1690), 311* (1691), 314* (1692–1693), 317* (1694),

320* (1695–1696), 332* (1701–1702), 334* (1702–1703), 335* (1703), 336 (1703–1704), 337 (1704), 338 (1704–1705), 346 (1708–1709), 347 (1709), 348 (1709–1710), 349 (1710), 350 (1710–1711), 360* (1715–1716)

    503: *Mémoires relatifs aux intérêts*
    11,149: *Finances du Parlement*

Parlement of Pau
Archives Départementales, Pyrénées-Atlantiques
Series B. *Parlement de Navarre*. 4,538: *Registres secrets, 1637–1683*; 4,540–4,543: *Livre secret . . . de Parlement de Navarre, 1688–1697*; 4,545–4,548: *Registres secrets, 1700–1721*. 6,017: untitled, contains royal legislation registered in Parlement
    Series C. *Délibérations des États de Béarn*. 731 & 733 (1670–1671 & 1672–1673)

Parlement of Rennes
Archives Départementales, Ille-et-Vilaine
Sub-Series 1B. *Parlement de Bretagne*. 1Ba: *Enregistrement*, 22–23 (1655–1674). IBb: *Délibérations du Parlement (registres secrets)*, 216–331 (1661–1718). 1Bb: *Registre littéraire. Correspondance politique du Parlement*. 1Bc1: *Remontrances et affaires politiques, 1578–1719*. 1Bc2bis: *Correspondance du Parlement, 1715–1732*
    Series C. *Fonds des États de Bretagne*. 2657–2658: *Procès-verbaux des délibérations des États* (1665–1677)

Parlement of Rouen
Archives Départementales, Seine-Maritime
Sub-Series 1B. *Parlement de Normandie. Registres secrets*, 192–195 (1661–1666), 199 (1670–1671), 221–239 (1701–1720). 5,276: *Chambre de la Réformation des Eaux et forêts, 1674*
    'F. Parlement'.: *Table chronologique des édits, ordonnnances, déclarations du Roy, 1516–1774*

Bibliothèque Municipale, Rouen, Manuscrits
Y. 63: 'Abrégé historique du Parlement de Rouen', 1499–1764, Pavyot de Bouillon, 4 vols
    Y. 91: 'Abrégé historique du Parlement de Rouen, depuis 1499 jusqu'en 1715', Pavyot du Bouillon, 1722
    Y. 214/24–214/26: *Recueil d'extraits des registres secrets et ordinaires du parlement de Rouen, par Cl. Pellot*, 1664–1676

Parlement of Toulouse
Archives Départementales, Haute-Garonne
Series B. *Enregistrement des Actes du pouvoir royal*. 1919–1920 (1667–1674)
    Sub-Series 51B. *Remontrances. Parlement*. 29–30 (1712–1789). *Lettres. Parlement*. 36 (1561–1790)
    Series C. *États de Languedoc*. 2316 (1667–1669). 2318 (1671–1672)

MAIN PRINTED SOURCES

Correspondence, journals, memoirs, treatises

André, Louis, ed. *Testament politique du Cardinal de Richelieu*. Paris, 1947.

d'Argenson, René Louis de Voyer, marquis. *Journal et mémoires du marquis d'Argenson*. Edited by E.J.B. Rathery. 9 vols Paris, 1859–1867.

Barbier, Edmond-Jean-François. *Journal historique et anecdotique du règne de Louis XV*. Published by A. de La Villegille. 4 vols Paris, 1847–1856.

Barthélemy, E. de, comte, ed. *Gazette de la Régence*. Paris, 1887.

Bigot de Monville, Alexandre. *Mémoires du Président Alexandre Bigot de Monville. Le Parlement de Rouen: 1640–1643*. Edited by Madeleine Foisil. Paris, 1976.

Boislisle, Arthur-Michel de, ed. *Correspondance des contrôleurs généraux des finances avec les intendants des provinces*. 3 vols Paris, 1874–1897.

Bornier, Philippe. *Conférences des nouvelles ordonnances de Louis XIV*. 2 vols Paris, 1694.

Boutaric, François de. *Explication de l'ordonnance de Louis XIV . . . sur les matières civiles*. N.p., 1743.

Brûlart de La Borde, Nicolas. *Choix de lettres inédites*. Edited by Lacuisine. 2 vols Dijon, 1859.

Buvat, Jean. *Journal de la Régence (1715–1723)*. Edited by Émile Campardon. 2 vols Paris, 1865.

Colbert, Jean-Baptiste. *Lettres, instructions et mémoires de Colbert*. Edited by Pierre Clément. 8 vols Paris, 1861–1882.

Cosnac, Daniel de. *Mémoires*. Edited by J. de Cosnac. 2 vols Paris, 1852.

Dangeau, Philippe de Courcillon, marquis de. *Journal du marquis de Dangeau, avec les additions inédites du duc de Saint-Simon*. 19 vols Paris, 1854–1860.

Depping, Georges, ed. *Correspondance administrative sous le règne de Louis XIV*. 4 vols Paris, 1850–1855.

D'Esmivi de Moissac, J.L.H. *Histoire du Parlement de Provence, 1501–1715*. 2 vols Aix, 1726.

Dorsanne, Antoine. *Journal de M. L'abbé Dorsanne*. 2 vols Rome, 1753.

Ferrière, Claude-Joseph de. *Dictionnaire de droit et de pratique*. 2nd edn. 2 vols Paris, 1740.

Flammermont, Jules, ed. *Remontrances du Parlement de Paris au XVIIIe siècle*. 3 vols Paris, 1888–1898.

Forbonnais, François Véron de. *Recherches et considérations sur les finances de France, depuis l'année 1595 jusqu'à l'année 1721*. 2 vols Basel, 1758.

Furetière, Antoine. *Dictionnaire universel*. 4 vols Reprint, Geneva, 1972.

Guyot, Joseph-Nicolas. *Répertoire universel et raisonné de jurisprudence civile et criminelle, canonique et bénéficiale*. 17 vols Paris, 1784–1785.

Isambert, François-André, *et al.*, eds *Recueil général des anciennes lois françaises depuis l'an 400 jusqu'à la révolution de 1789*. 29 vols Paris, 1822–1833.

Le Boindre, Jean. *Débats du Parlement de Paris pendant la minorité de Louis XIV*. Edited by Robert Descimon and Orest and Patricia Ranum. Paris, 1997.

Le Moy, Arthur, ed. *Remontrances du Parlement de Bretagne au XVIIIe siècle. Textes inédits*. Paris, 1909.

L'Hôpital, Michel de. *Discours pour la majorité de Charles IX et trois autres discours*. Edited by Robert Descimon. Paris, 1993.

Louis XIV. *Mémoires for the instruction of the Dauphin.* Translated and edited by Paul Sonnino. New York, 1970.

Loyseau, Charles. *Ordre des cinq livres des offices,* in *Les oeuvres de maistre Charles Loyseau.* New edn. Paris, 1678.

Mallet, J. *Comptes rendus de l'administration des finances du Royaume de France pendant les onze dernières années du règne d'Henri IV, le règne de Louis XIII et soixante-cinq ans du règne de Louis XIV.* Paris, 1789.

Marais, Mathieu. *Journal et mémoires de Mathieu Marais, avocat au Parlement de Paris sur la Régence et le règne de Louis XV (1715–1737).* Edited by de Lescure. 4 vols Paris, 1863–1868.

Molé, Mathieu. *Mémoires.* 4 vols Paris, 1855–1857.

Motteville, Françoise-Bertault de. *Mémoires de Madame de Motteville.* Vol. 10, 2nd ser., *Nouvelle collection des mémoires pour servir à l'histoire de France.* Edited by Joseph-François Michaud and Jean J.-F. Poujoulat. Paris, 1836–1839.

Mousnier, Roland, ed. *Lettres et mémoires adressés au Chancelier Séguier (1633–1649).* 2 vols Paris, 1964.

Orléans, Elisabeth Charlotte, duchesse d'. *A Woman's Life in the Court of the Sun King. Letters of Liselotte von der Pfalz, 1652–1722.* Translated and introduced by Elborg Forster. Baltimore, Md, 1984.

Ormesson, Olivier Lefèvre d'. *Journal d'Olivier Lefèvre d'Ormesson et extraits des mémoires d'André Lefèvre d'Ormesson.* Edited by Pierre-Adolphe Chéruel. 2 vols Paris, 1860–1861.

Pellot, Claude. *Mémoires sur la vie publique et privé de Claude Pellot.* Edited by Ernest-Marie-Jacques O'Reilly. 2 vols Paris and Rouen, 1881–1882.

Saint-Simon, Louis de Rouvroy, duc de. *Mémoires de Saint-Simon.* Edited by Arthur de Boislisle. 41 vols, plus index. Paris, 1879–1928.

Savignac. *Mémorial général de Mr. De Savignac, conseiller au parlement de Bordeaux, 1708–1713.* Bordeaux, 1931.

Sévigné, Marie de Rabutin-Chantal, marquise de. *Madame de Sévigné. Lettres.* Edited by Gerard-Gailly. 3 vols Paris, 1953–1963.

Talon, Omer. *Mémoires.* Vol. 6, 3rd ser., *Nouvelle collection des mémoires pour servir à l'histoire de France.* Edited by Joseph-François Michaud and Jean J.-F. Poujoulat. Paris, 1836–1839.

Torcy, Jean-Baptiste Colbert, marquis de. *Journal inédit de Jean-Baptiste Colbert, marquis de Torcy.* Edited by Frédéric Masson. Paris, 1884.

Political thought

d'Aguesseau, Henri-François. 'Fragmens sur l'origine et l'usage des remontrances', in Vol. 10, pp. 4–31, of *Oeuvres complètes.* 16 vols Paris, 1819–1829.

Bodin, Jean. *Les six livres de la République, avec l'apologie de René Herpin.* Paris, 1583.

Choppin, René. *Oeuvres de René Choppin.* 5 vols Paris, 1662.

Du Haillan, Bernard. *De l'estat et succez des affaires de France.* Paris, 1593.

Du Vair, Guillaume. *Les oeuvres du sieur du Vair. Garde des sceaux de France.* Paris, 1618.

Figon, Charles de. *Discours des estats et offices tant du gouvernement que de la justice et des finances de France.* Paris, 1579.

Grimaudet, François. *Oeuvres.* Paris, 1613.

La Bigotière, René de. *Commentaires sur la coutume de Bretagne*. 2nd edn. Rennes, 1702.

La Roche-Flavin, Bernard de. *Treize livres des Parlements de France*. Geneva, 1621.

Le Bret, Cardin. *De la souveraineté du roi*, in *Les oeuvres*. Paris, 1689.

Le Caron, Louis [Charondas]. *Pandectes ou digestes du droit françois*. Lyon, 1596.

L'Hommeau, Pierre de. *Les maximes générales du droit françois*. Rouen, 1614.

Pasquier, Étienne. *Les recherches de la France*. Paris, 1665.

Seyssel, Claude de. *The Monarchy of France*. Translated by J.H. Hexter and Michael Sherman. New Haven, Conn., and London, 1981.

Scholarly studies

Ames, Glenn Joseph. *Colbert, Mercantilism, and the French Quest for Asian Trade*. DeKalb, Ill., 1996.

Antoine, Michel. 'La chancellerie de France au XVIe siècle', in *Le dur métier de roi*. Paris, 1986.

——'Colbert et la révolution de 1661', in *Un nouveau Colbert*, directed by Roland Mousnier. Paris, 1985.

——*Le Conseil du roi sous le règne de Louis XV*. Geneva, 1970.

——*Le fonds du Conseil d'état du Roi aux Archives Nationales*. Paris, 1955.

——*Le Gouvernment et l'Administration sous Louis XV. Dictionnaire biographique*. Paris, 1978.

——*Louis XV*. Paris, 1989.

——'Les remontrances des cours supérieures sous le règne de Louis XIV (1673–1715)'. *Bibliothèque de l'École des Chartes* 151 (January–June 1993), 88–121.

Asher, Eugene L. *The Resistance to the Maritime Classes: The Survival of Feudalism in the France of Colbert*. Berkeley, Calif., 1960.

d'Avenel, Georges, vicomte. *Richelieu et la monarchie absolue*. 2nd edn. 4 vols Paris, 1895.

Basdevant-Gaudemet, Brigitte. *Aux origines de l'État moderne. Charles Loyseau, 1564–1627*. Paris, 1977.

Bayard, Françoise. *Le monde des financiers au XVIIe siècle*. Paris, 1988.

Beik, William H. *Absolutism and Society in Seventeenth-Century France. State Power and Provincial Aristocracy in Languedoc*. Cambridge, 1985.

——*Urban Protest in Seventeenth-Century France. The Culture of Retribution*. Cambridge, 1997.

Bély, Lucien, ed. *Dictionnaire de l'Ancien Régime. Royaume de France, XVIe–XVIIIe siècle*. Paris, 1996.

Bercé, Yves-Marie. *La naissance dramatique de l'absolutisme, 1598–1661*. Paris, 1992.

Bickart, Roger. *Les parlements et la notion de souveraineté nationale au XVIIIe siècle*. Paris, 1932.

Bien, David. 'Offices, Corps, and a System of State Credit: The Uses of Privilege under the Ancien Régime'. In *The Political Culture of the Old Regime*, edited by Keith Michael Baker. Oxford and New York, 1987.

——'The *sécretaires du roi*: Absolutism, Corps, and Privilege under the Ancien Régime', in *Vom Ancien Régime zur Französischen Revolution. Forshungen und Perspektiven*, edited by Ernst Hinrichs. Göttingen, 1978.

Bitton, Davis. 'History and Politics: The Controversy over the Sale of Offices in Early

Seventeenth-Century France', in *Action and Conviction in Early Modern Europe. Essays in Honor of E.H. Harbison*, edited by Theodore K. Rabb and Jerrold E. Seigel. Princeton, NJ, 1969.

Blet, Pierre. *Les assemblées du clergé et Louis XIV de 1670 à 1693*. Rome, 1972.

Bluche, François, ed. *Dictionnaire du Grand Siècle*. Paris, 1990.

——*Les magistrats du Parlement de Paris au XVIIIe siècle (1715–1771)*. Paris, 1960.

——*L'origine des magistrats du Parlement de Paris*. Paris, 1956.

——, and Jean-François Solnon. *La véritable hiérarchie sociale de l'ancienne France. Le tarif de la première capitation (1695)*. Geneva, 1983.

Bonney, Richard. *L'absolutisme*. Paris, 1989.

——'The Eighteenth Century. II. The Struggle for Great Power Status and the End of the Old Fiscal Regime', in *Economic Systems and State Finance*. Edited by Richard Bonney. Oxford, 1995.

——*The King's Debts: Finance and Politics in France, 1598–1661*. New York, 1981.

——*Political Change in France under Richelieu and Mazarin, 1624–1661*. Oxford, 1978.

——'"Le secret de leurs familles": The Fiscal and Social Limits of Louis XIV's *Dixième*'. *French History* 7 (no. 4; December 1993), 383–416.

Boscheron des Portes, C.-B.-F. *Histoire du Parlement de Bordeaux depuis sa création jusqu'à sa suppression (1451–1790)*. 2 vols Bordeaux, 1877.

Bourgeon, Jean-Louis. *Les Colbert avant Colbert. Destin d'une famille marchande*. Paris, 1973.

Briggs, Robin. 'Richelieu and Reform. Rhetoric and Political Reality', in *Richelieu and His Age*, edited by Joseph Bergin and Laurence Brockliss. Oxford, 1992.

Brown, Elizabeth A.R., and Richard C. Famiglietti. *The Lit de Justice. Semantics, Ceremonial, and the Parlement of Paris, 1300–1600*. Sigmaringen, 1994.

Cabasse, Prosper. *Essais historiques sur le Parlement de Provence, depuis son origine jusqu'à sa suppression, 1501–1790*. 3 vols Paris, 1826.

Campbell, Peter R. *Power and Politics in Old Regime France, 1720–1745*. London and New York, 1996.

Carcassonne, Élie. *Montesquieu et le problème de la constitution française au XVIIIe siècle*. 1st pub. 1927. Reprint, Geneva, 1978.

Carré, Henri. *Le Parlement de Bretagne après la Ligue (1598–1610)*. Paris, 1888.

Chéruel, Pierre-Adolphe. *Dictionnaire historique des institutions, moeurs et coutumes de la France*. 8th edn. 2 vols Paris, 1910.

Church, William F. *Constitutional Thought in Sixteenth-Century France. A Study in the Evolution of Ideas*. Cambridge, Mass., 1941.

——'The Decline of French Jurists as Political Theorists, 1660–1789'. *French Historical Studies* 5 (Spring 1967), 1–40.

Clamageran, Jean-Jules. *Histoire de l'impôt en France depuis l'époque romaine jusqu'à 1774*. 3 vols 1867–1876. Reprint, Geneva, 1980.

Clapier-Collonques, Balthasar de. *Chronologie des officiers des Cours souveraines de Provence*. Aix-en-Provence, 1909.

Cole, Charles Woolsey. *Colbert and a Century of French Mercantilism*. 2 vols New York, 1939.

Collins, James B. *The Fiscal Limits to Absolutism. Direct Taxation in Early Seventeenth-Century France*. Berkeley, 1988.

——*The State in Early Modern France*. Cambridge, 1995.

Colombet, Albert. *Les parlementaires bourguignons à la fin du XVIIe siècle*. 2nd edn. Dijon, 1937.

Communay, A. *Le Parlement de Bordeaux. Notes biographiques sur ses principaux officiers*. Bordeaux, 1886.

Cubells, Monique. 'Le Parlement de Paris pendant la Fronde'. *Dix-septième siècle* 35 (July 1957), 171–201.

——*La Provence des lumières. Les parlementaires d'Aix au 18eme siècle*. Paris, 1984.

Cummings, Mark. 'The Social Impact of the Paulette: The Case of the Parlement of Paris'. *Canadian Journal of History* 15 (no. 3; 1980), 329–354.

Desjonquères, Léon. *Le garde des sceaux Michel de Marillac et son oeuvre législative*. Paris, 1908.

Dessert, Daniel. *Argent, pouvoir et société au Grand Siècle*. Paris, 1984.

——, and Jean-Louis Journet. 'Le lobby Colbert. Un royaume, ou une affaire de famille?' *Annales. E.S.C.* 30 (no. 6; November–December 1975), 1303–1336.

De Waele, Michel. 'De Paris à Tours: la crise d'identité des magistrats parisiens de 1589 à 1594'. *Revue Historique* 299/3 (1998), 549–577.

Dewald, Jonathan. *The Formation of a Provincial Nobility: The Magistrates of the Parlement of Rouen, 1499–1610*. Princeton, NJ, 1980.

——'The "Perfect Magistrate": Parlementaires and Crime in Sixteenth-Century Rouen'. *Archiv für Reformationsgeschichte* 67 (1976), 284–300.

Doolin, Paul Rice. *The Fronde*. Cambridge, Mass., 1935.

Dornic, François. *Une ascension sociale au XVIIe siècle. Louis Berryer, agent de Mazarin et de Colbert*. Caen, 1968.

Doucet, R. *Les institutions de la France au seizième siècle*. 2 vols Paris, 1948.

Doyle, William. *The Parlement of Bordeaux and the End of the Old Regime, 1771–1790*. New York, 1974.

——'The Parlements', in *The French Revolution and the Creation of Modern Political Culture*. Vol. I of *The Political Culture of the Old Regime*, edited by Keith M. Baker. Oxford, 1987.

——*Venality. The Sale of Offices in Eighteenth-Century France*. Oxford, 1996.

Echeverria, Durand. *The Maupeou Revolution*. Baton Rouge, La., 1985.

Egret, Jean. *Louis XV et l'opposition parlementaire, 1715–1774*. Paris, 1970.

——'Note d'orientation de recherches sur les cours souveraines, particulièrement au XVIIIe siècle'. *Bulletin de la Société d'histoire moderne et contemporaine*. Paris, 1964.

——*Le Parlement de Dauphiné et les affaires publiques dans la deuxième moitié du XVIIIe siècle*. 2 vols Grenoble, 1942.

El Annabi, Hassen. *Le Parlement de Paris sous le règne personnel de Louis XIV. L'institution, le pouvoir et la société*. Tunis, 1989.

Engrand, Charles. 'Clients du roi. Les Colbert et l'état (1661–1715)', in *Un nouveau Colbert*, directed by Roland Mousnier. Paris, 1985.

Engelmann, Arthur, *et al. A History of Continental Civil Procedure*. Translated by Robert W. Millar. Boston, 1927.

Esslinger, Albert. *Le conseil particulier des finances à l'époque de la polysynodie (1715–1718)*. Paris, 1908.

Estignard, A. *Le Parlement de Franche-Comté de son installation à Besançon à sa suppression, 1674–1790*. 2 vols Paris, 1892.

Faure, Edgar. *La banqueroute de Law, le 17 juillet 1720*. Paris, 1977.

Filhol, René. *Le premier président Christofle de Thou et la réformation des coutumes*. Paris, 1937.

Floquet, Pierre-Amable. *Histoire du Parlement de Normandie*. 7 vols Rouen, 1840–1842.

Foisil, Madeleine. *La révolte des nu-pieds et les révoltes normandes de 1639*. Paris, 1970.

Ford, Franklin L. *Robe and Sword. The Regrouping of the French Aristocracy after Louis XIV*. 2nd edn. Cambridge, Mass., 1962.

Franklin, Julian H. *Jean Bodin and the Rise of Absolutist Theory*. Cambridge, 1973.

Fréville, Henri. *L'intendance de Bretagne (1689–1790)*. 3 vols Rennes, 1953.

Frondeville, Henri de. *Les présidents du Parlement de Normandie (1490–1790). Recueil généalogique*. Rouen and Paris, 1953.

Frondeville, Henri de, and de Odette Frondeville. *Les conseillers du Parlement de Normandie de 1641 à 1715. Recueil généalogique*. Rouen, 1970.

Germond, André. 'Les parlementaires Bretons de 1661 à 1720'. Diplôme d'Études Supérieures, Faculté des Lettres, Université de Haute-Bretagne (Rennes 2), c. 1964.

Glasson, Ernest-Désiré. *Histoire du droit et des institutions de la France*. 8 vols Paris, 1887–1903.

——*Le Parlement de Paris. Son rôle politique depuis le règne de Charles VII jusqu'à la Révolution*. 2 vols Paris, 1901. Reprint, Geneva, 1974.

Gresset, Maurice. *Gens de justice à Besançon, 1674–1789*. 2 vols Paris, 1978.

——*L'introduction de la vénalité des offices en Franche-Comté*. Besançon, 1989.

Hamilton, Earl J. 'Prices and Wages at Paris under John Law's System'. *The Quarterly Journal of Economics* 51 (1937), 42–70.

——'Prices and Wages in Southern France under John Law's System'. *Economic History (A Supplement to the Economic Journal)* 3 (1934–1937), 444–461.

Hamon, Philippe. *L'argent du roi: les finances sous François Ier*. Paris, 1994.

Hamscher, Albert N. *The Conseil Privé and the Parlements in the Age of Louis XIV: A Study in French Absolutism*. Philadelphia, Pa.,1987.

——*The Parlement of Paris after the Fronde, 1653–1673*. Pittsburgh, Pa., 1976.

Hanley, Sarah. *The Lit de Justice of the Kings of France. Constitutional Ideology in Legend, Ritual and Discourse*. Princeton, NJ, 1982.

Hardy, James D. *Judicial Politics in the Old Régime: The Parlement of Paris during the Regency*. Baton Rouge, La., 1967.

Harsin, Paul. *Les doctrines monétaires et financières en France du XVIe au XVIIIe siècle*. Paris, 1928.

——'La finance et l'État jusqu'au système de Law (1660–1726)', in *Histoire économique et sociate de la France, II*, Edited by Fernand Braudel and Ernest Labrousse. Paris, 1970.

Hartung, Fritz, and Roland Mousnier. 'Quelques problèmes concernant la monarchie absolue'. *Relazioni del X Congresso Internazionale di Science Storiche* 4 (1955), 3–55.

Hildesheimer, Bernard. *Les assemblées générales des communautés de Provence*. Paris, 1935.

Holt, Mack P. 'The King in Parlement: The Problem of the *Lit de Justice* in Sixteenth-Century France'. *The Historical Journal* 31 (no. 3; 1988), 507–533.

Hurt, John J. 'Les offices au Parlement de Bretagne sous Louis XIV, aspects financiers'. *Revue d'Histoire Moderne et Contemporaine* 23 (January–March 1976), 3–31.

——'La politique du Parlement de Bretagne (1661–1675)'. *Annales de Bretagne et des Pays de l'Ouest* 81 (1974), 105–130.

——'The Parlement of Brittany and the Crown: 1665–1675'. *French Historical Studies* 4 (no. 4; Autumn 1966), 411–433.

Jacquart, Jean. 'Colbert et la réformation du domaine', in *Un nouveau Colbert*, edited by Roland Mousnier. Paris, 1985.

Kaiser, Colin. 'The Deflation in the Volume of Litigation at Paris in the Eighteenth Century and the Waning of the Old Judicial Order'. *European Studies Review* 10 (1980), 309–336.

Kaiser, Thomas E. 'Money, Despotism, and Public Opinion in Early Eighteenth-Century France: John Law and the Debate on Royal Credit'. *Journal of Modern History* 63 (March 1991), 1–28.

Kelley, Donald R. *Foundations of Modern Historical Scholarship. Language, Law and History in the French Renaissance*. New York and London, 1970.

Keohane, Nannerl O. *Philosophy and the State in France. The Renaissance to the Enlightenment*. Princeton, NJ, 1980.

Kettering, Sharon. *Judicial Politics and Urban Revolt in Sixteenth-Century France. The Parlement of Aix, 1629–1659*. Princeton, NJ, 1978.

——'Patronage in Early Modern France'. *French Historical Studies* 17 (no. 4; Autumn, 1992), 839–862.

——*Patrons, Brokers, and Clients in Seventeenth-Century France*. New York and Oxford, 1987.

Kim, Seong-Hak. 'The Chancellor's Crusade: Michel de L'Hôpital and the *Parlement* of Paris'. *French History* 7 (March 1993), 1–29.

——*Michel de L'Hôpital. The Vision of a Reformist Chancellor during the French Religious Wars*. Kirksville, Mo., 1997.

Knecht, R.J. 'Francis I and the "Lit de Justice": A "Legend" Defended'. *French History* 7 (March 1993), 53–83.

Kossmann, Ernst Heinrich. *La Fronde*. Leiden, 1954.

Krugg-Basse, J. *Histoire du Parlement de Lorraine et Barrois*. Paris and Nancy, 1899.

Labatut, Jean-Pierre. *Les ducs et pairs de France au XVIIe siècle. Étude sociale*. Paris, 1972.

La Condamine, Pierre de. *Pontcallec. Une étrange conspiration au coeur de la Bretagne*. 3rd edn. Mayenne, 1988.

La Cuisine, M. de. *Le Parlement de Bourgogne depuis son origine jusqu'à sa chute*. 3 vols Dijon and Paris, 1864.

Lair, Jules. *Nicolas Fouquet, procureur général, surintendant des finances, ministre d'état de Louis XIV*. 2 vols Paris, 1890.

Lapierre, Eugène. *Le Parlement de Toulouse*. Paris, 1875.

Lavisse, Ernest. *Louis XIV. La Fronde. Le Roi. Colbert (1643–1685)*. Vol. 7, pt. I of *Histoire de France depuis les origines jusqu'à la Révolution*. Edited by Ernest Lavisse. Paris, 1905.

Law, John (?). 'Histoire des finances pendant la Régence', in *John Law. Oeuvres complètes*, edited by Paul Harsin, vol. 13. Paris, 1934.

Leclercq, Dom Henri. *Histoire de la Régence pendant la minorité de Louis XV*. 3 vols Paris, 1921–1922.

Lemaire, André. *Les lois fondamentales de la monarchie française, d'après les théoriciens de l'Ancien Régime*. Paris, 1907. Reprint, Geneva, 1975.

Le Moy, Arthur. *Le Parlement de Bretagne et le pouvoir royal au dix-huitième siècle*. Paris, 1909.

——, ed. *Remontrances du Parlement de Bretagne au XVIIIe siècle*. Paris, 1909.

Lloyd, Howell A. 'The Political Thought of Charles Loyseau (1564–1627)'. *European Studies Review* 11 (January 1981), 53–82.

Lüthy, Herbert. *La banque protestante en France, de la révocation de l'Édit de Nantes à la Révolution.* 2 vols Paris, 1959–1961.

Mahuet, A., comte de. *Biographie de la Cour souveraine de Lorraine et Barrois et du Parlement de Nancy (1641–1790).* Nancy, 1921.

Mailfait, Hubert. *Un magistrat de l'ancien régime. Omer Talon, sa vie et ses oeuvres, 1595–1652.* Paris, 1902. Reprint, Geneva, 1971.

Major, J. Russell. *Bellièvre, Sully, and the Assembly of Notables of 1596.* Transactions of the American Philosophical Society, n.s. 64, pt. 2. Philadelphia, 1974.

——*From Renaissance Monarchy to Absolute Monarchy. French Kings, Nobles, & Estates.* Baltimore and London, 1994.

——*Representative Government in Early Modern France.* New Haven, Conn., 1980.

Marchand, Pierre-Joseph. *Un intendant sous Louis XIV, étude sur l'administration de Lebret en Provence.* Paris, 1889.

Marion, Marcel. *Dictionnaire des institutions de la France aux XVIIe et XVIIIe siècles.* Paris, 1923.

——*Histoire financière de la France.* 5 vols Paris, 1927–1928.

Maugis, Édouard. *Histoire du Parlement de Paris.* 3 vols Paris, 1913–1916. Reprint, Geneva, 1977.

Mettam, Roger. 'France', in *Absolutism in Seventeenth-Century Europe*, edited by John Miller. London, 1990.

——*Power and Faction in Louis XIV's France.* Oxford, 1988.

Meyer, Jean. *Colbert.* Paris, 1981.

——*La noblesse bretonne au XVIIIe siècle.* 2 vols Paris, 1966.

——*Le Régent, 1674–1723.* Paris, 1985.

Michaud, Claude. 'Notariat et sociologie de la rente à Paris au XVIIe siècle: l'emprunt du clergé de 1690'. *Annales E.S.C.* 32 (November–December 1977), 1154–1187.

Michaud, Hélène. *La grande chancellerie et les écritures royales au seizième siècle (1515–1589).* Paris, 1967.

Michel, Emmanuel. *Biographie du Parlement de Metz.* Metz, 1855.

——*Histoire du Parlement de Metz.* Paris, 1845.

Momplot, F. 'Recherches sociales sur les conseillers au Parlement de Paris, 1685 à 1690'. Mémoire. Maîtrise, University of Paris IV, 1970.

Monnier, Francis. *Le chancelier d'Aguesseau. Sa conduite et ses idées politiques.* Paris, 1863. Reprint, Geneva, 1975.

——*Guillaume de Lamoignon et Colbert. Essai sur la législation française au XVIIe siècle.* Paris, 1862.

Moote, A. Lloyd. 'Law and Justice under Louis XIV', in *Louis XIV and the Craft of Kingship*, edited by John C. Rule. n.p., 1969.

——*The Revolt of the Judges. The Parlement of Paris and the Fronde, 1643–1652.* Princeton, NJ, 1971.

Mousnier, Roland. 'The Fronde', in *Preconditions of Revolution in Early Modern Europe*, edited by Robert Forster and Jack P. Greene. Baltimore, Md, 1970.

Mousnier, Roland. *The Institutions of France under the Absolute Monarchy.* 2 vols Vol. 1, *Society and the State.* Translated by Brian Pearce. Vol. 2, *The Organs of State and Society.* Translated by Arthur Goldhammer. Chicago, 1979–1984.

——*La vénalité des offices sous Henri IV et Louis XIII.* 2nd edn. Paris, 1971.

Murphy, Antoin E. *John Law. Economic Theorist and Policy-Maker.* Oxford, 1997.

Olivier-Martin, F. *Les lois du roi.* Reprint, Paris, 1988.

——*L'organisation corporative de la France d'ancien régime.* Paris, 1938.

Pagès, Georges. *La monarchie d'ancien régime en France (de Henri IV à Louis XIV).* Paris, 1932. Reprint, Paris, 1952.

Parker, David. *Class and State in Ancien Régime France. The Road to Modernity?.* London and New York, 1996.

——*The Making of French Absolutism.* New York, 1983.

Paulhet, Jean-Claude. 'Les parlementaires toulousains à la fin du XVII siècle'. *Annales du Midi* 76 (April 1964), 189–204.

Picot, Georges. *Histoire des États Généraux considérés au point de vue de leur influence sur le gouvernment de la France de 1355 à 1614.* 4 vols Paris, 1872.

Pilastre, E. *Achille III de Harlay. Premier Président du Parlement de Paris sous le règne de Louis XIV.* Paris, n.d.

Pillorget, René. 'Henri Pussort, Oncle de Colbert (1615–1697)', in *Le Conseil du Roi de Louis XIII à la Révolution,* edited by Roland Mousnier. Paris, 1970.

Pillot, Gabriel-Maximilien-Louis. *Histoire du Parlement de Flandres.* 2 vols Douai, 1849.

Pocquet, Barthélemy. *La Bretagne province.* Vol. 6, *Histoire de Bretagne.* Rennes, 1914. Reprint, Mayenne, 1985.

Poisson, Jean-Paul. 'Introduction à une Étude Quantitative des Effets Socio-Économiques du Système de Law', in idem, *Notaires et Société. Travaux d'Histoire et de Sociologie Notariales.* Paris, 1985.

——'De quelques nouvelles utilisations des sources notariales en histoire économique (XVIIe–XXe siècle'. *Revue Historique* 249 (January–March 1973), 5–22.

Ranum, Orest. *The Fronde. A French Revolution, 1648–1652.* New York and London, 1993.

——*Richelieu and the Councillors of Louis XIII: A Study of the Secretaries of State and Superintendents of Finance in the Ministry of Richelieu.* Oxford, 1963.

Rebillon, Armand. *Les États de Bretagne de 1661 à 1789: Leur organisation. – L'évolution de leurs pouvoirs. – Leur administration financière.* Paris and Rennes, 1932.

Richet, Denis. *La France moderne: l'esprit des institutions.* Paris, 1973.

Rogister, John. 'Parlementaires, Sovereignty, and Legal Opposition in France under Louis XV: An Introduction'. *Parliaments, Estates & Representation* 6 (June 1986), 25–32.

——*Louis XV and the Parlement of Paris, 1737–1755.* Cambridge, 1995.

Salmon, J.H.M. 'The Legacy of Jean Bodin: Absolutism, Populism, or Constitutionalism?' *History of Political Thought* 17 (no. 4; Winter 1996), 500–522.

——*Society in Crisis: France in the Sixteenth Century.* New York, 1976.

Saulnier, Frédéric. *Le Parlement de Bretagne, 1554–1790. Répertoire alphabétique et biographique de tous les membres de la cour, accompagné de listes chronologiques et précédé d'une introduction historique.* 2 vols Rennes, 1909.

Saulnier de La Pinelais, Gustave. *Les gens du roi au Parlement de Bretagne.* Rennes and Paris, 1902.

Sée, Henri. *Les idées politiques en France au XVIIe siècle.* Paris, 1923. Reprint, Geneva, 1978.

Shennan, J.H. *The Parlement of Paris.* Ithaca, NY, 1968.

——*Philippe, Duke of Orléans: Regent of France, 1715–1723.* London, 1979.

——'The Political Role of the Parlement of Paris, 1715–23'. *The Historical Journal* 8 (no. 2 1965), 179–200.

Smedley-Weill, Anette. *Les intendants de Louis XIV*. Paris, 1995.

Spooner, Frank C. *The International Economy and Monetary Movements in France, 1493–1725*. Cambridge, Mass., 1972.

Stocker, Christopher. 'The Politics of the Parlement of Paris in 1525'. *French Historical Studies* 8 (no. 2; Fall 1973), 191–212.

——'Public and Private Enterprise in the Administration of a Renaissance Monarchy: The First Sales of Office in the Parlement of Paris (1512–1524)'. *The Sixteenth Century Journal* 9 (July 1978), 4–29.

Stone, Bailey. *The Parlement of Paris, 1774–1789*. Chapel Hill, N.C., 1981.

Storez, Isabelle. *Le Chancelier Henri François d'Aguesseau (1668–1751)*. Paris, 1996.

Swann, Julian. *Politics and the Parlement of Paris under Louis XV, 1754–1774*. Cambridge, 1995.

Swart, Koenraad Walter. *Sale of Offices in the Seventeenth Century*. The Hague, 1949.

Thomas, Alexandre-Gérard. *Une province sous Louis XIV, situation politique et administrative de la Bourgogne de 1661 à 1715*. Paris, 1844.

Truchis de Varennes, A., vicomte de. *Le rétablissement du Parlement de Franche-Comté en 1674, suivi de la liste des membres de ce parlement de 1674 à 1789*. Besançon, 1922.

Vilar-Berrogain, Gabrielle. *Guide des recherches dans les fonds d'enregistrement sous l'ancien régime*. Paris, 1958.

Virieux, Maurice. 'Une enquête sur le Parlement de Toulouse en 1718'. *Annales du Midi* 87 (January–March 1975), 38–65.

Vuitry, Adolphe. *Le désordre des finances et les excès de la spéculation à la fin du règne de Louis XIV et au commencement du règne de Louis XV*. Paris, 1885.

Wolfe, Martin. *The Fiscal System of Renaissance France*. New Haven, Conn., 1972.

Zolla, Daniel. 'Les variations du revenu et du prix des terres en France au XVIIe et XVIIIe siècles'. *Annales de l'école libre des sciences politiques* 8 (1893), 299–326, 439–461, 686–705; 9 (1894), 194–216, 417–432.

Index